Advance reviews of *Unl*

"Imagine the founders of diverse therapy methodologies discussing how they achieve deep, lasting, transformational change and agreeing it's due to one basic process. Building on state-of-the-art neuroscience to identify that core process, the authors develop an approach that is theory-free, non-pathologizing, empathic, experiential, phenomenological, and nonspeculative, and that hones therapy while not cramping the therapist's unique contribution—an integrationist's dream!"

—Hanna Levenson, PhD
Author of Brief Dynamic Therapy

"Why do symptom complexes and negative narratives often persist, and how can therapists help clients get free of them? In this well-written book, the authors have provided a transtheoretical, effective and efficient approach, nicely grounded in recent neuroscience, for deep, transformational change in pernicious emotional implicit learnings across a wide variety of presenting problems and situations. This is a significant 'breakthrough' book that deserves careful study. I recommend it most highly!"

—Michael F. Hoyt, PhD
Author of Brief Psychotherapies: Principles and Practices
and editor of The Handbook of Constructive Therapies

"This is a unique, creative, and insightful book that shows how to utilize experiential methods to promote personal transformation. The authors back up their approach by showing how it fits with recent neuropsychological findings on how the brain can alter and even eliminate old painful memories. This book is on the forefront of books that are using neuropsychological findings to illuminate psychotherapy."

—Arthur C. Bohart, PhD
Professor Emeritus, California State University, Dominguez Hills,
and coauthor of How Clients Make Therapy Work:
The Process of Active Self-Healing.

"Drawing on the latest developments in neuroscience, Bruce Ecker, Robin Ticic and Laurel Hulley provide an innovative approach to psychotherapy that is very much of the 21st century. In this book filled with both groundbreaking neuroscience and provocative case examples, they describe how to tap into the reconsolidation process in therapy. If you want to know what's happening that is new in psychotherapy, this is the place to start."

—Jay Lebow, PhD
Clinical Professor of Psychology, Northwestern University
and editor of Family Process

Unlocking the Emotional Brain

Psychotherapy that regularly yields liberating, lasting change was, in the last century, a futuristic vision, but it has now become reality, thanks to a convergence of remarkable advances in clinical knowledge and brain science. In *Unlocking the Emotional Brain,* authors Ecker, Ticic, and Hulley equip readers to carry out focused, empathic therapy using the process found by researchers to induce memory reconsolidation, the recently discovered and only known process for actually unlocking emotional memory at the synaptic level. Emotional memory's tenacity is the familiar bane of therapists, and researchers have long believed that emotional memory forms indelible learning. Reconsolidation has overturned these views. It allows new learning to erase, not just suppress, the deep, unconscious, intensely problematic emotional learnings that form during childhood or in later tribulations and generate most of the symptoms that bring people to therapy. Readers will learn methods that precisely eliminate unwanted, ingrained emotional responses—whether moods, behaviors or thought patterns—causing no loss of ordinary narrative memory, while restoring clients' well-being. Numerous case examples show the versatile use of this process in AEDP, Coherence Therapy, EFT, EMDR, and IPNB.

Bruce Ecker and **Laurel Hulley** are the originators of Coherence Therapy and coauthors of *Depth Oriented Brief Therapy: How to Be Brief When You Were Trained to Be Deep—and Vice Versa,* the *Coherence Therapy Practice Manual and Training Guide,* and the *Manual of Juxtaposition Experiences: How to Create Transformational Change Using Disconfirming Knowledge in Coherence Therapy.* Ecker is codirector of the Coherence Psychology Institute, has taught for many years in graduate programs, and has been in private practice near San Francisco since 1986. Hulley is director of education and paradigm development of the Coherence Psychology Institute and co-founder of the Julia Morgan Middle School for Girls in Oakland, California.

Robin Ticic is director of training and development of the Coherence Psychology Institute and is in private practice near Cologne, Germany, specializing in trauma therapy and clinical supervision of trauma therapists. She has served as a psychologist for the Psychotraumatology Institute of the University of Cologne for many years, provides a low-fee counseling service for parents, and is author of the parenting guide *How to Connect with Your Child,* published in English and German.

Unlocking the Emotional Brain

Eliminating Symptoms at Their Roots Using Memory Reconsolidation

Bruce Ecker
Robin Ticic
Laurel Hulley

Routledge
Taylor & Francis Group

NEW YORK AND LONDON

First published 2012
by Routledge
711 Third Avenue, New York, NY 10017

Simultaneously published in the UK
by Routledge
27 Church Road, Hove, East Sussex BN3 2FA

Routledge is an imprint of the Taylor & Francis Group, an informa business

Library of Congress Cataloging in Publication Data
Ecker, Bruce.
    Unlocking the emotional brain : eliminating symptoms at their roots using memory recon-
    solidation / Bruce Ecker, Robin Ticic, and Laurel Hulley.
    p. cm.
    Includes bibliographical references and index.
    1. Emotion-focused therapy. 2. Emotions. 3. Memory. 4. Psychotherapy. I. Ticic, Robin. II.
    Hulley, Laurel, 1947- III. Title.
    RC489.F62.E35 2012
    616.89'14—dc23
                                                                          2012010794

ISBN: 978-0-415-89716-7 (hbk)
ISBN: 978-0-415-89717-4 (pbk)
ISBN: 978-0-203-80437-7 (ebk)

Typeset in Times New Roman
by EvS Communication Networx, Inc.
Printed and bound in the United States of America by Edwards Brothers Malloy, Inc.

For our children

Gustavo, Jesse, Jhon, Justine, Sierra, Zachary

Contents

Foreword   xiii
Robert A. Neimeyer, PhD

Preface   xv
Acknowledgements   xvii

PART 1
Emotional Coherence: A Unified Framework of Behavioral,
Emotional, and Synaptic Change   1

1 Maximizing Effectiveness and Satisfaction in Clinical Practice   3

Unlocking Emotional Memory   3
Emotional Learning, Coherence, and Symptom Production   5
The Emotional Coherence Landscape   8
Emotional Coherence and Your Clinical Development   11

2 Memory Reconsolidation: How the Brain Unlearns   13

After a Century, a Breakthrough   13
The Tenacity of Implicit Emotional Memory   14
Detecting Reconsolidation: From Indelible to Erasable   17
How Reconsolidation Works   20
The Behavioral Process for Erasing an Emotional Learning   25
Memory Reconsolidation in Clinical Practice:
     The Therapeutic Reconsolidation Process   27
The Neuroscience of Psychotherapy:
     Reconsolidation versus Emotional Regulation   31
The Interplay of Meanings and Molecules: A Prediction   35
Conclusion   37

3 The Focused, Deep Psychotherapy of Emotional Unlearning 39

Embodying the Therapeutic Reconsolidation Process 40
The Therapeutic Reconsolidation Process in Coherence Therapy:
Case Example of Anxious Low Self-Esteem 43
The Process in Summary 63
Markers of Change for Symptoms Dispelled at Their
Emotional Roots 64
Ubiquity of the Transformation Sequence in Profound Change 65
Conclusion 65

4 The Moments of Fundamental Change: Map and Methods 67

How to Identify Targets for Unlearning 68
Sources of Disconfirming Knowledge 70
Case Studies and Techniques 71
Obsessive Attachment to Former Lover 71
Pervasive Underachieving 77
Stage Fright (PTSD) 86
Summary of Techniques 92

5 Emotional Coherence and the Great Attachment Debate 93

Attachment, Other Domains of Emotional Learning, and Temperament 93
Attachment Learnings 97
Terms of Attachment 102
Optimizing Attachment Therapy:
Dyadic Reparative Work and Beyond 103
Varieties of Attachment Therapy in Action: Case Studies 105
Conclusion: A Coherent Resolution 124

6 A Framework for Psychotherapy Integration 126

Transformational Change and Specific Factors 126
Accelerated Experiential Dynamic Psychotherapy (AEDP) 130
Emotion-Focused Therapy (EFT) 136
Eye-Movement Desensitization and Reprocessing (EMDR) 141
Interpersonal Neurobiology (IPNB) 148
Envisioning Psychotherapy Integration through the
Therapeutic Reconsolidation Process 149
Common Factors, Specific Factors, and
Psychotherapy Process Research 153
Conclusion: Unlocking the Emotional Brain 155

PART 2
Coherence-Focused Therapy in Practice 157

7 **A Father's Tormenting Guilt:**
   Deep Resolution in Seven Coherence-Focused Sessions 159

   Paul Sibson

8 **Up on Top from Down Below:**
   Cessation of Compulsive Drinking Using Coherence Therapy 168

   C. Anthony Martignetti

9 **Bypassing Bypass Surgery:**
   Using Emotional Coherence to Dispel Compulsive Eating 181

   Niall Geoghegan

10 **Hearing Hostile Voices:**
   Ending Psychotic Symptoms at Their Coherent Roots 186

   Timothy A. Connor

Glossary 201
References and Further Reading 207
Online Supplements 219
Author Index 220
Subject Index 224

Foreword

Most experienced therapists from Freud onward will recognize in their work those spine-tingling moments of courage and honesty when a client suddenly hits upon and voices for the first time an emergent awareness, one that casts old problems in a new light, and that paves the way for their deeper consideration and eventual dissolution. Most therapists have experience with frustration the seeming unpredictability of such moments, the mystery of the encounter that ushers them in, and the fragility of the insights they generate, which so easily collapse again into the apparently automatic performance of the problem. Faced with this prospect of a long slog through a densely overgrown and unmapped terrain, punctuated only periodically by discovery of a high ground that affords a glimpse of true clarity and direction, it is understandable that some therapists move to a safely psychoeducational or interpretive distance, or alternatively simply walk alongside their clients on their wanderings, trusting that together they will find a path forward. The result in the former instance is often an intellectualized intervention that lacks specific resonance, and in the latter is an emotionally attuned therapy that may be only vaguely relevant. What seems needed in both cases is some means of wedding clarity of method to a deep form of companioning, in a way that prompts a client toward the articulation and transformation of those core forms of construing and doing that constitute the problem, in the container of a therapeutic relationship marked equally by efficiency and respect. Until recently, this happy conjunction has often seemed slippery and occasional, rather than reliably available.

It is precisely this therapeutic desideratum—swift and respectful transformation of a client's positioning in relation to the problem—that Ecker, Ticic, and Hulley elegantly address in *Unlocking the Emotional Brain*. Building on the twin pillars of cutting edge neuroscience and long experience in the facilitation of change in clinical practice, they offer not merely a vision but also a methodology for achieving what frequently may seem chimerical in psychotherapy: profound release from the roots of symptom production in the minimum number of sessions possible. What makes this often elusive goal feasible? One answer is found in recent, but well-replicated research on *memory reconsolidation*, the clearly specified circumstances in which emotional learning can be accessed, activated, and erased. Another can be found in the close process analysis of transformative sessions of psychotherapy, in which precisely the same procedures can be discerned in the consulting room as in the laboratory. Much of the genius of this volume lies in the lucid bridging of these two domains, conveyed with clarity through ample case studies that make vivid how the problems clients consciously resent and resist in fact issue from fully coherent learning at limbic levels, which, when discovered and held nonreactively alongside incompatible experience, can also be dissolved. Ecker and his colleagues adroitly lead the reader through these scientific and clinical accounts, and winnow their lessons for compellingly effective psychotherapeutic practice.

Although this—amounting to a fresh instruction manual for how to conduct life-changing psychotherapy—alone would more than justify acquiring this volume, the authors and contributors offer still more. Thus, they recast with uncanny clarity the great attachment debate in psychotherapy, offering helpful distinctions between client problems that merely arise in the *context* of intimate relational experiences and those that reflect their very *terms of attachment*, as when the existing, problematic adaptation unconsciously offers the best prospect for maintaining a critical bond that would feel threatened by the problem's dissolution. Furthermore, the book offers a persuasive argument for a new approach to common factors that account for the efficacy of different therapeutic procedures that on the face of it have little in common: at root, each of several experiential approaches is seen to offer alternative means of tapping into and transforming the symptom-generating learning that has perpetuated the problem. And finally, contributed chapters from the field demonstrate, in the context of complicated grief, substance abuse, compulsive eating, and even psychotic symptoms, the great scope and power of a practice centered on the deep coherence of implicit emotional learning. With characteristically spellbinding style, the authors weave through these and other themes with authority but without pretense, conjuring into tangible form the brain's own rules for transmuting the lead of insufficiently effective interventions into the gold of life-altering clinical work. I am a wiser, more focused, and more consistently effective therapist for having studied this remarkable volume, and I feel confident in predicting that it will have a similarly intensive, informative, and inspiring impact on you.

Robert A. Neimeyer, PhD
University of Memphis, March 2012

Preface

Several days before drafting this preface, we completed the manuscript for this book after an intensive year of writing, which followed two years of envisioning, designing, and redesigning what this book would be. For us it has been a labor of love and we are very happy that our paths have put us in a position to offer this contribution to the practice of psychotherapy. This is an exciting time in the evolution of our field.

We have organized the book so that readers can easily choose how much neuroscience they imbibe. Some therapists cannot get enough of the neuroscience of psychotherapy, while others have less interest in it, so we have put the rich trove of brain science technicalities in one place, Chapter 2, available for readers as and when they wish. All other chapters focus on the art, rather than the science, of unlocking the emotional brain for lasting change, while providing just enough "neuro lite" to inform our readers of the basic scientific underpinnings.

This book is not centrally about any one school, theory, or "brand" of psychotherapy. It describes a virtually theory-free methodology that can be fulfilled by many psychotherapies—as shown by case studies from AEDP, Coherence Therapy, EFT, EMDR and IPNB—or eclectically, without adherence to any particular therapy. For instructional purposes of illustrating in sharp detail the cross-platform framework shown in this book we use primarily Coherence Therapy, which was first described in the volume *Depth Oriented Brief Therapy* by Ecker and Hulley (1996). The name of the approach was changed from Depth Oriented Brief Therapy, or DOBT, to Coherence Therapy in 2005. (The DOBT book remains a basic source. Its many case studies and thorough treatments of therapist stance and discovery techniques are not replicated here; yet that book is significantly supplemented by the account of Coherence Therapy in this one, such as in the examination of moments of profound change in Chapter 4 and attachment work in Chapter 5.)

Acknowledgements

Help dearly needed is help most dearly appreciated, so our thankfulness toward the following individuals is heartfelt.

Publisher and archaeologist Mitch Allen scrutinized our book proposal and contracts and was unstintingly generous in sharing his astute knowledge of these matters; and he persistently pushed us to craft chapter and section titles that "tell a story." Psychologist and university professor Sara K. Bridges again and again tuned in to our evolving style and phrasing, deftly guided its shaping to reach our audience of psychotherapists and clinical graduate students, and helped make the table of contents do justice to the book's substance. These two angels turned on the lights for us at many key points—sometimes when we didn't even know we were in the dark.

Three others also contributed vitally to this book's creation. Psychologist, author, and editor Babette Rothschild guided us to think beyond particular systems of therapy, which pivotally led us to realize the full scope and integrative power of the framework we in fact held in our hands; not to mention her timely nudge and guidance in the direction of a well-structured book proposal. Psychologist and university professor Greg Neimeyer's vigorous, sustained, multifaceted supportiveness of Coherence Therapy was a major factor in maintaining our momentum on this project through its early stages. Psychologist and *Psychotherapy Networker* editor Rich Simon helped lay the foundation for this book through his early receptivity to the clinical importance of memory reconsolidation, his support for bringing news of it to psychotherapists, and his invaluable guidance in crafting the message. The creative contributions that these three dedicated psychologists have made to our field would fill a museum, with this book being just one of the items in that collection.

The subjective nuances as well as the objective processes involved in psychotherapy are a great challenge to a writer's skills, so we are grateful for expert help received on this level of the task. Life coach and music composer Elise Kushner critiqued every page of the growing manuscript, challenging us to clarify our phrasing and our thinking at certain critical points, contributing invaluable feedback, and often amazing us with her syntactical acuity. Author and speaker Zach

Davis shared generously of his knowledge, helping us to recognize and speak directly to our readers' needs and aspirations. Data processing consultant John Ticic supported us generously and contributed his technical expertise in various forms, whenever needed. English language instructor Fern Kushner edited our proposal and researched questions of language usage that arose during our writing process.

Connecting with Routledge editor Anna Moore was like coming home. The relaxed, respectful context she created has been for us, as writers, a real boon, and knowing that we could rely on her responsiveness and helpfulness has been terrific. We thank Brian Toomey for suggesting, almost a decade ago, a detailed study of the types of synaptic plasticity, an endeavor that has proven very fruitful. The steady, earnest moral support and interest in the manuscript's progress from therapist colleagues Jan van der Zwaag, Bret Lyon, and Merle Jordan have been a balm and a genuine enjoyment, whether over coffee or over the telephone; and we received helpful feedback from therapist colleagues Sheridan Adams, Steven Freemire, Nancy Friedman, Steve Kelly, Dana Locke, and Nora Wolfson, as well as from April Burns.

A special thanks is what we feel toward our contributing authors of the case examples in Part 2 of the book—for the beauty, skill and remarkable poignance of their work, for their courage in sharing it, and for their patience with our rounds of editorial feedback. That thanks extends also to other colleagues who submitted manuscripts that we would have included but for space limitations, and that we plan to publish in a future collection of case studies. And speaking of courage— that of our therapy clients is what has made it possible for us to learn, in living depth, literally everything presented in this book. What we have learned from books has become real knowledge for us solely through actually using it with our clients—and they have taught us so much about the mind, the heart, and change that was *not* in any books. Our gratitude to them could never really be sufficient. Similarly, we have been taught how to teach the material in this book by a legion of trainees, graduate students, and consultees over the past 20 years, and though they might not have been aware of that contribution, we were—and we thank them for it.

Each of the three authors also wants to express thanks here to the other two— for an unwavering spirit of good-natured collaboration and dedication to seeing what was best for the book, as distinct from attachment to particular ideas. It was a journey that went far beyond our initial vision and became a complex and creative unfolding that in many instances wove together our individual contributions, such that we ourselves cannot always tease them apart in the end. Experiencing this process with one another has been an honor and a great pleasure.

This book continues the reorientation of psychotherapy in terms of emotional implicit memory and its associated brain science and, in doing so, stands on the shoulders of the clinical writers who pioneered that revisioning and the enhanced effectiveness it bestows, starting with trailblazer Bessel van der Kolk and continuing with Allan Schore, Daniel Siegel, Babette Rothschild, and Louis Cozolino. And earlier still, it was Eugene Gendlin who identified the experiential emergence of implicit knowing into explicit awareness as a key ingredient of effective psychotherapy. Their contribution to our field and to the alleviation of suffering is of immeasurable value.

Finally, we want to express keen appreciation and real admiration for the many neuroscientists—named in citations in the text—who discovered memory reconsolidation and then went about revealing more and more of how it operates. We particularly want to give recognition here to neuroscientist Héctor Maldonado, founder of the Laboratory of Neurobiology of Memory at the University of Buenos Aires, who identified the particular type of experience required by the brain for unlocking an emotional learning at the synaptic level and who, with neuroscientists María Pedreira and Luis Pérez-Cuesta, first demonstrated this discovery empirically. We believe that the gift they have given humanity will prove to be far greater than is yet recognized in either field—neuroscience or psychotherapy. That discovery, published in 2004, was one of Professor Maldonado's many important contributions to the field of neuroscience. In 2010, at the age of 83 he continued working in his laboratory until his last moments, supervising his students, generating new projects and publishing research articles.

Bruce Ecker
Robin Ticic
Laurel Hulley
February 25, 2012

PART 1

EMOTIONAL COHERENCE: A UNIFIED FRAMEWORK OF BEHAVIORAL, EMOTIONAL, AND SYNAPTIC CHANGE

1

Maximizing Effectiveness and Satisfaction in Clinical Practice

All human beings should try to learn before they die what they are running from, and to, and why.

—James Thurber

What we therapists find most fulfilling are those pivotal sessions in which a client experiences a deeply felt shift that dispels longstanding negative emotional patterns and symptoms. Bringing about such decisive, liberating results for our clients sustains us, but the alchemy that produces these life-changing shifts has been something of a mystery, allowing them to come about only unpredictably in the course of many months or years of sessions.

In fact, the tenacity of emotional learnings—which arguably generate the vast majority of unwanted behaviors, moods, emotions, and thoughts addressed in therapy—is so strong that after nearly a century of research, even brain scientists had concluded by the 1990s that well-established emotional learnings are indelible, unerasable, for the lifetime of the individual. Learnings formed in the presence of intense emotion, such as core beliefs and constructs formed in childhood, are locked into the brain by extraordinarily durable synapses, and it seemed as though the brain threw away the key. No wonder therapists and clients often feel they are struggling against some unrelenting but invisible force.

Unlocking Emotional Memory

A major breakthrough has recently occurred, however, in our understanding of how emotional memory works. Neuroscience research since 2004 has shown that the brain does indeed have a key to those locked synapses: a type of neuro-plasticity known as *memory reconsolidation*, which, when launched by a certain series of experiences, actually unlocks the synapses of a target emotional learn-ing, allowing it to be not merely overridden but actually nullified and deleted by new learning. This research has shown that the brain is always capable of unlock-ing and dissolving emotional learnings and, remarkably, we now know what the required series of experiences is. With clear knowledge of the brain's own rules for deleting emotional learnings through memory reconsolidation, therapists no longer have to rely largely on speculative theory, intuition, and luck for facilitating powerful, liberating shifts.

This book provides a unifying account of:

- *emotional learning and memory*, with emphasis on its adaptive, coherent nature and the specific content and structure of symptom-generating emo-tional implicit learnings
- *the unlearning and deletion of emotional implicit knowledge* through the sequence of experiences required by the brain for memory reconsolidation
- *the therapeutic reconsolidation process*, which is the entire set of steps needed for putting into practice the required sequence of experiences in psychotherapy sessions

We call this unified body of knowledge the Emotional Coherence Framework, and we predict that it will expand your clinical vision and mastery invaluably, as it has ours. We see this happening for therapists who are already making use of this knowledge; there are examples of such work in Part 2 of this book.

The therapeutic reconsolidation process consists of steps that guide you as therapist without cramping your individual style. It involves richly experiential work that utilizes your skills of emotional attunement and focuses the use of your empathy so as to cooperate closely with the brain's rules for accessing and dis-solving the emotional learnings at the root of your clients' presenting symptoms. Major, longstanding symptoms can cease as soon as their very basis no longer exists, as shown in the many case examples in this book. All of the depth, inti-macy, and humanity of talk therapy at its best are preserved in this approach, for these valued qualities of therapy are key ingredients for successfully using the therapeutic reconsolidation process to free clients from entrenched negative reac-tions, old attachment patterns, unconscious core schemas, and emotional wounds.

New learning always creates new neural circuits, but it is only when new learn-ing also unwires old learning that transformational change occurs, and this is pre-cisely what the therapeutic reconsolidation process achieves. The process fulfills the brain's requirements for allowing a new learning to rewrite and erase an old, unwanted learning—and not merely suppress and compete against the old learn-ing. The result is transformational change, as distinct from incremental change and ongoing symptom management.

An extremely broad range of techniques can be used to carry out the process, which is largely why your creativity and individual style of working continue to have great scope of expression in this approach. No single school of psychotherapy "owns" the therapeutic reconsolidation process because it is a universal process, inherent in the brain. Quite a few existing systems of psychotherapy are compatible with carrying out this process—see Table 1.1—and carrying it out *knowingly* can significantly increase a practitioner's frequency of achieving powerful therapeutic results, as we have found for many years in our own clinical practices and in training therapists in this process. Later in the book, in case examples of several different clinical approaches—AEDP, Coherence Therapy, EFT, EMDR, and IPNB—you will see that the steps of the therapeutic reconsolidation process are present in each, and that there is sound reason to expect these steps to be present when therapy of any kind yields a lasting disappearance of a longstanding, learned, symptomatic response pattern, whether emotional, behavioral, or ideational.

Table 1.1 Focused, experiential, in-depth psychotherapies that are congenial to fulfilling the therapeutic reconsolidation process if the therapist applies them to do so

Psychotherapy	References
Accelerated Experiential Dynamic Psychotherapy (AEDP)	Fosha, 2000, 2002
Coherence Therapy (formerly Depth Oriented Brief Therapy)	Ecker & Hulley, 2008a, 2011
Eye Movement Desensitization and Reprocessing (EMDR)	Parnell, 2006; Shapiro, 2001
Emotion-Focused Therapy (EFT)	Greenberg, 2010; Greenberg & Watson, 2005
Focusing-Oriented Psychotherapy	Gendlin, 1996
Gestalt Therapy	Polster & Polster, 1973 Zinker, 1978
Hakomi	Fisher, 2011 Kurtz, 1990
Internal Family Systems Therapy (IFS)	Schwartz, 1997, 2001
Interpersonal Neurobiology (IPNB)	Badenoch, 2011 Siegel, 2006
Neuro-Linguistic Programming (NLP)	Vaknin, 2010
Traumatic Incident Reduction (TIR)	French & Harris, 1998 Volkman, 2008

Emotional Learning, Coherence, and Symptom Production

The Emotional Coherence Framework—this book's conceptual and methodological framework for psychotherapy—is an emotional learning and unlearning paradigm. It is applicable for dispelling a vast range of presenting symptoms and problems generated by existing learnings held in implicit memory—learnings, that is, that the individual is unaware of possessing, even as these learnings reactivate and drive unwanted responses of behavior, mood, emotion, or thought.

As you follow each of this book's case examples, you may be surprised by what you see regarding the inherently sophisticated nature of implicit (non-conscious) emotional learning. The emotional brain—particularly the subcortical emotional brain or limbic system—is often described as "primitive" and "irrational," and its unwanted, problematic responses are usually characterized as "maladaptive" and "dysregulated," but these pathologizing and pejorative terms prove to be fundamentally at odds with what research has revealed about emotional learning—a point to which we will return later in this chapter. The Emotional Coherence Framework emphasizes recognizing and utilizing the full extent of the coherence and adaptive functioning of emotional implicit learning because the therapeutic leverage gained is very great for both case conceptualization and methodology. The intention within this framework is to learn how to maximize our ability to cooperate with the brain's own powerful processes of change.

As later chapters cover in detail, emotional learning usually consists of much more than stored memory of the "raw data" of what one's senses were registering and what emotions one was experiencing during an original experience. Also learned—that is, stored in implicit memory—is a constructed *mental model* of how the world functions, a template or schema that is the individual's sense-making generalization of the raw data of perception and emotion. This model is created and stored with no awareness of doing so. It does not exist in words, but is no less well-defined or coherent for that. The emotional brain then uses this model or schema for self-protectively *anticipating* similar experiences in the future and recognizing them instantly when they begin (or seem) to occur. Emotional memory converts the past into an expectation of the future, without our awareness, and that is both a blessing and a curse. It is a blessing because we rely daily on emotional implicit memory to navigate us through all sorts of situations without having to go through the relatively slow, labor-intensive process of figuring out, conceptually and verbally, what to do; we simply know what to do and we know it quickly. It is easy to take for granted the amazing efficiency and speed with which we access and are guided by a truly vast library of implicit knowings. Yet our emotional implicit memory is also a curse because it makes the worst experiences in our past persist as felt emotional realities in the present and in our present sense of the future.

As a relatively simple example, consider a man who undertakes psychotherapy for social anxiety and for the first time becomes directly aware, and puts into words, that he lives and moves within the expectation of being shamed and rejected if he differs openly with another person about anything. All his life, this non-conscious expectation has wordlessly defined *how the world is*—or so it has felt to him because his emotional brain formed that implicit model of human beings based on childhood perceptions during family interactions. His social anxiety had seemed to him a mysterious affliction, but now, with this retrieval—this shift from implicit to explicit knowing—his anxiety makes deep sense as the emotion that naturally accompanies his living knowledge of how people respond. Yet his learned constructs had never appeared in his prior experience of that anxiety; nothing indicated that this was actually memory of the past. The constructs we form do not normally show up in conscious experience themselves, much as a colored lens just in front of the eye is not itself visible. (For a comprehensive account of this phenomenological, *constructivist* understanding, see, for example, Mahoney, 1991, 2003 and Neimeyer & Raskin, 2000.)

We easily see in discussing this man that what seemed and felt so real to him about the world was not an external reality at all, but rather a vivid illusion or mirage maintained by his own implicit constructs in emotional memory. It hardly seems an exaggeration to regard the limbic brain's power to create emotional reality as a kind of magic that immerses one in a potent spell that feels absolutely real and would last for a lifetime. However, thanks to a fortunate confluence of developments in clinical knowledge and brain science, we now know how to induce the emotional brain to use its power to break emotional spells that it previously created.

The emotional brain's completely nonverbal, implicit yet highly specific meaning-making and modeling of the world is innate and begins very early in life. For example, infants three months old form expectational models of contingency and respond according to these models (DeCasper & Carstens, 1981), and 18-month-old children can form mental models of other people as wanting things that differ from what they themselves want and will give the other what he or she wants (Repacholi & Gopnik, 1997), and can form models that distinguish between intentional and accidental actions (Olineck & Poulin-Dubois, 2005).

In this book's 16 case examples we will see the therapeutic power of creating direct cortical awareness of the emotional brain's knowings—the shifting of implicit knowings into explicit awareness. The retrieved learnings are always found to be specific and completely coherent: They make deep sense in light of actual life experiences and are fully adaptive in how they embody the individual's efforts to avoid harm and ensure well-being. Bringing these underlying learnings into awareness makes it unmistakably apparent to the client, on a deeply felt level, that the symptom exists as part of adaptive, coherent strivings. Pragmatically, it is through their coherence that the symptom-generating emotional learnings are most readily found and retrieved. In the clinical field there is already much recognition of the importance of coherence in an individual's conscious narratives of life experience. That, however, is neocortical coherence. Our emphasis in the Emotional Coherence Framework is on the coherence of the emotional brain—subcortical and right-brain coherence—the coherence that is intrinsic to implicit emotional learnings and, when retrieved into conscious awareness, creates new autobiographical coherence most meaningfully and authentically.

The timeless, unfading persistence of underlying, symptom-generating learnings across decades of life, long after the original circumstances that induced their formation have ceased to exist, is often taken as meaning that they are maladaptive and that the symptoms they produce signify a dysregulation of emotional brain networks. However, when symptoms turn out to have full underlying coherence and a positive, adaptive, urgent purpose in the context of a person's actual life experience, such pathologizing conceptualizations seem ill-founded (Ecker & Hulley, 1996, 2000b; Neimeyer & Raskin, 2000). Furthermore, as mentioned earlier, memory research has established that learnings accompanied by strong emotion form neural circuits in subcortical implicit memory that are exceptionally durable, normally lasting a lifetime. The brain is working as evolution apparently shaped it to do when, decades after the formation of such emotional knowledge, this tacit knowledge is triggered in response to current perceptual cues and launches behaviors and emotions according to the original adaptive learning. Such faithful retriggering is, in fact, proper functioning of the brain's emotional learning centers, not a faulty condition of disorder or dysregulation—unless one is prepared to say that it is a dysregulation of evolution itself, not of the individual.

Memory research thus supports a non-pathologizing, coherence-based model of symptom production in the wide range of cases where symptoms are generated by emotional memory. This is the central perspective of the Emotional Coherence Framework. Some symptoms have causes other than learning and memory, of course, whether genomic, such as the autism spectrum, or biochemical, such as depression caused by hypothyroidism. Viewing symptom production as dysregulation may be accurate in such cases, but they are a small minority of those encountered by psychotherapists in general practice.

The tenet that a person's unwanted moods, behaviors, or thoughts may be generated by unconscious emotional learnings or conditioning has figured in many forms of psychotherapy since Freud's day, but the approach in this book is new, firstly, in its swift and accurate retrieval of those emotional learnings, bringing them into direct awareness, and, secondly, in its non-theoretically based, research-corroborated methodology for prompt dissolution of those retrieved learnings at their emotional and neural roots.

The Emotional Coherence Landscape

Practitioners who are steeped in this framework use it largely by *feel* in their sessions, without excessive "up in the head" figuring out how to guide the process forward. If this framework is new to you, you may at first need to rely on a conceptual, step-by-step map without much sense of flow, in the same way that speaking sentences of an unfamiliar language is at first a thought-out, non-flowing experience until, with some experience over time, the know-how becomes second nature and fluid.

The following is a broad view of the territory ahead.

Chapter 2 tells the story of the dramatic scientific turnaround caused by the discovery of reconsolidation, showing why this phenomenon has extraordinary significance for psychotherapy and explaining selected, clinically relevant research findings. A clear distinction emerges between transformational change (in which problematic emotional learnings are actually dissolved and symptoms cannot recur) and incremental change (which necessitates the ongoing managing and effortful counteracting of symptoms). We then map out specifically how this research translates into clinical application, defining the set of operational steps termed the therapeutic reconsolidation process. The chapter ends by pointing out how the clinical implications of reconsolidation research since 2004 extend beyond and differ in some important ways from what was implied for therapy by neuroscience before reconsolidation entered the picture; and what emerging knowledge of brain epigenetics means—and doesn't mean—in relation to the psychotherapeutic framework of this book.

Chapter 3 addresses how psychotherapy can be conceptualized and conducted in order to carry out the steps of the therapeutic reconsolidation process for a given presenting symptom. This chapter also acquaints the reader with the basics of memory reconsolidation, so that the more detailed research review in Chapter 2 is not required in order to understand and use this framework. You will see that the richly human and humane qualities of the client–therapist relationship and the depth of personal meaning experienced by the client need not be sacrificed at all in order to follow a process of change confirmed by neuroscientists in the laboratory. If Chapter 2 of this book is its scientific bedrock, Chapter 3 is the heart of its vision for therapy: use of the therapeutic reconsolidation process with guidance from the Emotional Coherence Framework. The therapeutic reconsolidation process is an integrative and open-access methodology because it is phenomenological and avoids theory-based interpretations, and because it does not impose particular techniques to be used for guiding clients into the necessary sequence of experiences. Demonstrating the process for instructional purposes necessarily entails, therefore, showing how a particular set of techniques or system of therapy may be used to create the sequence of experiences. For this instructional purpose we use a particular form of therapy—Coherence Therapy—because the defining steps of this approach are explicitly and recognizably the same as the steps of the therapeutic reconsolidation process. It is especially easy and transparent, in other words, to see the therapeutic reconsolidation process in case examples of Coherence Therapy. The case study in this chapter addresses a man's chronic self-doubt, anxiety and lack of confidence in his professional role at his workplace—symptoms that reveal nothing of the underlying core emotional learnings driving them, though these hidden learnings soon come into the client's direct awareness in the retrieval work, in part through use of specialized mindfulness practices. Dissolution of the retrieved, problematic learnings follows and the anxious self-doubting at work ceases.

Chapter 4 puts the key moments of transformational change under still closer scrutiny in three case examples, so that you can see exactly what is involved and how well-defined and guidable the necessary experiences are. The examples—involving obsessive attachment, pervasive underachieving, and stage fright that is actually PTSD—all show the collaborative journey with each client and the therapist's creativity in finding how to guide each client into the crucial experiences. The journey metaphor is an apt one, because knowledge of the therapeutic reconsolidation process serves very much as a compass and a map for working effectively in the territory of the client's non-conscious emotional learnings. How to move from one point to another, however—the concrete mode of transportation in the metaphor—depends on the therapist's choice of methods. Coherence Therapy supplies the therapist with a set of versatile techniques designed specially for the steps of the therapeutic reconsolidation process, while always encouraging the therapist to improvise variations, adapt techniques from other therapies, or invent new techniques as best suits the unfolding process with each client.

Chapter 5 focuses on working with attachment patterns using the therapeutic reconsolidation process and the conceptualization of attachment work in the Emotional Coherence Framework. We will see that the fully experiential retrieval of a given symptom's underlying emotional learnings—the shift from implicit knowing to explicit knowing, as required for the therapeutic reconsolidation process—makes apparent whether these learnings are attachment-related, not attachment-related, or a combination of the two. This allows a non-speculative, non-theoretical determination of whether a given presenting symptom is based in attachment learnings—often a matter of considerable controversy among both clinicians and researchers. Such clarity regarding the nature of the underlying learnings in turn sheds light on the optimal role and use of the client–therapist relationship with a given client; there is quite a range of strongly held opinions about this, as well. Here, too, the Emotional Coherence Framework provides an illuminating perspective of a non-theoretical nature. Because this framework embodies a learning model of both symptom production and symptom cessation and is completely phenomenological and interpretation-free in its implementation, it can help steer us clear of theoretical biases in clarifying some of the more complex and thorny issues in psychotherapy.

Chapter 6, which concludes Part 1 of the book, shows the integrative, cross-platform nature of the therapeutic reconsolidation process by revealing the presence of its steps in representative case examples of several psychotherapies (AEDP, EFT, EMDR, and IPNB) whose defining features do not necessarily correspond to that process in an obvious manner. We propose that this process may prove to be a universal template for deep elimination of any existing learned response. This hypothesis is supported by the fact that memory reconsolidation is, as of this writing, the only type of neuroplasticity known to neuroscience that is capable of unlocking locked synapses and eliminating emotional learning from implicit memory. In the opening and closing sections of Chapter 6, we regard the steps of the therapeutic reconsolidation process as *specific factors* required for transformational change of existing, learned responses; we describe the challenge posed by the therapeutic reconsolidation process to non-specific common factors theory and why this may auger a fundamental shift in perspective on common factors theory; and we note the support that these possibilities have from psychotherapy process research.

Part 2 of the book consists of case examples contributed by practitioners of Coherence Therapy. We selected these cases because they complement and extend the illustrations of the therapeutic reconsolidation process in Part 1 in various ways: different types of symptoms dispelled (indicated in the table of contents), the therapists' diversity of styles and choices, larger numbers of sessions in most cases, and candid accounts of how the therapist grappled with challenges and obstacles along the way, including client resistance and the need for technique improvisation. We think you will be fascinated and inspired, as we were, by these true tales of therapeutic adventure and triumph.

The online supplements to this book include searchable copies of a glossary of terms in this book, the book's index, a list of the defining features of Coherence Therapy, and an index of published case examples of Coherence Therapy organized by presenting symptom.

Emotional Coherence and Your Clinical Development

In conducting trainings in this approach since 1993, we have seen that most psychotherapists and counselors—ourselves included—seek certain kinds of satisfaction in their practices in order to sustain the inspiration and meaningfulness that originally attracted them to this challenging, difficult work. To conclude this introductory chapter, we list common dilemmas that our therapist colleagues and trainees have described as developing over time in their clinical work, motivating them to seek some revitalizing approach. Along with each dilemma, we preview how this book helps meet these professional challenges.

As a therapist I feel I ought to know, in advance, the interventions that will eliminate my client's symptoms, and that is a burden. That assumption and the angst it generates are dispelled by understanding symptom production in terms of coherent, implicit emotional learnings that are unique to each client. In this approach, the therapist is comfortable in recognizing that a client's pathway to resolution is findable and is equipped to find it collaboratively, without needing to know in advance what the unique pathway will be.

My client's symptoms seem to be maintained by some powerful but elusive force that has a life of its own. Client and therapist can readily find and thoroughly demystify the source of the power driving unwanted states and behaviors—the unrecognized "part" consisting of implicit emotional learnings that are passionately committed to certain tactics for avoiding suffering and ensuring well-being. You can bring about transformational change through welcoming, valuing, and cooperating with these parts and learnings instead of battling them.

Searching for relevant information in a client's past too often feels like looking for a needle in a haystack. Bringing to light the truly relevant elements in your client's past can become quicker, easier and more accurate by using simple coherence-guided experiential methods designed for that purpose.

I feel that my efforts are too easily rendered ineffectual by clients' resistance. Like other seemingly negative responses, resistance is coherent and full of accessible emotional meaning that can pivotally assist the therapeutic process if it is honored and sensitively "unpacked" and understood.

I frequently help clients deeply understand the causes of their symptoms, yet no real shift occurs and their suffering persists. You can facilitate real change on an experiential, emotional level, rather than hoping that your clients' cognitive insight into the causes of their problems will somehow lead to change.

I want my sessions to provide me more often with learning experiences for growth of my clinical skill and understanding. Guiding clients to retrieve implicit emotional learnings into awareness involves steady tracking of a client's experience in each session, supplying you with ongoing feedback on your clinical choices, as does eliciting client feedback early in each session on the effects of the previous session and between-session task. Your learning is heightened also by the wide-open scope for creative use of techniques.

At the end of my workday, I seldom feel satisfied that I've facilitated new breakthroughs that end my clients' sufferings. You can become consistent in making each session effective and powerful by incorporating some learnable steps and ways of thinking, making new use of your existing skills. Real breakthroughs can be a frequent occurrence in your day-to-day practice, thanks to the knowledge we now have of the brain's built-in process for profound change of existing, core emotional learnings. For us clinicians, hearing a client report a decisive change in glowing terms is a moment of deep professional fulfillment. Imagine enjoying several such moments every week ...

2

Memory Reconsolidation: How the Brain Unlearns

Yesterday this day's madness did prepare.

—Edward FitzGerald (trans.), *The Rubáiyát of Omar Khayyám*

Psychotherapists, seeking to make their work exceptionally valuable for their clients as well as deeply and freshly satisfying for themselves, are eager to find ever more effective methods that build on existing skills. Fertile ground of that kind has been opened up by a major development in brain science reported initially in 2004, with fundamental and extremely positive implications for enhancing the effectiveness of psychotherapy. The new brain science of *memory reconsolidation* centers on the surprising discovery of the brain's ability to delete a specific, unwanted emotional learning, including core, non-conscious beliefs and schemas, at the level of the physical, neural synapses that encode it in emotional memory. Deletion of the emotional learning underlying a particular symptom eliminates that symptom down to its emotional roots. We will see in this chapter how psychotherapists can use skills of empathic attunement to guide the process that induces this potent form of change.

After a Century, a Breakthrough

Before 2000, based on nearly a century of research, neuroscientists believed that the brain did not possess the capability of erasing an existing, established emotional learning from memory. The detection of memory reconsolidation, a type of neuroplasticity or synaptic change that *can* erase emotional learning, was therefore both a breakthrough and a turnaround in our knowledge of learning and memory. In 2004, researchers identified how to induce reconsolidation behavior-ally, through a series of experiences required by the brain for erasure (Pedreira, Pérez-Cuesta, & Maldonado, 2004), but it was not until 2006 that this discovery and its clinical use began coming to the attention of psychotherapists (Ecker, 2006). As of this writing, there is no other process or type of neuroplasticity known to neuroscience that eliminates an emotional learning.

This new knowledge has enormous value for psychotherapy because prob-lematic emotional learnings so prevalently underlie and generate symptoms and problems presented by therapy clients. What are attachment patterns, PTSD, co-dependency, low self-esteem, perfectionism, or "unresolved emotional issues" (to name a few of the more obvious examples, and our case examples in this and later chapters will provide many non-obvious ones) but the expression of emotional learnings? Reliable knowledge of how to erase such learnings greatly expands therapists' ability to dispel suffering. A well-defined, experiential process has emerged in reconsolidation research for erasing a target emotional learning, and researchers have demonstrated that this process does not impair autobiographical memory or other closely related emotional learnings. Carrying out the process clinically involves sensitive, empathic attunement between therapist and client, as our case examples will show.

This chapter tells the story of the remarkable findings of reconsolidation research and explains in clear terms how reconsolidation works, as distilled from the original, highly technical research reports. The findings covered below are well established, but they are so recent that the topic of reconsolidation is absent or only barely mentioned in the many influential texts and articles that have been published on the implications of neuroscience for psychotherapy as of this writing (e.g., Arden & Linford, 2009; Badenoch, 2008; Cozolino, 2002, 2010; Folensbee, 2007; Fosha, Siegel, & Solomon, 2010; LeDoux, 1996; Panksepp, 1998; Roths-child, 2000; Schore, 2003a, 2003b; Siegel, 1999, 2006, 2010; Siegel & Solomon, 2003; van der Kolk, 1994, 1996). The clinical implications of neuroscience have certainly continued to develop at a rapid pace. Near the end of this chapter, we delineate how the implications of reconsolidation compare with and differ from those of pre-reconsolidation neuroscience.

The Tenacity of Implicit Emotional Memory

Underlying the diverse behaviors, moods, emotions, and thoughts for which peo-ple seek therapy are "implicit" emotional learnings—learnings that are not in conscious awareness and that entered into memory during experiences involving strong emotion (e.g., Milner, Squire, & Kandel, 1998; Roediger & Craik, 1989; Siegel, 1999; Toomey & Ecker, 2007; van der Kolk, 1996). Implicit knowledge is often termed *procedural* knowledge because it consists of knowing how to perform an action (such as knowing when and how to behave in a very pleas-ing manner in order to be safe) or knowing how the world functions (such as "knowing" that people become rejecting or attacking as soon as they are displeased in any way). Such knowledge consists of schemas (patterns, templates, or models) that have been abstracted and extracted from experience and stored in memory systems other than those that hold one's explicit, autobiographical, "episodic" knowledge of past events. Knowledge created by implicit learning remains out of awareness even as it generates behaviors, emotions, and thoughts in response to current experience.

As noted above, therapists grapple daily with many phenomena that are clearly recognizable as expressions of non-conscious, learned emotional knowledge, such as attachment patterns, family of origin rules and roles, unresolved emotional themes, traumatic memory, and compulsive behaviors and emotional reactions in response to external or internal triggers. These phenomena can manifest as panic and anxiety attacks, chronic or acute depression, addictive behaviors, shame, self-criticism, rage, sexual inhibition, fear of intimacy, post-traumatic stress symptoms such as hypervigilance or compulsive avoidance, and many other symptoms and sufferings.

Of course, there are many psychological and behavioral symptoms not caused by emotional learnings—for example autism, hypothyroidism-induced depression and genetically based addiction—as well as symptoms produced from the interaction of implicit emotional learning (which are "nurture" influences) with genetic tendencies. For example, the degree of expression of certain genetic predispositions toward depression may depend upon the load of depression-inducing learnings in emotional implicit memory ("I'm not normal," "Mom and Dad hate each other," "I'm unlovable," and so on; for discussion see Toomey & Ecker, 2009). However well such nature–nurture interactions may come to be understood, in practice it is the power of existing emotional learnings that confronts therapists and their clients, so a new level of effectiveness in dispelling memory-driven symptoms would be of far-reaching benefit.

The potency and relative ubiquity of implicit emotional learnings are a sizable clinical challenge, but the real problem is their remarkable tenacity. Therapists routinely witness the extraordinary durability of original emotional learnings, which persist in their unrelenting vice grip on mood and behavior decades after they were formed. In conventional in-depth psychotherapies, it is therefore assumed that many months or years of steady work are necessary for releasing that grip. The deeply ingrained quality of emotional learnings is the bane of psychotherapists and their clients, but it appears to be a survival-positive result of natural selection. Selection pressures during evolution apparently crafted the brain such that any learning that occurs in the presence of strong emotion becomes stored in specialized subcortical implicit memory circuits that are exceptionally durable (McGaugh, 1989; McGaugh & Roozendaal, 2002; Roozendaal, McEwen, & Chattarji, 2009).

In fact, a central conclusion of memory and brain researchers throughout the 20th century was that the neural circuits of emotional learnings were unchangeable and permanent for the lifetime of the individual once they became physically installed in long-term memory through the process known as *consolidation* (reviewed in McGaugh, 2000). There appeared to exist no form of neuroplasticity capable of unlocking the synapses maintaining consolidated implicit memory circuits. This conclusion was based on extensive research on extinction, which is the observed suppression of the behavioral response of an established emotional learning by repetitive counter-training experiences. Neuroscientists and psychologists beginning with Pavlov had amassed extensive evidence that even after complete suppression of an emotionally learned (conditioned) response by extinction, the original response was only temporarily suppressed, not fundamentally eliminated from memory, and was fairly easily retriggered in various ways (Bouton, 2004; Milner et al., 1998). Research showed that extinction training forms a separate learning in a physically separate memory system from that of the target learning, and that the extinction learning competes against, but does not replace, the target learning (e.g., Bouton, 2004; Foa & McNally, 1996; Milner et al., 1998; Phelps, Delgado, Nearing, & LeDoux, 2004).

Consolidated emotional learnings were therefore believed to be indelible in memory, encoded in neural circuits by synapses that were irrevocably locked. The tenet of indelibility became most solidly established with publication of a research journal article on extinction studies by neuroscientists LeDoux, Romanski, and Xagoraris (1989) titled "Indelibility of Subcortical Emotional Memories." It was then natural and appropriate for psychologists to follow the lead of this body of research. When van der Kolk (1994) published in the *Harvard Review of Psychiatry* his seminal article, "The Body Keeps the Score: Memory and the Evolving Psychobiology of Post Traumatic Stress," he was introducing clinicians to an understanding of emotional implicit memory as the basis of symptom production—a paradigm-changing step that would powerfully influence the evolution of psychotherapy. Indelibility was a prominent part of the picture in a section of the article titled, "Emotional memories are forever." Subsequently therapists were guided to think in terms of implicit memory and associated brain science also by Schore (1994, 1996, 1997), Siegel (1999), Rothschild (2000) and Cozolino (2002).

The conclusion that implicit emotional learnings last for a lifetime meant that people could never become fundamentally free of flare-ups of childhood emotional conditioning such as fear reactions and insecure attachment patterns, which can be so limiting throughout our lives. It meant that evolution made the brain's limbic system—the major, subcortical region of implicit emotional learning and memory—into a kind of psychological prison in which each of us serves a life sentence.

Indelibility implied also that the only possible psychotherapeutic strategy for preventing symptoms based in emotional memory was the use of *counteractive* methods—the class of methods (including extinction training prototypically) that compete against an unwanted learning by building up a preferred learning and response intended to override and suppress the unwanted response. The unwanted response remains relatively free to recur, so an ongoing counteractive effort is typically required indefinitely. Counteracting is the nature of any communication or procedure that is understood as intended to prevent the symptom by arranging for a more desired state to occur instead—such as teaching a relaxation technique to counteract anxiety, building up resources and positive thoughts to counteract depression, or use of oxytocin to enhance feelings of emotional connection and empathy. The strategy of counteracting predominates in the psychotherapy field and is carried out by a wide range of methods, such as the various forms of cognitive-behavioral therapy (CBT), solution-focused therapy, and the positive therapies. Counteractive methods do not necessarily appear overtly suppressive of unwanted responses and learnings, as when desired resources and responses are being fostered in an expansive, fully positive spirit; certainly the attitude or intention of the therapist is not necessarily suppressive in using such methods, yet that tends to be the effect on underlying emotional learnings. (See Toomey & Ecker, 2009, for a discussion of counteractive vs. transformational change.)

Our story continues with the downfall of indelibility through the discovery of reconsolidation—along with some increase in technical detail. Readers who choose at any point to skip to the fully clinical focus of Chapter 3 and subsequent chapters will find a seamless transition because no familiarity with this chapter's account of reconsolidation research is assumed. In the rest of this chapter we take a look "under the hood," but in Chapter 3 you will be in the driver's seat, learning how to create the series of experiences that launches memory reconsolidation.

Detecting Reconsolidation: From Indelible to Erasable

At the end of the 1990s, neuroscientists resumed a line of research neglected since 1982, by once again studying the effects of reactivating an implicit emotional memory. Between 1968 and 1982, a few researchers had reported unexplained exceptions to indelibility. Standard ECT (electroconvulsive therapy) procedures that had failed to dispel a learned emotional response became dramatically successful in some animal and human studies when the procedure was varied such that the target response and its underlying implicit learnings were in a state of strong reactivation at the time of the shock (Misanin, Miller, & Lewis, 1968; Rubin, 1976; Rubin, Fried, & Franks, 1969). In these and several similar studies (Judge & Quartermain, 1982; Lewis & Bregman, 1973; Lewis, Bregman, & Mahan, 1972; Mactutus, Riccio, & Ferek, 1979; Richardson, Riccio, & Mowrey, 1982), targeted emotional and behavioral responses ceased and could not subsequently be re-evoked. This striking result implied that the change was not due to extinction or some other, merely suppressive mechanism and, therefore, that a true elimination or deletion of the original learning from implicit memory apparently had been achieved. Reactivation of a well-consolidated, longstanding implicit memory appeared to have rendered the stored emotional learning susceptible to dissolution. This was a direct challenge to the prevailing model of memory consolidation. However, these few anomalous studies received scant attention from memory researchers or clinicians, the phenomenon was not investigated further, and the tenet of the indelibility of implicit memory persisted.

In 1997, researchers began applying sophisticated new techniques as well as advanced knowledge of exactly where in the brain certain emotional learnings form and are stored in implicit memory, in order to study the effects of reactivating an implicit emotional memory into behavioral expression in animals. They utilized chemical agents known to destroy new, unstable, unconsolidated synapses but not synapses already consolidated and locked. They applied such agents shortly before or after reactivation of a consolidated emotional learning and found that in some cases, well-learned, consolidated responses subsequently disappeared completely and could not be re-evoked (Nader, Schafe, & LeDoux, 2000; Przybyslawski, Roullet, & Sara, 1999; Przybyslawski & Sara, 1997; Roullet & Sara, 1998; Sara, 2000; Sekiguchi, Yamada, & Suzuki, 1997). This meant that consolidated synapses previously believed impossible to unlock had become unlocked—that is, physically converted to a de-consolidated, "labile," "destabilized," or "plastic" state, similar to that of synapses prior to initial consolidation—which allowed the chemical agent to disrupt them physically and render the neural circuits of the learned emotional response defunct, as if they had never existed. Nader et al. (2000), whose study is often regarded as the confirming breakthrough, concluded, "Even well consolidated memories are labile and subject to disruption when reactivated" (p. 724). We will see below, however, that neuroscientists' initial inference that reactivation in itself is sufficient to unlock synapses was premature.

These demonstrations that a consolidated memory could be de-consolidated were a major reversal of the canonical tenet of indelibility. Researchers reasoned as follows: Implicit memories are reactivated regularly in the course of normal (non-laboratory) circumstances, yet are generally observed to remain stable, as if locked, over long periods of time; therefore the new knowledge that reactivation can de-consolidate a memory into a labile state implied that the destabilized, labile state is a temporary one and is automatically ended by a natural relocking or *reconsolidation* that returns the memory to a stable state no longer susceptible to change or disruption until it is destabilized again. This temporary period of de-consolidation, or "reconsolidation window," was soon demonstrated empirically by Pedreira, Pérez-Cuesta, and Maldonado (2002) in animal studies and then in other animal and human studies (Duvarci & Nader, 2004; Pedreira & Maldonado, 2003; Schiller et al., 2010; Walker, Brakefield, Hobson, & Stickgold, 2003). It is a five-hour window during which the de-consolidated target learning is directly revisable by new learning and so can be radically unlearned and, as a result, no longer exist in memory—without using synapse-blocking chemical agents, nearly all of which are toxic for humans.

Thus, we now know that the consolidation of emotional learnings in memory is not, as had been believed for a century, a one-time, final process, and emotional learnings are *not* indelible. Rather, they can be returned temporarily to a de-consolidated state, allowing erasure not only by chemical means but also, as researchers subsequently showed and as described below, by new learnings before reconsolidation takes place.

The term "reconsolidation" is used by neuroscientists in two ways—to denote the relocking of synapses in the final step of the natural process of synaptic unlocking and relocking, but also to refer to the brain's overall process of unlocking and then relocking the synapses encoding a specific memory. In what follows, the term refers to the overall process unless the context makes it clear that only the final stage is meant.

Reconsolidation was described as "permitting reorganization of the existing memory as a function of new information in the retrieval environment" by researchers Przybyslawski et al. (1999, p. 6623). Similarly, Nader et al. (2000, p. 725) stated, "Reconsolidation may reflect the dynamic nature of the process by which new information is added to existing stores," and Nader (2003, p. 65) affirmed "the hypothesis that reactivation of a consolidated memory can return it to a labile, sensitive state—in which it can be modified, strengthened, changed or even erased!" Dudai and Eisenberg (2004, p. 93) maintained that reconsolidation is "of profound relevance not only to fundamental issues in memory research, e.g., the nature of memory persistence, but also to potential applications, e.g., targeted erasure of stubborn traumatic memories."

Of particular importance are the behaviorally observable, distinctive markers of erasure of an emotional learning. Neuroscientists rely on these markers as their primary evidence of successful erasure in both animal and human subjects (e.g., Schiller et al., 2010). The true disappearance from memory of a learning that previously generated behavioral responses has the following signature features.

- A specific emotional reaction abruptly can no longer be reactivated by cues and triggers that formerly did so or by other stressful situations.
- Symptoms of behavior, emotion, somatics, or thought that were expressions of that emotional reaction also disappear permanently.
- Non-recurrence of the emotional reaction and symptoms continues effortlessly and without counteractive or preventive measures of any kind.

According to current neuroscience, those markers can result only from memory erasure, that is, via reconsolidation. They cannot be produced by extinction or other counteractive/competitive processes, which are inherently susceptible to relapse, particularly in new or stressful situations. Likewise, whenever these markers are observed and firmly established in clinical work, erasure via reconsolidation is a valid inference. On the basis of that logic, proponents of several psychotherapies of focused, deep emotional change have inferred that reconsolidation must be the neurobiological mechanism of change induced by their methods: Coherence Therapy (Ecker, 2006, 2008; Ecker & Hulley, 2011; Ecker & Toomey, 2008), Emotion-Focused Therapy or EFT (Greenberg, 2010), exposure with acupoint tapping (Feinstein, 2010), Eye Movement Desensitization and Reprocessing or EMDR (Solomon & Shapiro, 2008), Interpersonal Neurobiology or IPNB (Badenoch, 2011), and psychoanalytic therapy (Gorman & Roose, 2011). In addition, the demonstrated effectiveness of an imaginal reenactment protocol for dispelling post-traumatic symptoms has been attributed to reconsolidation (Högberg, Nardo, Hällström, & Pagani, 2011). Chapters 3 through 10 of this book provide case examples of several of these and other therapies, showing how they fulfill the brain's requirements for inducing reconsolidation.

According to researchers, reconsolidation implies a psychotherapeutic strategy of transformational change of acquired memory—in sharp contrast to the counteractive strategy of change. Liberating, life-changing, lasting shifts are clinically observed to result from using the process identified by reconsolidation researchers, as we show throughout this book. The prison of emotional memory, built over the aeons by evolution, comes with a key, and that key has now been found. Synapses can be unlocked. The limbic life sentence can be commuted.

How Reconsolidation Works

Reconsolidation has been demonstrated with nematodes, honeybees, snails, sea slugs, fish, crabs, chicks, mice, rats, and humans, for a wide range of different types of emotional learning and memory as well as for non-emotional memory, such as motor memory and semantic (factual) memory, corresponding to memory networks in many different anatomical regions of the brain (reviewed in Nader & Einarsson, 2010). For clinical purposes in this book, however, we are concerned with emotional memory, so our discussion of reconsolidation is focused in that area. We do not go into detail regarding brain anatomy because the sequence of experiences that launches reconsolidation is the same for all regions and types of memory. Even our references to the major regions of the emotional brain—using terms such as subcortical, limbic, or right-brain—are meant largely heuristically. If some function or memory that we refer to as "subcortical," for example, were to be shown later to be actually a right-brain function or memory, this would not invalidate the substance of our point.

Requirements for de-consolidation: Reactivation plus mismatch

In 2004, reconsolidation researchers' early inference that memory reactivation alone destabilizes a memory's neural circuits was overturned by the demonstration, in an animal study, that in order for de-consolidation to occur, a critical additional experience must take place while the memory is still reactivated

(Pedreira et al., 2004). This second experience consists of novel perceptions that *mismatch*—that is, deviate saliently from—what the reactivated target memory expects and predicts about how the world functions. At least nine subsequent studies (listed in Table 2.1) also have demonstrated this requirement of mismatch for de-consolidating a well-established memory. These studies have shown that

Table 2.1 Studies reporting that both memory reactivation and memory mismatch are necessary for inducing memory labilization and reconsolidation

Year	Authors	Species	Memory type	Design and findings
2004	Pedreira et al.	Crab	Contextual fear memory	Reactivated learned expectation of visual threat must be sharply disconfirmed for memory to be disrupted by cycloheximide.
2005	Galluccio	Human	Operant conditioning	Memory is erased only by being reactivated along with a novel contingency.
2005	Rodriguez-Ortiz et al.	Rat	Taste recognition memory	Novel taste following reactivation allows memory disruption by anisomycin.
2006	Morris et al.	Rat	Spatial memory of escape from danger	After reactivation, only a change of the learned safe position allows disruption of original memory by anisomycin.
2006	Rossato et al.	Rat	Spatial memory of escape from danger	After reactivation, only a change of the learned safe position allows disruption of original memory by anisomycin.
2007	Rossato et al.	Rat	Object recognition memory	Memory is disrupted by anisomycin only if reactivated in presence of novel object.
2008	Forcato et al.	Human	Declarative memory	Memory of syllable pairings learned visually is labilized and lost only if reactivation is followed by learning revised novel pairings.
2008	Rodriguez-Ortiz et al.	Rat	Spatial memory of escape from danger	After reactivation, only a change of the learned safe position allows disruption of original memory by anisomycin.
2009	Perez-Cuesta & Maldonado	Crab	Contextual fear memory	Reactivated learned expectation of visual threat must be sharply disconfirmed for memory to be disrupted by cycloheximide.
2009	Winters et al.	Rat	Object recognition memory	Memory is disrupted by MK-801 only if reactivated in presence of novel contextual features.

the mismatch can be either a full contradiction and disconfirmation of the target memory or a novel, salient variation relative to the target memory.

If the target memory is reactivated by familiar cues but not mismatched in that manner, synapses do not unlock and reconsolidation is not induced. Absence of a mismatch experience is associated with failure to induce memory de-consolidation and reconsolidation in several studies (e.g., Cammarota, Bevilaqua, Medina, & Izquierdo, 2004; Hernandez & Kelley, 2004; Mileusnic, Lancashire, & Rose, 2005). Likewise, when reactivation was followed by memory reinforcement, which is the opposite of mismatch, reconsolidation was not observed (e.g., Forcato et al., 2008; Pedreira et al., 2004). Nevertheless, many science journalists (and even some neuroscientists) have, as of this writing, continued to write that reactivation alone destabilizes a memory and launches reconsolidation; they appear to be unaware of the well-established mismatch requirement, which may reflect the not uncommon time lag for widespread recognition of all findings to develop in any rapidly emerging field.

A computer analogy has been widely used to explain how reconsolidation allows a particular emotional learning to be updated (revised or erased): Reactivating a memory is likened to opening a document on a computer, which allows the contents of the document to be edited or deleted before the document is resaved and closed. In this analogy, opening the document corresponds to reactivating the target memory. However, according to the extensive research cited just above, that analogy is somewhat misleading. Whereas the single step of opening a computer document allows it to be modified, the single step of reactivating a target memory is not sufficient to render it labile and modifiable. Reactivating a memory is only the first of two steps needed to put the memory into a condition of being ready to be replaced by new learning. The needed second step is *a perception or experience that mismatches the target memory*, in the form of either a salient novelty or an outright contradiction. Only after those two steps will the memory be updated by a learning experience that occurs next.

Regarding the brain's requirement for a mismatch of the target memory in order to launch the reconsolidation process, Lee (2009, p. 417) noted in a review article, "It is not simply that memory reactivation must differ in some manner to conditioning ... Instead, reconsolidation is triggered by a violation of expectation based upon prior learning, whether such a violation is qualitative (the outcome not occurring at all) or quantitative (the magnitude of the outcome not being fully predicted)." Lee proposed that "the existence of a prediction error signal [from some brain region] might be a crucial pre-requisite for reconsolidation to be triggered" (p. 419). In another review article, Wang and Morris (2010, pp. 66–67) summarized, "reconsolidation occurs when there is new information at the time of memory retrieval. ... In the context of memory reconsolidation, novelty is likely derived from mismatch between consolidated and current information, which then re-engages the encoding process ... reconsolidation does not always occur after memory reactivation."

Based on the many reconfirmations of the mismatch requirement, as listed in Table 2.1, we may adhere to this principle: Whenever the markers of erasure of a learning are observed, both reactivation and a mismatch of that learning must have taken place, unlocking its synapses, or erasure could not have resulted. This logic can serve as a useful guide for identifying the critical steps of process in both the experiments of researchers and the sessions of psychotherapists.

Precision of erasure

When a de-consolidated memory is erased, erasure is limited to precisely the reactivated target learning, without impairing other closely linked emotional learnings that have not been directly reactivated. This was shown both in an animal study using chemically induced erasure (Debiec, Doyère, Nader, & LeDoux, 2006) and in a human study using behavioral erasure (Schiller et al., 2010). Furthermore, Kindt, Soeter, and Vervliet (2009) demonstrated in a human study that chemical erasure of a learned fear did not impair explicit autobiographical memory: After the learned fear response had been eliminated, subjects still remembered the experiences in which they had acquired the conditioned fear response, as well as the fact of having had the fear, but the fear was not re-evoked by remembering those experiences. These findings are understood as reflecting the well-established anatomical separateness of different types of memory, which allows erasure of a specific emotional implicit learning stored in an emotional implicit memory network without affecting the autobiographical, narrative learning of the same original events stored in a neocortical, explicit memory network. Thus the extent of the learnings erased via reconsolidation is highly defined and controllable, as necessary for safe clinical use of the erasure process.

Other aspects of reconsolidation research

Our interest is the pharmaceutical-free application of reconsolidation in psychotherapy, so we cover in this chapter selected aspects of the research relevant to that. However, reconsolidation is a complex phenomenon with many aspects that do not bear directly upon such clinical uses but are nevertheless important for the more fundamental understanding of learning and memory sought by neuroscientists. Areas not covered here include how the minimum strength of reactivation (intensity and/or duration) and the minimum strength and quality of mismatch experience required for successful de-consolidation of a memory are influenced by memory age, memory strength (the intensity and quantity of original learning experiences), and memory type. The complex relationships among those parameters, or "boundary conditions," are a major topic of ongoing reconsolidation research (as reviewed by, e.g., Lee, 2009; Nader & Einarsson, 2010).

Another type of boundary condition under study is that between reconsolidation and extinction, two phenomena that have distinctly different behavioral effects, as noted earlier. It has been established that they are neurologically distinct processes (Duvarci, Mamou, & Nader, 2006; Duvarci & Nader, 2004) and that they can occur either entirely independently of each other (Lee, Milton, & Everitt, 2006; Mamiya et al., 2009; Pedreira & Maldonado, 2003; Pedreira et al., 2004; Pérez-Cuesta & Maldonado, 2009; Schiller et al., 2010; Suzuki et al., 2004) or simultaneously and with a complex interaction (Eisenberg, Kobilo, Berman, & Dudai, 2003; Nader, 2003; Pedreira & Maldonado, 2003; Pedreira et al., 2004; Pérez-Cuesta & Maldonado, 2009; Rossato et al., 2006; Stollhoff, Menzel, & Eisenhardt, 2005; Suzuki et al., 2004; Tronson & Taylor, 2007).

Yet a different aspect of the distinction between reconsolidation and extinction comes into play in studies that use a behavioral procedure identical to extinction training during the reconsolidation window to serve as new learning that contradicts and erases the target learning (e.g., Monfils, Cowansage, Klan, & LeDoux, 2009; Quirk et al., 2010; Schiller et al., 2010; Xue et al., 2012). Robust, long-lasting erasure is observed to result, so it is apparent that the *neurological* effect created by this special use of "extinction training" is not extinction (creation of a separate, competing learning) but rather erasure via reconsolidation (updating of the target learning by the contradictory learning). Thus a particular behavioral learning procedure can have quite different neurological effects and behavioral consequences depending on whether or not it is carried out during the reconsolidation window. "Reconsolidation cannot be reduced down to facilitated extinction" was the conclusion of a study by Duvarci and Nader (2004, p. 9269). When the procedure traditionally termed "extinction training" is applied during the reconsolidation window and the result is unambiguously not extinction, the procedure in that instance could more appropriately be labeled "memory update training" rather than "extinction training" to avoid conceptual errors and confusion. Indeed, the beauty of the reconsolidation window is that during that window, to unlearn is to erase. The century-old, deeply familiar label of "extinction" has tenaciously stuck with this training procedure, however, even in this new context where the procedure does not result in extinction, and researchers (and science journalists) typically refer to this procedure as, for example, "extinction-induced erasure," "extinction training during reconsolidation," the "memory retrieval–extinction procedure," and "erasing fear memories with extinction training." We describe this potentially misleading situation here so that our readers may be spared some unnecessary confusion. The extinction training protocol fits well with research requirements because of its simple, structured format, but it is only one of a potentially unlimited number of forms in which new learning may occur during the reconsolidation window in psychotherapy, as the case examples in the book illustrate.

The biomolecular and genetic processes involved in reconsolidation are another major area of study; for a review, see Tronson and Taylor (2007). Of great interest to neuroscientists also is the question of whether the destabilized synapses are those of the encoded learning, the circuits serving retrieval of the encoded learning, or both (a question whose resolution will not affect the clinical implications and applications described in this book; for this area see, e.g., Hardt, Wang, & Nader, 2009; Matzel & Miller, 2009). Research on the chemical disruption of reconsolidation for psychotherapeutic purposes is also ongoing (e.g., Kindt, Soeter, & Vervliet, 2009; Soeter & Kindt, 2011; Tronson & Taylor, 2007).

The Behavioral Process for Erasing an Emotional Learning

We come now to the clinical heart of the matter: the sequence of experiences required by the brain for launching reconsolidation and then using new learning to erase a target learning, as identified in reconsolidation research. In this regard, both animal and human studies have yielded the same results. For clinicians, human demonstrations are perhaps most credible and reassuring, so we focus here on the findings garnered from studies in which learnings created in human subjects were erased, weakened, or revised via reconsolidation using natural, behavioral techniques of new learning. What neuroscientists sometimes term the "updating" or "rewriting" of specific learnings has been demonstrated in humans for several different types of memory:

- procedural, motor skill memory (Walker et al., 2003)
- operant conditioning (Galluccio, 2005)
- declarative memory (Forcato et al., 2007, 2008)
- episodic memory (Hupbach, Gomez, Hardt, & Nadel, 2007; Hupbach, Gomez, & Nadel, 2009)
- classical fear conditioning (Schiller et al., 2010)
- memory for cue-triggered heroin cravings (Xue et al., 2012).

(The inclusion of declarative and episodic memory in this list may seem to imply a contradiction of the finding, described earlier, that erasure of an emotional learning leaves autobiographical memory unaffected, but that is not the case. Reconsolidation is highly selective and affects only the memory that is experientially mismatched, whatever type of memory that may be. Thus if emotional memory is so targeted, as in the Galluccio and Schiller et al. studies listed above and as is the case for psychotherapeutic application, then autobiographical memory remains unaffected, but if autobiographical memory is targeted it will consequently be the memory affected.)

In each of these studies, the target learning was first destabilized by the two steps of being reactivated and then mismatched by a novelty or contradiction. Then, in a third step, the target learning was completely or partially "rewritten" by new learning within the five-hour reconsolidation window—the memory's labile period. The altered memory was then allowed to reconsolidate naturally (in contrast to eliminating the memory's neural circuits by chemically disrupting their reconsolidation). Behavioral tests then verified the erasure or alteration of the target learning. These demonstrations have confirmed what neuroscientists surmised soon after reconsolidation was discovered, namely that it is the brain's adaptive process for updating existing learnings with new ones. Reviewing these studies, Hupbach (2011) has inferred that whether the effect of the new learning is to completely replace, impair (weaken), or integrate into (supplement) the target learning depends upon "the degree with which the newly presented information [within the reconsolidation window] competes [i.e., is incompatible] with the previously encoded information." Our understanding will undoubtedly be refined by future studies of how new learning can be applied for the rewriting and updating of existing, unwanted learnings.

Thus, from the totality of research to date, we see that the natural, behavioral process of transformational change of an existing emotional learning—the brain's rules for unlearning and erasing a target learning—has three steps.

1. *Reactivate.* Re-trigger/re-evoke the target knowledge by presenting salient cues or contexts from the original learning.
2. *Mismatch/unlock.* Concurrent with reactivation, create an experience that is significantly at variance with the target learning's model and expectations of how the world functions. This step unlocks synapses and renders memory circuits labile, i.e., susceptible to being updated by new learning.
3. *Erase or revise via new learning.* During a window of about five hours before synapses have relocked, create a new learning experience that contradicts (for erasing) or supplements (for revising) the labile target knowledge. (This new learning experience may be the same as or different from the experience used for mismatch in Step 2; if it is the same, Step 3 consists of repetitions of Step 2.)

After this three-step sequence, researchers also conduct an erasure verification step consisting of behavioral tests of whether the target learning still exists in memory. We will refer to this as Step V (for verification).

The *erasure sequence*, steps 1–2–3 above, is a research finding that appears to have the potential to revolutionize the practice of psychotherapy. Reconsolidation research has identified this process for utilizing new learning to unlearn and erase all or part of an existing learning, including the emotional implicit learnings that so often underlie clinical symptoms. As of this writing, this is the only behavioral process known to neuroscience that achieves true eradication of an emotional learning, and it does so through the only known form of neuroplasticity capable of unlocking the synapses maintaining an existing learning: memory reconsolidation.

In this book we refer to the erasure sequence also as the *transformation sequence*, particularly in the context of psychotherapy, in order to help emphasize the distinction between transformational and counteractive change. Our clinical case examples are intended to show the potency of the transformation sequence for routinely achieving a level of clinical effectiveness well beyond current norms.

Importantly, the three-step erasure sequence is a series of experiences defined without referring to specific techniques for bringing about those experiences. This means that in its application to psychotherapy, it can be carried out by therapists using their own choices of experiential techniques from a range of possibilities that may well be unlimited—or rather, limited only by the inventiveness of therapists. The erasure sequence is a theory-independent, universal meta-process, and as such it can richly foster integration within the psychotherapy field. We address this topic in Chapter 6 by surveying several experiential psychotherapies with methods that differ greatly from one another, showing that all three steps of the erasure sequence are detectable in the implementation of each therapy and appear to be responsible for the effectiveness of each.

Dwell with us for a moment on the "new learning" that serves to rewrite and erase the target learning in Step 3 above. Quite differing forms of new learning were used in the studies listed at the start of this subsection. Researchers have yet to find how the form, duration, and intensity of new learning determine its effectiveness in rewriting the target learning. What is clear is that the new learning must feel decisively *real* to the person based on his or her own living experience. In other words, it must be experiential learning as distinct from conceptual, intellectual learning, though it may be accompanied by the latter. The case studies throughout this book provide many examples of new learnings that successfully nullified and permanently eliminated targeted emotional learnings. Some of the examples will show that it is often extremely useful to take advantage of the fact that the emotional brain hardly distinguishes between imagined and physically enacted experiences (as demonstrated empirically by, for example, Kreiman, Koch, & Fried, 2000).

Memory Reconsolidation in Clinical Practice: The Therapeutic Reconsolidation Process

Now we come to the pragmatics of carrying out the erasure sequence in therapy sessions. Clearly there are significant differences between the lab, where neuroscientists keep conditions well controlled and simplified, and the consulting room, where therapists encounter high levels of complexity which, by the very nature of the situation, cannot be well controlled procedurally. What are the main considerations for reliably importing the erasure sequence from the former domain to the latter?

We can find our way in this matter by recognizing that therapists face two main differences in the clinical situation relative to the lab: the *unknown content* of the target learning, and the *complexity* of the target learning.

Carrying out each step of the erasure sequence requires detailed knowledge of the target emotional learning, but a psychotherapist is completely in the dark in this regard with each new client. Neuroscientists, in contrast, know all details of the target learning from the start because in a reconsolidation study they design and create the emotional learning to be erased. Instilling that learning in subjects occurs on Day 1 of any given lab study. Then, on Day 2, they make detailed use of their knowledge of the target learning in every step of the three-step process of erasure—reactivation of the target learning; creation of an experience of mismatch of the target learning; and finally, creation of an experience of new learning that contradicts and rewrites (and thereby erases the content of) the target learning. Researchers could not carry out these crucial three steps for erasure if they did not know the specific content of the target learning.

In therapy, even the symptoms (the unwanted responses) are unknown to the therapist at the start. So, in order to become able to carry out the erasure sequence reliably and decisively, the therapist must first elicit accurate descriptions of (A) the symptom(s) to be dispelled and (B) the emotional learnings generating those symptom(s). Those are initial, preparatory steps that must be added in the clinical setting. As a rule, the emotional learnings maintaining therapy clients' symptoms are complex and are areas of deep vulnerability that consist of implicit memory and implicit knowledge, so they are not conscious at the start of therapy. *Retrieving* them into explicit awareness for Step B typically constitutes the greater part of the therapeutic work. Various psychotherapies (see Table 1.1) have developed specialized, focused methods for this in-depth retrieval work, and usually it can be carried out in far fewer sessions than was assumed necessary by most of the clinical field for most of the twentieth century. In all subsequent chapters of this book, readers will encounter examples of how implicit emotional knowledge is brought into explicit awareness in a focused, efficient manner for Step B. Often only a few sessions are needed for the retrieval work, though of course the number of sessions increases commensurate with the complexity and severity of the case.

The retrieval work reveals a target learning considerably more complex than those addressed in reconsolidation research. This turns out to be advantageous because within any one emotional learning, *several* components are potent targets for mismatch and erasure, and succeeding with any one of them is all that is needed. We will map out the rich makeup of human emotional learnings or schemas in Chapters 3 and 4, providing you with a clear guide for working with their complexity. What is relevant to our present discussion is that once the specific makeup of the retrieved, underlying learning is known to the therapist, he or she can then begin the task of *finding* suitable mismatch material to be used in the erasure sequence—and that is preparatory Step C (and the topic of Chapter 4, which provides case studies illustrating some of the many ways of addressing this task). Finding mismatch material means finding living knowledge available to the client from past or present experience that contradicts the target learning and can therefore serve as new learning that eradicates the target learning. As soon as the contradictory ingredients are identified in Step C, the erasure sequence can then be carried out.

Thus in the clinical situation, a preparatory process consisting of the following three steps is needed initially in order to carry out next the erasure sequence identified in reconsolidation research.

A. *Symptom identification.* Actively clarify with the client *what* to regard as the presenting symptom(s)—the specific behaviors, somatics, emotions, and/or thoughts that the client wants to eliminate—and *when* they happen, that is, the percepts and contexts that evoke or intensify them. This information, which in many cases may be obtained within the first session, is needed for embarking upon step B efficiently. It also subsequently helps the therapist to carry out step 1 of the erasure sequence, reactivation.

B. *Retrieval of target learning.* Retrieve into explicit awareness, as a visceral emotional experience, the details of the emotional learning underlying and driving the presenting symptom. This in turn allows the therapist to carry out Step C, identification of disconfirming knowledge, and also to carry out a deep, thorough implementation of Step 1 of the erasure sequence, reactivation.

C. *Identification of disconfirming knowledge.* Identify a vivid experience (past or present) available to the client that can serve as living knowledge that is fundamentally incompatible with the model of reality in the target emotional learning retrieved in Step B, such that both cannot possibly be true. The disconfirming material may or may not be appealing to the client as being more "positive" or preferred; what matters is for it to be mutually exclusive, ontologically, with the target learning. It may be already part of the client's personal knowledge or may be created by a new experience. It will be used to carry out Step 2 of the erasure sequence (the mismatch that destabilizes the target learning) and Step 3 (repetitions of mismatch in which the contradictory knowledge serves as new learning that erases the target learning).

We refer to the three preparatory steps, A–B–C, as the *accessing sequence* required in order to carry out Steps 1–2–3, the *erasure sequence*, knowingly and explicitly. (Steps 1–2–3 can also occur implicitly, i.e., unbeknownst to therapist and client, in some therapies, or even serendipitously, without Steps A–B–C taking place.) We term the entire series of steps, A–B–C–1–2–3–V, the *therapeutic reconsolidation process* (see Table 2.2).

Several sessions are usually needed for the accessing sequence, whereas the subsequent erasure sequence in itself requires only several minutes. (Schiller et al., 2010 carried out Steps 1–2–3 in 15 minutes to erase a purely subcortical, classical conditioning fear memory in humans.) However, complications of various types can arise in the accessing sequence, the erasure sequence, or both, increasing the number of sessions required. We describe these complications in Chapter 3.

Table 2.2   Steps of process for clinical application of memory reconsolidation

Therapeutic reconsolidation process	
I. Accessing sequence	A. Symptom identification B. Retrieval of target learning (symptom-requiring schema) C. Identification of disconfirming knowledge
II. Erasure sequence*	1. Reactivation of symptom-requiring schema (B) 2. Activation of disconfirming knowledge (C), mismatching symptom-requiring schema (B) 3. Repetitions of (B)–(C) pairing
III. Verification step	V. Observations of: – Emotional non-reactivation – Symptom cessation – Effortless permanence

Notes: Steps 1–2–3–V replicate the process identified in reconsolidation research for erasing a specific emotional learning from implicit memory, as reviewed in the text. In the clinical setting, additional initial Steps A–B–C are necessary in therapies of in-depth schema retrieval, so that the therapist acquires information needed for carrying out Steps 1–2–3.

* *Erasure sequence* is used interchangeably with *transformation sequence* in this book to refer to Steps 1–2–3. *Erasure sequence* is used in the neurological context and *transformation sequence* is used in the clinical context.

Neuroscientists follow steps 1–2–3 with a verification step—step V—consisting of a test that probes the status of the target learning by presenting a known cue or trigger that formerly strongly evoked a clear behavioral response from the target learning but would elicit no such response if erasure has occurred. The same is important to do clinically, both soon after erasure and at intervals thereafter, if possible. Absence of the client's former problematic response gives both therapist and client a clear indication that the sought-for change has been accomplished. Clear-cut verification in Step V is also necessary for documenting single case studies for empirical research purposes.

The seven-step therapeutic reconsolidation process summarized in Table 2.2 defines the direct translation of memory reconsolidation findings to psychotherapy, and it does so in technique-independent and theory-independent terms. It "belongs" to no single system, school or theory of psychotherapy or personality, though therapy systems differ widely in their native suitability for carrying out this process. The range of experiential methods and styles of working that therapists can use for carrying out the seven steps is open-ended, including verbally guided experiential methods (as in Gestalt-type chair work, Focusing, inner child work, Jungian active imagination, or guided visualization, for example), somatic and energy therapy methods, couple and family systems methods, trauma therapy methods, art therapy and sandtray methods, drama therapy methods, and bilateral (dual) stimulation methods. All following chapters of Part 1 describe various aspects of carrying out the therapeutic reconsolidation process: in Coherence Therapy (Chapters 3–5) and in AEDP, EFT, EMDR, and IPNB (Chapter 6).

The Neuroscience of Psychotherapy:
Reconsolidation versus Emotional Regulation

At the time of writing this book, reconsolidation and its psychotherapeutic implications were very new input from neuroscience into the clinical field. This new
input follows a lengthy prior phase during which the clinical field welcomed a
large influx of pre-reconsolidation neuroscience. Therefore, the understanding
that many therapists now have of the implications of brain science for psychotherapy is based on the pre-reconsolidation state of knowledge. Rapidly emerging
knowledge of reconsolidation has expanded the picture, however, by adding a
new type and process of change that differ significantly in certain respects from
what came before. In this section we review the pre-reconsolidation input from
neuroscience so that readers can acquire a clear perspective on how and why the
therapeutic reconsolidation process represents a different type of psychological
change.

Pre-reconsolidation brain science came to the attention of the clinical field, creating unmistakable benefit for advancing the evolution of psychotherapy, largely
due to the writings of van der Kolk (1994, 1996), Schore (1994, 2003a, 2003b),
LeDoux (1996), Panksepp (1998), Siegel (1999), Rothschild (2000) and Cozolino
(2002). Subsequent texts continued to develop the pre-reconsolidation vision of
how to enhance therapeutic effectiveness by being a "brain-based," "brain-wise,"
or "brain-savvy" therapist, such as those of Folensbee (2007), Badenoch (2008),
Arden and Linford (2009), Cozolino (2010), and Fosha et al. (2010). This infusion
of pre-reconsolidation brain science consisted of clinicians' recognition of the
following research findings.

- A basic characteristic of the brain is lifelong neuroplasticity. The brain can
  always "rewire" itself.
- The brain's neural circuits are changed therapeutically through new experiences, not through cognitive insights alone.
- New experiences that are imaginal can be effective for creating new neural
  circuits and new responses, because the emotional centers in the subcortex
  hardly distinguish between perceptions arising externally versus internally.
- Separate regions or subsystems of the brain handle psychological functions of different types, including learning and the forming and storing of
  memory of many different types. There is great plasticity in the degree
  of integration and sharing of information among these subsystems. The
  vertical structure of cortex, subcortex, and brain stem (the "triune brain")
  and left–right lateralization are large-scale approximations describing this
  localization of function, which is extremely complex on smaller scales.
- The personal, dynamic unconscious (the Freudian unconscious) consists
  largely of implicit memory of emotional learnings formed and stored by the
  subcortical limbic system and the right cortical hemisphere. Implicit emo-

tional learnings generate responses independently of conscious awareness, which is based in other cortical regions.

- Early life experiences within primary attachment relationships create potent emotional learnings in implicit memory, which can have a major influence on the degree of integration among brain systems, interpersonal responses, personality, and dominant mood.

The points listed above are general "truths of the brain" that have advanced psychotherapy invaluably and are not challenged by the subsequent findings of memory reconsolidation research. However, the following three additional implications of pre-reconsolidation brain science *are* challenged and do need to be reconsidered in light of reconsolidation research, because they represent limitations that no longer exist, given the expanded state of knowledge.

- Unwanted, emotionally-driven responses arising from subcortical, emotional brain centers can be therapeutically regulated and suppressed only by building up preferred learnings and responses in other brain regions that have regulatory neural linkages to the subcortical regions.
- Procedurally, replacing an unwanted response with a new, preferred response requires great numbers of repetitions of the new response over time, accompanied by mindful attention to choosing the new response each time, in order to establish the new neural linkages required. The need for many repetitions reflects the principle that "neurons that fire together, wire together," which is the popular formulation of Hebb's law.
- In order to change negative attachment patterns therapeutically, new positive attachment experiences are required in the client–therapist relationship.

The three points above, which express the paradigm of counteractive change, do not apply to facilitating change through the therapeutic reconsolidation process. For example, whereas counteractive methods rely centrally on Hebb's law for creating new neural linkages through extensive repetition over a prolonged period, transformational change through the erasure sequence does not rely on extensive repetition over time to effect change. The swiftness with which deep, decisive, lasting change occurs through the therapeutic reconsolidation process (and through therapies that embody it) challenges traditional notions of the time required for major therapeutic effects to come about. The important topic of attachment and how the transformational change of attachment patterns is understood in terms of the therapeutic reconsolidation process is addressed in detail in Chapter 5.

The changes sought in therapy are nearly always a matter of arranging for new learning to supersede old, existing learning. Both the counteractive change process and the therapeutic reconsolidation process use new learning to bring about desired change, but they do so in different ways and yield different results,

Table 2.3 Comparison of the therapeutic effects of the therapeutic reconsolidation process and emotional regulation

Therapeutic reconsolidation process	Emotional regulation
Eliminates source of problem: Uses new learnings to delete problematic learnings.	Competes against source of problem: Uses new learnings to develop preferred state.
Symptom cessation is rapid and complete.	Symptom reduction is slow and incremental.
Not subject to relapse.	Subject to relapse.
Remaining symptom-free is effortless.	Preferred state needs effortful ongoing maintenance.
Increased sense of unified self and wholeness.	Persistent sense of divided self and inner conflict.
Symptom production is understood as the normal functioning and expression of implicit memory.	Symptom production is understood in a pathologizing manner as a dysregulation of brain systems.

as summarized in Table 2.3, where the pre-reconsolidation, counteractive framework is labeled *emotional regulation*, the name by which it is widely known and taught (along with the variations *affect regulation* and *cognitive regulation*).

Of course, new learning of any kind creates brain change in the form of new neural connections; but it is *only* when new learning also unwires old learning that *transformational* change occurs, rather than counteractive change, and this is precisely what the reconsolidation process achieves. Examined in that way, we see that counteractive change and transformational change represent learning processes of two fundamentally different types.

In counteractive change or emotional regulation, new learning creates circuits and memory that are neuroanatomically separate from the existing circuits of unwanted old learnings. These new separate learnings compete against the existing old learnings and, if successful, the new circuits suppress and override the existing ones, so that preferred responses occur instead of unwanted responses. Both old and new learnings continue to exist in memory, so the old responses can still occur and an ongoing effort must be made to help the new responses predominate, though this is not always successful. For example, Heatherton and Wagner (2011, p. 132), in a peer-reviewed journal article titled, "Cognitive Neuroscience of Self-Regulation Failure," stated, "Cognitive neuroscience research suggests that successful self-regulation is dependent on top-down control from the prefrontal cortex over subcortical regions involved in reward and emotion." This is representative of the pre-reconsolidation implications of brain science for clinicians striving to practice neurobiologically informed psychotherapy.

In transformational change through the therapeutic reconsolidation process, new learning directly impinges upon and revises the circuits of the old learning, rewriting and updating them, as noted earlier. The synaptic encoding of the old learning is replaced by the synaptic encoding of the new learning through the neurological process of memory reconsolidation. As a result of new learning formed in this way, the original unwanted, symptom-generating learnings no longer exist in memory because their content is gone. Therefore the unwanted response driven by the old learning ceases permanently.

Both reconsolidation research and clinical experience have shown that the brain is always ready to update and erase existing learnings through the therapeutic reconsolidation process. The resulting profound change is effortless to maintain once it occurs because the old learning no longer exists. The circuits of existing learnings are erased only under the special conditions described by the erasure sequence (see Table 2.2), according to current knowledge in brain science. In contrast, *counteractive methods by definition cultivate desired new learnings and responses without fulfilling the brain's required conditions for erasure of old learnings.*

Counteractive methods, including therapies of emotional regulation, are broadly applicable across essentially all clinical situations. In contrast, although the range of applicability of the therapeutic reconsolidation process is very broad—in principle, covering all unwanted responses arising from emotional learning—there are several types of clinical situation in which its role should be, as a rule, only adjunctive to primary treatment through counteractive methods such as crisis intervention, skill-building, resource utilization, or pharmacological measures:

- situations of urgent crisis, danger or emergency
- conditions known not to consist of underlying emotional learnings (such as autism spectrum disorders, hypothyroidism-induced depression and genetically based addiction)
- individuals whose stability could be compromised by direct experience of underlying, unresolved emotional vulnerability or distress, or who are unable to attend to and maintain awareness of the content of their own subjective experiencing
- severe patterns of personality or character that initially make deeper emotional work and self-awareness impossible for all practical purposes
- clients who express a definite choice not to do in-depth work and want to cultivate preferred states or behaviors without addressing interior, underlying sources of the problem.

For example, with a client who presents PTSD and extreme characterological avoidance of emotional vulnerability, primary treatment would consist ideally of counteractive methods, such as relaxation techniques, supplemented gradually by adjunctive use of the therapeutic reconsolidation process, for example through empowered re-enactment to dissolve specific traumatic memories (an example of which is included in Chapter 4). In contrast, with a client who presents PTSD, depression or many other symptoms, but who fits none of the categories of counter-indication listed just above, the therapeutic reconsolidation process can be the primary approach and, in light of the therapeutic advantages of this approach as indicated in Table 2.3, it may warrant being regarded as best practice in this case.

The prototype of counteractive, regulatory methods is of course extinction training, which is directly applied clinically in various forms of exposure therapy (e.g., Foa & Kozak, 1986; Foa & McNally, 1996; Tryon, 2005). However, there are many other regulatory approaches, which differ in the type of resources and experiences utilized for building up preferred new responses. (For example, a spectrum of types of cognitive regulation of emotion is described by Ochsner and Gross, 2005 and reviewed by Toomey and Ecker, 2009.) The counteractive, regulatory strategy is predominant in the field of psychotherapy in such forms as CBT (e.g., Brewin, 2006; Dobson & Dobson, 2009; Hayes, Strosahl, & Wilson, 2003), solution-focused therapy (e.g., Miller, Hubble, & Duncan, 1996), and systems of positive psychology (e.g., Gable & Haidt, 2005). Arden and Linford (2009) regard CBT as emotional regulation and cite brain science to support that view; likewise Brewin (2006, p. 765) reviews memory retrieval research indicating "that CBT does not directly modify negative information in memory, but produces changes in the relative activation of positive and negative representations such that the positive ones are assisted to win the retrieval competition."

In-depth therapies, such as psychodynamic psychotherapy, also are usually conceptualized as regulatory. Therapy systems that concentrate on attachment disturbances by using the client's experience of the therapist for new learning are described by proponents as therapies of emotional regulation (e.g., Badenoch, 2008; Fosha, 2002; Della Selva, 2004). Methods used in this class of therapies tend to be richly experiential and emotionally deep and can yield either counteractive or transformational change, depending on how the methods are implemented by the individual practitioner.

The Interplay of Meanings and Molecules: A Prediction

Our increasing knowledge of the neural and molecular processes involved in learning and memory—as well as in thoughts, feelings and behaviors—freshly provokes ancient questions about the relationship between mind and matter. Our intent here is simply to touch briefly on certain aspects of this fascinating topic and offer a prediction.

Neuroscience researchers consistently refer to the identified neurobiological and biomolecular processes as "subserving" subjective psychological processes or as being "substrates" or "correlates" of such processes. They describe subjective or behavioral responses as "recruiting" neurobiological processes. These terms suggest an intricate, mutually dependent interplay of the "top" and "bottom" domains without implying that one is fundamentally the cause or source of the other. There are, of course, specific instances where one domain clearly drives effects in the other—such as a stroke destroying specific areas of subjective functioning, or (illustrating what neuroscientists term "experience-driven" neural effects) chronic despair and depression over major personal losses causing measurable changes in brain chemistry, synapse firings, and epigenetic alteration of gene expression. Use of the clinical methods described in this book lays bare what appears to be a top-down, meaning-driven causation of therapy clients' symptoms. Moreover, the clinical ability to retrieve the contents of emotional implicit memory, revealing its coherence, combined with our research-based understanding of the longevity of such a memory enable us to recognize that even in generating responses regarded as symptoms, a person's brain has functioned as it was set up to do by evolution and is not malfunctioning—suggesting again that the causation of symptoms based in memory is not bottom-up.

These issues may become particularly relevant in the context of *epigenetics*, an emerging field of great importance to the scientific understanding of learning, memory, and symptom production. The term refers to a complex system of molecular machinery that carries out experience-driven (that is, learning-driven) modifications of gene expression without mutating the genes themselves. In the complex interplay of nature and nurture, epigenetic mechanisms deliver the influences of nurture to our genes—in the form of molecular units or tags that are attached to or removed from genes or nearby structures, influencing the level of gene activity in response to environmental experiences. Researchers have made significant progress in delineating the detailed epigenetic markers and corresponding changes in gene expression in the brain that result from, for example, experiences that induce depression or attachment insecurity and distress (e.g., Franklin et al., 2010; Tsankova, Renthal, Kumar, & Nestler, 2007).

All meaning-driven behaviors, emotions and thoughts—including those regarded as clinical symptoms—undoubtedly do have a neural and molecular substrate, but what is a meaningful definition of causation? We suggest that depression- or insecurity-generating experiences, for instance, may drive epigenetic molecular tagging not directly but through the long-lasting negative meanings and constructs that these experiences set up in implicit memory (even in animals). It is these chronically operating, implicit, subjective meanings, we propose, that drive emotional and behavioral responses which, in turn, drive the epigenetic tagging process in a top-down manner. In this view, epigenetics research is showing us more of what's "under the hood." Knowing the molecular details of what's under the hood, though, does not logically imply a change in our recognition of top-down causation. In the car analogy, the *cause* of the car turning left continues to be the subjective desire and will of the person at the wheel, not the movements of the mechanical parts under the hood, because those movements are recruited by and subserve the driver's subjective world of meaning—and no less so if we know in detail what those movements are.

The view that the fundamental cause of many clinical symptoms lies in implicit emotional meanings, and that those same meanings drive changes at the molecular level, generates the prediction that if epigenetic tags created by depression-inducing events are removed by chemical agents, the tags and associated symptoms of mood and behavior would recur when the chemical agent ceases to be applied, because the causal meanings in implicit memory are not removed by the chemical agent and would therefore once again drive production of tags and symptoms in the absence of the chemical intervention. This prediction is supported by observations that the antidepressant imipramine removes or blocks some of the depression-related epigenetic tags and dispels symptoms of mood and behavior (e.g., Tsankova et al., 2007), and that symptoms return when imipramine is discontinued. The same prediction implies that the induced molecular tags would disappear lastingly as a result of erasure, through memory reconsolidation, of the learned meanings that generated them. To test this key prediction, methods already demonstrated by neuroscientists to erase a learned fear (Monfils et al., 2009; Schiller et al., 2010) could be complemented by epigenetic monitoring.

Conclusion

In this chapter we have seen how memory reconsolidation works and, as demonstrated in a large body of quite recent research by neuroscientists, how it unlocks the neural circuits of a targeted emotional learning, allowing that learning to be unlearned and erased by other learning. Emotional learnings are extremely tenacious and otherwise normally last for a lifetime. Based on these findings, we defined the *therapeutic reconsolidation process* as a general template for utilizing reconsolidation in psychotherapy for elimination of learned responses down to their emotional and neural roots.

Since the 1950s, the beliefs of psychotherapists regarding symptom causation have drifted ever farther away from psychological causation, and have increasingly embraced biochemical, neurological, and/or genetic causation of symptoms, often despite weak or faulty evidence for the latter views. (For example, see Toomey and Ecker, 2009 for a review of the invalid empirical evidence surrounding the rise of antidepressant SSRIs and the view that depression is caused by imbalances of neurotransmitters.) However, as reconsolidation and memory erasure enter more and more into clinicians' thinking and practices, and therapists repeatedly witness a symptom such as long-term depression or anxiety attacks ceasing permanently as a result of a process known to bring about erasure of emotional learnings, psychological causation will speak for itself compellingly, particularly when this is observed for many different kinds of symptoms (see Table 3.1 and supplemental online list of published case studies indexed by symptom).

Of course, we must not overshoot in this direction either; as we noted earlier in this chapter, there are important categories of symptom that we reliably can believe have genetic and/or neurobiological, but not psychological, causes. And it may be found in the future that, for example, most cases of depression are due to psychological causes—that is, emotional learnings in implicit memory—while some smaller fraction of depression cases may have physical, non-psychological causes that have not been identified as yet. Overall, as a result of reconsolidation research having put emotional memory erasure into the clinical picture, the psychological causation of symptoms can become clearly apparent to therapists as never before.

The rest of this book moves on to show a wide range of clinical methods, skills, and processes that are well suited for facilitating deep, transformational change based on these principles. Therapists who understand that the brain requires a definite process for erasing an emotional learning are in a position to use their preferred methods to fulfill that process, regularly deliver therapy of exceptional, liberating potency, and enjoy a level of effectiveness in day-to-day practice well beyond what previously seemed possible in the clinical field, as shown in the many case examples throughout this book.

This is a wonderful moment in the ongoing advancement of psychotherapy—the moment when, for the first time in the course of evolution, we understand how to free ourselves from limiting emotional learnings formed earlier in life. This book is dedicated to spreading that knowledge throughout the field of psychotherapy.

3

The Focused, Deep Psychotherapy of Emotional Unlearning

The heart has reasons of which reason knows nothing.

—Blaise Pascal

For a century, the fields of psychotherapy and clinical psychology have been searching for definitive knowledge of how ingrained, negative emotional learnings, which underlie a wide range of clinical symptoms and are extremely tenacious, can be truly dissolved and replaced by new learning. This is the very knowledge most needed for our clients' well-being and our own professional satisfaction and sustenance.

Research by neuroscientists since 2004 has provided the missing knowledge, so central to the psychotherapeutic enterprise, of a well-defined, behavioral process that achieves actual neurological deletion of a target emotional learning or schema without impairing autobiographical memory of past experiences. We now know that the brain has a built-in process of profound unlearning through a type of neuroplasticity called *memory reconsolidation*—described in detail in Chapter 2 and summarized briefly below—that can actually delete a specific, unwanted learned emotional response from memory. As a result of this unlearning and deletion process, the powerful grip of an existing emotional reaction disappears permanently.

With beautiful synergy, these research findings have confirmed the earlier clinical identification of the same behavioral process by two of the authors (Ecker & Hulley, 1996, 2000a). Thanks to this convergence of the applied art and the laboratory science of memory reconsolidation and erasure, extensive clinical experience and know-how already exist for enabling mental health professionals to utilize this built-in process that the brain possesses. In this chapter we want to give you a close look at the *therapeutic reconsolidation process* unfolding as a deeply human experience at the core of personal meaning.

Embodying the Therapeutic Reconsolidation Process

Below we will be describing and illustrating the therapeutic reconsolidation process in action. The steps of the process define essential experiences the client must have, without specifying methods or techniques for creating those experiences—just as a map does not impose a mode of travel when one is on a journey. This allows each therapist full freedom to choose and use preferred methods to fulfill the sequence of experiences required by the brain for shedding a targeted emotional learning. We show in Chapter 6 how several widely used systems of psychotherapy are well suited for this purpose.

In order to illustrate, for instructional purposes, the clinical use of the therapeutic reconsolidation process, its sequence of steps needs to be embodied in some chosen, concrete way. Best suited for this instructional demonstration is a therapy that implements the steps explicitly and recognizably. Across the various psychotherapies that are congenial to this process (see Table 1.1), there is a wide variance in the degree to which its steps are overtly apparent. In other words, if we were to observe such therapies being carried out successfully (as in Chapter 6), for most of them we would not easily recognize the steps of the therapeutic reconsolidation process occurring even when the client is, indeed, having the particular *sequence of internal experiences* that is the true essence of the process required by the brain.

To our knowledge, the only form of psychotherapy that has a procedural map or methodology that explicitly calls for and guides every step of the therapeutic reconsolidation process is Coherence Therapy—the approach developed by Ecker and Hulley in discovering the process clinically. For that reason, in this chapter and the next, the non-theoretical system of Coherence Therapy will serve to demonstrate the unlocking of the emotional brain through the therapeutic reconsolidation process.

Table 3.1 maps the steps of the therapeutic reconsolidation process and shows how the phases of Coherence Therapy are in one-to-one correspondence with those steps. This chapter will give you a basic grounding in understanding those steps of process—the sequence of internal experiences—that erase the emotional learnings underlying a given presenting symptom.

Coherence Therapy (originally called Depth Oriented Brief Therapy or DOBT) was initially developed from 1986 to 1993 by Ecker and Hulley (1996, 2000a, 2008a, 2011). Clinical training in this process began in 1993—more than a decade before reconsolidation researchers arrived at the erasure process in the lab—and it has been in use by psychotherapists since then (e.g., Ecker &

Table 3.1 Steps of clinical process for using new learning to nullify or update an existing emotional learning

Therapeutic Reconsolidation Process		Coherence Therapy
I. Accessing sequence	A. Symptom identification	Symptom identification
	B. Retrieval of target learning (symptom-requiring schema)	Discovery phase
		Integration phase
	C. Identification of disconfirming knowledge	Transformation phase: Juxtaposition experiences
II. Transformation sequence*	1. Reactivation of symptom-requiring schema (B) 2. Activation of disconfirming knowledge (C), mismatching sympton-requiring schema (B) 3. Repetitions of (B)–(C) pairing	
III. Verification phase	V. Observations of key markers: – Emotional non-reactivation – Symptom cessation – Effortless permanence	Verification of schema nullification

* *Transformation sequence* is used interchangeably with *erasure sequence* to refer to Steps 1–2–3. *Transformation sequence* is used in the clinical context and *erasure sequence* is used in the neurological context.

Hulley, 2000a, 2008a; Martignetti & Jordan, 2001; Neimeyer, 2009; Neimeyer & Bridges, 2003; Neimeyer, Burke, Mackay, & van Dyke Stringer, 2010; Neimeyer & Raskin, 2001; Thomson & Jordan, 2002) to dispel a broad range of symptoms, as listed in Table 3.2; for a listing of published case examples indexed by symptom, see the online supplement.

The steps of methodology of Coherence Therapy listed in Table 3.1 emerged as a result of culling from thousands of therapy sessions the outliers that contained the markers of profound, lasting change that later came to be associated distinctively with the erasure of an emotional learning. Those ultra-effective sessions were closely studied in order to identify the essential steps of process that they shared, across a wide range of symptoms and clients. Neuroscientists using the same markers of change identified the same steps of required process in research on memory reconsolidation published since 2004, as reviewed in Chapter 2; for readers who have bypassed that review of research, we note that brief, accessible accounts of reconsolidation research and its extension to psychotherapy are available online (Ecker, 2011; Van Nuys, 2010a). Researchers determined that change consisting of those markers corresponds on the neurological level to an unlocking of synapses, which allows the neural encoding of a well-established emotional learning to be erased from functioning memory through being rewritten and replaced by new learning.

Table 3.2   Symptoms observed that are dispelled by the therapeutic reconsolidation process through Coherence Therapy

Aggressive behavior	Grief and bereavement problems
Agoraphobia	Guilt
Alcohol abuse	Hallucinations
Anger and rage	Inaction
Anxiety	Indecision
Attachment-pattern behaviors & distress	Low self-worth
Attention deficit problems	Panic attacks
Codependency	Perfectionism
Complex trauma symptomology	Post-traumatic symptoms
Compulsive behaviors of many kinds	Procrastination
Couples' problems of conflict/communication/closeness	Psychogenic/psychosomatic pain
Depression	Sexual problems
Family and child problems	Shame
Fidgeting	Underachieving
Food/eating/weight problems	Voice and speaking problems

Note: For a list of published case examples indexed by symptom, see online supplement.

The fact that the same process emerged independently through such different approaches as the neurological study of learning and memory in animals and the examination of psychotherapeutic process signifies progress toward a synthesis of the neurobiological (bottom-up) and holistic (top-down) understandings of therapeutic change. The need for just such a binocular approach was emphasized by neuroscientist Eric Kandel (2001, p. 605) toward the end of his Nobel address, when he commented regarding a range of challenging unknowns in brain science, "These systems problems of the brain will require more than the bottom-up approach of molecular biology. They will also require the top-down approaches of cognitive psychology, neurology, and psychiatry. Finally, they will require a set of syntheses that bridge the two approaches." The convergence described in this chapter appears to be a step in the direction of fulfilling this vision of unification.

Coherence Therapy equips the therapist with extensive guidance for carrying out the therapeutic reconsolidation process, as well as offering a set of versatile techniques for doing so. It is defined by both the methodology indicated in Table 3.1 and a guiding conceptual framework consisting of the research-based knowledge of emotional learning and unlearning in the Emotional Coherence Framework, described in Chapter 1. This includes the central concept of *symptom coherence*, which, as demonstrated below, serves as Coherence Therapy's model of both symptom production and symptom cessation. The limits of applicability of Coherence Therapy are the same as were detailed in Chapter 2 for the therapeutic reconsolidation process. Being entirely a respectful process of guiding the client to attend deeply to his or her own emotional learnings and attributed meanings, Coherence Therapy is naturally applicable cross-culturally and across sexual orientations, socioeconomic levels and age groups. It can be conducted with individuals, couples and families, and with children, adolescents and adults.

In describing Coherence Therapy in the following case example, we assume that the therapist–reader already has sound skills of listening, communicating empathetic understanding authentically, attuning accurately, building emotional safety and trust, creating a good working alliance, and repairing ruptures. These relationship skills and qualities, known in the clinical field as "non-specific common factors," certainly are prerequisites for carrying out Coherence Therapy successfully. However, Coherence Therapy is not defined in terms of these common factors, and its specific process of profound change—the therapeutic reconsolidation process—is neither inherent in the common factors nor likely to result regularly from them alone (a point that is further discussed toward the end of Chapter 6).

The Therapeutic Reconsolidation Process in Coherence Therapy: Case Example of Anxious Low Self-Esteem

The case of "Richard," a mild-mannered man in his late 30s and the older of two siblings, is relatively straightforward as an introductory walk-through of the therapeutic reconsolidation process in Coherence Therapy. Richard described a chronically disturbing self-doubt and lack of competence and confidence during his workday at a company that creates websites for businesses. This self-doubting in turn caused him significant anxiety daily and often blocked him from expressing his knowledge, ideas, and opinions. The mystery deepened as it emerged that in terms of his actual performance and achievements in his work life, he had for many years been consistently successful and even impressive to co-workers and supervisors. Yet at work he regularly went into paralyzing doubt of his own knowledge and abilities.

Regularly regarding one's own knowledge and abilities as invalid or inadequate is a common form of low self-worth. Therapists are well acquainted with the great prevalence as well as the exceptional tenacity of low self-worth in its many forms. It is largely immune to conventional types of therapy, including counteractive or "positive" approaches, in which relapses of low self-worth often occur. As we will see, Coherence Therapy's effectiveness in this area is due to its focus on finding the unique underlying emotional learnings according to which it is adaptively *necessary* to go into negative thoughts and feelings toward oneself. Those symptom-requiring learnings are then the target for dissolution by the transformation sequence. The negative thoughts and feelings toward oneself cease to arise when the underlying need for them no longer exists, as we will see in Richard's case.

Symptom identification (Step A)

In his first session, Richard readily described recent examples of his symptoms of doubting his knowledge and abilities at work. He quoted self-talk such as "Who am I to think I know what's right?" and "This could be wrong" and "Watch out— don't go out on a limb." Such thoughts arose and stopped him from expressing himself when he had something to say, such as during daily technical meetings.

Richard's delineation of *what* responses constituted the problem and *when* the problem occurred accomplished *symptom identification* (the first step of Coherence Therapy and Step A of the therapeutic reconsolidation process). With some clients, this step is considerably more challenging than it was with Richard, and it is critically important to be persistent and diligent in clarifying with the client what experiential elements constitute the problem, even if this step requires multiple sessions. The therapist needs to understand in concrete, experiential terms which specific thoughts, feelings, and/or behaviors to regard as the person's symptoms, in order to be in a position, then, to pursue the discovery of the emotional learnings maintaining those particular symptoms. Clarity and ongoing mindfulness regarding the client's specific symptom(s) are the therapist's rudder in Coherence Therapy, allowing him or her to steer the process in a definite direction: toward and into the emotional learnings that generate the symptom(s).

Coherence of the symptom

The central principle in Coherence Therapy is that far more symptoms are produced by emotional learnings than is generally recognized, and learning-driven symptoms exist entirely because they are adaptively and compellingly *necessary* to have, according to at least one of a person's emotional implicit learnings for how to avoid suffering and have safety, well-being, or justice. That is the principle of symptom coherence, the model of symptom production in Coherence Therapy. It is not a theoretical position about the mind or personality, but is based on pragmatic clinical observation as well as a wealth of empirical research on learning and memory (as reviewed by Toomey & Ecker, 2007).

A symptom-requiring emotional learning is a schema that is usually largely if not entirely implicit (outside of awareness) at the start of therapy, but it proves to be coherent, well defined and efficiently findable. It also proves to be dissolvable by the transformation sequence (Steps 1–2–3 of the therapeutic reconsolidation process), as the work with Richard will show. Symptom coherence implies that as soon as each emotional learning maintaining a symptom has been dissolved, the symptom ceases and its non-recurrence is thereafter effortless, without any preventive measures. We have observed this with our clients many hundreds of times.

Coherence Therapy is of course by no means original in recognizing that symptomatic behaviors, moods, and thoughts may be an adaptive, coherent expression of unconscious emotional learnings. Many different methodologies and theories of psychotherapy incorporate that understanding in varying degrees, explicitly or implicitly, as articulated in the writings of, for instance, Bandler and Grinder (1979), Bateson (1951, 1972, 1979), Dell (1982), Dodes (2002), Freud (1916, 1923), Gendlin (1982, 1996), Greenberg, Rice, and Elliott (1993), Johnson (2004), Jung (1964), Kegan and Lahey (2001), Laing (1967, 1995), Mahoney (1991, 2003), Mones and Schwartz (2007), Papp and Imber-Black (1996), Polster and Polster (1973), Rosenberg (1999), Satir (1972), Schwartz (1997, 2001), Shapiro (2001, 2002), Sullivan (1948), and van der Kolk (1994, 1996), among others. Readers familiar with those writings and therapeutic systems will recognize Coherence Therapy's unprecedented utilization of the principle of coherence to retrieve accurately and then unlock decisively the unconscious emotional formations of a lifetime.

Discovery phase (Step B)

The therapist's mindfulness of the symptom continuously guides the discovery work, which is the beginning of step B. The discovery work needs to be primarily experiential—as distinct from the "talking about" mode—through the creation of *discovery experiences*. In each discovery experience, the client has an actual subjective encounter with the implicit emotional meanings and knowings coherently generating the symptom, and in this way becomes aware of this material directly and accurately, not through speculation, interpretation or theorizing.

For pursuing the discovery work, Richard's therapist applied the symptom coherence principle by internally holding the following basic question as his guide: What unconscious, learned emotional knowledge was making it necessary for Richard to generate self-doubt at work? Or, to put it the other way around: What implicit learning was making it important for Richard *not* to feel or act competent and confident at work, and important *not* to recognize viscerally the work history that strongly indicated his competence? These questions were not ones to express to Richard, because doing so would have risked his misunderstanding and feeling blamed or pathologized for being "self-sabotaging." Rather, these coherence-based questions served as the therapist's compass, giving clear direction for the discovery work.

In order to create a discovery experience that would begin to bring a symptom-requiring emotional learning into awareness, the therapist asked Richard to imagine being present at one of the daily work meetings, making a few brief, useful comments, and feeling confident in his knowledge while doing so. (The therapist added, "This is not a rehearsal for actually doing that at work; it's just an exercise to do here with me so we can find out some important things.") This is an example of *symptom deprivation*, one of several basic techniques often useful for the discovery work. If a client's symptom occurs in a particular situation because it is actually necessary in some unrecognized way, then having the client imagine being in that situation *without* the symptom is likely to give rise to some specific dilemma or distress, which the client normally avoids, unconsciously, by producing the symptom. The specific dilemma that arises when deprived of the symptom begins to reveal the client's unconscious knowledge of how, why, and when to produce the symptom in order to avoid suffering that particular distress.

Richard closed his eyes and imagined being in the meeting at work, making some useful comments and feeling confident about the knowledge he had shared. This is what ensued:

Cl: Now I'm feeling really uncomfortable, but—it's in a different way.

Th: OK, let yourself feel it—this different discomfort. *[Pause.]* See if any words come along with this uncomfortable feeling.

Cl: *[Pause.]* Now they hate me.

Th: "Now they hate me." Good. Keep going: See if this really uncomfortable feeling also can tell you *why* they hate you now.

Cl: *[Pause.]* Hnh. Wow. It's because—now I'm—an arrogant asshole—like my father—a totally self-centered, totally insensitive know-it-all.

Th: Do you mean that having a feeling of confidence as you speak turns you into an arrogant asshole, like Dad?

Cl: Yeah, exactly. Wow.

Th: And how do you *feel* about being like him in this way?

Cl: It's horrible! It's what I've always vowed *not* to be!

Notice that the therapist focused primarily on eliciting attributed *meaning* as well as the emotional quality of the experience. Construed meanings are key implicit learnings. At this point, an initial discovery experience has occurred. The client has been guided to "bump into," notice, and reveal to the therapist previously unconscious constructs, knowings, feelings, and purposes that strongly require his chronic self-doubting and the insecure, unconfident feeling that this self-doubting generates. Thus Richard has begun to *retrieve* his learned schema (Step B) consisting of the knowledge that speaking with any feeling of personal confidence equates to being brutishly insensitive and arrogant like his father and being hated for that by others, so it is intensely important not to let himself ever feel confident. He successfully accomplishes this with thoughts and self-talk that doubt and invalidate his own knowledge, preventing any confident self-expression.

Our example is already showing several other things. The particular way in which Coherence Therapy is "experiential" is apparent here: It consists of the client's subjective immersion in the symptom-requiring schema, which is essential in this approach. The therapist guides the client into speaking *from* and *in* the present-moment live experience of that material. In that way, the therapist learns accurately from the client what the symptom-requiring constructs are. Those constructs are a key part of the client's emotional learnings, and they will be the target of change through the therapeutic reconsolidation process.

The therapist watches and listens closely for *any and every emerging indication of how the symptom is necessary to have.* That *selection criterion* guides the therapist during the discovery work, and each such indication is what the therapist selects and focuses on next for a further emotional deepening of the discovery work. Closely observing the client's response to each attempted step of the discovery work is the key to an efficient process in this stage. In many cases, the emotional learnings and themes that emerge are outside the range of possibilities familiar to the therapist, so it is important for the therapist to adopt a "not-knowing" stance during discovery and be truly receptive to learning the makeup of the client's world of meaning. The therapist works as an anthropologist does, eliciting and learning the client's reality-defining constructs involved in symptom production just as they are, avoiding interpretive overlay, making as few assumptions as possible, and not at all attempting to change, fix, or correct anything.

Based on the discovery work described so far, it was apparent to the therapist that Richard's symptom of self-doubting had a function, because it was the very means by which he protected himself from being self-assertive, noxious and hated like his father. The self-doubting of course caused suffering of its own, but within Richard's world of meaning, the suffering it avoided would have been much worse. A fundamental feature of the symptom coherence model of symptom production is the recognition that the suffering due to a functional symptom is actually the lesser of two evils—the other, greater evil being the suffering that is unconsciously expected from *not* having the symptom. Those are *the two sufferings,* as they are called in Coherence Therapy; the client's emotional brain has full knowledge of them both and compels the production of the symptom in order to avoid the even worse suffering expected from being without the symptom. Richard's learned, implicit knowledge was that being *without* his symptom of self-doubting would bring the even worse suffering of being hated as a heavy-handed know-it-all, like Dad.

Prior to therapy, Richard's neocortical, conscious self was not privy to this tradeoff between the two sufferings, so he was mystified and felt afflicted by his insecure self-doubting, which seemed to have an insistent life of its own. However, as the discovery and integration work unfold in Coherence Therapy and the subcortical or right brain's implicit knowings are accessed and shared with the neocortex's conscious awareness and are verbalized, the client experiences directly how the symptom is actually *necessary to have*—according to the client's own emotional learnings—for the positive purpose of avoiding a worse suffering. As Richard was now beginning to experience, this is a lucid recognition of the client's own urgent purpose *for* having the symptom, termed the client's symptom— a position termed the client's *pro-symptom position* in Coherence Therapy. The client has become aware of the learned emotional knowledge that is *the emotional truth of the symptom*—a phrase used almost synonymously with the phrases pro-symptom position, symptom-requiring schema, and symptom-generating emotional learnings. This is new awareness of a major formative theme in the client's life, and it makes sense of the symptom in a whole new, non-pathologizing way. Clients often express strong relief over realizing that the symptom's existence is part of a coherent, sensible response to what they actually experienced in life and does *not* mean they are defective, irrational, weak, and so forth.

Not all presented symptoms are functional, however. Some are revealed in the course of discovery work to be functionless. A functionless symptom is produced because it is an inevitable result or by-product of a functional (but possibly unpresented) symptom—such as loneliness that results from the functional, unpresented symptom of avoiding relationships with people in order to be safe from abandonment, or anxiety that results from the functional, unpresented symptom of never asserting boundaries in order to be safe from a punitive withdrawal of love. Coherence Therapy is a movement into underlying causes, so it always converges to and focuses on the client's functional symptom even if the presented symptom was a functionless (though still fully coherent) by-product.

A symptom-requiring schema is a learned but durable mental object having its own definite structure and makeup (which we will examine more closely below). A different practitioner of Coherence Therapy could have used an experiential method other than the symptom deprivation technique for carrying out the discovery process with Richard, but the same material would have emerged. Other discovery techniques are described in case examples throughout this book. (For detailed instructional coverage, see Ecker & Hulley, 2011.) The discovery phase is defined not in terms of techniques or any formulaic protocol, but rather as the use of *any* experiential methods (including parts work, chair work, Focusing, dream work, bilateral stimulation, inner child work, etc.) to follow the links from the manifest symptom to the underlying personal constructs that necessitate it, drawing that normally implicit material into explicit awareness.

As we are seeing with Richard, this discovery process deepens emotionally directly into quite tender territory and areas of vulnerability. In order for the client to open to this process, the therapist must be an emotionally safe presence and communicate genuine, empathetic understanding and full acceptance of the emerging emotional truth of how and why the symptom actually feels necessary to have. A sustained focusing of empathy on *that* material is a specialized, primary use of empathy in Coherence Therapy; thus it has its own name: *coherence empathy.* Of course, the more common therapeutic empathy toward the suffering due to having the symptom and toward the client's wish to be rid of the symptom is also communicated in the course of Coherence Therapy.

We have found that in general practice, most Coherence Therapy clients have no problem holding the emotional experiences that develop in the course of the work. For some, however, care must be taken to follow a graduated process of *small enough steps* into the emerging material to limit the intensity of emotional accessing to levels that are not destabilizing or overwhelming. The need for such extra care usually becomes apparent quickly, for example in observing that the client dissociates (becomes wooden, glassy-eyed, confused, or shifts into shallow breathing) in reaction to early steps of experiential accessing. It is best practice to ask the client after each further segment of experiential work, "How is it for you to be in touch with this?" or, in the latter portion of the session, "How will it be for you to be in touch with this after you leave my office today?" in order to learn each client's emotional tolerances, detect any incipient destabilization or problematic reactions, and take measures to ensure safety and stability. A client's emotional experience during a session may feel tolerable due to feeling sensitively accompanied by the therapist, but being alone with the experience after the session may feel daunting. When a client indicates that such a dilemma looms, the difficulty can reliably be dispelled by the therapist saying, "I understand, and what I want to suggest is for you to forget all about these things between sessions, and only when we are together *during* sessions will we revisit them. How would that be, for you?" With such permission to re-suppress what was retrieved in the session, all clients to whom we have offered that option have been fully successful at utilizing it.

Integration phase (Step B continues)

Richard's fresh new awareness of why he avoids speaking with confidence occurred in an altered state—an area of emotional experience not normally connected to conscious awareness, as is typically the case with any newly conscious emotional truth—so it was likely to disappear from awareness again if no further steps were taken to help integrate it into routine, ongoing, stable awareness. The therapist therefore pursued integration, Coherence Therapy's next phase, through the creation of *integration experiences,* which are simply repeated experiences of the discovered material both during and between sessions. Stable integration into everyday awareness completes the retrieval of a symptom-requiring schema from implicit memory into explicit awareness (Step B of the therapeutic reconsolidation process).

The first integration experience that the therapist created for Richard consisted of inviting him to make a simple *overt statement* of what had emerged:

Th: So, let's see if it feels true to you to say this sentence: "Feeling *any* confidence means I'm arrogant, self-centered, and totally insensitive like Dad, and people will hate me for it, so I've got to *never* feel confident, ever."

Cl: Feeling *any* confidence means I'm arrogant, self-centered, and totally insensitive like Dad, and everyone will hate me for it, so I've got to *never ever* feel confident.

Th: Does that fit or feel true for you, in your body?

Cl: My body is *buzzing* with how true it feels.

Th: Mm-hm. A few minutes ago you seemed surprised by getting in touch with this—with realizing you have this powerful purpose for not getting anywhere *near* feelings of confidence.

Cl: Yeah. *[Pause.]* But it's kind of a relief, too. I mean, I feel so screwed-up at work and I thought that's just how I *am.*

Th: I see. And now you're in touch with the deep *sense* it really makes in your life to keep yourself feeling the *opposite* of confident.

Fullest emotional deepening occurs in the integration work. In that segment, notice that the therapist, in expressing coherence empathy, made comments reflecting Richard's own *purpose* and *agency* in producing his symptom of self-doubting. The therapist was simply making explicit the key elements that had already emerged in the prior discovery experience, not imposing an interpretation or getting ahead of Richard's own recognition of emotional truth.

The client's explicit, experiential recognition of his or her own purpose and agency behind a symptom is a key milestone of retrieval in the integration phase and key marker of integration. In Richard's last response, we can see that his new awareness of the underlying coherence of his self-doubting was quickly dispelling his previous pathologizing way of making sense of that symptom.

For Richard, making the overt statement above was an integration experience because it was a repeated, explicit, subjective experience of his own symptom-requiring emotional schema or pro-symptom position. The essence of an integration experience lies in having the client again speak *from* and *within* the felt emotional reality of the pro-symptom position, expressing it as his or her own emotional truth. What matters is for the client repeatedly to have a bodily experience of the emotional realness of the discovered material—not necessarily a cathartic, dramatic, or intense experience, but an unmistakably embodied, authentic one.

For that purpose of guiding truly experiential work, there is a style of phrasing that is particularly effective for verbalizing the retrieved emotional truth of the symptom—the style used in the overt statement offered to Richard above: "Feeling *any* confidence means I'm arrogant, self-centered, and totally insensitive like Dad, and people will hate me for it, so I've got to *never* feel confident, ever." That style of vivid, present tense, first-person, emotionally candid, highly specific phrasing for naming one's living knowledge of what is at stake, what one's vulnerabilities are, and what measures are therefore urgently necessary, is called *limbic language* in Coherence Therapy, referring to the brain's limbic system, the major seat of emotional implicit memory. Crafting this style of phrasing requires empathic attunement to the texture of subjective reality in the emotional brain. Such phrasing is important because it brings both the specific content and the native quality of the emotional material most fully and faithfully into direct experience. In contrast, everyday colloquial and social phrasing tends to intellectualize, minimize, depersonalize and avoid facing or contacting the living emotional vulnerabilities involved. For example, Richard's everyday phrasing for the same material, had he not been guided to use limbic language, would probably have been something like, "People won't like you if you're confident in what you say to them, so it's good to be careful." That phrasing would have yielded a quite weak accessing of his actual emotional knowings, possibly too weak for the subsequent transformation phase to succeed.

Emotionally deep experiential work requires, in addition to limbic language, comfort on the therapist's part in being in the presence of the client's emotional experiencing, as well as use of softer voice tones, slower pacing, and silences to facilitate emotional deepening in areas of vulnerability. If the therapist were to continue speaking in an ordinary voice during experiential work, emotional deepening would be limited or even discouraged, because an ordinary voice implicitly signals that the speaker is not attuning sensitively to the delicacy of the listener's experience. These elements are of course not apparent in the transcripts.

Perhaps most importantly, the deep retrieval work in Coherence Therapy requires the therapist to refrain from following any *counteractive reflex*—the urge to apply immediately all possible influence *against* the newly found pro-symptom schema to correct it, refute it, fix it, override it, avoid it, disconnect from it, or manage it, believing that this could yield lasting change. Such well-intentioned counteracting fails to produce profound change reliably, because counteracting quickly re-suppresses the material that has been brought to light, pushing it back into a dissociated, implicit state where it remains unavailable for transformational change. Instead, the coherence-focused approach follows a completely non-counteractive process of integration: The therapist guides the client simply to *stay* in touch with, and *keep* having experiences of, the symptom-requiring emotional truth, embracing and integrating the schema into conscious awareness *just as it is*. The integration motto in this approach is, "Once you have arrived at the symptom's emotional truth, *stay there*. Pitch a tent. Set up camp right there" (Ecker & Hulley, 2011, p. 36; emphasis in original).

The end of the session with Richard was now approaching, so the therapist created a simple between-session task that would "stay right there" and continue to create integration experiences. On a pocket-sized index card, the therapist wrote the same sentence that Richard had spoken as an overt statement: "Feeling *any* confidence means I'm arrogant, self-centered, and totally insensitive like Dad, and everyone will hate me for it, so I've got to *never ever* feel confident." Handing this card to Richard, the therapist suggested, "Read this once a day for a minute or two, and just let it bring you back in touch with how true this feels for you, just the way you're feeling it right now. Don't try to analyze or overcome any part of it. Just use the card to stay in touch with all of this on a feeling level." Use of an index card to guide a between-session task that maintains or even forwards the work is standard practice at the end of every session. For Richard, each reading of this card would be another integration experience as well as a practice of mindfulness of the retrieved material. The integration work is mindfulness training focused on the specific area of a newly conscious pro-symptom schema.

At the start of the second session one week later, the therapist needed to assess whether the index card task had successfully achieved further integration of the emotional truth written on it, and therefore asked Richard simply, "How was it to live with what we put on that card?" The absence of specifics in that question was deliberate, so that it would be apparent from Richard's reply whether *he* could now readily refer to the specifics of his pro-symptom position. Richard reported that he had read the card every day at first and then less often. He said it was something of a surprise to recognize "what a big deal it is for me to not be anything close to how heavy-handed and dominating Dad was—and he still is." He said it was also a surprise to find how "black and white" it was for him, meaning that "*any degree* of confidence or real assertiveness on my part *does* mean that, to me—which hasn't changed now that I know it." Richard's specific references to the key elements on the card were markers confirming that integration of this material had occurred.

Now that awareness had been extended "down" into the underlying emotional theme and purpose requiring the symptom, it was time for the return trip back "up" into experiencing the concrete, manifested symptom *with* this new awareness of its emotional necessity. This return trip, which largely completes the integration phase, took only a few minutes: The therapist invited Richard to return, in his imagination, to the moments of a recent occurrence of his self-doubting, self-invalidating self-talk at work, and simply to add onto that self-talk an overt statement (explicit verbalization) of his now-conscious need and purpose for it. The self-talk in this instance was, "How could *I* know what's right here? Who do I think I am?" In this replay the therapist now guided Richard to add, "I'm telling myself that so that I'll keep quiet and won't confidently say what I know and be hated as a domineering know-it-all, like Dad." This lucid linkage of purpose and symptom was full integration and ownership of his pro-symptom position.

The therapist then asked, "How does it feel to really stand behind your own deep purpose for doubting yourself?"

Richard replied, "I feel somehow more solid, but at the same time I'm surprised, again, to see how big this is to me," which confirmed the experiential quality of this further step of integration. The between-session task written on an index card near the end of the session was this:

> If I say anything with confidence, I'll be just like Dad—a know-it-all lording it over everyone. And then people will hate me for that, just the way I hate *him* for it. So I'd better keep myself quiet by thinking, 'What do *I* know?' even though that makes me feel so insecure that I don't express what I do know.

This phrasing felt resonantly true to Richard, and the therapist recommended reading the card immediately whenever he noticed self-doubting thoughts appearing. This mindfulness practice would continue to firm up Richard's integration of the pro-symptom emotional learning he had now largely retrieved (deepening of Step B of the therapeutic reconsolidation process).

The client's integration work in Coherence Therapy is a guided, persistent practice of mindfulness of the specific emotional learnings that have been brought into the foreground of awareness from the implicit background. The therapist works to build up the client's mindfulness as well as an *unreserved acceptance* of his or her own symptom-requiring emotional knowledge. This embracing of the very material causing all the trouble is exactly what it seems, a straightforward process of integration, not a paradoxical intervention. As Carl Jung famously observed, "We cannot change anything until we accept it. Condemnation does not liberate, it oppresses." In order to sustain the integration work for relatively complete retrieval of a pro-symptom schema, as illustrated here with Richard, clearly the therapist has to be able to refrain completely from the urge to counteract or oppose the symptom-necessitating theme—and that is a discipline that can require some cultivation for therapists steeped in using counteractive methods.

The anatomy of a symptom-requiring schema

The retrieval work with Richard had at this point revealed and put him directly in touch—emotionally, bodily, and cognitively—with enough of his learned, symptom-requiring schema to fulfill Step B of the therapeutic reconsolidation process. In order for the therapist to know when retrieval is complete, an understanding of the content as well as the structure or anatomy of emotional implicit schemas is valuable, as several clinical writers have emphasized (e.g., Badenoch, 2008, 2011; Ecker & Hulley, 1996, 2000b, 2011; Ecker & Toomey, 2008; Schore, 2003a, 2003b; Siegel, 1999, 2006). The various components of Richard's pro-symptom schema illustrate the schema map we find most useful, as follows.

- *Perceptual, emotional and somatic memory of original experiences:* his suffering from his father's heavily dominating, hyper-confident self-expression, plus related suffering from unmet needs for fatherly expressions of love, acceptance, understanding, validation. (This is the "raw data"; matching features in current situations are triggers of the whole schema.)
- *A mental model or set of linked, learned constructs operating as living knowledge of a problem and a solution:*
  - *The problem: knowledge of a vulnerability to a specific suffering.* Confident assertiveness in any degree inflicts crushing oppression on others and is hated by them. I would be horrible like Dad and hated by others, as he is, if I asserted my own knowledge or wishes confidently. (This is

a model of how the world *is*, and current situations that appear relevant to this model are triggers of the whole schema.)

○ *The solution: knowledge of an urgent broad strategy and concrete tactic(s) for avoiding that suffering.* Never express any confident assertiveness, to avoid being horrible and hated (general strategy and pro-symptom purpose), by vigilantly noticing any definite knowledge or opinions forming in myself and blocking them from expression by generating potently self-doubting, self-invalidating thoughts (concrete tactic and manifested symptom).

Mental models are recognized and studied by a number of overlapping disciplines (see, e.g., Held, Vosgerau, & Knauff, 2006) and have become a key aspect of advanced clinical practice. The mental models underlying clinical symptoms operate as an automatic set of instructions to the self for proactively avoiding the suffering or maintaining the reward experienced in the original learning experiences; the symptom is among the behaviors, thoughts and/or mood that such models launch. This learned mental model is the core material that necessitates and drives production of the symptom, so it is the therapist's target for dissolution (erasure) through the therapeutic reconsolidation process.

As is characteristic of the modular, schematic, and hierarchical manner in which the brain organizes and retrieves knowledge (Eichenbaum, 2004; Rumelhart & McClelland, 1986; Toomey & Ecker, 2007), the client's mental model operates as a multi-component whole, so integration of a pro-symptom schema or position is not complete, as a rule, until all of its components have been experienced emotionally and, while being experienced, verbalized accurately by the client, and then incorporated into everyday awareness. Richard had been guided to feel, recognize and verbalize all of his mental model's initially nonverbal, linked elements in an experiential (rather than intellectual) manner. It was now lucidly clear to him that his self-doubting thoughts and their resulting insecure, unconfident feeling at work were actually his *solution* to the previously unrecognized and implicit but now explicit *problem* of expecting to resemble his father and be hated for any degree of confident self-assertion.

Our mapping of symptom-generating mental models in terms of problem- and solution-defining sections is a phenomenological finding that is strongly consistent with many previous writings and findings in the field of phenomenology (e.g., Husserl, 2010) as applied to psychotherapy (e.g., Gendlin, 1996; Laing, 1995), such as this one by McLeod (2001, p. 40):

there are points in therapy where most therapists will encourage their clients to bracket off their assumptions about their problems, describe their experiences in detail, express their sense of their experience in fresh language, and in general 'overthrow and build anew' their understanding of self and relationships ... in seeking to bring to light the experiential data that constitute the 'problem' and its 'solution,' and in finding ways to uncover the 'essence' of the problem, the therapist can be seen as teaching, guiding or coaching the client in the self-application of phenomenological principles which were first identified by Husserl.

We have been describing a synthesis that combines well-established phenomenological principles with advanced knowledge of the subjective, structural and neurobiological processes of emotional learning and unlearning. This synthesis is a defining feature of the Emotional Coherence Framework, which serves as the guiding conceptual framework for Coherence Therapy.

The erasure of an emotional learning is the dissolution of certain constructs in use by the emotional brain, and this dissolution occurs only when these constructs receive such a direct and decisive disconfirmation through vivid new experience that the emotional brain itself recognizes and accepts the disconfirmation of its own constructs. In those moments of disconfirmation, what had seemed real is finally recognized as being only one's own fallible constructs. Only upon their experiential disconfirmation are the constructs that make up emotional learnings recognized by the individual *as* constructs, rather than reality. The result of construct dissolution is a fundamental change in one's experience and perception of the world. Something that seemed self-evidently true about the world no longer seems true at all. We will see below how this remarkable shift unfolded for Richard. This "constructivist" understanding of learning, meaning-making and change is extremely valuable for working with mental models in psychotherapy, in our experience, and is another defining element of the Emotional Coherence Framework. (Recommended readings on the constructivist perspective include Guidano, 1995; Mahoney, 1991, 2003; Neimeyer, 2009; Neimeyer & Bridges, 2003; Neimeyer & Raskin, 2001; and for a review of neuroscience research supporting this perspective, see Toomey & Ecker, 2007.)

As soon as the client's formerly implicit pro-symptom model has become conscious and explicit, revealing the specific constructs within it to therapist and client, the work can move next into Step C of the therapeutic reconsolidation process: finding living knowledge that sharply contradicts the pro-symptom model and can be accessible to the client. Only by first knowing the makeup of the pro-symptom model (Step B) can the identification of contradictory knowledge (Step C) be undertaken, launching Coherence Therapy's transformation phase.

Transformation phase begins by finding disconfirming knowledge (Step C)

Two weeks later, in his third session, Richard reported that on numerous occasions he had carried out the integration task: He had noticed his specific thoughts of self-doubt, then read the card and acutely recognized and felt his purpose for having such thoughts. Each of those instances was another integration experience. Richard was now routinely conscious of his pro-symptom position or schema.

The therapist therefore now began Step C, the search for contradictory knowledge that could then be used in the transformation sequence, Steps 1–2–3.

There are many pathways available to the therapist for finding the needed contradictory knowledge, as we will see in Chapters 4 and 5. Here we cover only the pathway that developed with Richard, the one we call an *opposite current experience*. It often happens that experiences in daily life provide living knowledge that is contradictory of a person's pro-symptom model, but because this model is normally unconscious, compartmentalized, and sealed off from contact with other knowings, the contradictory knowledge is not recognized as contradicting anything, use is not made of it, and the fleeting opportunity passes. However, when such an opportunity develops at the point in Coherence Therapy where the client's pro-symptom model is well retrieved and unsealed, as it was for Richard at this juncture, the client feels and notices the significance of the contradictory experience and the therapist can make highly effective use of it, as follows.

After reporting that he had carried out his last task of reading his index card and recognizing his own purpose for not speaking up many times, Richard wanted to describe an incident that had struck him. He said, "I was in a technical meeting at work and I thought of a good solution to a problem being discussed. But I went into 'What do *I* know?' and kept quiet … . A moment later, somebody else spoke up and suggested the same solution, and he said it pretty confidently. That jolted me, and immediately I looked around the room—and then I saw that everybody seemed glad to get this useful solution from this other guy. It was weird, how differently it went from how I expected it to go if *I* had said it confidently like he did."

Because Richard was aware of his pro-symptom model, this experience at work had struck a disconfirming chord quite noticeably. The therapist recognized that vivid contradictory knowledge was now at hand, which accomplished Step C and allowed the therapist to proceed directly to guide Richard through Steps 1–2–3, the transformation sequence in the therapeutic reconsolidation process.

Transformation via juxtaposition experiences (Steps 1–2–3)

To begin that sequence, the therapist asked, "Would you be willing to conjure up that scene at work in your mind's eye and sort of be back in the meeting for a few minutes, with me guiding you to try a few things?" Richard readily agreed, so the therapist, in a somewhat softened voice, began guiding an imaginal series of experiences: "The moment to revisit is that point during the meeting when you've squelched your own good idea to keep from being hated like Dad, because *any* expressing of confidence makes you resemble him. Just be back in touch with that, in your body, in that scene, to whatever degree you can." This was Step 1, the reactivation of the target emotional learning. It was fully deliberate on the therapist's part to re-evoke explicitly the key target construct, "*any* expressing of confidence makes you resemble Dad."

The therapist continued, "Do you have that? Good. And now the action continues: the other guy confidently comes out with the same solution that you've doubted away, and you're looking around the room and it feels really surprising and weird that folks are *fine* with hearing *him* put forward that same good idea with such confidence. *[Brief pause.]* Can you feel that moment, to some degree?" This was the concurrent experience or juxtaposition of mismatching, disconfirming knowledge needed in Step 2. As shown by neuroscientists, it is this step in the transformation sequence that unlocks synapses maintaining the target learning.

Richard had closed his eyes while listening to these instructions, and he now answered, "Mm-hm," in a much lower and slower voice, indicating that he was immersed in subjective experiencing, as needed.

"Good," replied the therapist, who then proceeded to guide him into repetitions of the same juxtaposition experience for Step 3:

Th: Stay with that. Stay with being surprised at what you're seeing—surprised because in your life, you've had such a definite knowing that saying something confidently to people will always come across like Dad, like an obnoxious know-it-all, and people will hate that. That's what you know, yet at the same time, here you're seeing that saying something confidently *isn't* always like Dad, and then people are fine with it. And it's quite a surprise to know that. *[That was an explicit prompting of another side-by-side experiencing of the two incompatible knowings, with the therapist expressing empathy for both, with no indication of any favoring of one knowing over the other. The therapist paused for several seconds, then asked:]* Does it feel true to describe it like that? Your old knowing right alongside this other new knowing that's so different?

Cl: *[Quietly, seeming absorbed in the experience.]* Yeah.

Th: *[Softly.]* All along, it seemed to you that saying something confidently could be done only in Dad's dominating way of doing it, and now suddenly you're seeing that saying something confidently can be done very differently, and it feels fine to people. *[This was another deliberate repetition of the same juxtaposition experience.]*

Cl: Yeah.

Th: Mm-hm. *[Silence for about 20 seconds.]* So, how is it for you be in touch with both of these knowings, the old one telling you that anything said with confidence means being like Dad, and the new one that knows you can be confident in a way that feels okay to people? *[Asking this question repeated the juxtaposition experience yet again, and, in addition, the "how is it" portion of the question prompted Richard to view the experience with mindful or metacognitive awareness, while remaining in the experience.]*

Cl: It's sort of weird. It's like there's this part of the world that I didn't notice before, even though it's been right there.

Th: I'm intrigued by how you put that. Sounds like a significant shift for you.
Cl: Yeah, it is. Huh.
Th: You're seeing *both* now, the old part of the world and this other part of the world that's new, even though it was right there all along. *[That cued the juxtaposition experience for a fourth time, followed by silence for about 30 seconds.]* So, keep seeing both, the old part and the new part, when you open your eyes in a few seconds and come back into the room with me. *[Richard soon opens his eyes and blinks a few times.]* Can you keep seeing both?
Cl: Yeah.
Th: What's it like to see both and feel both now? *[With the transformation sequence complete, this question begins the next step of verification— Step V—because it probes for whether the target learning still exists as an emotional experience.]*
Cl: *[Pause, then sudden, gleeful laughter.]* It's kind of funny! Like, what? How could I think *that*? *[This is an initial marker indicating that the pro-symptom schema may have been successfully disconfirmed, depotentiated, and dissolved by the transformation sequence.]*
Th: Do you mean, how could you think that simply saying what you know, or mentioning some good idea that you've had, would make you seem arrogant, insensitive and dominating like Dad and be hated for it?
Cl: *[Laughing again.]* Yeah!

In an empathic and natural manner, the therapist has guided four repetitions of the juxtaposition experience for Step 3 of the transformation sequence. Those juxtaposition experiences are the actual moments in which profound change occurs—the radical clearing away of troubled emotional learning with contradictory knowledge. Each juxtaposition experience consists of simultaneously experiencing the pro-symptom schema side by side with the sharply contradictory knowledge, with both knowings feeling vividly real, yet both cannot possibly be true. For the client, holding two utterly contradictory but equally real-feeling personal truths simultaneously is a peculiar experience, yet it is the experience required in order for new learning to nullify and replace old learning. This edgy *experiential dissonance* can be viewed as an enriched extension of the phenomenon of cognitive dissonance (Festinger, 1957). Reconsolidation research tells us that in these repeated juxtaposition experiences, the contradictory knowledge serves as new learning that rewrites and replaces the pro-symptom constructs.

Notice that the therapist gave recognition and empathy equally to both knowings—the knowledge that speaking confidently would make him noxious like Dad, and the knowledge that it would not have that effect. In fact, it was by empathizing explicitly with both of those knowings that the therapist again and again prompted Richard to bring both of them into his field of awareness together, as needed. For facilitating a successful juxtaposition experience, the client must be guided into feeling open to attending to both of the mutually incompatible knowings, and the therapist's welcoming attitude toward both is crucial for this. In contrast, any attempt by the therapist to use the contradictory knowledge to show the incorrectness of the pro-symptom knowledge would be unwelcoming and suppressive of the pro-symptom schema. Then neither genuine juxtaposition nor synaptic unlocking nor transformational change would occur, because juxtaposition creates the required mismatch only if both knowings are experienced as *true* and the dissonant impossibility of that is keenly felt. To take sides is to short-circuit the client's own process of determining what to regard as true. In setting up a juxtaposition experience, the therapist is simply fulfilling the condition that the client's brain and mind require for revising existing emotional schemas. The therapist's stance is one of cooperating with and trusting the client's inherent capability of revising emotional learnings.

When the juxtaposition experience was first defined by Ecker and Hulley (1996, 2000a, 2000b) as the inherent requirement of the mind and brain for transformational change of an existing learned response, the transformation sequence had not yet been identified by neuroscientists. Subsequently it became apparent that a juxtaposition experience, as defined in Coherence Therapy, fully embodies the transformation sequence identified in memory reconsolidation research. After a successful set of juxtaposition experiences lasting only a few minutes, the client finds that the pro-symptom emotional reality or schema no longer has its former emotional realness or grip. Though it had shaped and constrained life for decades, its strangle-hold is suddenly gone and the symptoms it maintained simply cease (unless there is more than one pro-symptom schema, in which case each such schema must be dissolved in order to arrive at symptom cessation).

Juxtaposition experiences in Coherence Therapy differ fundamentally from the techniques of cognitive restructuring (a major component of cognitive-behavioral therapy; see, e.g., Frojan-Parga, Calero-Elvira, & Montano-Fidalgo, 2009) and cognitive defusion (used in Acceptance and Commitment Therapy or ACT; see, e.g., Deacon, Fawzy, Lickel, & Wolitzky-Taylor, 2011). In both cognitive restructuring and cognitive defusion, the therapist typically describes the client's symptom-producing beliefs as "irrational," "maladaptive," or "pathogenic" and communicates to the client the counteractive intention to oppose and undermine either the content of the beliefs (cognitive restructuring) or their function (cognitive defusion). In contrast and as emphasized above, juxtaposition experiences are guided with no counteractive, invalidating notes whatsoever because such notes foreclose the emotional and neural processes necessary for bringing about transformational change (actual dissolution of symptom-generating constructs, not mere suppression of them). Cognitive restructuring, like cognitive reappraisal techniques, also tends to be carried out through a challenge of existing beliefs in a largely cognitive manner, in contrast to the fully experiential quality of process needed and used in juxtaposition experiences for achieving transformational change of emotional learnings.

Verification of schema dissolution (Step V)

After Step 3, the therapist's question "What's it like to see both and feel both now?" was the beginning of Step V, the first probe to verify whether or not dissolution of the symptom-requiring schema has occurred. If the schema has been dissolved, its familiar emotional grip is strikingly absent in the scene where it has always been present, and the client's response reveals this absence as well as the client's feeling about this surprising absence—which can range from a silent blinking of eyes, to an amused observation that now it seems "silly," "funny," or "absurd" to imagine "feeling that way," to gleeful laughter expressing true joy over suddenly feeling liberation and well-being, to a shout of amazed recognition of new meaning, to feelings of compassion for self or others; or, in some cases, to feelings of distress over a loss or disorientation entailed in the change.

The end of the session was approaching and the therapist asked, "How about if we write some of this new perspective on a card for you, so you can stay in touch with the felt sense of it?" The joint effort produced this card:

> All along it's been so clear that if I confidently say what I know, I will always come across as arrogant, insensitive, and dominating like Dad, and be hated for it. And it's so weird, looking around the room and seeing that it *doesn't* come across like that.

Richard was to read that card before he left for work each day and also once during any meeting over the course of the day. This practice would continue to create repetitions of the juxtaposition experience. This was desirable because, while only a few repetitions are often enough to yield lasting dissolution, some pro-symptom schemas have a large contextual range, so they exist in memory in a distributed manner involving several different memory systems corresponding to different contexts of experience. Therefore it is prudent to extend Step 3, the repetitions of the juxtaposition experience, as long as possible and into as many contexts as possible through use of a between-session task. The therapist emphasized, "The aim is only to stay in touch with what's on this card while you're at work, *not* to try to say anything confidently or do anything differently."

At his fourth session one week later, Richard reported, "Something has really changed. I feel really different at work, but it's not how I always thought I'd feel if I could stop feeling so shaky. I always thought I would feel super-confident, like some kind of genius, but I don't. The change is just that I don't feel uncertain any more, or insecure. That's a big relief, but there are no bells and whistles. It's kind of ordinary, actually. When I have something to say or contribute, I just say it, and it's no big deal."

The therapist replied, "Mm-hm. That's quite a change. I'm really glad to hear it." Dropping his voice to a quieter tone, the therapist added, "But tell me, when you have something to say and just say it, what about the danger of coming across as a know-it-all, like Dad, and being hated for that? What about your fear of *that* and how urgent it is to protect yourself from that?" The therapist deliberately implemented verification Step V again, applying cues that previously had been effective for evoking Richard's pro-symptom position into direct emotional experience, in order to probe for any remaining life in that schema. Erasure is reasonably well established only when a pro-symptom position is consistently no longer activated by cues and contexts that formerly did activate it prior to juxtaposition. This experiential way of verifying transformation by confirming the markers of erasure is an important final step in Coherence Therapy's methodology.

Richard took in the question, gazed at the therapist in silence for a few seconds, and then replied, "Well, I don't know what to tell you. All I can say is, that doesn't trouble me any more. And hearing you say it, it seems a little strange that it ever did—like, what was my *problem?*"

This reply once again had the characteristic quality indicating that the pro-symptom schema has thoroughly lost its former emotional realness. The withered lifelessness of the pro-symptom schema and the effortlessness of remaining free of the symptom are the hallmarks of the therapeutic reconsolidation process and the main signs of successful Coherence Therapy. The nature of the liberating shift was captured well by a different male client who had presented social anxiety and then described his new comfort in social settings by saying, "That feels really good. Something's shifted that's allowing that. I'm not doing something volitional and I'm not being brave. I'm not *overcoming* my fear; I *have less* fear."

Transformational versus counteractive change

Think of the start of the first session with Richard: A man whose knowledge, skills and contributions are already respected by his co-workers wants to stop doubting himself and feeling insecure at work. There is no awareness and no sign whatsoever that his wobbly lack of confidence is urgently important for being unlike his noxious, hated father. In counteractive therapies, that imperative emotional necessity would typically remain unrecognized and intact as the therapist works to build up Richard's trust in his proven knowledge and skills at work, aiming to correct his "incorrect" and "irrational" self-doubts. How likely is that to bring about a lasting shift, given that the underlying, passionate, urgent need for self-doubt remains in force? Counteractive overlays may take effect temporarily, but then they usually prove to be no match for the compelling intensity of the client's implicit pro-symptom position, and relapse occurs.

Richard came for two more sessions over the next six weeks. The therapist asked him to consider additional sessions to address any other, lingering aspects, such as grieving. Richard thought about it and said he felt no need to extend the work beyond the change for which he had come.

Complications and resistance

This case vignette has shown the process of Coherence Therapy unfolding in a straightforward manner, which is often the case and which makes the example of Richard useful as an introduction to this approach. There are, however, complications that arise with some clients. Retrieval of the pro-symptom schema may require several cycles of alternation between discovery and integration; the schema may contain feelings, knowings, meanings, or memories that initially are too distressing for the client to allow into awareness all at once, requiring a slower, small-enough-steps approach; similarly, the schema may be dissociated to an extreme degree (often the case for traumatic memory), requiring a more extended process of integration experiences to achieve steady awareness; there may be more than one symptom-generating schema, with each requiring discovery, integration and transformation; or resistance may develop at any stage and require its own process of discovery, integration and transformation in order to fall away. The methodology of Coherence Therapy can address all of these complications, though the work may unfold in a less clear-cut manner and the number of sessions can increase significantly relative to Richard's case. Some of these complications are prominent in the case examples in Part 2.

Resistance arises sometimes in response to the transformation sequence. Despite well-designed, well-guided juxtaposition experiences, the pro-symptom material can remain in force, as shown in the case of Ted in Chapter 4. This indicates that the process of disconfirmation and dissolution is being blocked by resistance to some reorientation, loss, pain or fear that the client expects, on some level, to result from dissolution of the longstanding pro-symptom model of reality. Dissolution of part of what has seemed to be reality can involve significant emotional adjustments. The dissolution of personal constructs is a top-down process, that is, it is allowed to proceed, or not, depending on whether the emotional results feel tolerable to the client's emotional brain in all areas, both consciously and unconsciously; the nature of the process is not simply mechanistic or neurological. Any resistance must therefore be sensitively respected and addressed, and in Coherence Therapy this is done by applying Coherence Therapy to the resistance itself: The therapist regards the resistance as a new "symptom" and guides discovery of the underlying coherent need for it by bringing into awareness the specific loss, pain, or fear that is making the dissolution of the pro-symptom schema too daunting to allow. When, as a result of this work, the ramifications of that dissolution do feel tolerable in all areas, the juxtaposition experience is repeated and now dissolution readily occurs. Using active, focused, experiential methods, usually this transformation resistance work on a single schema is accomplished in a small number of sessions. (For an instructional survey of techniques for working with resistance in Coherence Therapy, see Ecker & Hulley, 2011.)

Another type of complication that can extend the work is a target schema having a large contextual range. Compare, for example, one woman's retrieved schema based in the (newly verbalized) construct, "Expressing any anger makes me unlovable" with another woman's schema based in the construct, "All women are viciously competitive with each other and dangerous." The second schema comes into play in a far wider range of contexts than does the first, namely in every context in which women are present—at the workplace, at social events, visiting with friends, shopping in stores, attending classes, etc. A schema that is strongly relevant in many different contexts becomes part of each separate neural memory network corresponding to each context. Only one context at a time is addressed by the juxtaposition experience that fulfills the transformation sequence in the therapeutic reconsolidation process. Therefore, a schema may be erased in one context but remain in effect for others; complete erasure of the schema across all of its contexts may require separately carrying out the transformation sequence (see Table 3.1 on p. 41) in each context, in order to erase the schema in each memory network that has incorporated it. Life between sessions serves up useful instances in the various contexts very helpfully, but waiting for life to cover all relevant contexts is not actually necessary because the therapist proactively can guide either an experiential revisiting of past experiences or an imaginal new experience in each relevant context.

The Process in Summary

The case example of Richard provides a basic familiarity with the steps of the therapeutic reconsolidation process, labeled A–B–C–1–2–3–V in Table 3.1 for easy reference (p. 41). In review of what we have seen above:

The steps of the process are well defined, but they must be carried out uniquely with each client, requiring clinical skill as well as comfort with emotional processes. The process is experienced by the client first as a deeply felt, lucid recognition of core emotional learnings formed adaptively during potent experiences earlier in life—learnings that drive certain responses, including the presenting symptom(s). Then the client experiences a profound *un*learning and witheringaway of these problematic, unwanted learnings.

The process begins with the identification of the client's presenting problems or symptoms described in concrete, experiential specifics (Step A). The next step consists of drawing into explicit awareness the implicit emotional learnings underlying and maintaining the symptoms (Step B). These emotional learnings are the target for erasure and dissolution. Understanding the makeup of this newly conscious target learning then allows for the identification of contradictory knowledge that is emotionally real to the client (Step C; numerous methods for this step are described in Chapters 4 and 5). Steps A, B and C—the preparatory, accessing sequence—gather the information needed in order for the therapist to carry out the next phase, Steps 1, 2 and 3—the transformation sequence—that unlearns and nullifies (dissolves, erases) the target learning, following the same sequence of experiences demonstrated in neuroscientists' studies of memory reconsolidation.

In the transformation sequence, first the symptom-generating learning or knowledge is re-evoked and reactivated (Step 1). Then, concurrently, the contradictory knowledge is activated (Step 2) for a mismatch experience of two knowings, side by side, both of which cannot possibly be true. It is this step that actually unlocks synapses maintaining the target learning, opening a time window—the "reconsolidation window" of about five hours—during which the target learning is dissolvable by new learning. Repetitions of this both-at-once *juxtaposition experience*, as it is termed in Coherence Therapy, function as the new learning that rewrites and nullifies the target learning (Step 3), completing the transformation sequence. Then observations of key markers verify successful unlearning and symptom cessation (Step V). These markers are summarized in the next section.

Steps A–B–C–1–2–3–V are defined without reference to concrete techniques, which is a great strength because this means that the therapeutic reconsolidation process can be facilitated through all manner of experiential methods, limited only by our ingenuity and stylistic leanings. Therefore, although the process itself is well delineated, clinicians can exercise great freedom and creativity in using their preferred methods to fulfill it. Here we have used Coherence Therapy to embody and demonstrate the steps because the phases of Coherence Therapy's methodology correspond directly to all steps of the therapeutic reconsolidation process. Quite different methods that fulfill these steps in other therapies are the topic of Chapter 6.

Markers of Change for Symptoms Dispelled at Their Emotional Roots

Successful completion of the therapeutic reconsolidation process is unambiguously verified by a number of distinct markers that are observed in the final verification stage, as follows.

- *Non-reactivation.* A specific emotional reaction can no longer be reactivated by cues and triggers that formerly did so or by other stressful situations.
- *Symptom cessation.* Patterns of behavior, emotion, somatics, or thought that were expressions of that emotional reaction also disappear permanently.
- *Effortless permanence.* Non-recurrence of the emotional reaction and symptoms continues effortlessly and without counteractive or preventive measures of any kind.

The importance of these markers lies, of course, in their declaration of a therapeutic breakthrough. That is not all, however. Their importance also lies in the fact that, according to current neuroscience, these markers can result only from successful neurological erasure of the emotional learnings involved, and erasure results only from memory reconsolidation. Therefore, these markers serve as clear feedback to the therapist that she or he has carried out the therapeutic reconsolidation process successfully. If these markers do not appear, this is an equally clear signal to investigate how and why the process was incomplete or blocked. Thus the markers foster the therapist's effectiveness and learning.

Ubiquity of the Transformation Sequence in Profound Change

Transformational change of the kind addressed here—the true disappearance of long-standing, distressing emotional learning—of course occurs at times in all sorts of psychotherapies that involve no design or intention to implement the transformation sequence by creating juxtaposition experiences. Likewise, in the sessions of Coherence Therapy practitioners, such change sometimes comes about without any apparent signs of a juxtaposition experience having occurred. In such cases, inquiring into the process that took place internally for the client has consistently revealed that a juxtaposition experience *had* occurred, serendipitously, without being commented on by the client or recognized by the therapist until closely re-examining what happened. As we illustrate in Chapter 6, when we study closely the moment-to-moment process in case examples of various types of therapy, we can identify the steps of the therapeutic reconsolidation process whenever deep, lasting change was observed and verified. These clinical observations seem to reflect what the current state of knowledge in neuroscience (covered in Chapter 2) also tells us: According to current knowledge, the transformation sequence is the only endogenous, behavioral process that can induce the neurological erasure of an emotional learning.

This means that, in the course of any type of therapy, whenever we therapists happily observe the markers of erasure without knowing clearly why profound change came about, we can reliably infer that a juxtaposition experience has occurred, unrecognized, and we can then use open-ended enquiry to guide the client to find and articulate the juxtaposition experience explicitly. Doing so has much therapeutic benefit for the client: With explicitness of juxtaposition experiences comes the client's awareness of unlearning and evolving prior knowledge and of being *capable* of doing so. In addition there is a sizable benefit to the therapist, namely, the process of observing and learning first-hand how juxtaposition experiences take place and how to become skilled and efficient in facilitating them.

Conclusion

Our aim in this chapter has been to show the therapeutic reconsolidation process in action, illustrating its abundant value to therapy clients and psychotherapists both. It makes full use of the newly recognized power of the brain and mind to dissolve troubled emotional realities that were created earlier in life and persist as the root cause of a broad range of symptoms. This process dispels symptoms by deeply resolving chronic areas of core distress and, in doing so, depathologizes both symptoms and clients' sense of self, instilling a sense of the fundamental validity and coherence of self. Such liberating elimination of old learnings by new ones is the therapeutic ideal. Now that we largely understand such change both experientially and neurologically—through both the top-down and bottom-up lenses—it has become possible for this level of therapeutic breakthrough to be a regular occurrence in the daily practices of psychotherapists and counselors, rather than an occasional, unpredictable victory that depends too much on luck or intuition to happen regularly. It is a joy for us every time a client says, "All this time I thought I was broken. For the first time, I see that I've been responding to what I experienced—and responding in a way that now makes total sense. What a relief it is to know I can feel okay about myself!"

The next chapter focuses on techniques for creating the all-important juxtaposition experience that embodies the transformation sequence and nullifies troubling emotional learnings.

4

The Moments of Fundamental Change:
Map and Methods

Presume not that I am the thing I was.

—William Shakespeare, *King Henry IV, Part 2*

We have seen that when an emotional learning or schema is the underlying cause of a therapy client's presenting symptom, the schema can be retrieved into direct, explicit experience and then profoundly unlearned and dissolved by the same sequence of experiences that neuroscientists identified in reconsolidation research. And we have seen, too, that symptoms cease as soon as the schemas underlying and necessitating them no longer exist. The methodology for bringing about that retrieval and dissolution of schemas and symptoms is defined by the therapeutic reconsolidation process, summarized in Table 3.1 (page 41).

This chapter focuses on the actual moments of definite transformational change and on specific methods that configure such moments. In what follows, we assume that you have in mind, from Chapter 3, that the critical ingredient in moments of profound change is a juxtaposition experience, as well as: what preparation juxtaposition experiences require and when they come into play (after the accessing phase, Steps A–B–C of the therapeutic reconsolidation process); how they embody the process or series of experiences (Steps 1–2–3, the transformation sequence) that erases emotional learnings through memory reconsolidation; and what they yield as distinct markers of profound change.

Building on those foundations, you will learn in this chapter about techniques and pathways for creating juxtaposition experiences with your clients. This chapter is, in effect, an expanded view of a small region on the much larger map which is seen at a glance in Table 3.1. Here we are looking closely at one particular step within the full seven-step therapeutic reconsolidation process: Step C, finding a vividly felt knowledge that strongly contradicts key reality-defining constructs in the symptom-generating schema. That step sets the stage for a synapse-unlocking construct-erasing juxtaposition experience, repetitions of which complete the transformation sequence (Steps 1–2–3).

Our demonstration platform continues to be Coherence Therapy; the ways in which other psychotherapy systems can bring about juxtaposition experiences are the topic of Chapter 6. One of the examples in the current chapter addresses resistance to schema dissolution developing in response to the juxtaposition experience, showing how such resistance can be worked with and dissipated.

Your confidence in succeeding with the therapeutic reconsolidation process will grow as you relax into trusting in the availability of various pathways that are at your disposal for facilitating it. The process utilizes your skills of empathic attunement to clients' unresolved emotional vulnerabilities, combined with your cognitive ability to maintain focus on the needed series of steps. You will see for yourself in this chapter how clear, tangible, and non-mysterious the core steps of profound change are, making this versatile process learnable, usable, and verifiable.

How to Identify Targets for Unlearning

Finding the needed disconfirming, contradictory knowledge in Step C is based completely on having already revealed and identified, in Step B, the specific constructs in the client's mental model in the symptom-requiring schema. Familiarity with the retrieved pro-symptom constructs attunes the therapist, who develops, in effect, a sensitive "antenna" and mindfulness for spotting any signs of contradictory knowledge as it emerges. It is therefore useful in this context for us to review briefly the information in Chapter 3 about the makeup of mental models in pro-symptom schemas.

Every pro-symptom schema contains constructs that define a dire *problem*—a specific suffering that is urgent to avoid—and constructs that define the client's *solution* to that problem—a certain strategy and tactics that are compellingly necessary and purposeful for avoiding that suffering. This solution requires producing the presenting symptom either directly or indirectly. A directly required symptom is itself the necessary tactic and is therefore functional. An indirectly required symptom is an inevitable by-product of a necessary tactic being either carried out or disallowed, but in itself is functionless.

All of the problem-defining and solution-defining constructs are emotional learnings that exist implicitly and nonverbally until awareness reaches them and they are felt as emotional truths and then accurately verbalized. The construct selected as the target for dissolution can be in either the problem-defining or solution-defining part of the symptom-necessitating schema. (For a more detailed description of the structure of pro-symptom schemas and the nature of their constituent constructs, see Ecker and Hulley, 1996, 2000b, 2011.)

Consider, as an example, the pro-symptom model retrieved in the case of Richard, whom we met in Chapter 3: In terms of the two clusters of problem-defining and solution-defining constructs, what do we see? His presenting symptoms were self-doubt, anxiety, insecurity, and self-suppression while at his job, and his retrieved, symptom-requiring schema became verbalized in this way:

> I feel I'll be just like Dad, a know-it-all lording it over everyone, if I say anything that I'm confident is right. And then people will hate me for that, just the way I hate *him* for it. So I'd better keep myself quiet by thinking, "What do *I* know?," even though that makes me feel so unconfident and insecure that I don't express what I do know.

If you were the therapist and you had now become acquainted with that schema, you could then recognize that its problem-defining constructs are these: *I'll be just like Dad, a know-it-all lording it over everyone, if I say anything that I'm confident is right. And then people will hate me for that, just the way I hate* him *for it.*

You would also recognize that the schema's solution-defining constructs are these: *I'd better keep myself quiet by thinking, "What do I know?"* That includes a construct defining a *general strategy* for solving the problem (*I'd better keep myself quiet*) and a construct defining a *concrete tactic* for carrying out that strategy (*by thinking, "What do I know?"*). You can also see that in the solution-defining cluster there is a tacit construct that could be verbalized as: *By solving the problem in this way, I'll be much better off.* This construct is always present implicitly in any solution-defining cluster, though it is easy to overlook. It, too, can be made fully explicit in the retrieval work, as illustrated in the example of Charlotte in this chapter.

When you have become familiar with the constructs in a client's pro-symptom model, you then consider which construct seems the best one to target for disconfirmation and dissolution. To do that, ask yourself the following question as you review the constructs in each cluster separately: "Which construct do the other constructs arise from as the basis for their very existence?" In this way you will find the *master constructs*. As an exercise, you can try to answer that question in Richard's case on your own, before reading the next paragraph. The master construct is the best one to select as the target construct for unlearning and dissolution, because with its dissolution, the other, more subordinate constructs in the cluster dissolve, too. Targeting a master (superordinate) construct for erasure by a juxtaposition experience is the shortest path to a therapeutic breakthrough.

Richard's master problem-defining construct was, in our perception, his knowledge—for constructs operate as knowings—that *any degree of expressed confidence equals Dad.* That black-or-white, all-or-nothing construct is the one we regard as his master construct because if it were to dissolve—which means, if he were to know instead that there are degrees of overt confidence that are *not* the same as Dad and would *not* be hated—then none of the other constructs in the pro-symptom model would have any basis for existing, the entire schema would dissolve, and his self-suppression would no longer be necessary to avoid being hated. If the problem-defining cluster dissolves, the solution-defining cluster no longer has any basis and dissolves also. Such a *dissolution cascade* can yield several significant transformational shifts of various types, on various levels.

Richard's therapist, having identified *any degree of expressed confidence equals Dad* as the target construct, had become alert to contradictions of that specific construct and readily recognized an incident at work as providing Richard with a vivid experience of contradictory knowledge, which led directly to a successful juxtaposition experience. With dissolution and erasure of *any degree of expressed confidence equals Dad*, the problem simply no longer existed, ending Richard's need for symptoms of self-suppression and self-doubting. He now knew that the actual problem had not been any deficiency in his knowledge or confidence, as he had been feeling it to be, but rather his frightening expectation of being hated for it—and that expectation now no longer existed. In Richard's case, a problem-defining construct was targeted for dissolution. In some of the case examples below, we will see a solution-defining construct targeted.

Sources of Disconfirming Knowledge

You and your client can find a vivid knowing that contradicts a target construct either in the client's already existing, vast store of knowledge or in new learning experiences in daily life between sessions or in guided experiences during a session.

It may seem a paradox that many therapy clients are already in possession of living knowledge that contradicts their symptom-requiring schema. However, brain science readily explains this situation: Those two pieces of mutually antithetical knowledge have been held separately, in different memory systems. The symptom-requiring schema has existed all along only in implicit (non-conscious) emotional memory, whereas the contradictory knowledge typically is developmentally more recent and exists in conscious memory as a taken-for-granted, background item, so the two have never come into contact by being consciously and simultaneously experienced in juxtaposition, as required for disconfirmation and dissolution to take place. We estimate, based on our clinical experience, that between half and two-thirds of all clients (in a general, non-specialized therapy practice) already harbor some visceral personal knowing that can be used to contradict their pro-symptom schema.

The availability of both sources—existing knowledge and new experience—affords a great deal of flexibility and scope for your creativity within the guiding structure of the therapeutic reconsolidation process.

Case Studies and Techniques

In each case example below, the unfolding steps of the therapeutic reconsolidation process are sharply etched, with particular attention to the client's retrieved pro-symptom schema, the therapist's selection of the target construct within the pro-symptom schema, the method used for then finding the contradictory knowledge, and the way in which the therapist subsequently used the contradictory knowledge to create juxtaposition experiences, fulfilling the transformation sequence, Steps 1–2–3. You will also see the emotional depth and meaningfulness of the client's experience in the course of those steps. The unlearning of core, troubling emotional themes is remarkably rich work.

Many techniques for finding contradictory knowledge are used in Coherence Therapy, with over a dozen described in a manual of such techniques (Ecker & Hulley, 2012), and therapists undoubtedly will invent many more. We have seen the technique of using *opposite current experience* in Chapter 3, two other techniques are demonstrated in this chapter, and two more in Chapter 5. A chart at the end of the chapter reviews case examples to that point in terms of presenting symptoms, target constructs, contradictory knowledge found and technique used to find such knowledge, with a similar chart at the end of Chapter 5.

The three steps of the transformation sequence are reviewed here from Chapter 3 for ease of reference.

1. *Reactivate (re-evoke, re-trigger, guide client to re-inhabit) the symptom-requiring emotional knowledge,* with emphasis on the target construct that will be contradicted in the next step.
2. *Evoke vivid experience of contradictory knowledge* (initial juxtaposition experience, which unlocks synapses involved in the target construct).
3. *Guide a repetition of the juxtaposition* two or three more times (which rewrites and erases the target construct).

Obsessive Attachment to Former Lover

Preview of technique for finding disconfirmation

The simple experiential practice of guiding an *overt statement* of a discovered symptom-necessitating schema—so effective for fostering the integration of the schema, as we saw in Chapter 3—does double duty by also launching *mismatch detection*, which is a natural function of your client's brain that in many cases efficiently locates existing contradictory knowledge.

In the brain are specific regions and networks dedicated to detecting inconsistencies between current experience and existing conscious or near-conscious knowledge. This is a familiar experience, as when you encounter an acquaintance and sense clearly that something about his appearance has changed but cannot identify what the difference is, and you feel your mind persistently searching for it until suddenly you realize his moustache is gone. Neuroscientists usually describe this well researched function as "error detection," but in the more complex realm of psychotherapy it seems more fitting to regard it as detection of inconsistencies or mismatches.

From the viewpoint of your client's explicit memory networks, retrieval of a pro-symptom schema into explicit awareness presents entirely new information, which launches the natural search for mismatches, that is, any existing contradictory knowledge. (Indeed, as explained in Chapter 2, it is the perception of a salient mismatch that unlocks the synapses maintaining an ingrained emotional learning, allowing dissolution of that learning by a new learning.) As soon as your client is recognizing, feeling, and verbalizing the previously non-conscious, locked-away constructs making up a pro-symptom schema, his or her brain is actively submitting each of those constructs to mismatch detection—a kind of vetting of each retrieved construct in relation to a huge library of existing personal knowledge.

This process is powerful but not infallible—it can miss existing knowledge that would mismatch the pro-symptom constructs—but in a sizable fraction of cases the process succeeds and brings to the client's conscious attention the sought-after contradictory knowledge that can unlearn and dissolve the pro-symptom schema, ending symptom production. This built-in mismatch detector in a client's brain is one of the most important resources in the search for contradictory knowledge, and in this case example and the next we will see it in action.

Symptom identification

"Charlotte" was a 37-year-old single woman, the only child of a critical, over-involved mother and a rejecting, alcoholic father who divorced when she was 12. She wanted therapy to end her painful daily obsessing and ongoing "processing" with her former lover "Nina," all persisting even though it was now two years since her partner ended their eight-year relationship.

Early in her first session, Charlotte said, "The connection we had felt like one of those real primal connections that you don't get any other way except when you're in utero or something *[laughs]* and, um—it's just so painful, you know, to lose that." Soon she added, "I woke up this morning and I called her and I ended up sobbing uncontrollably, which is not unusual for me. I mean it doesn't happen every day, but dealing with her and dealing with emotional issues I cry pretty readily. And I was just really upset that she didn't understand me ... I'm too obsessed with connecting with her ... I need to be more at peace with living without that primal connection."

Finding the symptom's coherence

Charlotte's repeated references to a "primal connection" indicated to the therapist that the implicit emotional schema driving her obsessing consisted of an attachment pattern in which she relied on a deeply merged sense of connection for security. In order to begin to draw the schema into awareness, the therapist tried a simple sentence completion exercise by asking her to say, "If I let this end—", allowing the sentence to complete itself spontaneously without pre-thinking the ending. (Sentence completion is an experiential, projective technique with a long history of use in various fields (Lah, 1989; Rhode, 1957; Soley & Smith, 2008), and has been adapted to serve as one of Coherence Therapy's basic techniques for discovery work.)

Charlotte said the words, reached the blank, and tears came; the sentence that had formed was, "If I let this end—I lose *me*." This surprised her and felt significant. To the therapist, it confirmed Charlotte's reliance on merging for attachment, but when the therapist asked her whether she knew what her words meant, she said no. Continuing to focus on the meaning of those words later in the session, she said, "I couldn't look at *my* life [during the relationship] because I was busy, you know, kind of tumbling around in *hers*." In response the therapist tried out, "If you become *her* and then you *lose* her—". This had immediate resonance and clarity for her, and she replied with new vigor, "Right. That's a good connection! Yeah."

As a step of integrating this new recognition, the therapist then invited Charlotte to try out picturing her former partner and making an overt statement directly to that image: "An important part of me wants to be you and doesn't want to give that up." Becoming teary-eyed again, she spoke those words and then confirmed, "Yeah, yeah. It fits." The therapist wrote the words of that overt statement on an index card for daily reading, a task which, at each reading, would be another integration experience of this new awareness of purposefully seeking merging.

For Charlotte to feel her own purposefulness and agency in merging was a key milestone in Coherence Therapy and good progress in Session 1 toward retrieving a symptom requiring schema. However, a pro-symptom schema defines both a problem and a solution, and only Charlotte's solution of merging had been identified in the session. There had been no discovery of the problem being solved by merging—the specific suffering in primary attachment relationships that she was urgently trying to avoid by merging. The therapist anticipated that in Session 2 the discovery work would extend to the problem, completing retrieval.

Finding a disconfirmation: Mismatch detection

Session 2 began, however, with the following exchange, in which Charlotte reported an experience of a contradictory knowing that had emerged forcefully in response to her between-session index card task of reading the overt statement, "An important part of me wants to be you and I don't want to give that up." Evidently, her brain's mismatch detection systems had gone to work and brought a strong mismatch to her attention.

Th: So, I'm interested in hearing how the sentence on the card was for you.

Cl: I, um—*[long pause]*. When we were splitting up, I remember having these feelings sometimes that there were two of me. There was a me by myself, and there was a me in relationship, and—anyway, that was a strong feeling at times when we were splitting up. And, I've kind of gone back to that feeling and—*[pause]*.

Th: You mean, since our last session?

Cl: Yeah, in the last two weeks. It's like, that "me" that doesn't have any separation from her—it's like—*[becoming emphatic]* I see this as kind of like, you know, the slogan, "Silence equals death"? You know, I just see that *no boundaries equals death*. I mean, this has been this very, kind of, epiphany for me, in this last couple of weeks. I've just been thinking, "No, that [merging] doesn't work; that's not right."

This illustrates how the simple experiential practice of inhabiting an overt statement of one's pro-symptom schema launches the brain's mismatch detection activity. The therapist had no idea that Charlotte's conscious, adult self or ego-state was already in possession of the contradictory living knowledge that "no boundaries equals death"—that losing oneself by merging with another for attachment purposes is ruinous for oneself. This was already emotionally real to Charlotte, not merely an intellectual understanding, as is absolutely necessary in order for a contradictory knowing to be effective for dissolving a symptom-necessitating schema.

Her emotional knowledge in her pro-symptom schema, which could be expressed as "well-being is having no boundaries—as in utero—so I'm much better off by merging," was old and familiar within the world of emotional knowings held in her implicit memory, but it was new to her conscious, cortical, adult self, which inhabited a different world of explicit knowings. For her conscious self, her own adaptive tactic of merging was not only new but also startling and disturbing because consciously she regarded the costs of merging as fatal to her selfhood. This was a suitably sharp contradiction of her solution-defining construct, *I'm much better off this way,* which is an implicit construct in the solution-defining section of every pro-symptom schema. Thus the juxtaposition that had formed was the side-by-side experience of the two emotionally vivid knowings, *I'm much better off by merging* and *I'm much, much worse off by merging.* We call this the *solution's unacceptable costs* type of contradictory knowledge and juxtaposition.

If Charlotte had not already possessed any such contradictory knowledge, the therapist would have continued, as planned, with discovery of the problem-defining part of her pro-symptom schema, and this would have revealed other constructs as effective targets for dissolution.

Guiding a series of juxtaposition experiences

When a client's communications indicate that contradictory knowledge and a juxtaposition experience have arisen in response to overt statements (or any other step of integration) of a pro-symptom schema, this is the therapist's cue, firstly, to elicit more completely, if necessary, the contradictory knowledge that emerged and then, using this sharpened understanding of the contradictory knowledge, to guide a few explicit repetitions of the juxtaposition experience, fulfilling the requirements of the transformation sequence.

Clarifying the contradictory knowledge, if needed, can be done straightfor-wardly—in this case by the therapist saying, "When you said, 'No boundaries equals death,' I could see from your whole manner that you know this in a way that is very real to you, not just as some idea you've come across. Can you tell me some more of this personal knowledge you have of how lacking boundaries and merging with someone has very, very severe costs?" This elicited additional content: "Well, it's just so clear that if I have no boundaries in order to feel con-nected, I'm actually giving up the possibility of ever being seen for who *I* am by the other person—ever. I mean, that's what the 'death' is—never being seen because I avoided ever really showing up."

With those particulars, the therapist could now begin guiding repetitions of the juxtaposition experience. This was done simply by revisiting the two incompat-ible knowings in an empathic manner:

Th: So, let's go over what has emerged—these things you're in touch with now. If you can *feel* them emotionally as we go over them, that would be good. What I'm understanding from you is that *one* part of you *pictures Nina* and knows that in order to have the feeling of strong *connection* that's so important and so good to feel, you have to *go over* into *her* feel-ings and needs, and leave yourself behind. This part of you really yearns for that primal kind of connection and feels it's *good for you* to merge like that. And at the same time, *another* part of you has a very *different* knowing, a very clear knowing that merging into her world gives up the possibility of ever being seen for who *you* are. This part of you feels that merging is a kind of living death and is *not* good for you. And these two realities about merging are *so different*, and yet each feels so *real and true* to you. *[Pause. The first repetition of the juxtaposition is now complete.]* How is it to be feeling both of them together, like this? *[That question cues renewed attention to the both-at-once experience for a second repetition.]*

Cl: It feels like, how could I possibly have thought it could work to leave myself out like that? It's kind of puzzling right now to even see why I actually thought that could be good for me.

Notice the complete absence of any suggestion from the therapist that one of the knowings is more correct or valid than the other. This is critically important for successfully facilitating the dissolution of the symptom-requiring schema.

We noted in Chapter 3 that the therapist's question *How is it to be feeling both of them together, like this?* begins to probe for whether the pro-symptom schema still retains or has already lost emotional force. Charlotte's response, above, indicated the latter (i.e., non-reactivation). With that initial marker of possible dissolution of the schema, the appropriate homework task was an index card with sentences that would guide her yet again into the juxtaposition experience at each reading. The collaborative process of crafting those sentences—a process which itself induced yet another repetition of the juxtaposition—led to this card:

I really want merging because I'm sure that primal connection will make me feel happy and secure, the way it feels to be in utero; and at the same time, it's so clear to me how lost, invisible, and miserable the grown-up me actually feels in that kind of connection.

Outcome

Charlotte subsequently reported that she continued to feel free of her former attraction to the merged, in utero state. However, she was still contacting her former partner regularly because of a persisting urge to do so. When a pro-symptom schema is dissolved but symptoms continue, this indicates the existence of at least one other pro-symptom schema—that is, some other implicit emotional learning(s), according to which the same symptom is necessary. In the course of Sessions 2 through 9, which occurred at two-week intervals, the therapist guided Charlotte to retrieve two other, entirely different pro-symptom schemas requiring her to hold on to her connection with her ex, one of which we describe here. It consisted of an unconscious problem and solution that she formed at age 12 and that now became verbalized as, "Mom and Dad's divorce means that maybe love isn't strong enough to keep together people who love each other. I've got to prove that isn't so! I've been struggling to prove it isn't so since I was 12, and if I let go now of this relationship, I've failed and it means love fails to keep people together. So I won't let go!" In that schema, the master problem-defining construct is, "Love alone *should* be enough to keep people together, and it's a horrible world if it isn't." With Charlotte explicitly feeling and affirming that view, the therapist guided her to revisit a number of terminated couple relationships within her circle of close friends and relatives. She knew people who still loved each other dearly after separating due to incompatibility. This was vivid contradictory knowledge of the *opposite current experience* type (like Richard's in Chapter 3): What keeps people together is not love alone, but love plus compatibility, and the world isn't "horrible" because of that. The ensuing juxtaposition experience deeply revised her early, idealistic model of love and attachment, so the ending of her relationship no longer had a dire, intolerable meaning about love or the kind of world it is and was acceptable.

In her tenth and last session, she reported that she had ceased making contact with her ex-partner and felt a calm acceptance of having no further contact even though she and her ex-partner had made no progress on reaching a satisfactory mutual understanding. She said, "Now I just feel like, no, we don't have to get anything worked out. We just don't ... Well, it just shows me that I have a greater distance now if I'm willing to say, no, we don't have to work it out." Markers of non-reactivation and symptom cessation seemed steady. When she returned a year later for a different matter, she said the obsessing had not recurred.

At no time did the therapist attempt to counteract or prevent the obsessive attachment by, for example, teaching thought-stopping, building up her social support system, addressing her self-worth or insecurity, or carrying out reparative relationship therapy. The work never focused on intervening upon the obsessing *per se*, but rather on the underlying emotional learnings that had been requiring obsessive involvement as the necessary way to avoid various sufferings.

Pervasive Underachieving

Preview of technique for finding disconfirmation

Here we will see once again the simple technique of overt statement used for launching the client's mismatch detection, focused this time on the master solution-defining construct in a case of complex trauma. In a completely natural manner, this subjects the construct to a high level of truth-evaluation in relation to existing conscious knowledge, resulting in a disconfirmation that opens a pathway of deep resolution.

Symptom identification

"Ted," 33, was a scruffy-looking man who called himself a "drifter" and explained that he had dropped out of vocational training 10 years earlier and had never held a job or had a girlfriend for more than a few months. He was regularly in trouble with landlords over late rent. He said he wanted therapy because "I'm getting nowhere. It's like I just can't keep at it in anything. Kinda like, what's the use, you know? And then I give up and change to something else and then it goes the same with that."

Finding the symptom's coherence

In initial discovery work using the symptom deprivation technique, Ted was guided to imagine holding a steady job, and he commented ironically that this would "probably get my father off my back." The therapist, enquiring into Ted's experience of his father, learned that Ted was mired in hurt and bitterness toward his father over what he described as a childhood full of frequent, severe, and rageful criticism, denigration and shaming by him. There was not one expression of fatherly warmth or love that Ted could remember. Hearing this, the therapist now decided to focus the discovery work on revealing any connection between Ted's suffering of his father's emotional abuse and his presenting symptom of pervasive underachieving and marginality. To do that, the therapist continued the symptom deprivation experience, but now situated the imaginal experience within Ted's relationship with his dad, as follows:

Th: If you're willing, let's go a little further with imagining you've held a job. See if you can imagine it's now over a year at this job, and you've been doing good work, and you've gotten a raise. *[Pause]* And then, you tell your Dad the good news. Imagine actually telling him—maybe by phone, maybe face-to-face, whatever feels right—telling him, "Dad, I've done good work this whole year and I've been given a raise. And I wanted you to know how well I'm doing." See how it feels to tell that to Dad. Right to Dad.

Cl: *[Gazes at floor in silence, then gives a short laugh.]* You know, I don't know why, but what you're asking me to say makes me really edgy. I can't even remember it, what you're saying. *[The exercise is beginning to reveal, experientially, an unwelcome effect of being seen as successful by his father.]*

Th: Edgy? You get real edgy when you start to tell Dad you're doing well?

Cl: Yeah, like—can't even focus on the words.

Th: Okay. Sounds like telling Dad some good news about success is *very* uncomfortable in some way. Makes you feel edgy. *[Pause.]* I'm curious about what comes up if you complete this sentence to Dad. Just picture him again, and try out saying, "If you think I'm doing well—." Just say those words and when you reach the blank at the end, see what comes up to complete the sentence, without pre-thinking it. "If you think I'm doing well—."

Cl: If you think I'm doing well, then—*[pause]*—you'd stop being on my case all the time.

Th: Good. Okay, run it through again, and see what comes up next. "If you think I'm doing well—."

Cl: If you think I'm doing well—then when I visit home I wouldn't have to get torn down at some point.

Th: Good. Again.

Cl: If you think I'm doing well—that would prove him right. That would like—something about his ways, how successful he is at everything—oh, yeah, I know what it is! It would like prove he's been successful as a *parent*, too! *[Pause]* It would say that since I went after what I wanted and got it and became successful, that would prove he's a successful parent, he did okay, and how he treated me is no big deal 'cause I've gone out there and done okay and so he's like blameless. He could say, "Well look, you turned out okay."

Th: What *do* you want him to feel about how he did as your dad?

Cl: *[With an angry tone]* I want him to see what a fucking *asshole* he was and to feel like *shit* about it. He made *me* feel like shit, then he walks away like it's nothing, it's no big deal.

Th: I see. He really mistreated you, made you feel horrible, really hurt you, and you want him to *know* it and see that he *failed* as a father and feel bad about it.

Cl: Yeah, you bet.

Th: And so if he sees you going off and doing things that look so successful—?

Cl: Then forget about it—he'll *never* know what a lousy father he was.

Ted's last three responses have revealed both the problem and the solution that make up his symptom-requiring schema: His problem is the raw distress he chronically feels over receiving no accountability or justice for his father's hurtfulness and lovelessness toward him, all his life. His solution is to shape his own life to be the glaring evidence of the massive injury his father has caused, sending a constant message of rebuke and accusation intended to elicit accountability, remorse, and apology. Right at this point, Ted has emotionally deepened into recognizing and feeling his own powerful purpose for underachieving. The therapist's immediate next aim is to *stay right there* and create integration experiences to establish ongoing awareness of purposeful underachieving.

Th: So, try out completing this sentence: "The way I can make Dad realize what a lousy father he's been is——." Just say it out loud to me and see what comes up.

Cl: The way I can make Dad realize he's been a lousy father is— *[Falls silent without completing sentence. Gazes at floor.]*

Th: What's happening?

Cl: *[Angry edge is gone; voice now lower and slower.]* Well, when you asked me to say that, the words I heard in my head were, "Me being a mess." *[Pause.]* And it was kind of a shock. *[This was the moment of recognizing his own* agency *in relation to his symptom of underachieving. This experiential recognition of agency is a basic characteristic of Coherence Therapy.]*

Th: *[Pause; in a gentle tone:]* So, it's a shock to realize you may be *keeping* your life a mess, making sure success *doesn't* happen, for this crucial purpose—making Dad realize how bad he treated you.

Cl: Yeah.

Th: So, I wonder if you'd be willing to picture Dad again and try out saying it right *to him*—something like, "To me what's most important is getting you to see that you failed at being a father because you treated me so bad. That's so important to me that I'm willing to keep my life a mess to get you to see that." *[With that overt statement, the therapist is continuing to create integration experiences.]*

Cl: You want me to say that to him?

Th: Yes, because that seems to be the emotional truth of it. I'm asking you to picture him and say it right to him, and see for yourself if it feels true to say that.

Cl: But it's really screwed up to deliberately keep myself so messed up.

Th: Well, I understand it's not at all that you *like* keeping your life a mess. It's not that you like it. It's that you seem to have this powerful purpose of getting Dad to *get* it and care about how he hurt you. And the mess, the lack of any success, is your way of trying to make that happen.

Cl: Right, right. That helps—putting it that way. Okay, what is it I should say?

Th: Whatever words are true about what you suddenly realized, that shocked you—in really personal terms, right to your image of your father. If it makes it easier, you could start with, "I hate to admit this, but—."

Cl: *[Laughs.]* Yeah. *[Pause.]* I hate to admit this, but—*[pause]*—if I do okay and make big bucks—*[pause]*—you'll think you did fine and you'll never get it how bad you messed me up. And how *you* screwed up as a father.

Th: Good. Do you want to add that part about, "I'm hoping that seeing my total lack of success is what will make you get it"?

Cl: Yeah, right. What I'm hoping will make you get it is seeing my total lack of success.

Th: Want to change the wording in any way?

Cl: No, no, it fits. Kind of weird, though. *[Pause]* I mean, it's actually a relief, in a way, 'cause like I said, it's always seemed like something must be really wrong with me that I never get anywhere.

Ted's relief over the de-pathologizing of his underachieving, and his emerging sense of purpose and agency in relation to underachieving, were key markers of good integration of his pro-symptom schema. To end the session, the therapist set up a between-session integration task by giving him an index card that read:

> The most important thing to me is to get Dad to see that he *failed* at being a father to me. I hate to admit it, but that's *so* important to me that I'm willing to keep my own life a mess, and get nowhere, to get him to see how badly he screwed up by tearing me down all the time.

As instructions for using this card, the therapist said, "Read it each day just to stay in touch with that as you go through the day, until our next session. Just stay in touch with it; don't try to change anything, for now."

This productive first session had retrieved an emotional schema in which the problem was the complete absence of acknowledgment, apology, or accountability from his father for great emotional harm inflicted, and the urgent solution was for Ted to make such a visible mess of his own life that his father would have to see and acknowledge this shambles as clear evidence of his own wrongdoing and failure as a father. Therapists who work from an attachment perspective could view this schema as an attachment pattern, with Ted's solution being his attempt to induce his father to meet his needs by making amends properly. In Chapter 5 we discuss more extensively how attachment work is understood and carried out in the context of the therapeutic reconsolidation process and Coherence Therapy.

In Ted's pro-symptom schema, the solution-defining section is representative of the class of solutions consisting of an envisioned ideal, happy-ending outcome that is (unconsciously) expected to end a particular vulnerability, heal a grievous injury, deprivation or injustice, and restore well-being (as distinct from solutions that are only self-protective tactics for avoiding a particular suffering). Once conscious, solutions consisting of an ideal happy ending tend to be readily susceptible to disconfirmation by the client's existing knowledge, as we will see below.

Finding a disconfirmation: Mismatch detection

The second session began with a follow-up on the index card task.

Th: How'd it go with the card?
Cl: Well, at first I'd look at that card and, y'know, like it's so true but it would just make me feel down, y'know? But then, after a few days it changed, and I got more like pissed over it—like, how long am I just gonna keep my life on hold, y'know? Waiting for my father to get it, y'know?
Th: Waiting for him to get it. Sounds as though you believe he *could* get it.

In that interaction, the therapist recognized the master construct within Ted's solution: His previously unrecognized and unquestioned assumption that his father is a man who *could* face, feel, and acknowledge his own grievous wrongdoing—a magical fantasy of a wished-for, ideal outcome that was formed early in life. If Ted's fantasy assumption—that his intensely self-absorbed, rejecting father was capable of being remorseful and making amends—were to be disconfirmed and dissolved, the impossibility of his underachieving bringing about the intended result would become apparent to Ted, so the need for that solution of underachieving would disappear, allowing symptom cessation.

As we have seen already in the previous case example of Charlotte's obsessive attachment, there is a simple way to turn a target construct into a potent magnet that attracts existing contradictory knowledge: Guide the individual to make an overt statement of the construct, openly affirming the newly conscious knowledge, which activates the brain's mismatch detector networks. That is what the therapist immediately did next with Ted.

Th: Would you try out saying this sentence to me? Just try it out, even if it's mechanical at first, to see if it fits for you: "My father is a man who's *willing* to recognize his own big mistake."

Cl: My father's a man who's willing to admit he made a big mistake. *[Looks down into his lap shaking his head]* Fuck!

Th: Or trying out saying, "My father is a man who's *willing* to openly admit his mistake and apologize for causing me harm."

Cl: *[Still looking down and shaking his head. Low voice]* Oh, man! *[Rueful laugh]* I mean, what could I be thinking? He never does any of that with *anybody. Never. [Pause. Snorts]* What a joke.

Mismatch detection was immediate in this case. Ted's response clearly indicated that he was now experiencing a strongly felt knowing that his long-wished-for solution to his attachment ordeal with his father was an impossible, unobtainable fantasy (without the therapist saying anything of the kind). The first disconfirmation of the pro-symptom construct and a contradictory knowing was occurring in those moments, presumably unlocking synapses in the implicit memory circuits of that learned solution. Ted's distress here was a marker indicating that the disconfirmation was experiential, as needed. The yearnings for caring understanding from a parent and for accountability from an abusive parent are of course very deep, so Ted's distress was natural and inevitable in this process.

At the core of idealized fantasy solutions is the deeply implicit, unquestioned assumption or construct that the yearned-for outcome is *possible*. This construct of possibility is so tacit and fundamental that it is easy for the therapist to overlook. Upon noticing such a construct, as a rule it is also easy for a therapist to guide the client to make an overt statement simply affirming the long-standing assumption that the desired outcome is possible. The client then immediately becomes aware of a vivid, contradictory knowledge—his or her adult knowledge that the expected outcome is not actually possible. This juxtaposition experience is created without any counteractive message from the therapist whatsoever suggesting that the sought-after fantasy outcome is unobtainable.

Guiding a series of juxtaposition experiences

Several repetitions of a well-formed juxtaposition experience constitute the transformation sequence that dissolves an emotional learning, so Ted's therapist proceeded to guide a repeated, explicit juxtaposition experience by saying:

Th: Would you try out saying to me some words for what it seems you just saw? Maybe, "I see that my father can never give me the true apology I most want from him." *[The purpose of this was to make the emerging contradictory knowing fully explicit.]*

Cl: *[Long pause]* My father can never give me the true apology I most want from him.

Th: *[Pause]* How is it to get in touch with that?

Cl: I just want to fight it! It's fucking outrageous!

Th: Yes. Outrageous. Tell that directly to Dad. Picture Dad and tell him, "I *refuse to accept* that you can't give me the acknowledgment and apology and honesty I want from you, and I'm going to fight to *make* you come up with that for me." *[This invites an overt statement of his resistance to the contradictory knowing that his long hoped-for outcome is not possible. Note that the contradictory knowing is in this way kept at the center of attention and Ted is kept in the juxtaposition experience even while resisting it.]*

Cl: *[Gazes at his lap in silence, now looking melancholy instead of angry]*

Th: *[Pause]* What's happening now?

Cl: *[Sighs]* When you said "apology and honesty"—like, yeah, that's *exactly* what I want, and that's *exactly* what he'd never do. With me or with anybody.

Th: The sound of your voice and how you look—you seem kind of down, right now.

Cl: Well, yeah. *[Big exhale]*

Th: Mm-hm. *[Pause]* Would you try out saying to me, "If I really get it that my father will *never* have the emotional honesty to see what he did to me—." *[Sentence completion intended to invite verbal expression of the grieving that Ted has begun to allow himself to feel. Previously he had resisted this grieving by going into anger.]*

Cl: Then, it's like I got no father. I mean, it feels like that—like I got no father. *[Pause]* Never really did. *[Pause]* And never *will*, that's the thing. Never will. And I just want to fight that, y'know?

Resistance to transformation: Its coherence and dissipation

The session segment above is an example of resistance developing in response to the transformation sequence. As discussed in Chapter 3, even with well-guided juxtaposition experiences, the client allows the dissolution of personal constructs to take place only if the emotional results feel tolerable both consciously and unconsciously. If resistance arises, blocking dissolution of the target construct, the therapist then works to make fully explicit what it is that does not feel tolerable and sensitively guides the client to examine and process this area until construct dissolution does feel tolerable. In short, the therapist approaches the resistance in the same manner as any other specific symptom and applies the usual methodology of Coherence Therapy to it. In many cases of resistance to transformation, as in Ted's, it emerges that the client is protecting himself or herself from painful feelings of loss and grief that would accompany construct dissolution.

The therapist and Ted then co-wrote an index card that would capture the two knowings in juxtaposition as well as foster integration of his refusal to allow dissolution of his core construct. The following card resulted and Ted agreed to read it every day, especially whenever he saw or spoke to Dad:

> Even though keeping my life a mess is starting to really scare me, it would feel even worse to accept that Dad will never change, never face how he treated me, never apologize. I don't accept that! It feels too outrageous and too fatherless. I *will* keep trying to make him come up with the apology and honesty I want from him, in the one way I have: me being a mess.

This card would maintain the juxtaposition as well as Ted's awareness and ownership of his resistance to it, which was now the focus of the work. This was just the beginning of the resistance work in this case. Ten more sessions spanning six months were required for bringing to light and shifting all of Ted's specific emotional themes and purposes making it necessary for him to resist accepting and grieving his father's intractability—a process of applying Coherence Therapy's methodology to the resistance itself. Some of the index cards given to Ted in the course of these sessions capture his encounters with this material:

- Since Dad would think my success proves his fathering was a success, I refuse to *have* any success. How he thinks and feels is more important to me than how my own life goes.
- I *don't want* it to be true that Dad can't ever admit he treated me wrong, or feel bad about it, because then I'd know I've been wasting my life for *nothing*. And I'd have to accept being completely powerless to get the acknowledgment I deserve. No way!
- My only way to feel connected with Dad is by struggling to get him to understand and care about how he hurt me. If I drop that struggle I feel so disconnected, alone, and on my own that my stomach clenches up.
- Even though being so wired into Dad keeps my life on hold while I wait for him to finally have a change of heart and apologize, it feels even scarier to go forward without him, without a father behind me.
- If I go on without Dad and decide to get somewhere on my own, then I'm responsible for my own life. That feels really scary, so I'm holding back.

Ted avoided frightening degrees of aloneness, grief, injustice and self-responsibility by maintaining the hope that Dad would apologize, which is why he needed, at first, to block the juxtaposition experience and not allow his fantasy outcome to be dissolved. By making each of his emerging themes of resistance conscious in an experiential manner, Ted was able to evolve his relationship to them, dissolving some of them and beginning to accept others as the inherent uncertainties of life. Ted's shift on each of these themes entailed, in a natural manner, new knowings and juxtaposition experiences that dissolved existing problems and/or solutions.

When all themes of resistance seemed largely dissolved, the therapist guided Ted back into the primary juxtaposition experience again through asking him to make this overt statement of it: "Now I see that Dad can never admit that he hurt me real bad or apologize for it, like I always expected I would get him to do by being a mess." Ted could now stay with the emotional truth of that statement without fighting it, even along with continuing, natural feelings of sorrow over this outcome. His new level of differentiation and separation from his father was understandably a bittersweet achievement. He said that he had accepted that "my father will go to his grave never *getting* it. He's just living in his own world of 'ain't I great!'" This completed the transformation sequence.

What we have seen with Ted is that when an ideal fantasy solution is disconfirmed and dissolved, the problem still exists. Then the therapist guides the client to respond to the problem with a new and different solution, one that actually comes to terms with the problem and resolves it in a direct, deep, and authentic manner—such as through grieving.

Verification step

For several years, Ted had been considering a vocational training course in electronics and recently had been wondering again about signing up for it. The therapist now used Ted's lingering interest in this course as an opportunity to check concretely for whether there remained any unconscious vestiges of needing to avoid tangibly developing his life. The method for this probing consisted of guiding Ted to envision himself completing the course successfully and, in conjunction with that scenario, to try out saying, in turn, several of the sentences from his "deck" of index cards from previous sessions, sentences which bluntly expressed his various themes of needing to avoid being successful. These overt sentences now had little or no emotional resonance or grip. Some remained active, existential issues, but Ted was now dealing well with them. Envisioning successful completion of that course was the type of cue that formerly would strongly reactivate his several schemas that had powerfully opposed any success, but no such reactivation occurred now. That marker was a satisfactory completion of the verification step and of the therapeutic reconsolidation process with Ted. For readers who relate to psychotherapy largely in terms of attachment, we note that this case example illustrates how an attachment pattern can be transformed through the emotional effects of new, disconfirming experiences other than the therapist's safe, reliable empathy. This greatly expands the range of therapeutic options in working with attachment disturbances, as discussed in Chapter 5.

Outcome

Of course, the real measure of therapeutic success was Ted's behavior in his life outside of sessions. At the beginning of what turned out to be his final session, Ted mentioned he had finally signed up for the vocational training course in electronics. Just over two years later, Ted called for another session—a couple session with his girlfriend. They had been together for a year and had decided to marry, and wanted to do some relationship work. The therapist learned that Ted had completed the basic level of his electronics training program and had landed a job in the quality control testing department of a large manufacturer. He'd had "a few bouts of losing interest, but it didn't really throw me off any more, because, like, I knew what was going on, you know? Those cards still come in handy. Haven't lost steam for quite a while now." There were further markers of lasting change.

Stage Fright (PTSD)

Preview of technique for finding disconfirmation

This case example shows an application of our framework to trauma and post-traumatic stress disorder through using the technique of *empowered re-enactment* to create the new knowledge that contradicts and dissolves a client's symptom-generating knowledge. This technique makes full use of the fact that the emotional brain responds in essentially the same ways to imaginal experiences as to externally perceived experiences, as was demonstrated by Kreiman, Koch, and Fried (2000). Thus for the emotional brain, the imaginal experiences during re-enactment are real. Re-enactment summons the client's existing resources into expression in new ways. Within Coherence Therapy, the therapist tailors the re-enactment to create new knowledge that specifically contradicts a retrieved, pro-symptom schema's target construct.

Symptom identification

"Brenda," a woman in her mid-30s, was an aspiring stage performer. After working with the therapist over the course of a year on several different problems and symptoms, in her 22nd session she described for the first time a recently occurring problem of feeling such intense anxiety during rehearsals for a leading role she would play in two months that the rehearsals were an ordeal and largely useless. She also explained that her struggle with stage fright had a long history. In eighth grade when she was 13, she had a starring role in the school play, but on the morning of the play she was too terrified to go to school and stayed home. During high school, her stage fright was so strong that she did no performing despite wanting very much to do so.

Finding the symptom's coherence

Brenda also described a high-anxiety dream from the previous night in which she was driving her car and suddenly the brakes failed completely. In a session three weeks earlier, she had described a terrifying dream of being trapped in a careening high-speed bus and feeling doomed. The therapist was struck by the emergence of these high-fear dreams in motor vehicles during this period of preparing for her show, and wanted to see if the dreams could reveal something important about the underlying coherence of her stage fright. He therefore guided her into experiential dreamwork of the Gestalt therapy type, involving an eyes-closed, fully experiential re-immersion in the dream scene.

In the course of this work, suddenly Brenda said that an image was intruding persistently—the image of what she was seeing as an eight-year-old from the back seat of the family car as her drunk father drove her, her mother and sister on a careening, lurching trajectory at high speed toward a bridge that was visible in the distance. The therapist, understanding that this was the surfacing of a traumatic memory, immediately cooperated with shifting the focus to this emerging material and actively helped elicit it as fully as possible.

Already absorbed in the traumatic scene, Brenda described her whole-body tension and desperate attempt to control the car's motion with her will, magically. The car grazed the side railing; she felt she was going to die. As this memory module became known to the therapist, he understood that what made the event traumatic was, specifically, feeling helpless and powerless to protect herself in that situation. He therefore selected as the target for disconfirmation and dissolution this model of herself as powerless that had lived on in emotional memory and had re-emerged in Brenda's two recent dreams. The therapist wondered, but could not know at this point, whether Brenda's traumatic memory of the car experience was somehow being retriggered by her rehearsals as "stage fright." His plan was to guide her to dissolve this frozen memory through the therapeutic reconsolidation process and then see whether the stage fright would diminish as a result.

Finding a disconfirmation: empowered re-enactment

Given that the target selected for dissolution was the problem-defining construct, "I'm helplessly trapped in this car that is carrying me to my death," the therapist recognized that the technique of empowered re-enactment, widely used by trauma therapists (see, for example, Ogden, Minton, & Pain, 2006), would fit this clinical moment well because re-enactment can create a vivid experience of *having* power to protect oneself in a scene in which one initially felt completely powerless. In such re-enactment work, consideration of whether or not Brenda at eight years of age could have been more assertively self-protective would not at all be involved because the technique consists only of juxtaposing her original and persisting emotional knowledge of herself—being powerlessly trapped—and a present opposite experience that sharply contradicts that knowledge.

With Brenda already immersed in and re-experiencing the original scene of being in the lurching car's back seat and heading toward the bridge, the therapist moved naturally into the re-enactment by saying, "I'm going to help you through this situation in a whole new way." The re-enactment took less than four minutes and developed as follows.

Th: In that scene I want you to start to scream at your father, if necessary, "Stop the car right now! I've got to get out! I can't stay in this car!"

Cl: *[Loudly]* Stop the car! Dad, stop the car, I'm getting out! *[Voice tone is somewhat stiff, as if the re-enactment at this early point is feeling contrived and not emotionally real to her yet.]*

Th: *Make* him stop the car.

Cl: *[Louder]* Stop the car! Stop! I'm getting out!

Th: This is too dangerous.

Cl: This is too dangerous! I'm getting out! Stop!

Th: Does he stop it yet? Is he taking you *seriously* yet?

Cl: Not exactly.

Th: Keep going! Do what you've got to do!

Cl: *[Very loudly]* Stop! Stop the car! I'm opening the door! That's making him stop. *[Voice tone indicates that the action feels emotionally real to her.]*

Th: Good. Great. You're doing it! Keep going.

Cl: Stop! I'm getting out! He stopped when I opened the door.

Th: Great! Run out!

Cl: I'm on the wrong side, I'm on the traffic side.

Th: Okay.

Cl: I have to climb over my sister—

Th: Go ahead.

Cl: —and open her door. I'm getting out! I got out. I got out of the car. They want me to get back in.

Th: No.

Cl: My mother is yelling at me, "Get back in the car!"

Th: Take care of yourself! It's too scary for you in that car. It's traumatic.

Cl: No! No! No! I'm not getting in! Send a taxi for me.

Th: What needs to be said? "He's going to kill us!" "How can you let him drive like that?" "You're not protecting us!"

Cl: Yes.

Th: What do you need to say?

Cl: *[Suddenly crying; loudly through her tears]* How could you do this? We're
         going to *die*, don't you *get* it? God, I *hate* you! Go get out of here! Leave!
         You get in the car! I'm not getting in.
Th: Great!
Cl: I'm not getting in. I'm not getting back in the car. Fuck *you*.
Th: Great.
Cl: Fuck you. *You* get back in the fucking car. Now I'm walking in the other
         direction. Oh God, I hate her so much. I *hate* my mother for this.
Th: Feel it, feel it.
Cl: I hate her. I want *her* to get in the car and die. I hate her for this. I'm walk-
         ing the other way. And my mother's yelling, "You get back in this car!"
         No! No! Fuck you! *You* get back in the car! I'm leaving!
Th: Good.
Cl: And I won't get back in the car.
Th: Good. Good, you're really protecting yourself.
Cl: But she—they're bigger than me and they're starting to drag me.
Th: Then scream for help. Get some other adults to protect you.
Cl: *[Screaming:]* NO! NO! NO! I won't get back in the car! NOOOOOOO!
Th: Somebody help me, my father's driving drunk!
Cl: Help! Help! My father's driving drunk! HEEELLPP!
Th: Good!
Cl: Other adults are coming.
Th: Good—of course they will. Tell them; tell them what's happening.
Cl: My father's driving drunk! I won't get back in the car. There he is; he's
         drunk. We're careening around the road; I'm not getting back in the car.
         [Pause.] They call the police.
Th: They call the police; great.
Cl: The police are coming. And they won't let him drive.
Th: That's right.
Cl: And they won't make me get back in the car. *[This utterance and her
         next two are the moments when her new experience of having the power
         to protect herself feels sufficiently true and reliable to serve as a contra-
         dictory knowing that is juxtaposing with and dissolving the constructs
         of powerlessness and mortal danger originally linked to this context of
         approaching a bridge in the car.]*
Th: That's right. Are the police coming?
Cl: They're there. And I'll never get in the car with him drunk again.
Th: Good.
Cl: And they can't make me.
Th: Right.

The empowered re-enactment was complete at that point. It had guided Brenda
from her experience of the target problem-defining construct—the emotional

learning that consisted of *I am helplessly trapped in this car*—to an intense dis-confirming experience of contradictory knowledge of *having* the power and free-dom to get out of the car immediately for safety. A juxtaposition of those two incompatible knowings had taken place decisively and repeatedly, though tacitly, within the re-enactment. It is best practice, however, to guide an explicit experi-ence of the juxtaposition, continuing and completing the work as follows.

Th: You've done a wonderful job of protecting yourself and keeping yourself safe in this situation. Take a moment to simply feel good about using your power and freedom to protect yourself like this. *[Pause, 20 seconds]* And you can also reflect back on how at first you had been feeling so *powerless* to get yourself out of that car, and feeling helplessly trapped in it; but this experience you've now had is so different, because now you're so aware of *having* the power and freedom to protect yourself like this. *[Pause, 20 seconds]* And you can keep that awareness as you get ready to open your eyes and come back into the room with me.

Outcome

In her next session, 11 days later, Brenda said, "I've been much less scared since last session ... I've been thinking, well, something must have really shifted ... It really strikes me that something has shifted. I haven't been hugely afraid of doing this performance. I'm *somewhat* afraid; I think I'm *normally* afraid. I think anybody in my position would have some—concern or trepidation. But I think it's normal and manageable." Later she added, "I really think that session last week—there was a way that I was always psychically sitting in that back seat in the car, trying to hold on to something. To not have that responsibility now, of controlling a careening car, is very freeing ... I'm in a good place to be doing this show, thank God." These are clear markers of non-reactivation and symptom cessation.

She said she wanted to call for another session only if needed. She did so four months later for one session on other matters and in that session said her perfor-mance had gone well. After that it was again four months between each of her next two sessions, which were her last.

The fact that Brenda's stage fright was dispelled by transforming the stored, frozen memory of helplessness in the car confirmed that each episode of stage fright had been a flashback of the memory of that terrifying ride (an affective flashback as distinct from a perceptual-memory flashback; her perceptual mem-ory began emerging during the in-session dreamwork). In the session following the re-enactment work, the therapist asked Brenda if she was aware of how or why approaching the performance resembled and retriggered the memory of approaching the bridge in that car. The shared, triggering feature was now clear to her immediately; she explained that the two approaches were "the same, because once I'm on either one—the bridge or the stage—*I can't get off.*"

In that same session she described a dream since the re-enactment session in which she is saying goodbye to family and others who are with her at a table outdoors in a "colorful, enlivening" mood and setting. "This was very powerful, saying goodbye to my parents and more particularly my father ... just profound saying goodbye and ... I was crying, but it wasn't sad exactly, just touching, very touching ... I was just going away, going away someplace. It has a very positive kind of feel ... There was a way that the dream was really empowering, like I was making a break. And I wonder that I would have that dream after getting out of the back seat of that car ... Saying goodbye and getting the life-force back—there was just something very empowering about that."

This dream continued a major theme that developed during the re-enactment, in addition to the physical escape from the car: Brenda's powerless confinement in that life-threatening car at age eight was but one manifestation of her powerless confinement in a family system that felt life-threatening to her in its own ways. As with the frozen experience of being trapped in the car, her implicit emotional knowledge of being trapped in that family system had persisted intact into adulthood. In the re-enactment, her experience of her adult, current power to refute and differentiate from the rules and roles dictated to her by her parents was itself new contradictory knowledge. The dream consists of various markers of transformational change of Brenda's implicit model of herself as powerless to exit the prison of her parents' attachment rules, a big shift of separation/individuation.

Commentary: re-enactment

We have illustrated how the re-enactment technique can be applied for the creation of a juxtaposition experience. Trauma therapists have defined various change mechanisms to explain how re-enactment acts upon traumatic memory—for example, allowing the originally disallowed expression of the body's natural, self-protective response ends the blockage of that response and releases locked energy, among other mechanisms (see, for example, Levine, 1997). As understood in terms of the therapeutic reconsolidation process, enacting the natural, self-protective response is de-traumatizing because the experience of the empowered response creates new knowings that disconfirm and dissolve the model and the feeling of being powerless that had formed in the original traumatic learning experience.

It is important to note that the re-enactment technique is appropriate only if the original situation in fact gave the client early signs of danger or trouble, so that in re-enacting, the client can respond sooner and more assertively and self-protectively, and in that way can experience the ability to avoid harm. An example of a trauma that is inappropriate for re-enactment is the experience of a bomb exploding. In that case there is no way to respond more self-protectively, so re-enactment would only be re-traumatizing. In such cases, different techniques of traumatic memory transformation are needed.

Table 4.1 Case examples of Coherence Therapy in Chapters 3 and 4 described in terms of the target symptom-generating construct retrieved, the contradictory knowledge found, and the technique used for finding it in Step C of the therapeutic reconsolidation process

Client's symptom	Target construct	Contradictory knowing	Source	Technique
Anxiety, lack of confidence at work (Richard, Chapter 3)	Problem-defining: Toxicity of any expressed confidence	Others' comfort with expressed confidence	New experience outside of sessions	Identify opposite current experience
Obsessive attachment (Charlotte, Chapter 4)	Solution-defining: *I'm better off this way, merging*	Solution's unacceptable costs	Existing knowledge	Overt statement drives mismatch detection of opposite existing knowledge
Pervasive underachieving (Ted, Chapter 4)	Solution-defining: Model of father as capable of apology, accountability	Solution's impossibility	Existing knowledge	Overt statement drives mismatch detection of opposite existing knowledge
Stage fright (Brenda, Chapter 4)	Problem-defining: Traumatic model of physical and interpersonal helplessness	Actual powers of assertion, self-protection	New experience during session	Empowered imaginal re-enactment

Summary of Techniques

Table 4.1 provides an overview of our case examples thus far in the book by listing for each one the retrieved symptom-necessitating construct(s) targeted for disconfirmation, the contradictory knowledge found or created, the source of the contradictory knowledge and the technique used for finding or creating the contradictory knowledge.

These case examples of dissolving a pro-symptom schema have illustrated three different techniques for finding contradictory living knowledge, which is Step C of the therapeutic reconsolidation process. These demonstrated techniques are only an introductory sampling of the many verbal, imaginal, and body-oriented techniques available for this pivotal step in the process; additional techniques are described in the next chapter on attachment-focused work and summarized in Table 5.2 on page 125. There is probably no limit to the number of methods that inventive therapists can devise. For a more extensive and detailed coverage of such techniques plus clinical guidance for creating juxtaposition experiences in Coherence Therapy, see Ecker and Hulley (2012).

5

Emotional Coherence and the Great Attachment Debate

> *Psychotherapy should be formulated to meet the uniqueness of the individual's needs, rather than tailoring the person to fit the Procrustean bed of a hypothetical theory of human behavior.*

> —Milton H. Erickson

The importance of attachment in human life and in psychotherapy has been described in a wealth of publications on research and theory (e.g., Cassidy & Shaver, 2008; Schore, 1994, 2003a, 2003b; Siegel, 1999, 2001, 2006). However, as noted by Prenn (2011, p. 308), "There has been a gap between the prolific attachment theory and research literature and a relative paucity of guidance about how to apply attachment theory to clinical practice." Additionally, the degree to which attachment vicissitudes influence individual development and symptom production has been a quite controversial matter among researchers as well as clinicians, with highly respected voices on various sides of the debate (see, e.g., Wylie & Turner, 2011). It is a debate to which the Emotional Coherence Framework supplies a novel and comprehensive contribution along with a clinical methodology, case conceptualization, and modeling of attachment dynamics that help bridge the gap between theory and clinical practice.

Attachment, Other Domains of Emotional Learning, and Temperament

On one side of the controversy are those who cite extensive research in support of the idea that attachment experiences and dynamics determine the course of both individual psychological development and symptom production so power-fully that virtually all psychotherapy would best be defined and practiced so as to address attachment issues (e.g., Badenoch, 2008, 2011; Cassidy & Shaver, 2008; Connors, 2011; Fosha, 2000, 2002; Lipton & Fosha, 2011; Schore, 2003b; Siegel, 1999, 2006). For example, Schore (1997, p. 829) expressed his agreement with another author that "all psychopathology constitutes primary or secondary disorders of bonding or attachment." A view of attachment relationships as the ruling influence in development similarly was expressed by Lipton and Fosha (2011, p. 255):

> Early attachment relationships shape an infant's neurobiology and set the course for his or her future biopsychosocial self (Schore, 1996, 2009). Mediated by the greater social environment, this bidirectional, dyadic process directly influences the final wiring of our brains and organizes (or disorganizes) our future social and emotional coping capacities.

On another side of this debate are those who object to monopolization of psychotherapy by such a strong emphasis on attachment and maintain that both research and clinical experience show that attachment, though important, is just one among several other strongly influential determinants of development and symptom production—which would be neglected or mishandled, to the detriment of many therapy clients, if psychotherapists were to presuppose that attachment issues underlie all symptoms.

For example, psychologist Jerome Kagan, on the basis of his more than four decades of research on personality, the interaction of biology and psychology, and inborn temperament, emphasizes

> the profound influences of social class, gender, ethnicity, and culture on personality development. These factors, independent of a mother's sensitivity, can be as significant as the quality of the early attachment ... Research has demonstrated that social and economic factors have a powerful influence on development. The strongest predictor of adult depression or anxiety in many cultures is growing up in a disadvantaged social class ... In fact, if two groups of psychologists were asked to predict the personality traits and incidence of pathology in 5,000 randomly selected 30-year-olds, and the first group knew only the social class in which the child had been reared, while the other group knew only the mother's sensitivity and the nature of the child's attachment during the first two years of life, the first group would make far more accurate predictions about personality and mood disorders.
>
> (Kagan, 2011, p. 50)

That point—that social conditions outside the domain of dyadic attachment relationships can be of major influence—has been similarly stressed by Salvador

Minuchin, a primary figure in the family therapy field: "Certainly a stable early environment is important, but focusing so much attention on attachment issues can make compelling social and racial issues simply disappear. It can ... deny the full familial and social reality of children's lives, as well as obscure our understanding of the context in which they grew up" (Wylie & Turner, 2011, p. 27). Influential negative social experiences include bullying, racist or ethnic oppression, betrayal by friends or colleagues, layoff and unemployment, living in a war zone, or having and then losing popularity or fame.

Both Minuchin and psychologist and sex therapist David Schnarch have also expressed concerns that in the reparenting or reparative approach of attachment-focused therapy, "the therapist ... can become *too* important as the central, perhaps only, reparative figure in the client's life" (ibid.), encouraging dependency and codependency and failing to advance the individual's level of differentiation.

The picture expands further if we look closely at *existential* experiences, which in many (but not all) cases are meaningfully distinct from both social and attachment experiences. Examples include experiences of illness or injury causing disability or loss of desired pursuits, a change from affluence to poverty, accidentally causing a death, living through ordeals due to natural disasters, and the felt sense of mortality and the finite time period of one's life. In response to such experiences, people with secure attachment can and do form non-conscious, problematic emotional schemas and adaptations that generate symptoms presented in therapy.

Yet another major influence on personality development is inborn temperament. Kagan and colleagues have identified "high reactive" and "low reactive" types of temperament in four-month-old infants and have demonstrated the persistence of these predispositions to 18 years of age in males, using brain imaging to reveal amygdala activity (Schwartz et al., 2011). According to these researchers, "This is the earliest known human behavioral phenotype [visible expression of genetic makeup] that predicts individual differences in patterns of neural activity at maturity. These temperamental differences rooted in infancy may be relevant to understanding individual differences in vulnerability and resilience to clinical psychiatric disorder."

Kagan calls attention to the fact that Mary Ainsworth—whose attachment research is regarded by attachment advocates as foundational—came to the conclusion regarding her study of Ugandan mother–infant interactions that "We must concede that there are genetically-based individual differences between babies ... It is quite impossible to differentiate genetic, prenatal, and perinatal influences from environmental influences" (Ainsworth, 1967, p. 387). She further stated, "Therefore, the warmth of the mother and her observed affectionate contact behavior do not explain the differences between these groups" (p. 394).

The influence of genetic factors on how infants and children respond to parenting styles has become ever more apparent with subsequent research. For example, Dick et al. (2011) tracked children from ages five to 17 who had inattentive parents and found that those who inherited certain variants of a gene involved in learning and memory displayed higher rates of delinquency and aggression. Among children who had involved parents, those carrying the gene variants misbehaved less often than the non-carriers. Thus, the same gene variants correlated with heightened sensitivity to both nurturing and neglectful parenting; and the degree to which a child is affected by the parenting style is significantly influenced by the child's inborn sensitivity. Barry, Kochanska, and Philibert (2008, p. 1313) found that for infants carrying the short form (allele) of a serotonin transporter gene, the mother's "low responsiveness predicted particularly high risk for insecure attachment, [but a mother's] high responsiveness offset that risk" whereas for infants having the gene's long form "there was no association between [mother's level of] responsiveness and attachment organization." Pluess et al. (2011), studying the same gene's variants, reported that maternal anxiety during pregnancy was followed after birth by significantly greater negative emotionality of the infant for infants carrying the short allele as compared to infants who did not have that gene variant.

It appears, then, that attachment history is but one of several different major influences that complexly form an individual's emotional and interpersonal style. This means that attachment history may be the predominant influence generating some of an individual's symptoms, but not others; or it could generate all of the symptoms of some therapy clients, but none of the symptoms of others. In the debate over attachment, it seems that all sides are correct some of the time.

Our intention in this chapter is to show how the Emotional Coherence Framework can help to depolarize and reconcile this evolving debate. Like different rivers converging to one delta to enter the ocean, all of the domains of learning described above converge to the same locus of influence, namely the contents of the individual's emotional implicit memory. Attachment, social, and existential experiences (and others such as artistic, athletic and spiritual experiences) create emotional learning consisting of implicit schemas and adaptations, and it is through these persisting schemas that those experiences have their ongoing, personality- and life-shaping effects—as William Faulkner captured in writing, "The past is never dead. It's not even past." When a schema is erased, however, the original experiences that formed it lose their control over current responses, as the case examples in previous chapters have shown. Genetic factors that influence emotional responsiveness can cause an individual to form certain emotional learnings (schemas) in particular life experiences—schemas that perhaps might not have formed if genetic factors had been different—but once such a schema is subsequently nullified clinically, that *particular* instance of genetic influence is also nullified. Of course, erasure of a particular emotional learning does not eliminate a contributing genetic predisposition.

Therefore, because each domain of experience has its ongoing effect through specific emotional learnings created, we regard the dissolution of these learned implicit schemas as the most fundamental and effective therapeutic strategy for liberation from the effects of each domain. The retrieved, symptom-generating schema of some clients is recognizably a clear case of just one zone of learning—whether attachment, social, existential or some other—but many retrieved schemas point to original experiences that involved a complex mixture of two or more areas that cannot and perhaps need not be teased apart. What guides the therapist in facilitating transformational change is not the conceptual category of learning involved, but rather the actual retrieved content of the client's schema—the explicit, component constructs of the mental model in the schema. Knowledge of that content is what the therapist needs in order to guide the client into an experience of contradictory knowledge and then into a construct-dissolving series of juxtaposition experiences. By retrieving schemas fully and accurately and working with the unique schema's particular component constructs, the effects of the original contributing influences are therapeutically nullified inherently. When a distress-generating schema no longer exists, even genetic factors can no longer amplify its effects.

For consistent success using the Emotional Coherence approach, it is critically important for the therapist not to assume *a priori* what the original influences or types of learning were—such as a therapist assuming from the outset of therapy that social narratives of gender underlie the problem, or that insecure attachment underlies the problem and requires reparative attachment work. Rather, in this framework the therapist works from a stance of not knowing, and proceeds to *learn from the client* what the contents of the symptom-generating schema(s) are, working as an anthropologist would. Then, suitable methods can be chosen for guiding the client into experiencing contradictory knowledge—reparative attachment work being indicated at times as a viable possibility but at other times not relevant to the target schema, as case examples show later in this chapter.

The resolution and synthesis of the opposing views regarding attachment therefore need to consist, in our view, of a comprehensive, meta-level framework that recognizes the roles of both attachment-based and non-attachment-based learning and guides the therapist to *learn from the client* the content of the learnings involved *for a given retrieved schema*. Knowledge of that content then guides a suitable facilitation of transformational change (completion of the therapeutic reconsolidation process). For schemas found to contain attachment-based learnings, the Emotional Coherence Framework guides the therapist to transform attachment patterns and wounds either *with* or *without* reparenting or reparative attachment types of work. This allows the therapist a clinical choice that is sensitive to each client's unique characteristics as regards dependency, codependency, and differentiation.

Attachment Learnings

Understanding attachment patterns in terms of coherent emotional learning is helpful to therapists in various ways. One advantage, as we will see, is having a conceptual tool for discerning whether attachment learnings are involved in a client's symptom-generating material. To that end, we provide a brief review of what attachment theorists and researchers have identified as the emotional learnings that constitute each of the main attachment patterns.

Certain criteria define the personal, emotional bond constituting an attachment relationship. As summarized by Connors (2011, p. 350):

> The bond is emotionally significant and persistent, involves proximity seeking, and takes place in a very specific fashion with a particular individual. The infant uses the attachment figure as a secure base from which to explore and seeks greater proximity under conditions of stress, danger, or novelty. Although actual physical nearness is important, the goal of attachment seeking is "felt security" (Sroufe & Waters, 1977) and the maintenance of the attachment figure's accessibility and responsiveness (Kobak, 1999). Although other motivational systems are also important for human beings, the attachment system might be seen as fundamental in its promotion of survival and engagement with others (Howe, 2005).

In light of these criteria defining attachment relationships, we can recognize problematic *non*-attachment-related experiences had by securely attached children, adolescents and adults, and thereby recognize as well that such experiences can produce powerful implicit emotional learnings that endure and generate unwanted moods, emotions, thoughts, and behaviors as strongly and lastingly as learnings created by attachment experiences do. As noted in the previous section, influential non-attachment-related learnings form in social, existential and also other domains, such as those of art, interior self-awareness and spirituality. John Bowlby, the founder of the attachment-oriented school of psychology and psychotherapy, himself appears to have recognized this broader spectrum of experiences when he wrote, "Experiences of separation and loss and threats of being abandoned are only a few of the much larger class of events that are usually described as major changes in the lifespace" (Bowlby, 1998, p. 370).

Individual clinical case examples provide direct evidence of the reality of different domains of emotional learning. Here is a short one: "Raoul" was 36, married, and had two young children. He began therapy for his hair-trigger, excessive anger that flared unpredictably in a wide range of situations and with a wide range of people, including strangers, acquaintances, friends, and family members. The therapist and Raoul revisited a number of these instances of anger in some detail, particularly the moments just prior to Raoul's burst of anger, which revealed that they all had a common theme: In each case, his anger had flared in response to Raoul's perception that the other person had departed from what had been agreed upon, even if only in some seemingly minor way. The therapist recognized this as a dyadic dynamic and therefore began to expect that attachment issues would soon come to light.

Raoul was struck by this new, explicit recognition of the previously implicit theme of broken agreements. After several seconds of registering this new awareness, he went into a trance-like, blinking gaze into the middle distance. Soon the therapist asked softly, "What's coming up?" It was a montage of images, thoughts and feelings from a terrible experience from five years earlier, when he had been shocked to discover that a business partner had taken actions that grossly violated key agreements between them. Raoul soon found that the partner had thereby robbed him of his sizable investment in the business. This led to the dissolution of the business, which had embodied Raoul's professional aspirations. In the emotionally deepening retrieval work of the next few sessions (of Coherence Therapy), Raoul had direct experiences of the implicit emotional learnings he had formed in that ordeal, which became verbalized in the following ways.

- Breaking agreements ruins lives.
- Anyone who breaks an agreement with me doesn't care about ruining me and is my enemy.
- I'm furious at the person who did this to me and at anyone else who tries to break *any* agreement with me.
- Without my anger, I would feel powerless and defenseless against being betrayed again like that, so I *need* my anger.
- Without my anger, I would feel such intense grief and heartbreak over what I've lost that I might be swept away by it and not be able to function, so I *need* my anger.
- Without my anger, I would feel he totally got away with it and there's no accountability or justice in the world. To let go of my anger would be to let go of my demand for accountability and justice—and that is totally unacceptable to me.

Given that Raoul had been surprised to notice the "broken agreements" theme in his incidents of anger, the reader can well imagine how surprised he then was to find, within himself, the coherent emotional truths listed above and realize that his anger was functioning as his vitally needed solution to three big problems of feeling powerless, grief-stricken, and despairing over an unjust world.

Part of coherence thinking is an internal practice by the therapist consisting of asking himself or herself the question "And what's under *this*?" with regard to each newly discovered layer of pro-symptom schema. This practice guides the therapist to keep pursuing the discovery work into the deepest layers of the schema being retrieved. Invoking that question, Raoul's therapist thought it likely that the broken agreements theme had still deeper layers formed in childhood attachment relationships. The therapist therefore continued the discovery work in that direction by asking Raoul, "Is there something *familiar*, in your life, about this jolting experience of broken agreements? Anything of this kind from way back, when you might have felt this kind of betrayal?"

Raoul scanned his emotional memory and was open to the therapist prompting him to look for various possibilities, but could find nothing either as a memory or as bodily resonance, and finally said, "You know, I think it's the opposite sort of thing: Being honest and reliable and keeping your word was so natural and taken for granted in my family that I was just totally unprepared and bowled over by this kind of thing happening to me." Other such probes involving Raoul's relationship history continued to indicate that he experienced secure attachment in childhood and that his problematic emotional learnings regarding broken agreements were formed just five years earlier in the domains of social and existential experience, not in childhood attachment experience. Therefore, a therapy of reparative attachment would not and could not be effective for dispelling his anger. That is, experiencing a therapist's sensitive, accurate empathy could not, in itself, disconfirm and dissolve Raoul's anger-necessitating schemas listed above.

Raoul's example shows that in order for a therapist to know whether or not attachment issues underlie a client's symptom, what is required is the use of experiential, phenomenological methods of schema retrieval, not theorizing. The truth of the matter resides in the client, rather than in psychological theories, so it is necessary to use methods of retrieval designed to bring the implicit learnings into explicit awareness cleanly, without imposing external interpretations. This fundamental point is well known to phenomenologists in psychotherapy and other fields (e.g., Gendlin, 1966, 1996; Husserl, 2010; Laing, 1995).

When attachment learnings *are* identified in a client's retrieved schemas, what is their specific content? To answer that question, first we will summarize briefly the types of emotional learning that have been described by attachment researchers and clinicians, and then supplement this with some concepts from the Emotional Coherence Framework and some clinical findings from Coherence Therapy.

"Attachment theory emphasizes the importance of early relational learning" states Connors (2011, p. 357). According to Mary Main, whose research is foundational for the attachment perspective, an infant or child with a problematic, distress-generating caregiver actively organizes perceptions of this attachment figure's responses and availability, forms constructs and mental models (schemas) of the contingencies involved, and develops specific strategies of behavioral and emotional self-expression for maintaining some degree of proximity and preventing the caregiver's particular negative responses (Main, 1995). That process of learning forms the various types of attachment pattern.

The *insecure-avoidant* type of attachment develops with a mother who is consistently rejecting. The infant learns to expect a rebuff in response to any direct emotional expression of distress or need or any direct physical approach for contact. That learning identifies and models the *problem* with which the infant is confronted. The infant then also learns that his or her own distress is kept to a minimum by *not* seeking to communicate or connect, *not feeling* the need to connect or have attention (accomplished by dissociation or dis-integration of feelings), and actively avoiding direct interactional contact when the mother seeks it. That learning identifies a *solution* to the problem. The infant has intelligently formed the implicit knowledge that to feel the need for contact or to seek contact is to suffer rejection, aloneness, fear, and helplessness. The solution of avoiding both feelings and contact is an adaptive strategy because in this way the infant has and feels control over keeping his or her own emotional state more or less unperturbed and out of those torments. Thus the learned emotional schema defines both a problem and the solution for that problem—which, as we saw in Chapters 3 and 4, is the structure of emotional schemas retrieved by adults in psychotherapy. In adults, this attachment style is often termed *dismissive* because in this category people downplay the impact or importance of relational events, have few memories of childhood, and typically give brief responses that affirm the normality of their experiences of deprivation (Main, 1995).

The attachment pattern known as *insecure-ambivalent* or *insecure-resistant* uses the opposite strategy of maximum emotional display, which is in this case an adaptive solution to a very different problem: a caregiver who is inept and/or self-preoccupied, but has been responsive at times when the infant's behavior was intense enough to attract the distracted parent's attention. That pattern of learning is an intermittent schedule of reinforcement, which is known to produce particularly tenacious learning. This infant understands—subcortically—that showing intense neediness and emotionality—such as throwing a tantrum—is what is required, but is not reliable, for getting the self-absorbed parent to respond as needed, and that whether needed interaction occurs at all depends on the infant *making* it happen. Thus, the infant has, by adaptive necessity, learned a fundamentally controlling, manipulative style of interacting, one aspect of which is an anxious, hypervigilant attention to the presence and emotional state of the caregiver. In adults, this attachment style is often termed *preoccupied* to characterize a consistent, high level of emotional involvement in relationship matters.

A third form of disturbed attachment is termed *insecure-disorganized* because of these infants' lack of any adaptive strategy or solution to the attachment dilemma within which they live: a mother or caregiver who behaves in unpredictable, extreme and punitive ways, arousing severe distress in the infant but not providing comfort or help. The insoluble problem facing these infants is that the parent is needed for security while at the same time is perceived as a dangerous source of arbitrary aggression (Main & Hesse, 1990), a condition of "fear without solution" (Hesse & Main, 2000). These infants appear disoriented, frozen, or fearful—coherent but functionless expressions of helplessness and desperation in the face of harm and endangerment with no known self-protective response. The Emotional Coherence Framework emphasizes that although the infant's response is disorganized and helpless, coherent learning is occurring in the formation of an implicit emotional schema or model of dyadic relationships in which the Other is expected to do extremely hurtful, terrifying things and oneself is completely defenseless. It is through the lens of that expectation that the individual then perceives and responds to significant others in subsequent relationships.

This attachment pattern, which is sometimes termed *unresolved* in adults, has been linked to subsequent aggression, dissociation and over-controlling behavior (Solomon & George, 1999) and to lapses in reasoning and collaborative discourse (Hesse, 1999). We would add, based on our clinical experience, that when such infants become children, in many cases they do develop an adaptive strategy or solution that combines extreme codependency (compulsive pleasing, with suppression of their own wants and needs, accompanied in some cases by a parent–child role reversal) and invisibility (various skills of going unnoticed, even in plain sight), which persist into adulthood. The child's anxiety remains chronically high, however, even with this solution, due to awareness of the caregiver's capacity for eruption at any time, with or without apparent cause.

The emotional learning that infants develop in insecure attachment relationships produces emotional and behavioral styles in adults that are often described as "dysregulated" and "maladaptive," which indeed they seem to be when viewed externally in relation to conventional (culture-specific) norms of behavior and rationality. However, when these styles are viewed in the context of the life experiences and emotional learnings that generate them, their adaptive and coherent nature is apparent. The Emotional Coherence Framework maintains that, rather than being out of control—as "dysregulated" and other such pathologizing terms connote—these emotional and behavioral styles are fully under the regulatory control of the person's emotional brain and implicit knowledge, which "know" to manifest these styles just as they are, to avoid suffering.

Terms of Attachment

Terms of attachment is the phrase used in the Emotional Coherence Framework to refer to a person's learnings that define the forms of available connection with significant others and the specific behaviors, thoughts and feelings required and forbidden in order to participate in such connection. They are the individual's detailed, living knowledge of the conditionality of love. A child's or adult's complete, implicit mental model of the rules of primary-bond connection consists of the terms of attachment that caregivers imposed or that the individual has construed in response to interactions with caregivers. Examples of terms of attachment that have been verbalized after retrieval are: I must never like something that Mom or Dad doesn't like (or I'll be humiliated for it); I must never think I matter or try to tell Mom what I feel or need (because then I'm disgusting and she'll ignore me for hours); they'll pay attention to me and include me only if I say something clever and funny; don't cry no matter what happens (or I'll be slapped); don't have energy or strong feelings, negative or positive (or I'll be screamed at); Dad pays attention to me only if I talk about what *he* likes; I'm acceptable if I do things exactly how Mom wants, and if I do one thing wrong I'm totally unworthy.

Each of the standard types of insecure attachment described in the previous section has, of course, its own distinctive terms of attachment in a general sense, but each person with any one type of attachment has a unique set of specific terms of attachment.

Terms of attachment can be regarded as *primary* attachment learnings, but they are only a subset of the life-shaping learnings that develop in attachment relationships. Many other potent learnings created within attachment relationships in childhood are not terms of attachment, and in that sense are *secondary* learnings. For example, Richard in Chapter 3 learned from his father that expressing views confidently is horribly oppressive of others and elicits their hate, a fate he avoided (non-consciously) by doubting away his own valid knowings, causing himself perpetual insecurity and lack of confidence at work. These were learnings acquired within an attachment relationship, but not terms of attachment.

Terms of attachment define how the connection between self and other works, whereas secondary attachment constructs are learnings that do not model how the connection *per se* works but were learned from experiencing an attachment figure. This difference is usually easy to recognize once the therapist knows to look for it. The next section gives further explanation of this distinction.

Optimizing Attachment Therapy: Dyadic Reparative Work and Beyond

Attachment learnings operate in the same manner as other emotional learnings: constructed and learned in the past, they generate responses in the present. Thus, attachment schemas are disconfirmed, dissolved and replaced by new learning in the same way as other emotional schemas are: through the creation of juxtaposition experiences in which a vividly felt, contradictory knowledge is brought into awareness alongside a reactivated experience of the target attachment schema—that is, through the therapeutic reconsolidation process described and illustrated in Chapters 2, 3, and 4.

The makeup of the contradictory knowledge is the critical, operational clinical issue here. What does it need to consist of and how is it to be created when the target constructs are attachment learnings? These are the questions that concern us in the rest of this chapter.

According to attachment advocates starting with Bowlby, therapy for attachment problems has to consist of new learning experiences of what originally was missing, namely positive experiences of secure attachment, with the therapist now being the attachment figure (e.g., Bowlby, 1988). The logic of this reparative attachment or reparenting approach appears to be that it is necessary to build up the preferred, healthier condition of the client in the very manner that would have created secure attachment in the first place. The fact that a client's insecure attachment schema was formed in childhood within a dyadic relationship is taken to mean that only a dyadic relationship of the secure attachment type can now, in adulthood, create new learning that revises the original learning of insecure attachment; and that, although the original learning took place in infancy and childhood, new attachment learning can occur effectively in adulthood.

Within the Emotional Coherence Framework, we re-examine those assumptions and ask these key questions: What determines whether dyadic reparative attachment can succeed with a given client in creating transformational change? What criteria can therapists use to rule in or rule out reparative attachment in a given clinical situation?

Answers to those questions are provided by the logic inherent in the therapeutic reconsolidation process—that is, the logic of the process through which implicit schemas are dissolved. Those key questions need to be addressed in a schema-specific manner. A therapy client may have some emotional schemas that *are* possible to dissolve through reparative attachment and some that are not. The following decision path clarifies whether reparative attachment is suitable for a given retrieved schema.

1. *Does the schema consist of learnings formed in an attachment relationship?* See if schema was in effect in early family (as was done with Raoul). If *yes*, go to Question 2; if *no*, reparative attachment work is unsuitable.
2. *Does the core problem defined in the schema consist of terms of attachment?* This too is clearly apparent from the content of a fully retrieved schema. If *yes*, go to Question 3; if *no*, reparative attachment work is unsuitable.
3. *Are the specific terms of attachment in the schema disconfirmable by any feasible client–therapist interactions?* If *yes*, reparative attachment is suitable; if *no*, reparative attachment is unsuitable.

Use of the above decision-making process is illustrated in case examples below. We have found from long experience of using the therapeutic reconsolidation process that a client's new experience of secure attachment with a therapist can indeed dissolve an existing insecure attachment schema—*if* the new experience both *contradicts* and *occurs in juxtaposition with* an experience of the existing, insecure expectations (terms of attachment). Importantly, *the client's experience of secure attachment with the therapist does not in itself guarantee that such a juxtaposition experience is occurring.* In other words, the client's insecure attachment schema can remain intact and insulated from the in-session enjoyment of secure attachment unless the therapist prompts the activation of both at once for an actual juxtaposition experience. That insulation occurs, for example, when attempts at such juxtaposition experiences encounter resistance because strong emotional distress accompanies the conscious contrast between being regarded as worthy of empathy from the therapist but not so regarded by one's own parents. Clients can transiently feel and welcome the therapist's empathy while blocking the distressing juxtaposition experience that would induce liberating change. It is only when the juxtaposition experience occurs that transformation of the attachment schema takes place.

What the Emotional Coherence Framework contributes most significantly and expansively to the conventional approach to attachment work, we believe, is the recognition that the contradictory experience needed for dissolving a problematic attachment schema is not limited to experiences of secure attachment with the therapist. This recognition follows from the actual content of clients' retrieved schemas of insecure attachment, not from theoretical considerations. The actual content allows for disconfirmation by experiences other than experiences of the therapist's empathetic, validating understanding. Therefore, the range of options for transformational new learning is far wider than reparenting and reparative attachment methods. This opens up a large field of clinical methods for transforming attachment patterns. Having such an expanded palette of concrete options puts therapists in the strongest position to facilitate decisively effective work.

The relatively recent development of phenomenological clinical methods for retrieving emotional implicit schemas accurately, thoroughly and promptly (Ecker & Hulley, 1996, 2000a, 2011) makes it possible to know the content of a symptom-generating schema in detail in nearly all cases. This allows therapists to determine whether or not the schema consists of attachment learnings (as illustrated by the case vignette of Raoul above) and whether or not a schema that *does* consist of attachment learnings can or cannot possibly be disconfirmed by experiences of secure attachment with a therapist. If not, then other methods must be used for creating or finding contradictory knowledge to incorporate in a juxtaposition experience. However, in the existing body of literature on attachment work there is no recognition of the need for such triaging, to our knowledge; the pervasive assumption appears to be that *any* attachment learning can be revised therapeutically through positive experiences in relationship with the therapist.

Varieties of Attachment Therapy in Action: Case Studies

The examples below illustrate the use of the therapeutic reconsolidation process for disconfirmation and transformational change of problematic schemas learned in attachment relationships. The first case shows disconfirmation by the therapist's empathy, through the approach often termed reparative attachment, reparenting or the dyadic regulation of affect, but here done in a manner so as to create definite, explicit juxtaposition experiences that fulfill the therapeutic reconsolidation process. The second case demonstrates the *optional* use of *non*-dyadic methods of disconfirmation, even though the client's attachment schema is also amenable to change through reparative attachment. The third and fourth cases demonstrate the *necessary* use of non-dyadic methods of disconfirmation because the client's symptom-generating schema is not possible to disconfirm using reparative attachment. We continue using Coherence Therapy as the demonstration vehicle. How other therapies achieve transformational change of attachment patterns through the therapeutic reconsolidation process is illustrated in Chapter 6.

Use of reparative attachment to disconfirm schemas

The following vignette—a few segments of work, not a full case example—is adapted from Toomey and Ecker (2009). It shows how the therapist can at times choose to use a communication of empathetic understanding to create a juxtaposition experience by prompting the client to focus mindful attention on two contradictory experiences at once: that of original sufferings in relation to caregivers and that of the therapist's empathetic understanding and acceptance. Steps of the therapeutic reconsolidation process defined in Table 3.1 on page 41 are indicated as the work unfolds.

A 42-year-old man, "Travis," was in therapy because none of the marriages or other couple relationships in his life had ever developed intimate emotional closeness, and he had finally realized, "What they all have in common is me. It must be my fault." The therapist figured that if avoiding emotional closeness was the presenting problem (identification of which is Step A of the therapeutic reconsolidation process), then Travis's construction of terms of attachment, learned in his family of origin, was likely to be the symptom-requiring schema, so retrieving those emotional learnings became the therapist's initial focus for discovery work (Step B).

Travis was the middle of five siblings, with overwhelmed authoritarian parents whose range of behaviors did not include supplying children with personal understanding or emotional attunement. In a guided visualization he was back in that family at six years of age. When he was absorbed in the scene and describing details, the therapist asked him, "What's it like for you, there in your family, when you're scared or hurting over something?" The therapist was looking for indications of specific terms of attachment that Travis had to obey in order to be included in his family as one of them. Persisting with this focus for five minutes yielded swift emotional deepening and his first explicit awareness of a lifelong, implicit emotional truth, verbalized with tears as, "This is not a world where anyone will pay attention to what I feel or give me understanding for how I'm hurting. I don't matter, and I'm all on my own." This verbalized retrieval of core emotional learning (Step B) illustrates once again that what is learned consists largely of construed meanings that form a coherent mental model of a dire problem.

The therapist reflected Travis's meanings back to him empathetically by saying softly, "There you are, a little boy of six, and sometimes you're really hurting or really scared, and you need a grown-up to understand that and take care of you, but it never happens, so you feel very alone, you feel you're all on your own in this world. Is that right?" Tears welled up as he nodded assent. The therapist allowed a short silence and then, recognizing that the empathy just received and felt by Travis could serve as contradictory knowledge (Step C), created an experience of disconfirming juxtaposition by asking, again in an empathetic manner, "And how is it for you right now to be so in touch with that—your certainty that you will *never get caring understanding for what hurts* [Step 1]—and at the same time, recognizing that you are actually getting that kind of emotional understanding from me, right now? [Step 2]."

At this, Travis released into deeper crying, feeling both his long-suppressed anguish and also (as he subsequently indicated) a kind of amazed and bittersweet relief that the impossible was actually happening. When he was able to speak again, the therapist repeated the same question, guiding him once again into the juxtaposition experience (Step 3).

Travis thought for a moment and replied, "If it's possible for that to happen, then why did I get parents who couldn't do it?" Here he again cried quietly. His question indicated that he was now allowing the emotional truth of his childhood suffering to be present in his awareness and to generate a process of finding new, coherent meanings for what he experienced—meanings that would begin to replace the meanings and model that he had verbalized as, "This is not a world where anyone will pay attention to what I feel or give me understanding for how I'm hurting. I don't matter, and I'm all on my own." Those problem-defining constructs are an example of the generalization of an original attachment learning from caregivers to all other people—a phenomenon of emotional memory that we have observed with many clients. As many attachment writers and constructivist psychotherapists have noted, one's adaptive solutions to attachment problems tend to operate as self-fulfilling prophecies. Capturing that full, generalized construction of meaning about the kind of world one inhabits is important in the retrieval work, in order to guide the finding of suitable contradictory knowledge—in this case, Travis's experience of actually receiving tender understanding from the person sitting across from him, the therapist. It is important to note, however, that the Emotional Coherence Framework emphasizes the primacy of accurate construct disconfirmation, not the primacy of the therapist's person.

In subsequent sessions during the next two months, the therapist continued to find opportunities to disconfirm Travis's terms of attachment and the kind of world he inhabited, in juxtaposition with the client–therapist relationship. For example, when Travis gave a dry, matter-of-fact account of being yelled at demeaningly by his boss at work, the therapist said, "I notice that you mention nothing at all about how you *feel* from being treated that way by him. And I don't know if you're expecting I might be like your *parents* and *won't pay any attention* to what you're feeling—or if you're remembering that *I'm different from them* and *will* pay attention and *take seriously* what you're going through because *you matter.* Could you tell me about both sides of that?" In that way (and in other instances, not shown here) the therapist was again deliberately guiding him to hold the two contradictory emotional realities side by side, juxtaposed. That processing was again emotional for Travis. Following this, the therapist immediately guided a second juxtaposition experience by saying, "You know, I'm also really wondering about this: If you bring to mind the scene—there you are in your boss's office and he's yelling at you and saying those shaming things—you could make sense of his behavior either in the way you originally did with your parents—'I don't matter; being respectfully understood just doesn't exist in this world'—or, you could make sense of his behavior with the new knowings you've been getting in touch with: 'I *do* matter, and *he's* really screwing up and failing to do the right thing here; this is mistreatment that I don't deserve.' Can you be in touch with those two parts of you, each with such a different way of making sense of his behavior?"

That juxtaposition experience brought Travis's "new knowings"—which had emerged from the previous reparative attachment work—directly into the context of his relationship with his boss at work, in order to disconfirm his old attachment-based knowings in that context. The contextual range of attachment schemas varies widely across therapy clients, we find. One client's attachment schema comes into play (generating certain thoughts, emotions, and behaviors) only in romantic love relationships, but another client's attachment schema comes into play in many contexts—for example, in relation to all authority figures or in trying to turn all workplace relationships into *personal* relationships in which the client is well liked and therefore safe. When an attachment schema has a broad contextual range, juxtaposition experiences in each relevant context tend to be necessary in order to dissolve the schema in each of the corresponding memory networks. (The same is also true for non-attachment-based schemas that have broad contextual range.)

At the start of Travis's therapy, he regarded his lack of emotional engagement in couple relationships as a personal defect. In the course of becoming experientially aware of his learned terms of attachment—which defined him as a self who doesn't matter, so what he feels would always meet a deaf ear or worse—he was relieved to recognize that keeping his own feelings suppressed and hidden was actually his way of very effectively protecting himself, not a defect at all. This awareness of the function of his behavior in turn became a sense of agency; that is, it allowed Travis to feel his power to *choose* whether or not to protect himself in that way in a given situation. After a few successful experiments in choosing to matter and voice his feelings—first with the therapist and then with carefully selected others in his life—the therapist joked, "You've turned an involuntary muscle into a voluntary muscle." That progression is characteristic of how attachment work unfolds in Coherence Therapy: The individual becomes acutely aware of striving for attachment (connection, love, belonging) and/or self-protection according to certain rules and tactics learned in childhood, and this in turn brings the experience of agency and choice in relation to those rules and tactics.

According to the understanding of reparative attachment work in the Emotional Coherence Framework (and in Coherence Therapy), the therapist's empathy is not in itself directly curative of attachment problems, but rather it serves to create new experiences that disconfirm and dissolve troubled attachment schemas via juxtaposition with them (a role that can also be played by a wide range of other disconfirming experiences, as shown below). The therapeutic power of the therapist's empathy resides not so much in the client's agreeable experience of it, but in how that agreeable experience very specifically disconfirms the client's particular, problematic models of self, relationship and world. What is curative is the client's internal act of retrieving non-conscious, implicit constructs into explicit, subjective awareness and submitting them to experiential disconfirmation in a juxtaposition experience. No matter how much empathy is delivered by the therapist and enjoyed by the client, an attachment schema will not be transformed by the experience of the therapist's empathy if it does not come into a disconfirming juxtaposition with the experience of that empathy. For that reason, the Emotional Coherence Framework requires the therapist to orchestrate a definite juxtaposition experience and not merely *assume* that the client's experience of the therapist's empathy is having the needed disconfirming effect on existing attachment learnings. As described earlier, that assumption can fail to be accurate for various reasons. Through explicit, guided juxtaposition experiences, the therapist can ensure also that the disconfirmation reaches and transforms not only the terms-of-attachment constructs as they pertain to the family of origin, but also any generalized, "whole world" constructs such as Travis held.

Within the work described above with Travis there is another juxtaposition experience that took place, as it does in reparative attachment work with many clients. On one side of this juxtaposition is the lifelong implicit knowledge, "How I really feel in this suffering is too intense to bear and would crush/drown/shatter me, so for survival I've *got* to disconnect from my feelings and stay that way!" On the other side of the juxtaposition is the experience of remaining intact and functional after allowing those feelings to come out of suppression and be felt—and even feeling significantly restored to wholeness by feeling them. The therapist's understanding and accompaniment are indispensably catalytic in bringing about that juxtaposition, but it is the client's experience of his or her own capacity to *feel* and to *know* that is liberating and dissolves the attachment-based schema that models oneself as incapable of surviving feeling and knowing. This is an important therapeutic shift out of a dis-integrated mode of adaptation.

Other, separate attachment schemas still continue to exist, however. For example, a female client had learned in childhood that being smart or saying what she knows would evoke shaming and denigration from her parents and make her unlovable. After making the freeing shift into feeling and knowing what she had suffered, she said in response to an enquiry from the therapist, "It's safe to tell you what hurt me back then because that's what I'm *supposed* to do here. But no, I *don't* feel safe showing you how smart I am because, why wouldn't you hate me for that?" Dissolving such other attachment schemas requires juxtaposition experiences crafted uniquely for each.

Optional use of non-dyadic methods

Retrieved attachment-based schemas that are amenable to reparative attachment work can also undergo transformational change through methods other than reparative attachment. The work with a woman we will call Regina, age 36, exemplifies this. We will describe some representative segments of work, but not cover all aspects of Regina's therapy, which spanned 18 sessions. She sought therapy for relief from frequent episodes of strong anxiety or panic during or right after interacting with others in many contexts, had no idea what was causing this, and was troubled that it meant she was "crazy."

The therapist learned that Regina was an only child and, throughout childhood, her mother frequently and unpredictably erupted into a rageful tirade of disgust and denigration toward her over anything in Regina's behavior, big or small, that displeased her. Even innocent, ordinary actions could bring this on, such as being found with crayons and papers spread about for drawing ("making a mess"), bumping into a tree while riding her tricycle, or asking to go play with a girl who lived next door. The tirade often included a sharply unfavorable comparison of Regina to the neighbor's daughter, extreme verbal abuse ("You're a piece of shit!" was frequent), and sometimes took place in front of visiting uncles, aunts, and cousins, deeply humiliating and shaming her. Being put in her room alone for hours was the most dreaded of the punishments. Sometimes it took days before her mother's punishing negativity would end and life would be normal again. So, the moment of seeing her mother begin to be displeased with her was one of blind, helpless panic over the unstoppable ordeal to come. Regina's father was benign and at times tried, surreptitiously, to comfort and support Regina through these episodes, but he was fearful of his wife and did nothing to actually protect his daughter. This was a case of severe complex trauma and, given the nature of her mother's behaviors, it seems clear that Regina suffered the insecure-disorganized type of attachment. She now lived far from her parents but phoned every week and similar patterns continued, though "milder" than in the past.

In the discovery work it became apparent that Regina's bouts of anxiety always began with a perception or construal that someone had become even slightly displeased with her. That first moment of seeing possible signs of displeasure or cooled feelings was a strong trigger of her implicit emotional learning that a brutally punishing rejection would now ensue, but this linkage, so obvious once accessed, had never before come into awareness. The therapist guided her to compare a recent instance of that first moment in a social setting with a memory of Mom, and Regina, looking very small in her chair, nodded waif-like that the two felt the same. It was quickly clear from this plunge of emotional deepening into traumatic memory that affective flashbacks were easily retriggered, so the retrieval work needed to proceed in small-enough steps.

By the end of her third session, one of Regina's main attachment-based, implicit emotional learnings had been retrieved, verbalized, and written on an index card in this way:

> The slightest imperfection makes me completely disgusting and unlovable, so Mom starts hating me and wants to get rid of me and have some other girl instead, and I'm really scared that she might actually get rid of me. I'm acceptable and lovable only if I do everything *perfectly*. Everyone I ever know will reject me whenever some imperfection becomes visible, and I'm always dreading that and feel panic each time I think it's happening.

This schema was the underlying, coherent cause or emotional truth of the symptom of social anxiety as well as perfectionism. In it is a mental model of herself as unlovable, of terms of attachment that are the problem (with a generalization to all people, as we saw above for Travis), of specific, expected sufferings that must be avoided, and of a tactical solution of perfectionism.

The cluster of constructs inscribed on her index card was an important target for dissolution. To that end, the main clinical task—in Coherence Therapy in particular and in the therapeutic reconsolidation process more generally—was to guide Regina to find or create contradictory knowledge that felt so real that it would disconfirm the target constructs in a juxtaposition experience. Would reparative attachment work be suitable? In the decision path on page 104, the answer to the first two question was *yes* because the symptom-necessitating schema consisted of terms of attachment. This left the third question: Do the particulars of this schema allow for the *possibility* of disconfirmation by the client's experience of interacting with the therapist? The answer was *yes* because it was possible to imagine experiences of direct disconfirmation taking place in the client–therapist relationship; for example, when Regina was late for a session or when she accidentally spilled coffee on the therapist's rug, the therapist could have interacted with her to have her see and feel that these "imperfections" were not having the expected negative effects on the therapist's regard of her.

However, the therapist did not use methods of reparative attachment and opted instead to create contradictory knowledge by employing the *overt statement* technique (as illustrated in Chapter 4) in Regina's next session.

Th: How in touch do you feel, with what we found and put on the card last time?

Cl: Pretty much in touch with it.

Th: How would you say it to me in your own words—the way it feels to you right now?

Cl: Well—any imperfection in what I do is really disgusting, and my mother is right about me, so my only hope is to hide all imperfections and show only perfection, or else I'll always be rejected by everyone.

Th: By everyone; mm-hm. *[Therapist now thinks for a few seconds, sees a possible way of guiding her into an experience of strongly contradictory knowing through an overt statement, and proceeds to pursue it.]* Do you have a grandparent or an aunt or uncle who's special to you?

Cl: Mm-hm.

Th: Who is it?

Cl: My Uncle Theo—my dad's younger brother.

Th: Good. So, picture Uncle Theo. And you're with him, and it's really nice. *[Pause]* Do you have that?

Cl: *[She has closed her eyes.]* Yes.

Th: *[With a somewhat slower, softer voice suitable for guiding inner imaginal process]* And you're feeling such a warm fondness for him; all the little things about how he talks, how he gestures, his sense of humor—

Cl: The special little wink he gives me.

Th: Yeah. And you can actually feel the warmth of your love for him in your heart area—yeah?

Cl: Yeah.

Th: Good. And now say to him—either out loud or internally, whichever feels more natural—the words of your emotional truth, "But you love me only because I seem perfect, and you'd *stop* loving me if I let any of my imperfections show." *[That is a use of the* overt statement *technique for bringing an existing contradictory knowledge into awareness through mismatch detection.]*

Cl: *[Silence for about 15 seconds as she says it internally to Uncle Theo. She is very still and appears to have stopped breathing.]*

Th: What's happening now?

Cl: *[A tear slides down her cheek. In a quieter voice]* I said it, and then the look on his face—he was so hurt by it.

Th: He's hurt by it. How do you understand him being so hurt by it?

Cl: *[Silence for 10 seconds]* It's like—it was a deep insult to his love for me.

Th: I see; a deep insult. Can you say more about *why* it was an insult to his love?

Cl: It's because I'm saying his love is lightweight and superficial, and he knows it isn't.

Th: *He* knows that his love is—*[leaving the sentence incomplete, for her to finish it].*

Cl: *[Eyes tear up and overflow; softly crying as she says]* He knows he really loves me with all his heart—*[cries]*—and imperfections wouldn't change that. So it's like I'm totally wasting his love if I think it's only because I seem perfect.

Th: *[Silent for about 30 seconds, allowing client's conscious knowledge systems to incorporate this new knowing]* You're seeing that *he* knows he really loves you and your imperfections wouldn't change that. How is it for *you* to see and *feel* that? *[Pause]* Does it feel true?

Cl: *[Nods yes while dabbing her eyes with a tissue]*

Th: It does feel true. He really loves you whether or not your imperfections show up. *[She nods again.]* *[Client is now having a vivid experience of contradictory knowledge, as needed for creating a juxtaposition experience, so therapist now proceeds to guide her into the juxtaposition experience.]* So just look at him, knowing that he really loves you even when your imperfections show up; and knowing that, to him you're lovable, and that doesn't change because of imperfections. Can you just look at him, knowing and feeling that?

Cl: Mm-hm. Yeah.

Th: Good. And now keep him in view and keep knowing that, as you widen the picture and also see, maybe over on the other side of the room, your mom. Can you do that?

Cl: Yeah.

Th: And what you know about *her* love is *so different*, because *her* love quickly disappears and turns into disgust and rejection when any imperfections show up, yes? *[Client nods yes.]* So, just see how it is for you to be in touch, like this, with *both kinds of love at once*, and each is so clear, but they're so different: On one side, there's Mom with love that's so fragile and so quickly flips into rejection over any imperfections that displease her; and you could easily expect that's how it would be with *anyone*. *[That is a deliberate, explicit re-evoking of the target construct.]* And on the other side, there's Uncle Theo with love that is so steady and reliable and *unaffected* by imperfections, and he just sees and feels how lovable you are and *nothing changes that*. And both kinds of love feel so real, but they're so different. Can you feel both at once? *[Client nods yes.]* Good. What's that *like* for you—seeing so clearly that both kinds of love exist, and that you're actually *experiencing* both kinds?

Cl: *[Silence for many seconds]* I never thought of it like this before. *[Pause]*

Th: Yes, it's very new to see it this way—that you actually already experience both kinds of love. *[Pause]* And as you *look back and forth* at your Mom and Uncle Theo, what happens? *[Prompting her to look back and forth at them is a repetition of the juxtaposition experience.]*

Cl: *[Silence for about 15 seconds]* It's strange, but my Mom looks smaller. *[This is a first marker of a transformational shift in her construction of Mom.]* And it's like—what's wrong is in *her*, not in me. *[Pause]* It's over there in her, not over here in me. *[This is a marker of a transformational shift in the meanings she has attributed to her mother's harsh, rejecting behaviors.]*

Th: Mm-hm. And how does it *feel* to know that?

Cl: It feels scary—because, you know, then I can't have any control over it.
       If it's in me, I have a chance of controlling it. *[Her own purpose and
       agency for maintaining self-blame has now come into awareness. This
       is further retrieval of implicit knowledge (Step B): her solution to the
       problem of terrifying powerlessness has been to blame herself rather than
       her mother.]*

Th: Control it by hiding everything imperfect?

Cl: Right; and being really, really good. But if the reason she blows up at me
       is that *she's* messed up, then I can't possibly control it, and that's scary.
       [Silence while gazing into her lap] But I'm also feeling *relief*, too.

Th: Relief because—?

Cl: —because if *she's* the problem, then maybe there's nothing seriously
       wrong with me after all; and maybe I *won't* be rejected forever by anyone
       who gets to know me.

Th: Does Uncle Theo know you pretty well?

Cl: *[Grins happily]* He does, yeah.

Th: So, look at him again and this time, try out saying to him, "You love me
       with my imperfections, and that means the world to me."

Cl: *[Silence as she says that to him]* Yeah.

Th: It fits and feels true?

Cl: Yeah, it does. And he smiles at me; he's happy that I understand.

The therapist and Regina then worked on writing some simple limbic-language
sentences to put on an index card to help her stay in touch between sessions with
key elements of this work. The card read:

> Mom's kind of love, and Uncle Theo's kind of love. With Uncle Theo, I don't
> have to be perfect to be lovable and loved. Mom's love is so fragile because
> of trouble inside *her*, not because of *me*. That means I don't have control over
> getting her to stop rejecting me, the way I thought I had, and that feels scary
> and sad.

Read daily, those sentences would prompt repeated experiences of the juxtaposition and of the knowings that emerged from it. The therapist also asked Regina
to read the card just before phoning her mother and to keep the card in front of
her during the conversation.

Regina's juxtaposition experience had begun to dissolve her implicit mental
model that love operates *only* in her mother's manner and that the cause of her
mother's eruptions of hostility was her own defectiveness. Those models were
replaced by a new, expanded model that included her mother's type of love but
also recognized the existence of her uncle's type of love, as well as the view that
the cause of her mother's eruptions was something "messed up" in her mother, not

in herself. She was therefore now beginning to inhabit a world in which steady, secure love was possible and available to her, and she was worthy of it and intact.

In the next session, the therapist invited and guided her to identify who else, among her relatives, friends, teachers, and work colleagues, would similarly feel hurt by learning that Regina sincerely believed that their fondness of her was only a superficial enjoyment of how perfectly she pleased *them*. She was surprised by how many people were in this group. This exercise, understood in terms of the therapeutic reconsolidation process, was an accessing of the same contradictory knowledge in many different contexts so that the target constructs would undergo a disconfirming juxtaposition experience in each context, which, as noted above, tends to be needed for thorough dissolution when a target schema operates in different contexts that have different memory networks. This work continued nonlinearly across about 10 sessions, alongside and alternating with other lines of coherence work that had developed.

Imaginal work, such as was done with Regina, is of enormous value for guiding strong experiences of both attachment schemas and contradictory knowledge, as needed for successful schema-dissolving juxtaposition experiences. Creative use of imaginal process gives therapists virtually unlimited avenues for guiding such experiences beyond the limitations of relying solely on the client's experiences of the therapist for reparative attachment work. Imaginal work can be so effective because the emotional brain responds to imagined experiences almost indistinguishably from how it responds to physically enacted experiences (see, for example, Kreiman, Koch, & Fried, 2000).

In another form of experiential work, the therapist guided Regina into a practice that created both integration and juxtaposition experiences. We refer to it as the *I'm in memory* practice. At the start of her fifth session, Regina described a particularly strong panic attack that had occurred on the previous day as soon as she left a lunch meeting with several co-workers and returned alone to her car; she was still, one day later, feeling quite shaky from it. At lunch there had been more than enough snide comments made and ambiguous social signals sent to trigger Regina's expectation of disastrous rejection several times over. In fact, in re-telling the incident to the therapist, she became retriggered into a significant level of anxiety, and said so.

The therapist then said, "Okay, I'll guide you to try something that could help with this, and I'll explain it first. In our previous sessions, we've learned a lot about what it really means when your anxiety or panic ignites: It means somebody's behavior has at least *looked like* a possibly negative response toward you, and we know why that perception is so charged and scary for you: it's all those hundreds of times when you first saw a negative response starting in your mom, and then whammo! Really painful, humiliating, scary things would happen—a grueling ordeal that could keep going for days. Your emotional brain learned that the first moment of displeasure toward you means that now a horrible ordeal is coming. All of that emotional learning and suffering went into your *emotional memory*, and emotional memory just doesn't fade out over time—that's how the brain evolved. Someone seeming to become displeased with you in the present closely enough *resembles* that terrible moment of your mom becoming displeased with you that it retriggers all of that emotional memory, and to your emotional brain this means that the ordeal is about to happen again right now! The emotional brain mixes up the past and the present. It uses the past to make sense of what's happening in the present, and expecting the same ordeal to happen again now triggers an anxiety or panic attack. So here is what I want you to do right now:

"Put one of your palms on your heart, the way you might do if you were comforting a child who's terrified. Good. Next, softly but out loud say this sentence to yourself about that lunch meeting: 'This situation is *reminding* me of what I suffered *back then,* when Mom would start to get displeased with me.' [Regina said the words.] Good. Now say, 'This raw fear I'm feeling is my *living memory* of what I felt and suffered back then.' [Regina said the words.] Good. Now, as you say this next sentence, gently pat your heart area with your hand: 'It was so awful; it was so horrible for me—and this situation is reminding me of it.' [She did this.] Good. Then say all of it one more time; I'll lead you again ..."

After saying those self-compassionate sentences a second time, Regina said with surprise that her anxiety had already diminished greatly—on a scale of 0 to 10, it was down to 2 from 8—and she added, "It has *never* faded out so fast once it's triggered!" She also commented—and this was particularly indicative that the technique was working as intended—that "saying those words made something shift in my whole perspective—it was such a relief to realize that something awful *isn't* really happening now, and also that this crazy feeling is actually *coming from something* and I'm *not* crazy."

The therapist then assigned the *I'm in memory* practice to Regina as a between-session task by giving her an index card with these instructions written on it:

> Whenever you notice that either the fear or the pain has been retriggered, put the palm of one or both hands over your heart and say to yourself: This situation is reminding me of what I suffered back then, with Mom suddenly turning against me. I'm feeling my living memory of what I felt back then. [With patting:] It was so awful for me; it was so horrible; and this situation is reminding me of it. [Then say it one more time.]

In each session, Regina described the latest incidents of retriggering and how she used the *I'm in memory* practice in response. Each time, the therapist asked her to say a bit more about the living memory that had been evoked, and in that way, in small steps, Regina continued the process of revisiting and integrating what she originally suffered. Across several sessions she became able to enter deeply and unhurriedly into strong emotional recall of childhood experiences that initially had been too raw to re-contact even lightly for more than a few seconds. Feeling closely accompanied by the therapist in these deepening immersive recalls was a crucially important condition that made this work possible.

Regina's increasingly clear, direct awareness of what she endured in childhood had powerful, natural effects. Her retrieved knowledge directly turned into new, coherent narratives for major areas of life experience that previously had been baffling, unrepresented, or covered over with rationalizations. For example, she said, "My feelings get hurt *so deeply* so easily, all my life, and I could never tell anybody *why* or even tell *myself* why I'm so, you know, delicate or something. It never crossed my mind that that's the hurt I always felt when my mom would tell me I'm *so bad* even though I didn't do anything wrong and was trying so hard to be so *good*. But now I remember feeling that same hurt [indicating her heart area] as a little girl, alone in my room for so many hours until I'd be allowed out again."

Another area of new, coherent narrative was expressed by Regina in terms of new awareness of "so much that I *didn't* get," meaning warmth, cherishing, understanding, and feeling taken care of and secure. This in turn opened a process of self-compassionate grieving that was the indispensable, further emotional processing of so much high-distress experience that had been stored raw in emotional memory.

Development of coherent autobiographical narrative is widely regarded as an important goal of psychotherapy (e.g., Schore, 2003b; Siegel, 1999, 2001). The viewpoint within the Emotional Coherence Framework is that the most authentic and therapeutic narrative is formed through retrieving and verbalizing what the client's emotional brain already coherently knows in implicit memory. Nothing is invented in that process, only discovered.

The *I'm in memory* practice is a specialized form of mindfulness applied for bringing implicit memory into explicit awareness. It is often highly useful for facilitating the integration and transformation of emotional implicit memory containing traumatic levels of severe distress, including complex trauma within attachment relationships as well as trauma in other areas. The technique has been shaped into the particular experiential form described above for use in Coherence Therapy, but the essence of the practice—maintaining mindful recognition of being in a triggered state of reactivated emotional memory—has its origins in the human potential and self-awareness movement of the 1970s, to the best of our knowledge. The most obvious effect of this practice, as Regina demonstrated, is to spare oneself the experience of unknowingly projecting the reactivated memory of suffering onto the present external situation and suffering the present situation as if the original raw ordeal were happening again. That would be immersion in a flashback (retriggered traumatic memory) without awareness of it as a flashback. Instead, the *I'm in memory* practice utilizes each such episode of reactivation for further, mindful integration of the retriggered emotional memory, which in turn allows retrieval of meanings, constructs, and models formed and learned in the original sufferings. These then become targets for disconfirmation and dissolution in juxtaposition experiences, completing the therapeutic reconsolidation process. A suppressed emotional memory is sealed off and unavailable for such work and so remains preserved and retriggerable during daily living.

In addition to the *integration* of traumatic memory that is gently but steadily achieved through the *I'm in memory* practice, this deceptively simple exercise also creates three different juxtaposition experiences, as spelled out in Table 5.1. The rapid reduction of emotional distress observed to result from this practice can readily be understood as a direct effect of these juxtaposition experiences dissolving (a) the view and feeling that something truly terrible is happening right now, (b) the view that the extreme feelings and thoughts I'm having mean there is something terribly wrong with me, and (c) the presupposition (implicit knowledge) that living my life in an internally cut-off, dissociated, dis-integrated state is my only viable option. Being freed of those three states of mind is a big relief.

Naturally, this calming, comforting effect is what makes the *I'm in memory* practice so appealing to clients, but from the more technical viewpoint of clinical methodology—specifically, in relation to the therapeutic reconsolidation process—it is the integrative effect plus the three juxtaposition experiences that make this practice so valuable. It shifts the perceived source of presently felt distress from the present to the past, but notice how this shift comes about: It results from the prior, deep work of emotionally revisiting original sufferings, giving the client direct, *experiential* awareness that the actual source of the present distress is living memory of *past* sufferings. If, without that prior work, the therapist instead merely *explains* reassuringly to the client that his or her ordeals are safely in the past and are not happening or possible now in the present, this cognitive-insight form of the past/present distinction typically proves to have little therapeutic potency or holding power.

Table 5.1   Juxtaposition experiences created by the *I'm in memory* practice carried out when traumatic memory has been retriggered

Symptom-generating construct (existing, old implicit knowing)	Contradictory knowledge (new knowing created by I'm in memory practice)
Something terrifying [or hopeless, devastating, desolating, etc.] is happening to me right now.	What I'm feeling is my emotional memory of what happened to me *back then*. The present situation is only *reminding* me of that. It isn't happening to me again.
These extreme feelings and thoughts mean I'm crazy [or defective, dysfunctional, irrational, etc.].	These extreme feelings and thoughts are parts of my living memory of what actually happened to me *back then*.
I would be undone by facing, knowing and feeling what I suffered and still carry inside me! I need to live disconnected from knowing or feeling what I have experienced.	I am capable of knowing and feeling the truth of what I have experienced. I can fully inhabit my body, my feelings and my knowledge.

Returning to the work with Regina: In response to perceived interpersonal setbacks, her self-blame and her anxiety or panic decreased fairly steadily after her fifth session, as did her perfectionism (a solution less and less needed). She was largely free of symptoms by her 16th session, felt well equipped to continue working on her own with the occasional situation that still "tweaked" her, and saw no need for therapy after her 18th session.

Regina's therapy shows that in cases where the client's problematic attachment learnings could, in principle, be transformed by utilizing the client–therapist relationship reparatively to create contradictory knowledge, other sources of disconfirming, contradictory knowledge exist and can be equally or more effective. Another example of this type is the use of empowered reenactment in Chapter 4 with client Brenda, who suffered stage fright based on traumatic memory. The attachment rules governing her emotional world could have been disconfirmed in reparative attachment work but were dissolved instead by working imaginally with her interactions with her parents. Similarly, in the case of Richard in Chapter 3, reparative work in the client–therapist relationship *could* have been used to disconfirm his expectation that if he were to express his knowledge or views with any confidence, he would be hated for being a dominating know-it-all, as his father was. Instead, the therapist utilized a group interaction at Richard's workplace as the source of disconfirmation. The case example of Emotion-Focused Therapy (EFT) in Chapter 6 also shows core, attachment-based learnings and symptoms dispelled by being juxtaposed with living knowledge sourced outside of the client–therapist relationship.

We emphasize this point not to diminish the value or importance of reparative attachment work, but to expand the range of effective options available for attachment work so that more therapists can be more effective more of the time in more settings. Of course, the client–therapist relationship *was* an important catalytic ingredient in the work with Regina and Brenda, but not through a reparative attachment function.

Necessary use of non-dyadic methods

Positive experiences of a therapist cannot possibly disconfirm and dissolve some attachment-based, symptom-generating schemas. In such cases, reparative attachment work would necessarily fail to create transformational change of the schema. Methods other than reparative attachment are then necessary, not optional.

The case in Chapter 4 of Ted, who had, with unconscious purposefulness, made his life a shambles in order to rebuke his father, provides our first example. His presenting symptom of pervasive underachieving was maintained, it was found, by an emotional implicit schema that became verbalized in the following way.

The most important thing to me is to get Dad to see that he *failed* at being a father to me. I hate to admit it, but that's *so* important to me that I'm willing to keep my own life a mess, and get nowhere, to get him to see how badly he screwed up by tearing me down all the time.

That the content of this schema consists thoroughly of attachment learnings and memory of attachment experiences is clear. However, this particular schema does not consist of terms of attachment, so Ted's experience of the therapist's empathic attunement and acceptance could not disconfirm this material, and therefore reparative attachment work was not appropriate. To see in detail why this is so, one considers each way in which the client could have an experience of the therapist that might possibly be relevant either to *disconfirming* the schema's component constructs or *fulfilling* needs or solutions specified in the schema.

- If Ted deeply recognized and felt that he was utterly safe from being torn down by the therapist as he was by his father, and even that the therapist strongly wanted to *protect* Ted from being torn down by anyone, would this knowledge either disconfirm his need for accountability and justice from his father or somehow end that need by satisfying it? No, it would not.
- If Ted experienced the *therapist's* (instead of Dad's) genuine, empathetic understanding that he had been horribly hurt and harmed by his father and that his father was therefore a complete failure as a father, would this experience either disconfirm his need for accountability and justice from his father or somehow end that need by satisfying it? No, it would not.

With reparative attachment ruled out, the therapist used a different method for guiding Ted into experiencing the needed contradictory knowledge.

A second example is the brief but deep work conducted by psychologist Sara K. Bridges to address the marital sexual aversion of a mid-30s woman called Carol, the mother of an 11-year-old daughter, Dana (Neimeyer & Bridges, 2003, pp. 291–292).

Carol had no idea why she always felt so avoidant of sex with her husband despite their emotional closeness, other than to say that she "just didn't like to have sex very much." Using Coherence Therapy, Carol's symptom-necessitating schema was soon retrieved and found to be built upon the raw data of perceptual and emotional memory of much suffering due to her parents' flagrantly erotic behavior during her childhood.

In a quiet tone, with her legs crossed and her head in her hands, Carol then recalled a time when she was about 15 years old when her mother walked into the bathroom and found her masturbating. Far from being angry, her mother was so pleased that she not only told Carol's father but also called several friends and told them about this "beautiful good news."

Carol identified her decision to shut out sexual feelings from that very point. Discussing this series of memories and associated feelings, she also realized that enjoying sex with her husband subjectively meant being like her mother, and closer to risking mortifying her own daughter, Dana, in the same way.

At the end of that session, Carol left carrying an index card with the following sentences expressing the emotional truth of her newly conscious compelling purpose for avoiding sexuality. Reading these words would create integration experiences each time.

I hate to admit it, but experiencing sexual pleasure with my husband makes me more like my mother. So, even though it is hurting my marriage, I will continue to avoid sexual contact, because it is better to sacrifice pleasure and intimacy than to risk doing to Dana what my mother did to me.

Before that therapy session, Carol (non-consciously) expected that for her to engage in *any* marital sexuality would cause her own daughter the same sorts of harm and suffering as were inflicted on her by her parents' eroticism, making it urgent for her to avoid feeling or being sexual with her husband.

Was Carol's sex-avoiding schema amenable to reparative attachment work? To answer that question, we use the reparative attachment decision process. Clearly her schema was forged in the crucible of her attachment relationships with her parents, but are the constructs in this schema terms of attachment, i.e., primary rather than secondary (other attachment-related) learnings? In our view the answer is yes, they are primary, which is apparent as follows. Her mother's terms of attachment, as learned by Carol, could be verbalized approximately as, "Be erotic like me, out in the open where I and my friends can delight in it. This is what most strongly gets my attention and fondness and connects you to me. There must be no boundaries hiding your sexual behavior from me." The essence of these terms of attachment is: Sexuality must have no boundaries of privacy between us. That implicit construct defined Carol's understanding of how sexuality operates in a family. Inhabiting that problem-defining construct, Carol was implicitly expecting her sexuality to violate her daughter's boundaries.

The last question in the decision process is this: Is it conceivable that Carol's experience of her therapist's empathy, sensitivity, validation, safety, and so on could disconfirm those terms of attachment? Only if the answer were a clear *yes* could reparative attachment be a suitable approach for working with Carol. There is no reliable form of such disconfirmation that we can envision, though there is the following possibility that is an uncertain *maybe:* Carol's female therapist, upon learning the makeup of Carol's symptom-necessitating schema and recognizing the involvement of the terms of attachment described above, could have begun to express sensitive, overt recognition and respect for the fundamental privacy of Carol's sex life in relation to herself, the therapist. This might have created for Carol a secure attachment experience in the sexual area, in sharp contrast to her experience of her mother. For example, the therapist might have said, "Naturally, you're here to address a sexual problem so you are telling me about your sex life, but I just want to say—in case there is *any part of you* that might be wondering, from a certain angle, about *our* interaction—that I'm feeling *no need of my own* to hear about your sex life, and I deeply regard your sex life as *your private domain.* And *only* with your permission and wish for me to hear about it will we talk about it, because otherwise I feel it is *your private domain.*" That would be followed at some later point by asking, "How is it for you to see and understand that I'm so different from your mom in this way?"

Whether work along those lines would have been a sufficiently strong, relevant disconfirmation to achieve dissolution of the terms of attachment binding Carol is too uncertain to predict; and even if it had done so, it is also uncertain whether that shift would have brought about a dissolution of the construct that was directly maintaining Carol's aversion to marital sex—her expectation that her own sexuality would harm her daughter, as she was harmed by her mother's sexuality. Thus, we do not see any clear, decisive disconfirmation of that master construct developing within the client–therapist interaction, so the result of the decision process in this case is, for us, a ruling-out of reparative attachment work. The contradictory knowledge that would successfully disconfirm Carol's expectations would have to be found outside of the client's experiences of the therapist. How the schema was dissolved was described by Neimeyer and Bridges (2003, p. 292) in this way:

> In the next session, Carol reported that the statement [on her index card] began to seem almost silly to her during the week, and although she knew it would take time and practice, finding a new way to understand her sexuality as her own and not her mother's was a freeing experience for her and also for her relationship with her husband. Once held as a conscious rather than unconscious position, the previously prevailing view soon lost much of its power, permitting the client to relinquish it as her governing emotional reality.

In that account are two markers of transformational change. One is her reporting that "to understand her sexuality as her own and not her mother's was a freeing experience." That is a description of contradictory knowledge—my sexuality is *not* the same as my mother's—that came into Carol's awareness in response to her overt statement task on the index card, which maintained her awareness of her retrieved presupposition that her sexuality was identical to Mom's. (Emergence of contradictory knowledge in that manner is the fruit of the brain's mismatch detection activity, as described in Chapter 4.) The other marker is the report that emotional truths on the card that had felt deadly serious to Carol when first retrieved into direct awareness a week earlier now felt "almost silly" to her. That indicates that the disconfirming knowledge had successfully created a juxtaposition experience and dissolved the terms-of-attachment construct of identical sexualities and the associated expectation that her sexuality would harm her daughter.

The examples of Ted and Carol illustrate the class of clinical cases in which a retrieved schema is not disconfirmable through reparative attachment work, so utilizing other sources of disconfirmation is necessary. Another type of situation in which reparative attachment work is infeasible warrants mentioning here. It occurs with adult clients who seem to be good candidates for reparative attachment therapy—in that they have a full-blown history of insecure attachment, feel the emotional woundedness that that entails, and have opened up without resistance to experiencing deep areas of emotional distress and vulnerability in their sessions (indicating the presence of adequate emotional safety, trust, and empathy in the client–therapist relationship)—but they find the prospect of having attachment needs met through interactions with a therapist to be utterly unsuitable, unreal, non-credible and impossible. As one such client, "Tomás," a man of 45, honestly put it to his older male therapist, "Look, you're a professional practitioner who offers expert services that I'm paying you for. We might do five or 50 more sessions, but then you won't be in my life any more. So, when you ask me how it is to be feeling so understood and seen and validated by you after never getting *any* of that from my mother or father, no, it *doesn't* fill those empty slots that should have been filled by them doing it right. That's just not how this could work for me. Maybe it could work with someone who's in my life for real." Of course, it is possible that responses such as Tomás's might be a rationalized expression of unconscious resistance to the emotional dependency that accompanies allowing an attachment relationship to develop. However, we have observed this response from clients with whom such resistance was not a very plausible explanation, given their openness to deep, painful emotional work in prior sessions. Rather, it seems more likely to us that these are individuals who have a well-developed and authentic adult identity, and that reparative attachment can take place in therapy most readily for adults who lack a firm state of adult identity and are based largely in a child identity or ego state, which allows the therapist to be a plausible attachment figure.

Tomás's example drives home to us that the fully adequate presence of the non-specific common factors in the client–therapist relationship (trust, empathy, alliance, shared therapeutic goals, etc.) and the full, emotional engagement of the client in the work do not mean that the client necessarily experiences the therapist as an attachment figure or is having an experience of secure attachment. A therapy client can experience secure attachment with the therapist only if he or she experiences the therapist as an attachment figure. However, trusting a health care professional enough to cooperate with treatment, including putting oneself in a vulnerable position, is not, in itself, an attachment relationship. Thus, the common factors may be fully present without an attachment relationship or secure attachment experience being present. In other words, the common factors are a necessary but not sufficient condition for an attachment relationship and secure attachment to occur, because for that, conditions in addition to the common factors are required.

Further, as we have discussed in this chapter, if an attachment relationship and secure attachment *are* present, this does not necessarily mean that reparative attachment work is taking place, because reparative attachment requires, in addition to secure attachment, the fulfillment of the therapeutic reconsolidation process, with the client's experience of secure attachment serving to disconfirm his or her insecure attachment expectations in juxtaposition experiences.

In this way, the therapeutic reconsolidation process helps us to clarify the relationship between the presence of the non-specific common factors, the occurrence of secure attachment experiences, and the carrying out of reparative attachment work in therapy.

Conclusion: A Coherent Resolution

Our examples of Raoul's anger, Ted's underachieving, Carol's aversion to marital sex, and Tomas's "can't work for me" suggest that reparative attachment therapy—also termed the dyadic regulation of affect—is widely but not universally applicable and, as such, does not provide a sufficiently inclusive framework for integrating the field of psychotherapy. Attachment dynamics and relationships are vitally important to virtually all emotionally functional human beings, but people in their complexity also have other dimensions and other areas of learning from which clinical symptoms can arise and require psychotherapy.

The Emotional Coherence Framework enables therapists to distinguish between symptoms that are generated by attachment learnings and those that are not, and to utilize reparative attachment work as one important option among many different methods for guiding therapy clients into the living, contradictory knowledge that unlocks the emotional brain and breaks the spell of ingrained emotional learnings. Table 5.2 summarizes this chapter's three case examples illustrating that process—the therapeutic reconsolidation process—which appears to have the comprehensive scope required of a framework of psychotherapy integration, as the next chapter addresses.

Table 5.2   Case examples of Coherence Therapy in Chapter 5 described in terms of the target symptom-generating construct retrieved, the contradictory knowledge found, and the technique used for finding it

Client's symptom	Target construct	Contradictory knowing	Source	Technique
Emotionally distant couple relationships (Travis)	Problem-defining: Caring understanding is not available from others.	Caring understanding was not available from my parents.	New experience during sessions	Reparative attachment (therapist's empathy)
Social anxiety, panic (Regina)	Problem-defining: For the slightest imperfection I'm unlovable and so disgusting to everyone that condemnations, humiliations, punishments and rejection will come, as with Mom.	1. Uncle Theo's love for me doesn't change because of my imperfections. 2. Mom is so rejecting because of trouble inside *her*, not because of *me*. 3. This situation is only *reminding* me of what I suffered back then with Mom.	Existing knowledge	For 1 and 2: Overt statement in imaginal interaction drives mismatch detection of opposite existing knowledge. *For* 3: The *I'm in memory* practice
Marital sexual aversion (Carol)	Problem-defining: My sexuality would inflict eroticism and exposure on our daughter just as my mother's sexuality did to me.	My sexuality is *not* the same as my mother's and would *not* harm our daughter.	Existing knowledge	Overt statement drives mismatch detection of opposite existing knowledge

Note: This table can be seen as an extension of Table 4.1 and adds three techniques for finding a contradictory knowledge in Step C of the therapeutic reconsolidation process.

6

A Framework for
Psychotherapy Integration

Out of intense complexities intense simplicities emerge.

—Winston Churchill

In previous chapters we examined case studies that demonstrate the use of the therapeutic reconsolidation process. This gave us a close-in, clear look at the moment-to-moment experience of producing deep, lasting change in the implicit emotional schemas underlying and driving symptoms. In this chapter we widen our scope for a view of what the therapeutic reconsolidation process might also show us about integration of the panoply of psychotherapeutic systems. Here, for ease of reading, we will be using the acronym TRP to refer to the therapeutic reconsolidation process.

Transformational Change and Specific Factors

The TRP specifies the sequence of experiences that the brain requires for fundamental dissolution of existing, problematic implicit knowledge. The TRP's capability to play a unifying role in the psychotherapy field is based in its inherent qualities: It is empirically grounded in neuroscience, non-theoretical, technique-independent, and can be used in dispelling emotional implicit learnings of all clinically relevant types, whether formed in attachment, existential, social, traumatic, or other experiences. Furthermore it provides an intuitively appealing understanding of how subjective experiencing and neurological processes operate together, intricately and coherently, to revise learning and memory. The therapeutic reconsolidation process embodies the brain's rules for profound unlearning, and the existence of those innate rules means that each one of us is equipped to outgrow and shed the constraints of our earlier learnings and to continue evolving our knowledge, our relationship to life and our world of meaning.

The steps of the TRP are defined in Table 3.1 on page 41; in addition, here is a simplified listing for ease of reference when the steps are mentioned in the rest of this chapter.

- *Step A:* Symptom identification
- *Step B:* Retrieval of symptom-necessitating emotional schema
- *Step C:* Identification of accessible contradictory knowledge
- *Step 1:* Reactivation of symptom-necessitating emotional schema
- *Step 2:* Juxtaposed, vivid experience of contradictory knowledge
- *Step 3:* Repetitions of the juxtaposition experience in Step 2
- *Step V:* Verification of change by observation of critical markers

The TRP yields transformational change, which we have defined by the same criteria or markers (Step V) that neuroscientists use in lab studies of the erasure of emotional learnings: abrupt, lasting cessation of symptoms and lasting absence of symptom-generating emotional reactions in the presence of cues and contexts that formerly induced their strong reactivation, with cessation persisting without effort or counteractive measures. Because TRP Steps 1, 2, and 3—the transformation sequence—are the only way currently known to neuroscience for bringing about those markers, we may infer that Steps 1, 2, and 3 must have occurred whenever the markers are observed in therapy, whether or not the therapist or client was cognizant of this sequence of experiences taking place.

The TRP is therefore well suited for demystifying the process of deep, lasting change in therapy and for being understood as a set of *transformation-specific factors* shared by psychotherapies of transformational change, as distinct from psychotherapies of counteractive change. TRP Steps 1–2–3 may be considered transformation-specific factors in the strict sense of being necessary for erasing an emotional implicit memory, but Steps A–B–C (the accessing sequence) may also be regarded as transformation-specific factors in the somewhat softer sense that, although Steps 1–2–3 can take place fortuitously *without* completing A–B–C first, as a rule A–B–C are pragmatically necessary in order to fulfill 1–2–3 as a deliberate methodology. Thus, as a rule we expect all six steps to be detectable in any series of psychotherapy sessions that yields the markers of transformational change, and in that way to merit being deemed the required factors for transformational change. The case examples in this chapter—sessions conducted by different clinicians using widely different methods—are offered as an initial demonstration of our consistent observation that whenever therapy yields the markers of transformational change, the presence of the TRP steps is detectable. The relationship of the TRP steps as transformation-specific factors to the widely familiar non-specific common factors is itself an important topic that we address in a section toward the end of this chapter.

Therapists who knowingly practice according to the TRP guide their clients to find and transform all existing implicit learnings generating a given symptom, with no pre-assumptions as to the category of experience in which those learnings arose. As noted in earlier chapters, all steps of the TRP are defined abstractly as process functions, without being tied to any particular techniques for implementing them or to any particular clinical school, theory, or system. Clinicians who opt to guide their work using the TRP therefore have a full range of choices of concrete methods and personal styles for implementing the process.

The authors prefer to conceptualize and use the TRP within the larger context of the Emotional Coherence Framework described in this book because of the naturalness and seamlessness of the relationship between the two—specifically their shared, non-pathologizing view of the coherence of the emotional brain and of implicit-learning-based symptom production. However, therapists are, of course, free to understand and use the TRP within any preferred meta-psychological framework.

It is worth noting that the category of counteractive psychotherapies can also be defined in terms of the TRP: A counteractive methodology is one that cultivates a desired state of mind or behavior using methods that do not fulfill the brain's requirements—TRP Steps 1-2-3—for dissolving symptom-generating emotional schemas. Those schemas continue to exist but are kept in a suppressed condition in successful outcomes of these therapies.

In short, the therapeutic reconsolidation process potentially can contribute to psychotherapy integration in a number of ways by providing:

- a unified understanding of the transformational change of emotional schemas formed by all types of learning—attachment, existential, social, and other
- a clarification of how the mechanism of deep, lasting change operates in a given psychotherapy system on both the subjective and neurological levels
- a cross-platform template and language that therapists of diverse orientations can share in order to understand and discuss each other's methodologies and methods, without challenging any system's conceptualization of itself
- a therapist's meta-map that positions him or her to have a flexible choice of methods and approaches with a given client, and guides the use of those methods for efficient, transformational work
- a lens for discerning therapy systems that have an inherent capacity to produce transformational change as distinct from those that inherently produce counteractive (incremental, relapse-susceptible) change.

Yet there remains a pivotal question if the therapeutic reconsolidation process is to be a useful advance for psychotherapy integration: Are its component steps detectable in a wide range of psychotherapy systems whenever transformational change clearly takes place? In other words, does the TRP actually do the job of revealing a deep structure shared by psychotherapies of transformational change?

We address that question in this chapter by demonstrating the previously undocumented presence of the steps of the TRP in published case examples of several focused, in-depth psychotherapies:

- Accelerated Experiential Dynamic Psychotherapy (AEDP)
- Emotion-Focused Therapy (EFT)
- Eye-Movement Desensitization and Reprocessing (EMDR)
- Interpersonal Neurobiology (IPNB).

In earlier chapters, the steps of the TRP were illustrated as they take place in Coherence Therapy, which we utilized as a demonstration platform because of the transparent and explicit match between Coherence Therapy's methodology and the TRP steps (as laid out in Table 3.1). In the examples that follow, we view an unfolding of each of the above-mentioned therapy systems and identify how each carries out the steps of the TRP detectably. Our aim is to show readers the TRP's integrative value in action; for more extensive considerations of psychotherapy integration see, for example, Norcross and Goldfried (2005) and Stricker and Gold (2006). In selecting case examples, our sole criterion was a written account having sufficient detail to allow identification of the steps of experiential process taking place. For each system of therapy represented here, we used the first published example we found that met that criterion.

In presenting each case example, we have extracted the concrete, observable client–therapist interactions and their accompanying phenomenology of experience. Only the client's and therapist's quoted, spoken words are verbatim from the original publication. *All additional explanation of and commentaries on the unfolding process are the writing of this book's authors.* Our added commentary primarily points out where the steps of the TRP take place as the work proceeds. There is some degree of paraphrasing of original comments describing the client's moment-to-moment tone and manner; we have striven for complete accuracy and encourage the reader to consult the original for further clarifications. We do not attempt to provide the conceptual or theoretical account of the system of psychotherapy that its founders or exponents provide. This too is readily available in the original article or volume for each example. Our treatment here is not in any way a replacement for studying each system in its own terms, but rather is a supplementary meta-conceptualization meant to be respectful of each particular system of psychotherapy—as the TRP itself is.

The examples below are also intended to serve in a heuristic, anecdotal manner to illustrate our hypothesis that markers of deep, lasting change in any form of therapy will be found to correlate strongly with the detectable occurrence of the TRP's steps—particularly Steps 1, 2, and 3, the transformation sequence with its juxtaposition experiences—even when those steps do not seem to be specified in a particular therapy system's description of itself. In other words, we believe it is likely that the TRP will prove to consist of the deep-structural ingredients or transformation-specific factors operating in most, if not all, therapies that yield transformational change as defined by the universal markers of such change.

Accelerated Experiential Dynamic Psychotherapy (AEDP)

Defined by its founder, psychologist Diana Fosha, as a system for bringing about transformational change in attachment trauma, AEDP is based on a synthesis of attachment theory, neurobiological research and mother–infant studies (Fosha, 2000, 2002, 2003). It is a non-pathologizing approach that aims to mobilize the individual's inherent capacity and strivings for well-being. It emphasizes experiential, emotional work and equips the therapist with innovative strategies for carrying out reparative attachment work, with a particular focus on moment-to-moment creation of explicit experiences of secure attachment in the client–therapist dyad.

In the following study of therapeutic work done by clinical social worker Benjamin Lipton and described by Lipton and Fosha (2011), we point out the steps of the therapeutic reconsolidation process occurring within the methodology of AEDP. For Lipton's and Fosha's commentary on this case in terms of AEDP concepts, we hope readers will refer to their article. Here, all utterances of client and therapist are exact quotes.

The 40-year-old client, "Daniel," was a recently divorced father of a young son. As a boy he had been socially awkward and lonely during a "latchkey childhood of neglect and isolation," with parents who were "emotionally shutdown, career driven scientists." In junior high school at age 11, Daniel had skipped two grades and was much younger than other students, and a teacher who seemed to take a paternal interest and offer a refuge from loneliness instead perpetrated sexual abuse for a year. Daniel began therapy six months after ending a 20-year drug dependency, one year after his mother died of cancer, and two years after a divorce.

Daniel stated his goals for therapy in terms of wanting now to deal honestly with his life and face a range of emotional issues he had been avoiding all along. He wanted to "come clean and be brutally honest about who I am and how I got to where I am so I can figure out how to get out of this mess." (His reference to past non-openness about himself contributes to the first step of the TRP, *Step A*, symptom identification.)

In his second session, Daniel gave a long description of his parents that was candid but rambling, disorganized, and at an emotional remove—saying of his father, for example, "he's impossible to talk on the phone with. It makes you uncomfortable every second because he doesn't respond to anything. He's completely detached and he doesn't engage you." (Daniel's depersonalized phrasing contributes further to the symptom picture for *Step A*.)

When that long ramble ended, the therapist replied, "Daniel, what are you feeling inside right now *as you share this with me*? So that *we*, right away, *in our work*, Daniel, work against the sort of detached, talking head experience and really help you stay connected to your body and your emotions? Which is what *I really want to help you with and think you never really got help with before?*" In that response, we have italicized how the therapist sought to create a very personal, dyadic experience of secure attachment for Daniel—a key feature of AEDP that would be repeated many more times. In terms of the TRP, this initial creation of a secure attachment experience, contradicting and in juxtaposition with Daniel's reactivated expectations of insecure attachment, was *Step 2*. In AEDP the therapist undertakes Step 2 from the outset of therapy because the core strategy of the approach is reparative attachment. In other words, an AEDP therapist assumes in advance that, whatever the client's specific symptoms are (Step A), retrieval of symptom-generating schemas (*Step B*) will uncover insecure attachment learnings. This in turn, according to AEDP, identifies experiences of secure attachment with the therapist as being what would bring about transformational change of the existing insecure attachment learnings (fulfilling *Step C*, identification of disconfirming knowledge).

In addition, simply sitting across from the therapist and engaging in dyadic interaction tends to reactivate a client's insecure attachment learnings and responses—a particular model or schema consisting of a set of rules, roles, meanings, others' expected responses, self-protective tactics, and associated emotions (and this reactivation fulfills *Step 1*). Thus, within AEDP's assumptive framework, TRP Steps C and 1 are fulfilled automatically early in the first session, leading the therapist to embark upon the creation of a concurrent contradictory experience (secure attachment, *Step 2*) from the very outset of therapy.

Then, additional experiences of secure attachment have two effects that we will soon see: They tend to draw into awareness the client's underlying insecure attachment learnings and memories (*Step B*) and they create repetitions of the juxtaposition experience (fulfilling *Step 3*). Markers of transformational change then begin to appear (*Step V*) because the juxtaposition experiences have dissolved the client's insecure attachment schemas. Thus, in AEDP the steps of the TRP tend to be carried out in the sequence C–1–2–B–3–V, with Step A occurring intermittently throughout. This is how AEDP may be understood through the lens of the therapeutic reconsolidation process, not how it is described by its exponents.

In response, Daniel answered, "It's sad." With that, at least for the moment he accepted the invitation to engage with the therapist in intimate, vulnerable emotional self-revealing, presumably a new experience that contradicted insecure interpersonal expectations (TRP *Step 2*, the initial juxtaposition experience).

Soon the therapist again focused Daniel on the relational moment by suggesting, "If you just imagined here with me for a minute that we just shared the feeling of sadness together ... ." Daniel then uttered a few reflective but intellectualized comments—holding back this time—and in response the therapist persisted by asking, "So what's it like to have me inviting you to be sad with me?" Daniel answered again in a depersonalized style, explaining at length that he feels guarded and shameful about expressing his sadness and depression to others, expecting negative responses to such feelings, and usually covers up his unhappiness with humor or good cheer (adding more to *Step A*).

The therapist, undeterred in his mission, asked, "So could we take literally like a minute to check out what it would be like not to try to make me happy, but just to feel ...?" This was a straightforward invitation to Daniel to put aside his pressing, familiar expectations of insecure attachment and, instead, to open himself to experiencing secure attachment by expressing his own true feelings to the therapist (which would be a disconfirming juxtaposition experience contributing to *Step 3*).

This time, accepting the therapist's overture, Daniel said, "I'll just fall apart" and began to cry, and then added through tears, "I spend most of my time feeling like I could burst into tears." Daniel could no longer resist his true feelings spilling into (safe) expression.

The therapist then repeatedly found opportunities to guide Daniel into both having and mindfully *recognizing* that he was having a dyadically intimate emotional experience (fulfilling *Step 3* and completing the transformation sequence). Daniel soon commented, "I think there's just so much—the reservoir of sadness is just so huge and I steel up."

The therapist replied, "I was just thinking that. No wonder you steel up. There's so much to steel up against."

"And I want so much not to feel this way," Daniel admitted, going a bit further into open vulnerability than before.

"What way?" asked the therapist.

Daniel, going yet further, clarified, "I don't want to feel alone."

Seeing his next opportunity for dyadic deepening (another *Step 3* experience), the therapist asked, "Do you feel alone right now?"

"Less so," Daniel acknowledged.

Perhaps sensing Daniel's increasing receptivity, the therapist now ventured to ask, "Do you feel my presence with you?"

"Yeah," Daniel confided (confirming yet another *Step 3* experience).

To maintain and perhaps even further deepen Daniel's emotional experience of safe dyadic connection, the therapist asked next, "What's that like for you? What's it like to have another man not abandoning you and also not having an ulterior motive with you?"

Daniel replied, "Unique"; the therapist said, "I bet"; and Daniel added, "I've had people who wanted to be there for me. It's—but, unless you—most people who want to be there for you then need you to tell them what to do, and its hard then not to feel like you're putting people out or dragging them along when you can't really explain it to them."

The AEDP therapist, ever sifting the client's response for opportunities to focus the client yet more fully on his emotional experience of the therapist's empathy, now asked, "Are you sensing that from me?"

"No," said Daniel. This was both another *Step 3* experience and also an initial marker of change (*Step V*), because Daniel was reporting that he was not having an emotional reaction that would normally have occurred at this point.

The therapist prompted, "So if you stay with me right here in this moment ..." At this, Daniel began to cry deeply and powerfully, and the therapist said softly, "I'm right here, Daniel. Right here." Daniel sobbed, and as he did the therapist added, "So much grief, so much held in for so long." These were secure attachment (*Step 3*) moments of great depth and intensity, and they did therapeutic double duty in also allowing Daniel to feel his long-suppressed feelings of grief, which represented a new degree of integration and movement toward emotional resolution.

Daniel wept for some time, and finally looked up shyly into the therapist's eyes and said, "Thank you. Wow!" followed by a deep sigh and visible bodily relaxation (additional markers of the profound absence of the target emotional reactions of insecure attachment and a shift into well-being).

"You are so welcome," replied the therapist, who then asked, "What are you thanking me for?"

"I think I've been needing to do that my whole life," Daniel explained. "I knew it, but I didn't know it. Whew." After a long, introspective pause, he added with a warm smile, "So this is what it's like, huh?"

With a warm smile in return the therapist confirmed, "Yes, this is what it's like. It feels very good to share this with you, Daniel."

Daniel said, "It's like a new beginning. Hard, strange—but good. Thank you." His last few utterances seemed to be spoken from a subjective vantage point that had shifted—a position of inhabiting secure attachment and the emotional freedom it bestows, while looking back at his former insecure positioning in his entire earlier life. Insofar as these utterances may be understood as markers of the dissolution of that insecure positioning, they contributed to *Step V*, the verification of change.

In this session Daniel had a sizable number of experiences of secure attachment that were sharply contradictory of his reactivated insecure attachment learnings—juxtaposition experiences that the therapist deliberately orchestrated, abundantly fulfilling TRP *Steps 2 and 3* and completing the transformation sequence. Most of these juxtaposition experiences took place tacitly—that is, without explicit recognition or verbalization of the juxtaposition *per se*—but, in light of the clear markers of change that appeared, their effectiveness was reduced very little, if at all, due to their tacitness. An AEDP practitioner who is aware of the therapeutic reconsolidation process and the critical role played by the juxtaposition itself could easily prompt its explicit recognition and verbalization. The therapist could in that way confirm that the client's current experience of secure attachment is in fact occurring in juxtaposition with his or her live expectations of insecure attachment (which, unbeknownst to the therapist, may be split off and suppressed in these moments, preventing actual juxtaposition).

In the same vein, Lipton and Fosha note that in AEDP, at times the client's original learnings and sufferings of insecure attachment come into his or her awareness explicitly (*Step B*) due to their "contrast" with the new, positive experiences of secure, emotionally intimate connection with the therapist. For example, "Recognizing and integrating a new, positive relationship in the here-and-now organically evokes its historical contrast—the painful experiences of the original relational trauma. In so doing, it also allows traumatic memories to be worked through in the service of positive psychological transformation" (Lipton & Fosha, 2011, pp. 254–255). Some degree of that contrast effect is apparent in Daniel's session above, but for the most part it appears to be distinctive of AEDP that its reparative attachment methodology carries out the TRP transformation sequence (*Steps 1, 2 and 3*) largely through tacit juxtapositions. This tacit mode can work reliably in reparative attachment therapy with clients who have strongly insecure attachment, for the reason that the therapist often can accurately enough foresee both the target learnings of insecure attachment *without* their explicit retrieval (*Step B*) and the needed sharply contradictory experience (pre-assumed to be secure attachment with the therapist), as noted earlier. However, there are many therapy clients whose target, symptom-generating implicit learnings are not of the insecure attachment type, as discussed in Chapter 5. For this major category of clients, a suitable contradictory knowledge is *not* a priori known to the therapist and cannot be identified (*Step C*) until explicit retrieval of the target learnings is carried out (*Step B*). Only then—following Steps B and C—can the work proceed to juxtaposition experiences in Steps 1–2–3.

Because the transformation sequence appears to have been well fulfilled in Daniel's session above, it is not surprising that markers of resulting transformational change began to appear during the session, tentatively verifying (*Step V*) that the entire therapeutic reconsolidation process had been carried out successfully. Daniel continued to report significant markers of change in his next session, as described just below.

In the latter half of his next (third) session, two weeks later, Daniel began describing shifts that had been occurring since the previous session. "It's like there's some pit and you're telling me I can walk across and I'm like, 'No, it's a pit.' And you're like, 'No, there's an invisible glass floor.' [Laughs with mixture of anxiety and evident delight] I'm like, 'OK, there's an invisible glass floor.' [Pause] And I'm starting to walk across it ... in my time. I'm starting to believe more and more there's an invisible glass floor ... . I feel like in many ways I'm coming out of a nightmare, but I'm not all the way there. Um—it's almost like I have this smidgeon of hope or something, or light [gestures upward], like ceilings are cracking … [Long pause] It's like I'm evolving …"

A few minutes later, in a step that is an important characteristic of AEDP, the therapist guided Daniel to focus on the emerging sense of well-being that he had mentioned by saying, "And I'm just wondering, when you kind of tune in to that idea that you are evolving and that you're being more compassionate with yourself, what does that feel like, what's it like to just take a moment to connect with that? To not think about it, but to feel it—to drop down below the neck and breathe?" Daniel's successful dissolution of his symptom-generating target learnings naturally had restored him to aspects of native well-being that he was beginning to experience directly. By guiding him to focus more fully on and verbalize these new, positive experiences, the therapist was seeking to optimize their emergence as well as their integration into Daniel's identity and conscious narratives. In terms of the TRP, this is seen as additional (and here, largely tacit) juxtaposition experiences that dissolve existing negative constructs of identity and life story. What matters in the TRP picture is that the establishment of the client's new identity and narratives also dissolves the old, negative ones, rather than being installed as separate learnings that compete with them. It is through the *juxtaposition* of the new and old that the old is dissolved, and the more explicit the juxtaposition, the better.

With a big sigh, Daniel answered, "It's a relief." He laughed with delight and added, "It's like the monster that's been stalking the neighborhood is caught."

"Wow!" exclaimed the therapist, surprised by the magnitude of the change suddenly verified by Daniel. "Will you just stay with that for a second? That's a powerful statement. I just want you to tune in to what that's like to be saying."

"It's freeing," Daniel explained. "It's, um, it doesn't have to be that bad, y'know."

Maintaining the emotional and somatic focus, the therapist asked, "Where do you feel it?"

"It's like a deep breath," said Daniel with a big inhalation and a gesture to his lungs. "It's in the lungs. It's—it's—" and he took another deep breath.

"It's like a deep breath," repeated the therapist.

Daniel continued his thought: "—and, I guess, it's what it's like to not feel so anxious all the time; I guess whatever physical state that is that you're not being hunted, y'know," and Daniel chuckled in recognition and relief. Both somatic and metaphorical markers of the dissolution of previously distressing emotional meanings and constructs were emerging richly (*Step V*) and reflecting a new sense of well-being.

Soon the therapist returned to one of those important markers and guided a deepening experience there by asking, "So, can we come back to—we're near the end of our time today, but I want to just come back to just this moment, just one more moment of that [therapist takes a deep breath] feeling. [Daniel too takes a deep breath.] I just wonder what it's like to be not only feeling that feeling that the monster that's stalking the neighborhood has been caught, but also what's it like to be sharing the experience here with me? To have that experience with me?"

Previously that question had served to guide Daniel to open up to the very new and tentative experience of a secure dyadic connection (creating juxtaposition experiences in fulfillment of TRP Steps 2 and 3), but now, because evidently Daniel had successfully reorganized significantly around secure attachment, it served a different function, that of verifying the shifts that had taken place (*Step V*), for Daniel answered in a clear, declarative manner, "Comfortable. Easy." This alone would have been a significant indication of transformational change because, as Lipton and Fosha comment (p. 275), "He is allowing himself to have an experience that—based on his procedural attachment history—we (and he) would have never thought possible." Several other such indicators then emerged (*Step V*) as Daniel continued to described his recent experiences: "I think I've suppressed so much that a lot of emotion that was leaking out of me—or stored up pain—is just going away in many ways. Y'know, I think there are still wounds, but the sort of like thick, black blood from the infection that's been collecting is gone. Y'know it's hard. I still have lonely feelings, but it's less urgent. There's less panic. That's it, there's less panic." With a smile he added, "I'm having a much better time enjoying. And I got better anti-inflammatories finally for my shoulder, too." Daniel had a long history of neglecting self-care for health issues.

"So, you're taking better care of yourself," the therapist acknowledged.

"I am," Daniel confirmed, "and it feels good. I'm not destroying myself. And I don't want to destroy myself. I've done that—and it didn't help—and it hurt a lot. God knows what the long-term ramifications are going to be from all that."

Bringing the session to an end, the therapist said, "That really touches me, Daniel. You've really accomplished something amazing here. You are speaking your truth in such a deep, honest way. This touches my heart."

With a beaming smile, Daniel agreed, "I know. Me too. Me too." His new capacity for well-being and his relative freedom from previous, symptomatic forms of distress were strikingly apparent in his utterances (firmly accomplishing *Step V*). The changes he described were qualitative and transformational rather than incremental.

Emotion-Focused Therapy (EFT)

Based in humanistic theories of psychotherapy and utilizing experiential techniques of Gestalt therapy, EFT works toward deep change through feeling and expressing avoided emotion and by embracing the adaptive role of emotion (Greenberg, 2011; Greenberg & Elliott, 2002; Greenberg & Watson, 2005; Johnson, 2004). Psychologist Leslie Greenberg, one of EFT's founders, explained in an online interview (Van Nuys, 2010) that "the emphasis in EFT is … on how to work with people's actual feelings in the session and then how to work with changing emotions in the session, so that the real emphasis is on trying to understand emotional processes and how emotions change." Other developers of EFT include psychologists Robert Elliott, Susan Johnson, Laura Rice, and Jeanne Watson. EFT practitioners guide clients to experience their emotions in the safe setting of therapy so that, rather than avoiding or controlling their feelings, those emotions serve to create awareness of what is important or needed in their lives. The approach is also known as Process-Experiential Psychotherapy.

Our case example here, drawn from Greenberg (2010, pp. 39–41), reveals the therapeutic reconsolidation process as it develops in EFT. For Greenberg's own commentary on this case, please see the original publication.

In an initial assessment interview, the client, a 39-year-old woman whom we are calling "Trish," tearfully described herself as feeling depressed, as she had felt for most of her life but significantly more so in the past year, causing her to stop working and rarely leave her house or answer the phone or doorbell. Her relationships with members of her family of origin had become particularly difficult and painful. (Identifying symptoms of depression and associated isolation began TRP *Step A.*) The therapist also learned that Trish and her three sisters no longer had contact with their alcoholic mother and that her father, a concentration camp survivor, had always been emotionally removed from the family and perceived as often being critical and judgmental. Physical punishment had been the norm throughout her childhood.

The therapist observed that although Trish was able to focus on her internal experience when receiving empathic responses that helped her to focus inwardly, she tended to avoid painful and difficult emotions, sinking into states of helplessness and hopelessness whenever she began to feel primary emotions of sadness or anger or her need for closeness and acceptance. Trish also mentioned having feelings of resentment and sadness toward her father as well as a self-blaming, shameful view of herself as a "failure." At times she minimized her father's physical abusiveness with the view that "being slapped was just normal." (Feelings of helplessness, hopelessness, self-blame, and shame contributed further to *Step A*, the symptom picture.)

Based on Trish's presentation of symptoms, the therapist was now inferring that in childhood and into adult life Trish had often felt unsafe, abandoned, alone and shamed by verbal and physical blows (indicating complex trauma and contributing to *Step B*, retrieval of underlying emotional learnings).

In the third session, with the support of the therapist's empathic attunement, Trish talked about not receiving approval from her father and added, "I believe I'm a bad person, but deep down inside I don't think I'm a bad person … yeah, I'm grieving for what I probably didn't have and know I never will have." ("I believe I'm a bad person" added to the symptom picture, *Step A*. Her comments yielded important *Step C* information about contradictory knowledge in three areas: The client has indicated that she possesses the contradictory knowledge that she is not a bad person; that her emotional distress is due to an actual emotional hardship that she has suffered—absence of caring attention and loving acceptance and connection from parents—rather than due to any deficits or defects in herself; and that trying to get those emotional supplies from her parents is futile, so only grieving will free her, not maintaining hopes that her parents will change.)

The therapist then guided Trish into an empty-chair dialogue with her father. Picturing him in the chair across from her own, she began to voice the specific meanings of her painful emotions directly to him: "You destroyed my feelings. You destroyed my life. Not you completely, but you did nothing to nurture me and help me in life. You did nothing at all. You fed me and you clothed me to a certain point. That's about it." (Saying what had never been said before was retrieval work, *Step B*.)

The therapist, drawing on some of Trish's previous comments, guided her by saying, "Tell him what it was like to be called a 'devil' and have to go to church every ..."

She said to her visualized father, "It was horrible. You made me feel that I was always bad, I guess when I was a child. I don't believe that now, but when I was a child I felt that I was going to die and I was going to go to hell because I was a bad person." (The client has been guided efficiently into the sequence of experiences of TRP *Steps 1 and 2*: visceral reactivation of an unwanted emotional learning, "I'm bad," and, simultaneously, the experience of contradictory, disconfirming knowledge.)

As Trish continued, she began to depart from her usual self-protective adaptation of avoiding her own unmet needs, by telling her father, "It hurts me that you don't love me—yeah—I guess, you know, but ... I'm angry at you and I needed love and you weren't there to give me any love." (She could now tolerate the emotional pain of attending to her unmet, core needs because the therapist's empathetic accompaniment kept her from feeling alone as she did so. Recognition of the validity of her need for love is another knowing that contradicted the target learnings, so it fulfilled *Step C* and also *Step 3* by creating a tacit but effective juxtaposition with her original model, "Dad is unloving toward me because I am unworthy of love," which is being replaced by knowing that "Dad's negative behavior means he failed to be a loving father to me." This repeated the essence of her previous juxtaposition experience, so it is TRP *Step 3*. A learned model or construct of oneself as bad, unworthy, and unlovable is the very source of the feeling of shame, so its dissolution through the TRP brings cessation of shame.)

Later, with more encouragement from the therapist, she told the image of her father about her fear: "I was lonely. I didn't know my father. My father, all I knew you as, was somebody that yelled at me all the time and hit me. That's all—I don't remember you telling me you loved me or that you cared for me or that you thought that I did well in school or anything. All I know you as [*sic*] somebody that I feared." (Trish was continuing to tolerate retrieving her emotional knowledge of the specific forms of suffering that she had endured with her father. This again furthered *Step C* and *Step 3* as in the previous paragraph, because expressing this inventory of ordeals to him as the evidence of *his mistreatment of her* continued to disconfirm her self-blaming, self-shaming ways of understanding his behavior, creating the same tacit juxtaposition as before. Her next statements to him did more of the same.)

"Tell him how you were afraid of being hit," prompted the therapist.

"Yes, and you humiliated me," Trish continued. "I was very angry with you because you were always hitting me; you were so mean and I heard Hitler was mean, so I called you Hitler." At one point she added, "I guess I keep thinking that yeah, you will never be a parent, that you would pick up the phone and just ask me how I'm doing. It hurts me that you don't love me—yeah." Later in the session she confronted him particularly forcefully: "I'm angry at you because you think you were a good father, you have said that you never hit us and that's the biggest lie on earth, you beat the hell out of us constantly, you never showed any love, you never showed any affection, you never ever acknowledged we were ever there except for us to clean and do things around the house." She ended the session by saying, "I needed to be hugged once in a while as a child or told that I was OK. I think that's normal." (Those last four words may have been an initial marker of change, *Step V*, indicating that her negative model of herself was dismantled to some significant extent.)

In the next (fourth) session, the therapist used two-chair work, in which the client sits alternately in each chair, inhabiting and speaking from a different part or subpersonality in each. The aim here was to guide Trish to access, feel and express her inner critic (further retrieval of target learnings, or *Step B*) and to engage in dialogue with that part of herself (bringing the emotional schema(s) of the critic into juxtaposition with disconfirming knowings held by Trish apart from the critic's knowings, for *Steps 1 and 2*). The voice of the critic softened in this process (suggesting successful dissolution of the critic's mental models) and, no longer suppressed by self-invalidation, she began to feel a sense of her inherent worth and to express her grief over not being loved. This included a revisiting of the knowings that had become prominent in the previous session: "Even though Mom and Dad didn't love me or didn't show me any love, it wasn't because I was unlovable; it was just because they were incapable of those emotions. They don't know how to—they still don't know how to love." At this point, nowhere in evidence was the feeling of hopelessness that had been predominant in earlier sessions (a significant marker of dissolution of old models, *Step V*).

Here the original account moves to Session 7, in which the work began to focus on Trish blocking her feeling of wanting to be loved to protect herself from the pain of having that need not be met. The part of herself that protected her in this way became named the "interrupter." This work continued through Session 9 where, in two-chair work, while enacting her interrupter in one chair, Trish said to herself visualized in the other chair, "You're wasting your time feeling bad cause you want them; they are not there. So it's best for you to shut your feelings off and not need them. That's what I do in my life. When people hurt me enough I get to that point where I actually can imagine, I literally cut them out of my life like I did with my mother." (This was *Step B*, retrieval from implicit to explicit knowledge of the learnings making up the "interrupter" part.) In the other chair, Trish inhabited and expressed the self that needed and wanted to experience being loved and accepted. (The interaction of those two retrieved parts appears to have been largely an encounter between the part of herself that wanted to meet her need for love and get relief from the pain of not receiving love, and another part that had learned that actually seeking love results in even worse pain. These dialoguing parts held different knowings, but these were not actually mutually *incompatible* models of reality, so experiencing them simultaneously was not a juxtaposition experience.)

The therapist observed in Session 9 that "The hopelessness that was so dominant in the early sessions now is virtually nonexistent. The voice that wants love and acceptance becomes stronger, and the critic softens to express acceptance of this part of her. At the same time she is feeling much better and activation of her negative feelings decrease[s]." (Those several markers verifying change contributed significantly to *Step V.*)

In another round of empty chair work with her father in Session 10, Trish felt and gave voice to a more compassionate understanding of him (which Greenberg emphasizes is "a key empirically demonstrated process of change," hence an important further contribution to *Step V*). Trish stated to her visualized father, "I understand that you've gone through a lot of pain in your life and probably because of this pain, because of the things you've seen [in the concentration camp], you've withdrawn. You're afraid to maybe give love the way it should be given and to get too close to anybody because it means you might lose them. You know—and I can understand that now, whereas growing up I couldn't understand." She was continuing to hold him accountable for the ways that he had failed her and hurt her, while also allowing her compassion to be central in a new, more complete understanding of how their life together had unfolded. (No longer in the grip of her previous emotional reactions, she was able to access other knowings about her father that were juxtaposing with and dissolving yet more of her earlier ways of making sense of his behaviors. This was a new round of TRP *Steps 1, 2 and 3.*) Commenting on that dialogue at the end of the session, Trish said, "I feel relief that I don't have this anger sitting on my chest anymore." (This was a particularly decisive, somatic marker of change for *Step V.*)

In addition, the original account states that "By the end of this 14-session therapy ... needing to be loved no longer triggers hopelessness ..." Trish was more able to communicate her needs and was now in closer contact with her sisters (all *Step V* markers). The account of Trish's therapy ends here, so we presume that her original symptoms had ceased, because these last-mentioned changes indicate she was no longer isolating herself and, free from hopelessness, was no longer feeling depressed.

EFT typically carries out the steps of the therapeutic reconsolidation process in the sequence A–B–C–1–2–3–V.

Eye-Movement Desensitization and Reprocessing (EMDR)

EMDR was developed by Francine Shapiro originally for the treatment of post-traumatic stress symptoms and is now used to address a wide range of presenting symptoms (F. Shapiro, 2001; R. Shapiro, 2005). It is a comprehensive approach that utilizes structured procedures and protocols, along with aspects of psychodynamic, cognitive behavioral, interpersonal, experiential, and body-centered therapy methods. A major procedural element employed in EMDR is "dual stimulation," during which the client focuses attention on two experiential areas at once—a cluster of linked internal elements (specific images, emotions, body sensations, and thoughts) and an external physical stimulus that guides a bilateral oscillation of perceptual attention (whether through eye movements, audio tones, or physical taps).

The cornerstone of EMDR's conceptual model is what Shapiro terms the brain's Adaptive Information Processing System, which is understood as always striving for survival and adaptive mental health. In that context, EMDR is understood as functioning to update the client's memory network by bringing about a genuine resolution of negative emotional experiences rather than engaging in counteractive managing of symptoms.

Our EMDR case example comprises a series of five sessions conducted by licensed professional counselor Beverly Schoninger. Our account is drawn from Shapiro and Forrest (1998, pp. 74–88) and from Schoninger (personal communication, July 25, 2011). The commentary on the unfolding EMDR process is ours, with the aim of making apparent the embedded steps of the therapeutic reconsolidation process. The therapist carried out the entire EMDR protocol, including SUDS (Subjective Units of Distress Scale) ratings; our account, however, includes only the dual stimulation work and the client's immediate responses to it. We encourage readers to refer to the original publication for full details and to the EMDR literature for information on concepts and methodology.

The client, "Susan," was in her early 40s and second marriage, with two adult sons from her first marriage. Susan sought EMDR for relief from over four years of symptoms that she knew to be panic attacks stemming from a traumatic experience 10 years earlier, while living with her first husband, "Keith," and their younger son, "Ernie," in a dairy-farming village with a population of 600 in the USA's Midwest.

In her first session, as she began to tell the therapist about that trauma, her face flushed and she began hyperventilating, on the verge of a panic attack, but she managed to continue. She explained that at bedtime on June 7, 1984, the wind was blowing violently. She had grown up in the Midwest, was keenly alert to the danger of tornadoes, and had herded her family into their basement for safety on many occasions—though she once wished their house *would* blow away so they would receive the insurance money and be able to start new lives. Keith had come to the Midwest with Susan only a few years previously and had a patronizing attitude toward her vigilance for storms, regarding her as alarmist. On this night, Susan convinced Keith that they should abandon their air-conditioned bedroom upstairs for the night and sleep downstairs in the guest room, where the constant howling of the wind would be muffled.

At 12:50 a.m., a loud clap of thunder and flash of lightning awoke Susan. She could hear pouring rain and a persistent low whistling, like wind blowing in the eaves or a car horn driven by a weak battery. Then Ernie ran into the room because the sounds had awakened him, too. At first Susan thought the whistling might be the tornado alarm from the next town. Looking out the window, she saw total darkness. There were no lights on in town, not even at the fire station next door. She realized that the whistling was not a tornado alarm; it was the tornado itself.

Susan shouted, "Keith, come on! We're going to the basement!" and started running, followed by Ernie. Keith was awake but in no hurry. Susan saw him reaching for his pants as she hurried toward the kitchen, flung open the door to the stairs that led to the basement, and raced down to safety. Right away she heard a loud cracking as the siding on the house started to break up, and then she was unconscious.

When awareness returned, Susan was in complete darkness, soaking wet and buried in three feet of rubble in her basement. Rain was still pouring down, drenching her in her thin nightgown. The air was acrid with the smell of heating oil oozing from a break in the basement oil tank. The stairs were no longer there. The rows of shelves up to the ceiling, once stacked high with belongings, were gone also. The ceiling was gone. There was no house above her. Ernie was beside her, but Keith was not. When the rain finally subsided, Ernie crawled out from under the rubble, climbed up out of the cavity that had been their basement, and ran for help. A team of paramedics eventually arrived and, in the near-total darkness, brought Susan up to ground level and to shelter for the night, while Ernie joined rescue workers. That there was no sign of Keith was troubling but Susan assured herself he was all right.

In the morning Susan returned to the scene. The devastation by the tornado's 300-mile-per-hour winds was beyond comprehension. Eleven of the 12 houses in their immediate neighborhood were flattened, and so was the town itself. As *Time* magazine later chronicled, in only 20 seconds the town had been "wiped right off the map."

Visiting the recovery command center, Susan and Ernie were taken to see their local policeman. He looked haggard and sad and said, "Susan, Keith's dead." So were eight others, seven of them Susan's immediate neighbors, including her best friend, Jill, Jill's husband, and their eight-year-old daughter. Many more in the town had been injured.

This first session included initial training in safe place imagery, which is used in EMDR for self-soothing and for ensuring the client's emotional stability in the event that an unworkable level of distress becomes reactivated during the work or between sessions. (Safe place imagery is used for emotional deactivation if and when necessary. Its content is not necessarily matched to that of the client's traumatic memory and is not intended as part of the EMDR process for therapeutic change of memory contents.)

On the following day, the second session consisted of another rehearsal of using safe place imagery and of taking a thorough inventory of Susan's panic symptoms: anxiety; lump in the throat; light-headedness; dizziness; spacey disorientation; pain in chest, neck, and shoulders; and tingling in hands and feet. In answering the question, "When are you most likely to lose control of your body?" Susan replied, "When something happens in my body I don't understand, pain that is not explained, or in crowded stores or at the office." (This was TRP *Step A*, a detailed identification of both the *what* and the *when* of Susan's symptoms.)

Two weeks later, the third session began with EMDR's step of selecting a "target" to serve as the initial subjective focus for the first set of eye movements. The therapist asked Susan to select from her memory of the event the moment or image that she felt to be the most distressing part of it all. Susan identified the image of her husband putting on his pants as she hurried toward the steps to the basement. The therapist then guided Susan to identify the "negative cognition" associated with that image and, for that purpose, soon asked her gently, "Susan, do you have any feelings of guilt about what happened to Keith?"

"No. No, I don't feel guilty," Susan said without hesitation.

The therapist persevered and explained, "Well, some people might feel guilty about this. You know, when people die, very often their loved ones feel it was their fault in some way, even if it wasn't. Even if it couldn't have been. Check deep inside. Let your gut answer, not your mind. Do you think you might have any feeling that it was your fault?"

"Oh!" Susan exclaimed, wide-eyed, and after a long pause she acknowledged, "My gut *does* feel like that, like it was my fault, like I was the cause of Keith's death." Tears were now running down her cheeks. Susan identified the accompanying negative feelings as sadness and, asked where in her body she felt this, she indicated her chest and throat. (This was TRP *Step B*, retrieval of the implicit meaning, "It was my fault," which was a mental model that Susan had formed for making sense of her husband's death, with no awareness of forming it until now.)

The therapist asked, "What would you like to believe instead?" This was the next step of the EMDR procedure, the client's identification of a preferred "positive cognition" that defines what the client wants to experience as true instead of experiencing the negative cognition as true.

Susan said she would like to believe and feel, "I did the best I could." The client's articulation of a positive cognition in EMDR often proves to have accomplished TRP *Step C*—the identification of the knowing that will contradict and dissolve the existing symptom-maintaining knowings. The challenge is to bring this mere idea of a positive cognition into vivid emotional realness so that it can serve as an actual *experience* of contradictory knowing (in TRP *Step 2*). The EMDR process arrives at that vivification in sometimes surprising ways, as we will see.

The first set of eye movements began with Susan focusing on the target image and its accompanying elements—the conviction, "It was my fault," and the feeling of sadness and its sensations in her chest and throat. Immediately Susan began crying, and as set after set unfolded she roller-coastered through a wide range of emotions and meanings. "I didn't want him to die," she moaned, gasping for breath through her tears. Then, "I caused his death," which brought with it feelings of guilt and chest pain. After the next few sets she felt lighter, but then went on to ask, "Why didn't I die too?" and felt frustrated and angry with herself for being unable to protect Keith, since she was the one who knew about tornadoes. Later, she felt a fresh wave of guilt welling up in her throat because the tornado had broken every bone in Keith's body, yet she had walked away without a scratch. After the session's final set of eye movements, Susan said, "There's a piece inside about my being a no-good person. It doesn't make sense to me. I don't know where I got this stuff that I was bad."

It was her panic attacks that had led Susan to seek EMDR therapy, but the key underlying material that had now come into awareness (TRP *Step B*) during this initial session of bilateral work focusing on memories of the tornado experience consisted of constructs of angry self-blame and self-condemnation (I could have protected Keith but failed to do so; I caused his death; I'm a no-good person) and guilt for surviving unharmed. How these specific meanings and feelings might be related to the panic attacks was not yet apparent.

Two days later, at the start of her next session, Susan commented that she'd had "no idea that feeling was in me," referring to the self-blame that had surfaced and that continued to feel true, for she added, "I should have been able to make Keith understand the seriousness of the situation." After a long pause, in a sad voice she said, "Someday he would have learned to listen to me," and tears came.

The therapist then asked her to focus on those words—"I should have been able to make Keith understand"—for this session's first set of eye movements. After the set, Susan said her feeling of grief was even stronger. After another set the emotion of grief reached a peak of intensity, and Susan said she was feeling sadness and frustration in her chest and throat. Crying, she asked, "Why did he leave me alone?"

The therapist could not yet know, but in those moments Susan retrieved her suppressed emotional distress in its full depth (TRP *Step B*: experiential retrieval of symptom-generating emotion and emotional meanings). Over the next few sets, she reported feeling calmer.

A point now came, following a set, where Susan calmly said, "It was a choice he made. It had nothing to do with me. Our soul chooses." Having allowed the full intensity of her blocked grief to flow through her body and mind, suddenly Susan was now experiencing and voicing a very different knowing that sharply contradicted the constructs of self-blame that had been distressing her deeply until just minutes earlier (TRP *Step 2*: initial experience of contradictory knowing in juxtaposition with the target learnings). The quality of the experiential knowing expressed in Susan's last utterances will be recognizable to readers who are experienced EMDR practitioners, but to readers unfamiliar with this approach, those words may read as mere affirmations or positive thinking. However, it is characteristic of EMDR that new knowings contradicting the target construct can suddenly and unpredictably emerge during a set as an experiential, whole-body experience of a lucid truth, not just an idea. The typical quietude of the experience of this contradictory knowing in no way diminishes its compelling quality. In some cases, the content of the contradictory knowing feels completely new and unprecedented to the client, in which case it does not really seem to be a compartmentalized piece of prior learning. Phenomenologically it is as though the individual's inner being possesses a hidden store of intuitive knowledge that has been precisely tapped for a needed unit of illumination. Whatever its actual source, the newly emergent contradictory knowing has the specificity and compelling realness required for successfully disconfirming and dissolving the target construct. This is EMDR's distinctive way of fulfilling TRP *Step C* and *Step 2*.

The therapist immediately recognized the transformational value of what had just emerged and said to Susan, "Stay with that," and then conducted another set of eye movements.

After this set Susan said, "I can take care of myself" and again cried, and then said, "But it was his choice to live or die, and he was ready to go." (This was TRP *Step 3*, a first repetition of the same juxtaposition experience that achieved Step 2.)

Here again, the therapist could not be expected to recognize the nature of Susan's moment-to-moment process, namely that the transformational change had now been accomplished with just one repetition of the juxtaposition experience for Step 3. Susan's constructs of self-blame no longer felt emotionally real to her. She had created them in the aftermath of the tragedy and now she had dissolved them through a juxtaposition experience created by her new knowings. The juxtaposition consisted of the side-by-side experience of "I was responsible for Keith's actions and should have been able to make him listen to me and get to safety; so it is my fault he died in the tornado, and I am a very bad person" and "He made his own choice, beyond my range of influence, about how to respond when I summoned him to safety; I did the best I could, I cannot control everything in life, and it is not my fault that he made the choice he did and died as a result."

The only hint that this change had now actually occurred was Susan's immediate shift of attention to a new and less pressing area of emotional distress: After another set she said, "I'm feeling sorry for myself." Then a set focused on that feeling led to her saying, "I'm feeling abandoned by my family. They've pretty much dismissed what happened to me." Susan explained that in the initial period after the tornado, her parents and extended family members gave her a great deal of caring attention, but their expressions of sympathetic concern had tapered off much too soon. With a few more sets, these thoughts and feelings receded and were replaced by yet a different area of distress when she said, "I feel guilty about the money. I benefited: We had homeowners' insurance." The next set began with a focus on those words and led to Susan saying, "I do feel he did the best he could. He was a dreamer, you know, 'Don't think about it and it will just go away.' I was the practical one." She had returned to and was further articulating her lucid recognition of Keith's autonomy, again disconfirming her self-blame (*Step 3*, another repetition of the juxtaposition experienced earlier in the session; the TRP's transformation sequence was now complete).

After a set focused on her last utterances, she said, "What is there about me that I can still trust?" Asked what she meant, she explained, "I'm not the person I thought I was. I'm not the totally competent person who handles things and gets things done. That was the basic me. Now who am I, anyway?" Susan was now grappling with the implications or ripple effects of recognizing Keith's role in choosing how he acted that night. Perceiving his choicefulness was now leading her to accept the (existential) limitations of her own power to influence what happens—and *this* new knowing directly challenged and disconfirmed her long-standing model of herself as having essentially unlimited ability to make things happen as she sees best (which is TRP *Steps B, 1 and 2* in relation to her learned model of personal identity). Susan's comments, "I'm not the person I thought I was ... Now who am I?" were a marker of a transformational shift in her identity constructs (*Step V*) and signaled that she was undergoing new growth in her sense of self.

The session's final set began with a focus on her question, "Now who am I?" Following that set, Susan rated her distress to be zero and, when also asked by the therapist to rate the felt truth of her originally articulated, desired positive cognition, "I did the best I could," she gave it the highest possible score of "completely true."

Susan came for her fifth and last session, a half-hour follow-up, three days later. She said she was feeling great and her symptoms almost completely gone. She explained, "The things that were happening in my body don't happen any more. Even at work, where I'm now doing the job of two people, I can let things roll off my back." The absence of her previous emotional and somatic reactions in the presence of their formerly strong triggers was a clear marker verifying successful change (TRP *Step V*).

She had felt one minor panic attack since the last session, but this experience itself fed directly into the (TRP) change process because it happened "in a store, of course," and Susan realized that the department store, like some parts of her workplace, presented her with strong reminders of the tornado trauma: high shelves overhead stocked with items (as those along her basement walls had been), the general din of shoppers and PA-system announcements (like the surrounding roar of the tornado's winds ripping the house apart), and the visual turmoil of many things happening all around her. Susan's realization that these features were only present *reminders* of a *past* ordeal was a vivid, felt experience in itself, not just a cognitive insight, so this realization was essentially equivalent to the *I'm in memory* practice described in Chapter 5 and had the same freeing effects through juxtaposition experiences (as detailed in Table 5.1 on page 118). Susan's own words to the therapist described the liberating effect: "I still don't like those big mega-stores but I think I'm allowed to not like them. I don't have to have a panic attack over it." Even the multiple reminder cues in huge, crowded stores had now lost their power to drive Susan into a state of panic (*Step V*).

As Susan's sessions illustrate, the typical process of therapy in EMDR is non-linear. There is no predicting what material will emerge next at any given point, and seemingly discontinuous shifts into unexpected or even seemingly unrelated material can be about as frequent as recognizable continuity. Reviewing how Susan's material unfolded is therefore particularly useful.

If we use the *ad hoc* but intuitive principle that the sequence in which the client's material emerges in EMDR reveals something about the architecture of how the material is layered in implicit memory, as well as the relative emotional intensity or urgency of the material, we would infer that Susan's constructs of self-blame, which emerged first and foremost, were in some sense "in front" of the intense grief that came forth next. After self-blame came her knowledge that her extended family had withdrawn sympathetic attention much too soon for her, so she felt abandoned by them. Then her guilt over benefiting from the insurance money came into awareness, and finally she was feeling the shift in identity wrought by realizing that her husband had chosen his own fate, beyond her range of influence. Facilitated by bilateral stimulation work, Susan's mind and brain "unpacked" a series of five distinct areas of troubled meaning and feeling: self-blame, grief, abandonment, guilt, and identity.

It is noteworthy that during the eye movement work, nothing clearly related to Susan's presenting symptom of panic attacks emerged. No moments or images evoking terror came into awareness despite focusing directly on the traumatic event. In fact, in her short final follow-up session she reported having a mild panic attack since the last of the eye-movement sessions three days earlier, which meant that the eye movement work had not yet completely dispelled her panic symptoms. Yet, from that panic attack Susan recognized experientially for the first time—after more than four years of panic attacks—that the environmental perceptions triggering her panic were merely reminders of an ordeal that was in her past, not in her present, and *this* recognition unlocked and dismantled the panic-triggering linkages. Clearly, this liberation from panic attacks was made possible by the eye-movement-induced, powerful shifts in the five areas summarized in the previous paragraph—but how, exactly?

The principle of emotional coherence guides us to answer that question by relying on the emotional brain's coherence and asking this one: How did it *make deep sense emotionally* for Susan to cease having panic attacks only after she was no longer mired in self-blame, ungrieved grief, forlorn abandonment, guilt over gain, and an identity of having control?

If we think about each of those themes, we see that each was keeping the experience of the tornado emotionally and timelessly present for Susan. Blaming herself and feeling herself deeply bad for failing to save Keith from the tornado, she could not bear to be free of the catastrophe herself. With her intense grief blocked and unfelt, she had not arrived at acceptance of losing Keith to the tornado and was emotionally parked in mid-event, almost as if it were still possible to get him into the basement and save him; and her clinging to the identity of having unlimited control of events kept her in this limbo, as well. Feeling abandoned by her own family in her massive loss prevented closure of the episode in its own way, as did her guilt over the house insurance payment. With awareness and emotional processing in each of those areas, it had become *acceptable* to Susan to disengage emotionally from the tornado, allowing her to use her very next panic attack to recognize that the tornado was in the past, not the present.

Such key dynamics sometimes remain implicit during the mind's complex, nonlinear processing in EMDR, but the initially puzzling flow of a client's experiences can often be clarified by thinking in terms of the emotional coherence of the brain and mind. Case conceptualization is often assisted greatly by applying the principle of emotional coherence, we have found. For example, in our clinical experience a client's self-blame for negative events is always found to be coherently needed (non-consciously) in order to preserve the person's identity, role, or anxiety management strategy of *having* control over events, as in Susan's case; and/or in order to maintain attachment with caregivers who communicate much blame, criticism, contempt, or disgust.

To generalize about EMDR in relation to the therapeutic reconsolidation process, we note that the TRP's steps are typically carried out by EMDR in the sequence $A–(C)–B–1–2–3–V$, where (C) represents the identification of the client's desired positive cognition, which may or may not prove to represent the true contradictory material that finally emerges in *Step 2*.

Interpersonal Neurobiology (IPNB)

A primary aim of psychotherapy guided by IPNB, founded by psychotherapist and child psychiatrist Daniel Siegel, is liberation from the grip of emotional implicit memory formed in response to problematic attachment experiences in infancy and childhood. Prominent in IPNB is the recognition that specific mental models formed by the individual are a major part of symptom-generating implicit memory, and that early and ongoing attachment relationships can significantly impair brain organization and integration. The clinical implication, as understood in IPNB, is that the use of the same potent influence—dyadic relational experience, now in the client–therapist relationship—creates reparative attachment experiences that can undo the negative effects caused by the original, harmful attachment experiences. Key features of the therapeutic process in IPNB include the client's felt experience of the therapist's sensitive emotional attunement and accompaniment; guidance from the therapist for attending to and verbalizing neglected right-brain and subcortical activity comprising implicit emotional knowledge and responses; guidance for identifying how current triggers resemble past experiences; and cultivation of integrated awareness of what was suffered in the past, ending projection of the past onto the present situation.

Siegel's emphasis on the retrieval of the contents of implicit memory into explicit awareness and direct, emotional experience has made a substantial contribution to the clinical field (e.g., Siegel, 1999, 2006). He has described the effects of that implicit-to-explicit reorganization in terms of emotional and neurological integration, and has mapped out several distinct functional areas of integration so that therapists can knowingly cultivate them and thereby induce therapeutic change (e.g., Siegel, 2001, 2010). Siegel teaches a style of informing therapy clients about brain functioning that de-pathologizes symptoms, largely eliminating the stigma and shame that many clients feel regarding their symptoms and fostering the client's hopefulness and motivation in therapy.

In Table 6.1, a case vignette by marriage and family therapist Bonnie Badenoch illustrates IPNB and shows how the therapeutic reconsolidation process is fulfilled detectably within this methodology. The succinctness of Badenoch's clinical account permits verbatim reproduction here and we provide, in parallel, keyed comments that indicate where the steps of the TRP occur. This also shows the use of the TRP as a meta-framework for illuminating and discussing the operation of any system of psychotherapy in a manner that is free of theoretical biases. For Badenoch's or Siegel's own accounts of the concepts and methods of IPNB, we encourage readers to refer directly to their writings.

As this example shows, IPNB typically carries out the steps of the therapeutic reconsolidation process in the sequence A–B–C–1–2–3–V.

Envisioning Psychotherapy Integration Through the Therapeutic Reconsolidation Process

We have examined representative case examples of several different forms of focused, in-depth psychotherapy in this chapter and shown that the steps of the therapeutic reconsolidation process are identifiable, in some cases with distinctive variations in the sequence of preparatory steps, A–B–C, as summarized in Table 6.2. The presence of the transformation sequence—TRP Steps 1–2–3—in each type of therapy supports the central message of this book: The unlocking and transformational unlearning of problematic learning in the emotional brain's memory networks occur when the target learning is reactivated and, during that reactivation, the individual vividly experiences fundamentally contradictory knowledge. In that way, core, non-conscious, disturbing emotional themes of a lifetime can be deeply resolved and dispelled in a highly time-effective manner.

The same kind of TRP mapping as illustrated in this chapter's case examples could be done for other systems of psychotherapy as well, such as those listed

Table 6.1   IPNB case vignette (Badenoch, 2011, pp. 73–74)

Original text	Therapeutic Reconsolidation Process
Cerise came to me because all of her close relationships ended in her pulling away when emotional intimacy became intense [1]. We worked our way through a number of childhood memories in which she had felt overwhelmed by her mother, but this work did not produce much change in her relational apprehensions [2]. We began to ask her deeper mind to guide us toward the source of her unchanging fear [3]. Almost immediately, she felt the behavioral impulse of backing away while she saw an image of her parents in their ballet of mutual avoidance [4]. We began to focus our attention on these two internalized dancers. Much as we did in working with her child states of mind, we asked both inner parents, in turn, what was hurting or scaring them [5]. Requesting inner guidance again, she got the sense that we could begin most easily with her father. Waiting in receptivity after her question about what was happening inside him, Cerise began to sense in her body the same behavioral impulse to pull away that she felt when a lover wanted increasing connection [6]. Staying with this movement and letting her father know that we would remain with him, she began to have an intuitive sense of his frightening loss of connection with his depressed mother [7], experiencing it not in a cognitive but in a visceral way. We offered understanding, comfort, and continuous connection—key elements of what had been missing for him throughout his childhood, and thus a disconfirming experience [8]. In her body, she could feel his emotional tension release [9] as the brain circuitry holding this locked-away pain opened to the new relational experience we were offering.

We then moved on to do the same work with her mother. However, Cerise | [1] *Step A*, symptom identification: Client flees as emotional intimacy develops, abandoning and ending relationships.

[2] A first attempt at *Step B*, retrieval, is made, addressing an area of early emotional learning that appeared likely to be driving the symptom but turns out not to be doing so.

[3] *Step B* is pursued further by assuming an underlying emotional coherence and, in attentive stillness, submitting an overt request to the implicit system for an indication of relevant content.

[4] Retrieval of that content begins: The client feels the symptom (a pulling away) occurring in response to an image of her parents avoiding each other—revealing some of the "raw data" that seem to have produced the symptom-generating emotional learning.

[5] The same technique of simply asking is used to continue the discovery work. Notice that the question again arises from assuming emotional coherence.

[6] The repeatedly invited flow of knowings from implicit memory into explicit awareness now reveals that the father was a source of the client's learning of fearful withdrawal. The discovery work for *Step B* is proceeding well.

[7] The image of the father is the representation through which the client's implicit emotional knowledge of him is flowing into her explicit awareness. The inner father's suffering of insecure attachment is the problem for which his tactic of self-protective withdrawal is the solution. This largely completes the initial discovery of this emotional schema. Schema contents are now understood sufficiently for immediate completion of *Step C*, the therapist's identification of how to guide an experience of contradictory knowing, namely by |

experienced these wounds as so much more complex and variegated that many inner experiences were required before her inner mother began feeling a relaxation [10] similar to what she had experienced with her father. We can trust this inner process to unfold in its best way, even when it takes a long time. Sometimes the tangled implicit memories that hold a particular inner state in place require us to simply be present over and over again as we make our way through the layers. In the presence of safety and care, through the kind and gentle holding that creates a cradle in which painful experience can emerge, the healing will happen as quickly as it can, even when that is slowly.

As we worked with Cerise's mother, we noticed that her inner father watched the process between us and his wife. Instead of backing away, he seemed curious and open to understanding the nature of the wounds underlying her behavior [11]. As soon as her mother came to peace, she and her husband were able to form a more connected relationship internally. Their implicit dance of avoidance was over … . After completing this round of resolving experiences, Cerise's encounters with her parents in other memories that had originally contained this same emotional valence of avoidance now showed them softened and more available to one another [12]. It was as though working with them around their pains and fears had soothed similar pangs throughout the system. The resolution of her inner parents' avoidance turned out to be the key to change in Cerise's outer life. Once the two inner parents gained empathy for and connection with one another, her fear of closeness became a distant memory that she experienced as a brief behavioral impulse to back away that she no longer needed to follow [13].

creating experiences of secure attachment for the internal father figure.

[8] The therapist seamlessly proceeds to do so using the technique of imaginal interaction for communicating messages of secure attachment to the inner father. *Steps 1–2–3* of the TRP unfold smoothly in that manner: The reactivated, insecure expectations of abandonment are repeatedly experienced in juxtaposition with secure attachment in the present interactions.

[9] The client's own somatic experience of the inner father's release of tension indicates her empathic, vicarious participation in his (perceived) emotional state. This initial release is a natural expression of suddenly having attachment needs met that have been forever unmet, so this release may be only a transitory response and is not necessarily a marker of a transformational change. Such markers appear subsequently, however.

[10] In the face of greatly increased complexity of learned implicit material, the therapist works with persistence to guide the same process for the inner mother as for the inner father; that is, *Steps B, C, 1, 2 and 3.*

[11] The inner father's previous problematic emotional reaction of fearful withdrawal is no longer occurring in a situation where formerly it would have done so. That is a marker of a transformational change and is therefore a unit of verification that the therapeutic reconsolidation process has been carried out successfully (*Step V*).

[12] This similarly indicates additional markers of transformational change (*Step V*).

[13] This is the most important marker of transformational change: The client's behavioral and emotional freedom from the presenting symptoms in actual situations that previously would have evoked them— *Step V* in full form.

Table 6.2   Identified sequence of steps of the therapeutic reconsolidation
process in case examples from five psychotherapies of deep, lasting change

Psychotherapy	Typical sequence of TRP steps
AEDP	C–1–2–B–3–V (A throughout)
Coherence Therapy	A–B–C–1–2–3–V
EFT	A–B–C–1–2–3–V
EMDR	A–(C)–B–1–2–3–V
IPNB	A–B–C–1–2–3–V

in Table 1.1 on page 5. It is the detection of TRP Steps 1–2–3 in these therapies
that is critical for corroborating the value of the TRP for psychotherapy integration, and our hypothesis that the experiences defined by Steps 1–2–3 are transformation-specific factors shared by therapies of deep, lasting change. In other
words, we predict that any system of psychotherapy (or series of therapy sessions)
will be found to produce deep, lasting change only if the sequence of experiences described by TRP Steps 1–2–3 takes place successfully—independently
of whether the therapist is aware of these steps taking place and irrespective of
whether they occur explicitly or tacitly.

Imagine a panel of leading practitioners of, for example, EFT, EMDR, IFS
(Internal Family Systems therapy), Self Psychology, and Coherence Therapy
discussing how their diverse therapeutic approaches carry out the component
steps of the therapeutic reconsolidation process—which itself is not and cannot be the possession of any one therapeutic system. The panelists' use of the
TRP would create a shared, empirically based frame of reference and a shared
vocabulary, allowing these practitioners to discuss their methods in a manner
meaningful to each other and to practitioners of yet other clinical systems. That
scenario, in concrete terms, is the paradigm of psychotherapy integration we
envision through the TRP. Such use of the therapeutic reconsolidation process
can potentially provide the fields of psychotherapy practice and research with a
universal language and unifying framework through which seemingly dissimilar
approaches to transformational change can be compared meaningfully, revealing their metapsychological and methodological common ground. Indeed, any
authentic formulation of the brain's rules for transformational change of implicit
emotional learnings must necessarily have the kinds of integrative utility that we
have described here. (Of course, the psychotherapy field consists of at least *two*
universes, that of therapies of *transformational* change and that of therapies of
counteractive change, as discussed in Chapter 2 and in this chapter's first section. Readers interested in a candidate framework for integrating counteractive
therapies, based on the neuroscience of emotional regulation, may wish to consult Toomey and Ecker, 2009.)

Common Factors, Specific Factors, and Psychotherapy Process Research

Proposing that the steps of the therapeutic reconsolidation process can meaningfully be regarded as transformation-specific factors raises the question: What is the relationship of these newly proposed factors to the well-known non-specific common factors and to "common factors theory"? That prevalent view posits, on the basis of over 75 years of psychotherapy outcome studies, that the beneficial changes resulting from psychotherapy are due almost entirely to the qualities of the client and the client–therapist relationship, and are due very little (about 15 percent) to *specific* factors, namely the particular methods, processes, or theories brought to bear by the therapist (as described, for example, by Duncan, Miller, Wampold, & Hubble, 2009; Wampold, 2001). In this section we offer, in a heuristic spirit, an indication of what we believe the TRP, regarded as a set of transformation-specific factors, means for common factors theory, along with mention of therapy process research supporting these possibilities.

There is an observation that occurs regularly in the course of conducting Coherence Therapy that is intriguing and potentially significant regarding specific factors: After a client's symptom-generating emotional schema has been retrieved into direct awareness, but prior to any attempt at guiding a disconfirming juxtaposition experience, the pro-symptom schema continues to maintain its compelling quality and grip from session to session, as it did for Richard in Chapter 3, Ted in Chapter 4 and Regina in Chapter 5. Bringing the schema from implicit memory into explicit emotional experience is found, in itself, not to diminish or dispel it necessarily, even though the therapist skillfully supplies empathy, emotional safety, a good working alliance, and the other non-specific common factors for any number of sessions. Only when contradictory knowledge has finally been found and the therapist guides a juxtaposition experience successfully—and thereby carries out the transformation sequence, Steps 1–2–3— does the pro-symptom schema dissolve, often abruptly and decisively, as we have seen. Then the client reports that subsequently the associated symptoms ceased to occur. (In cases where a schema loses emotional potency very soon after retrieval, with no further in-session process work, it is found that a juxtaposition experience occurred due to the action of the brain's mismatch detector, as described in the case of Charlotte in Chapter 4.)

In addition to those observations, Chapter 5 demonstrated that the client–therapist relationship can play a wide range of roles in the process of change, even in attachment work: The qualities of that relationship—which are non-specific common factors—may play a merely catalytic role, making possible the necessary experiential work in key areas that are themselves unrelated to empathy or attachment; or in some cases the therapist's empathy *in addition* is itself the very substance of a new learning experience that disconfirms and dissolves the original, problematic learnings.

Taken all together, these clinical observations suggest that, while the non-specific common factors are generally necessary as a catalyst for the overall therapeutic reconsolidation process—and *can* play a critical role at the core of that process—they seem not to be inherently capable of dissolving an emotional schema in and of themselves, apart from the therapeutic reconsolidation process. What appears fundamentally necessary and indispensable for transformational change of an existing, acquired response, according to the brain's own requirements, is the transformation sequence in the TRP. In other words, the transformation sequence may possess a significant level of what clinical outcome researchers term a "specific treatment effect," meaning a symptom-dispelling effect that is *not* due mainly to client–therapist relationship factors but rather to a specific procedure (Steps 1–2–3) recruiting a well-defined mechanism of change, namely memory re-encoding via reconsolidation. (For further discussion of common factors theory in light of memory erasure via reconsolidation, see Ecker & Toomey, 2008.)

Common factors theory generalizes from the history of efficacy measurements and maintains that no particular procedure and mechanism of change can have a truly significant level of specific treatment effect. This view has come to be so widely accepted by therapists and researchers that our suggestion that the transformation sequence could have a significant specific treatment effect may seem to some to be a heretical departure from what is assumed to be the established fact of the matter. We suggest, nevertheless, based on our extensive clinical observations combined with rigorous studies of the transformation sequence by neuroscientists, that the series of experiences that we refer to as the transformation sequence warrants serious consideration as a possible breakthrough in this longstanding status quo.

Some critics of non-specific common factors theory have maintained that the theory emerged as an artifact of the particular prevailing form of psychotherapy outcome research, the randomized controlled trial, or RCT. In RCTs, the outcomes of large groups of individual therapy cases are compared statistically. The "outliers," or individual cases in which exceptionally effective, transformational change occurred, are buried in the statistical averages in RCTs and are not closely studied to identify the specific factors or ingredients associated with such results.

However, specific ingredients *are* identified in psychotherapy process research studies that examine individual cases. Numerous process studies indicate the existence of specific factors that correlate strongly with an outcome of decisive, lasting change, in contrast with the central prediction of common factors theory. For example, McCarthy (2009) found that specific factors, but not common factors, predicted outcome in studies of behavioral and psychodynamic therapy, and that the best outcomes in psychodynamic therapy were correlated with the specific factor of using process-experiential methods to facilitate emotional experiences that clients were suppressing and avoiding. In studies of both individual and group therapy, Oei and Shuttlewood (1996, 1997) found that specific processes were more strongly correlated with symptom reduction than were common factors. A meta-analysis by Weinberger (1995) found that one of the most widely emphasized common factors, the therapeutic alliance, accounted for only 11 percent of the variance in therapy outcomes, whereas 40 percent of variance was due to the specific factor of guiding clients to face what they had been avoiding.

The facilitation of richly emotional experience previously blocked, combined with conscious reflection on the emotional meanings that have emerged through this experience, appears to be a particularly important specific factor for successful therapeutic change. (Guiding attention to bring awareness to what has not been in awareness is a specific process that is not inherent in the non-specific common factors.) Many studies have demonstrated this factor's therapeutic effects (e.g., Baikie & Wilhelm, 2005; Elliott, Greenberg, & Lietaer, 2003; Gendlin, 1966; Greenberg, Warwar & Malcolm, 2008; Missirlian, Toukmanian, Warwar, & Greenberg, 2005; Pennebaker, 1997). This factor is centrally built into the TRP in the requirement for experiential retrieval of emotional learnings from implicit memory into explicit experience (Step B) and reactivation of that experience to start the transformation sequence (Step 1). The TRP would fit naturally within an "empirically supported principles of change" (ESPs) system (Rosen & Davidson, 2003).

Conclusion: Unlocking the Emotional Brain

Guiding our way through Part 1 of this book has been the central understanding, derived from both clinical experience and laboratory studies of the brain and behavior, that we humans are deeply coherent, adaptive beings—so much so that our coherence extends far beyond our perpetual striving for well-knit conscious narratives, deep down into our unconscious worlds of emotional learning. This understanding is the foundation of our broad paradigm, the Emotional Coherence Framework, and it challenges us as clinicians to move beyond our field's conventional view of symptoms as maladaptive or irrational disorders and pathologies—and instead to perceive and honor the coherent knowingness and complexly adaptive responsiveness that permeate the mind, no less in its nonconscious activities than in its conscious ones. Within this expanded view of our nature, the therapeutic reconsolidation process describes how new experience can interact with the depths of our implicit, coherent learnings to allow us to unlearn them. Whether implemented in one set of concrete methods or another, the TRP appears to be an invaluable key that unlocks the emotional brain and opens up a new level of effectiveness and satisfaction in the practice of psychotherapy.

We invite our readers to sample, in Part 2, some wonderful coherence-focused TRP work carried out by colleagues who, over the course of studying and practicing this approach for several years, have developed their own styles of using this therapeutic key.

PART 2

COHERENCE-FOCUSED THERAPY IN PRACTICE

7

A Father's Tormenting Guilt: Deep Resolution in Seven Coherence-Focused Sessions

Paul Sibson[1]

On first meeting "John"—a brown-haired, 40-year-old man of powerful, stocky build—I was struck immediately by his highly tense physical presence. In our initial discussions he was rigid in his seat, repeatedly pulled his clothes away from his sweating body, and personified a man in deep conflict with himself.

Session 1

John described a cluster of symptoms that centred upon deeply punishing feelings of guilt regarding his daughter's loss of a leg following meningitis seven years earlier. Internal blood clots caused by the meningitis had cut off the blood supply to one of her legs, causing the portion beneath the knee to necrose and require amputation. John blamed solely himself for not spotting the signs of this notoriously difficult-to-recognize condition. His additional symptoms included feelings of depression, sleeplessness, and outbursts of aggression towards his wife, son, work colleagues, and friends when they tried to talk to him—outbursts that had progressively isolated John from them all. "I just don't want to talk to them," he said. John had also curtailed his usual sociable sporting activities of running and golf.

---

1 Paul Sibson, Dip-Counselling, Dip-Psychotherapy, is in practice in Sunderland, UK and is a Licensed Psychotherapist under the British Association for Counseling & Psychotherapy (BACP) and the UK Council for Psychotherapy (UKCP).

We agreed that the initial focus of our work would be John's pervasive experiencing of guilt.

Session 2

With John having described so vividly his guilt-driven behaviours, moods, and thoughts, early in our second session I opted to use the discovery technique of symptom deprivation: I guided John to "try on" imaginally the state of being without his guilt and resuming his curtailed sporting, social, and work life. He immediately began to contact a potent pro-symptom position, which he expressed forcefully with the words, "My daughter's life stopped, so now mine has to!" In actual fact, his daughter's life had moved on very fully some years earlier.

Further discovery work focusing upon this felt imperative revealed that, in John's mind, if others saw him as moving on with his life they would judge him even more viciously and punitively than he already believed they were doing, and he himself would agree with their judgements of him: "a waste of space," "beneath contempt," "the worst thing a father can be," "a total disgrace." Subsequently I requested that John picture the people he felt these judgements would most come from—predominantly his work colleagues and family—and that he experiment with voicing to them an overt statement of his emotional truth: "I agree with you all. I am to blame for what happened to Ann, and I deserve never to move on with my own life." John reported that this felt true and that in his imagination they all were in agreement about his culpability and responded with silent nods.

I intended for this overt statement of John's position to begin to integrate these implicit meanings and purposes into his conscious attentional field. I now recognized the ferocity of his self-blame and understood that the idea of moving on in any way served only to heighten his feelings of self-loathing. At the end of the session I wrote two sentences on an index card to help John stay in touch between sessions with what we had brought into awareness, his own purpose for staying in tortured self-blame:

> Though my guilt over Ann is a daily torture, to stop blaming myself would be even worse. It would be "beneath contempt" to carry on with my life after the mistake I've made and would make me "a total disgrace."

I suggested that John read the card daily, and our session came to a close.

Session 3

This session opened with John reporting that he'd read the index card daily and that it continued to feel true in its description of his impossible predicament. He went on to explain that the card had reminded him that throughout his life he had hardly made mistakes and had always taken immense pride in all he did, and that he was something of a perfectionist. In fact, integrating the emotional truth on his index card had made him newly aware of other facets of the phenomenology he was now describing. He related vividly the importance he attached to being well-groomed, punctual, meticulous in his working life, and generally correct and orderly throughout his life.

I went on to inquire how it was, then, for him to be around people, feeling that he had made such a huge mistake. He said that it was deeply uncomfortable and that he wanted never ever to make another mistake. He added, "If I could make one that big, then what's next?"

Sensing this palpable fear of making another mistake, I invited John to imagine the specific kind of mistake that he feared most. He immediately described his recurrent fears of leaving an important and confidential file out of its locked cabinet at work and remembering it only after arriving home from work. As a symptom deprivation, I guided him into imagining this scene in full detail—the file still on his desk and his being at home, knowing he had forgotten to put away the file. He reported a deep anxiety and an overwhelming urge to return to work immediately "to cover my mistake before anybody finds out." Imagining the mistake being corrected without anyone knowing what had happened, John relaxed visibly.

Subsequently I invited him into a further step of this discovery work, through again imagining that the mistake at work had been made, but this time it had come into the full view of his work colleagues before he could do anything about it. Someone arrived before he did on the next morning, saw that the file was missing from its place in the cabinet, and then found it on John's desk in his "Out" basket. Other colleagues were told of John's mistake and word spread. I encouraged John to imagine their faces as he arrived at work the next day, knowing they were aware of his mistake.

His face tightened into a pained grimace, his head bowed, and he blushed intensely, commenting how uncomfortable it was even to imagine this situation. John reported feeling that people were laughing at him and that he felt "humiliated and inadequate." As a next step of discovery, I then asked if he felt any connection between his angrily cutting himself off from people—moving now into his world of guilt—and his fear of being seen by them to be making another mistake. The connection immediately resonated with him, as indicated by a categorical "yes" and a nod of the head. A further overt statement, spoken to his visualized work colleagues and family, confirmed and integrated the truth of this new-found pro-symptom position: "Feeling guilty, cut off, and angry is better than risking your seeing me make another mistake. You'd see me as totally inadequate then, and that's just too humiliating."

Sensing that the word "inadequate" had a special relevance, I sought John's personal, idiosyncratic meaning of that term, as is standard practice in Coherence Therapy. This brought his perfectionism into clearer focus: for him, "inadequate" meant not being 100 percent in control of a situation, not being able to protect his daughter regardless of any circumstantial factors.

A between-session index card simply verbalized John's newly discovered pro-symptom position, so that he could stay in touch with it during the week. It read:

> I'm worthless if I make mistakes, and all of you have already seen me make an unforgivable one. If you see me make yet another mistake, you'll see me as totally inadequate. I can't risk that! With my anger I've got to keep all of you away from me forever, so you'll never see me make another mistake.

John confirmed that this verbalization fit and felt true to him. He was now in touch with this particular purpose and his own agency in maintaining his anger and isolation—the minimum level of depth of retrieval needed as a prelude for change to occur in Coherence Therapy.

Writing in hindsight about these sessions with John, I can see that his constructs were generating feelings of shame in addition to guilt, creating a complex emotional brew that John labeled with the single word "guilt." It may or may not have proved possible or useful for John to tease those emotions apart, had we tried to do so. However, in carrying out Coherence Therapy, the particular words used by a client to name an emotion are less important than guiding the client to *feel* the emotion and then go beneath it to become aware of the unique personal constructs or meanings that are its very basis. At the end of Session 3, I felt that we had made good progress of that kind. The constructs at the root of his guilt, his shame, and his anger were becoming clearly apparent to him.

Session 4

John began this session reporting that he had felt less punished by his guilt over the course of the week, though the blaming internal voice was still there. He also said that he had experienced less of his fearful angriness when around his work colleagues and family. He was palpably less tense. These changes, coming in response to living with the card from Session 3, were an indication that the card had successfully forwarded John's integration of the emotional truths it put into words.

John's fearful expectation of the judgement of total inadequacy was now what I was regarding as his "symptom." I again guided his attention into his felt sense of being inadequate. When I requested that he recall a particular circumstance in which he had felt enormously inadequate, he described first an image of his daughter as a beautiful toddler, and then how that image compared to an image of her after her leg amputation. The contrast painfully highlighted John's feeling of inadequacy, especially that he "couldn't stop it happening." While he remained fully immersed in this painful sense of being inadequate, I invited him to complete the sentence: "If I accept fully that I couldn't stop what happened to Ann, then …"

His initial endings were overtly positive: "I wouldn't be to blame" and "I could move on with my life again." I therefore persisted, and his third and fourth endings were "I couldn't do anything" and "I'd feel helpless at how unfair it all is." I guided John's attention more fully toward these meanings by asking, "And how is it to acknowledge fully that there is nothing you could have done to prevent what happened to Ann?" John's eyes glazed with tears of grief, saying that Ann was his daughter and that it was so unfair. In an attempt to guide John more deeply into his experiencing of authentic grief, I invited him to visualize Ann and make an overt statement of his newly discovered emotional truth directly to her: "I was helpless to prevent what happened to you, Ann." Instantly he resisted moving further into his grief and moved back into the position that there must have been something he could have done to prevent what happened, and that in some way he was to blame.

For a highly competitive, perfectionist man—one who prided himself on not making mistakes and on being in total control—blaming himself and regarding himself as inadequate was a suffering that unconsciously was preferable to the suffering that would come with *not* blaming himself: knowing that life doesn't allow control over what happens to loved ones. His self-blame preserved his core, cherished construct that saving Ann had been *possible*. According to that construct, feeling his helplessness meant he had failed unforgivably. Though his self-blame caused misery, he stayed in it because releasing it would have brought a different and even worse suffering—the recognition of existential powerlessness, which John called "defeat." That was the coherent emotional truth of his resistance to feeling his grief more deeply, and that was what John took with him on an index card, to integrate further into his conscious awareness:

> Though blaming myself and feeling guilty and inadequate over Ann is terrible, really feeling my helplessness in the situation and the unfairness of what happened to her would be an admission of defeat, and that's just too painful. I have to keep punishing myself.

He said that the statements on the card felt true, and that this was a new feeling.

Session 5

The session began with us reviewing thoroughly the discovered, integrated, and now conscious purposes beneath John's self-imposed, guilty exile. His not accepting what had happened to Ann—and subsequently making sure he didn't appear to be moving on with his own life—prevented others from judging him even more harshly than he believed they did already. Keeping everyone at a distance curtailed the possibility that people might witness him making yet another mistake and then see him as more severely inadequate than he already felt he was. This maintained his sense of control over contingincies that felt urgent to avoid.

John reported that the first two of these integrated positions felt right but that he still just couldn't accept the idea that there was nothing he could have done. In his words, he had "been defeated."

I believed that his intense resistance to the idea that it was not possible for him to control what happened to Ann served the purpose of protecting him from fully feeling and grieving over the tragic unfairness of what happened to her. Each time I guided him experientially into "trying on" the experience of not being in control over what happened, he momentarily contacted his grief, then immediately moved back into resisting that feeling.

After numerous unsuccessful attempts at discovering why it was so important for him not to feel his grief and to maintain his sense of control at whatever cost to himself, a breakthrough finally came. With John imagining himself at Ann's bedside, visualizing her after her operation, I asked him to focus on feeling his need to avoid feeling his grief, and then asked him to complete a sentence stem from within this resistance, saying, "If I let myself really feel the tragedy of what's happened to you, then ..."

Following two or three completions about how upsetting it would be, another ending came up, angrily: "you can do everything right and bad things still happen." Sensing the deep meaning of this statement for him, I guided him in staying connected for a while with the idea that "if you do everything right, bad things still happen." In exploring what this statement meant to him, he quickly began to describe a long-held conviction that was in direct conflict with that idea: "If you do everything right, bad things don't happen." This was John's fundamental model of the world, and it would be contradicted and shattered if he faced and accepted the idea that he had been helpless to prevent the loss of Ann's leg. It was now clear that protecting that world view was a key, coherent purpose of his resistance.

Through the overt statement "If you do everything right, bad things don't happen" followed by serial accessing of other, linked beliefs, John quickly came into deeper contact with this presupposition about the world, and he identified it as having come from his father. With this realization John started to remember numerous times as he was growing up, when his dad had justified harsh punishments of John's mistakes with exactly this rationale. Particularly poignant was a football incident in which John had broken his leg in a tackle. His dad responded that John must not have tackled properly for that to have happened. According to his dad, John could and should have successfully controlled everything by acting correctly.

Based on this belief, in John's mind it was actually impossible for what happened to Ann to have happened without it having been his fault. In addition, his unquestioned model of others was that they held this same view of how the world works. Our new awareness of these constructs now made total sense of John's perception of others as being so damning of him, as well as his terrible fear of making another mistake.

In what seemed a rather sudden and surprising shift, both John and I now found ourselves consciously face to face with a totally coherent set of constructs that inevitably produced John's experienced symptoms of punishing guilt and angry withdrawal. Sitting there in touch with his newly conscious model of the world—"If you do everything right, bad things don't happen"—he seemed a little disoriented, which I took as a marker of successful accessing of constructs that were quite foreign to his conscious world. I could see that he was experiencing his newly conscious model alongside other more familiar, conscious knowledge that contradicted it. A juxtaposition experience was occurring immediately, at least to some degree, because of the mismatch.

In order to facilitate and further deepen this juxtaposition, I crafted a sentence stem for John to take with him on an index card:

If you do things right but bad things still happen then ...

My aim was to elicit further constructs that would juxtapose consciously with his newly discovered emotional truth about having control, which was written on the other side of the card:

If you do things right, bad things don't happen.

That was clearly a core, master construct in John's world. A change in that kind of construct tends to yield many lasting shifts in mood, thoughts, behaviour, posture, and energy. Being a definition or model of how some aspect of the world works, it is a fourth-order or deepest-lying construct in Coherence Therapy's map of interior depth (Ecker & Hulley, 2000b, 2011).

Session 6

"It's a tragedy but it wasn't my fault, was it, Paul?" With that rhetorical question, John began our sixth session. His utterance indicated a major shift. Through an empathic shake of my head, I wordlessly validated the truth of what he had said. John began to cry deep tears of grief. He subsequently reported having cried often during the week, though in private, both over the sheer unfairness and tragedy of what had happened to Ann and from the deep relief of knowing, finally, that it wasn't his fault. He had punished himself for seven years.

John reported that after our previous session he had driven to the nearby seaside and read the two-sided card over and over again. During this rereading, he said, he had thought of examples throughout history where everything had been done correctly but bad things had still happened. He cited runners who trained as well as they could for the Olympics but still did not win gold, golf shots hit perfectly that were blown off course by unpredictable winds, even the sinking of the *Titanic* after such careful preparation. In his mind, the juxtaposition of these undeniable, compelling examples with his deeply held, implicit belief that "if you do things right, bad things don't happen" served to disconfirm and dissolve that core construct and its implications. And with this shift, finally John's deep sadness over what had happened to his beautiful daughter was allowed to be felt, and his self-inflicted guilt could dissolve along with the construct that had required it.

John was now visibly more relaxed than I had ever seen him before, and he looked as if he had lost the bodily tension of a man perpetually holding onto something—his ungrieved grief. He described feeling lighter than he could remember ever feeling and said that much of his usual energy had returned. He also commented on having had "a good cry" over how hard his dad had been on him at times. *This* long-held grief, too, seemed to be releasing through our work.

With some difficulty, he described an emerging awareness of feeling more vulnerable to fate than he ever had before, feeling less in control. In addition, he described a growing sense of how awful it must have been for others, over the last few years, to be around him in his snappy, angry state.

Session 7

Within moments of beginning this session, John was recounting his week of activities, which he referred to as "reparative." He was relaxed, proud of the actions he had taken over the week, and smilingly surprised at his own behaviour, repeatedly commenting that the way he was behaving was "totally new to me."

The day after our previous session, John had spoken with his work colleagues and asked their honest opinions of how he had been to work with over the last few years. They said, unanimously, that he had been "terrible," and that they had long since given up trying to communicate with him. John fully accepted this from them and then apologized to them all, with a short explanation of his reasons for being the way he had been—blaming himself for his daughter's fate and feeling similarly judged by everyone else—and requested a fresh start with them all. Since then, John had enjoyed again feeling part of the team at work and was visibly moved, as well as relieved, at being so accepted by his colleagues. He had been terrified by the prospect that they might reject him, but felt he must attempt to mend relationships, regardless of what response he might get.

Subsequently John had repaired, apologetically, the relationships with his old golf colleagues, and with friends and family members—most notably with his daughter Ann herself. In the first open family discussion in years, John's daughter and wife told him how difficult it had been to live with him. He said that this was very painful to hear. Ann herself had stopped visiting them, such was John's brooding angriness. When he explained his newly discovered reasons for being as he had been, both his wife and daughter were shocked. Neither of them had ever considered any of what had happened to Ann to have been John's fault at all, and they told him so.

That was yet another powerful juxtaposition disconfirming John's previous self-blaming, guilt-ridden position. He described his work, as well as his social and family life, as subsequently "getting back to what it all was" in many ways. He also described what he felt was a permanent change in his way of dealing with his feelings—a much greater tendency to share with his wife and family how he felt, rather than to cut off from them and go it alone—and how this seemed to ease the initial vulnerability he had been experiencing in his new position.

Upon revisiting our initial work contract and our description of how we would know if our sessions had been effective, John and I agreed that the piece of work we had set out to do had come to effective completion. A brief communication with him eight weeks later confirmed that this remained the case. Seven years of tormenting guilt had come to an end in seven sessions.

8

Up on Top from Down Below: Cessation of Compulsive Drinking Using Coherence Therapy

C. Anthony Martignetti[1]

Norma, the secretary in the outpatient unit of our suburban psychiatric hospital, prided herself on her ability to diagnose patients at a glance. She heralded the arrival of "Cliff" on the intercom to my office: "Your next appointment is here. He's cute and really nervous, which makes him even cuter as far as I'm concerned." A tall, fit, casually well-dressed man, Cliff did seem tense, a bit shy, uncomfortable, and self-conscious as he entered my office. I caught Norma's eye from over his shoulder. She winked at me and, characteristically, whispered too loudly, "Cute, cute, cute." Sometimes getting the patients past Norma was a bit like running a gauntlet in which victims were pelted with untimely opinions instead of rocks.

Cliff, a 42-year-old married father of two girls (age seven and nine), wanted treatment, he said, because he had "a problem with alcohol." After undergoing the initial medical assessment, including having blood drawn to screen his liver functions, he was entered into the program by one of our psychiatric nurse practitioners. We typically used a combination of medication to block cravings and cognitive-behavioral techniques in a highly structured protocol to help reduce or discontinue drinking. Although my responsibility to the clinic, as Senior Clinician for the outpatient department, consisted only of managing a treatment formula and monitoring Cliff's alcohol use week to week, my interest was more in helping him discover the meaning and coherent emotional logic of his overuse of alcohol.

1 C. Anthony Martignetti, PhD, is in practice in Lexington, Massachusetts. He is a Licensed Mental Health Counselor, a Certified Diplomate of the American Psychological Association, and a Doctoral Addictions Clinician of the National Board of Addiction Examiners.

He described himself as a "stay-at-home dad" who had opted not to work outside the home, despite a good career and earnings of his own, because his wife, a senior partner in a large East Coast law firm, had a salary more than five times his. "It seemed a better plan," he stated flatly, that he should fulfill the primary home and childcare responsibilities rather than hiring outside help.

I asked Cliff to describe a typical day. After getting the girls up, fed, and off to school, he said, he did a number of household chores, such as laundry, vacuuming, emptying the dishwasher, and making the beds. Sometimes he did yard work or repaired the family vehicles. He'd pick up the dry-cleaning, take the ancient cat to the vet when needed, attend to the various requirements of their four other pets, shop for household needs, and buy groceries for dinner. By the time he got to the supermarket, he would feel pressure building that he might not get everything done before he could start drinking. It had become routine for him to buy bottles of whiskey at the liquor store adjacent to the market. Once he had them in the trunk, he could think calmly about picking up the kids after school and spending time with them for a while as they ate their snacks. He could even enjoy helping them get started with their homework because he knew that by five o'clock, about an hour before his wife returned from work to take over the evening schedule, it would be time to drink. I began to think of this as his "second shift."

Cliff's drinking pattern included 10 to 12 shots daily, averaging about seventy-five drinks each week. Three years earlier, he had been prescribed an antidepressant as a treatment for both anxiety and depression by a psychiatrist whom he visited every eight weeks for medication monitoring. He reported that despite a number of attempts over the years to control his alcohol use—including idiosyncratic self-fashioned attempts, abstinence support programs, and psychiatric and psychotherapeutic interventions—he had not been successful in stopping or reducing his drinking.

As our conversation shifted to Cliff's understanding of his alcohol use, he pointed out that he often found himself unable to attend social events with his wife because of a debilitating anxiety. She was a board member of a local museum, a member of fund-raising groups for the public school system, and an active church member who was required to attend benefits, dinners, and church events and services. Cliff felt unable to attend most of these events. This was distressing to his wife, but Cliff said she was very supportive, understanding, and "always trying to help" him. He came across as resigned to powerlessness while telling his story, but not at all depressed or anxious. He was more matter-of-fact, as if simply reporting the details of a life and circumstances he was bound to continue living. I noticed this and asked him how he felt about his situation and he replied, "It's just the way things are. I can't change my life."

After the first week of taking the medication prescribed by the clinic, measuring and recording his drinks, and agreeing to adhere to the other protocol components, Cliff reported that he found no difference in his alcohol use.

During this second meeting Cliff revealed to me that, in fact, he had not followed the instructions as given and said that these had not been made clear to him by the prescribing nurse practitioner. That may have been true, but I thought it unlikely. I carefully explained the timing and dosages of the medication and made sure he had all the program literature to refer to if he had any questions. Cliff went off to try his luck with the method for another week. Upon his return, the story of his drinking was unchanged. Again he revealed that he had taken some creative license with the prescribed method and that, although he had adhered more closely to the protocol, his drinking pattern remained uninfluenced. His attitude seemed in line with the powerlessness I noticed in our first meeting. It was as if he were saying, "See, I told you. It's no use. I can't change." I did not know, and could not have anticipated at this time, that "I can't change" was actually "I *mustn't* change."

As I pondered Cliff's situation, I wondered what the coherence of his drinking might be—its meaningfulness and its unrecognized, necessitating logic. I needed to get to know and accept, "make friends" with the realities in Cliff's emotional world, in the hope that something in that hidden world would come forward enough to let me understand his behavior. I suspended our focus on the treatment protocol in the third session and attempted, instead, to find the hidden purpose and emotional truth of his alcohol use. I did, however, tell him it was okay to take the medication in the following week, if he wished, and to measure and record his drinks if that seemed important to him.

In order to discover the hidden meaning of a client's drinking behavior, I generally begin with methods such as symptom deprivation to investigate what would be experienced if the symptom did *not* occur.

My initial use of this approach did not prove effective in the first 15 minutes or so, however, so I tried pursuing symptom deprivation with the help of Eugene Gendlin's process of Focusing to foster awareness of a felt sense initially experienced bodily (Gendlin, 1996). My aim was to reach the out-of-awareness meaning of the presenting symptom of alcohol abuse with work that was as experiential as I knew how to make it.

The following transcription was taken from the notes I had written during the session and is accurate within those limits.

Th: Would it be okay if we try something else right now? Would you be willing?
Cl: I think so; it depends on what it is.
Th: Well, I thought that it might be useful if we—together, one more time—tried to get at some of this difficulty, and maybe even the importance of drinking in your life, as bad as it can sometimes be for you. I'd just like you to try some imagining of physical feelings.
Cl: Imagining?
Th: Yes.
Cl: Importance?

Th: Yeah, I'm thinking it's got to be important to you, no?

Cl: Yeah, okay.

Th: Yeah?

Cl: Yeah, whatever. It's fine, I'll imagine.

Th: Okay, so I'll just try to create a picture here. Get comfortable. You can even lie down on the couch if you want; just make yourself as comfortable as you're able. *[Cliff sank into the couch and stared up at the ceiling with an expression that seemed about to break into an adolescent eye-roll.]* Okay, there you are at home, before your wife Melissa gets in, and the girls are there and all the stuff of the day is around you. Melissa is going to come home soon, all happy and helpful and hard-working, and this is the time when you start to pour down some bourbon, knowing that you'll still be able to look after the girls for a little while and be okay until she gets home to take over, right?

Cl: Right. *[Not seeming enthusiastic about this experiment]*

Th: Okay then, right there, right then and there, try to imagine what you would feel, in the middle of your body, somewhere in there, if you didn't have a drink. There it all is, you're perfectly ready for the drink, the cold, crystal glass filled with square rocks, just the way you like them, and the bottle of bourbon, just opened and ready to pour, and you don't even go there. No bourbon. The stage is perfectly set for it, but no bourbon. What would you feel in your body?

Cl: Oh, well, I've done that before.

Th: Okay, yes, of course. I didn't mean to imply you hadn't. I guess what I'd like you to try this time, just for the exercise we're doing ... I want you to imagine it's a drinking day. A day where you fully expect to drink and it's all set and you're all ready to go, but you don't. Sort of take it away, the bourbon, the whiskey, at a time when you expect to have it.

Cl: Oh, okay ... *[A minute elapsed.]* What was the question again?

Th: Ahh, in that moment of not having the drink you fully expected to have, what feeling comes up somewhere in the middle of your body? What physical sensation do you get?

Cl: *[Another minute elapsed and Cliff sank deeper into the couch.]* Well, I think I'd feel a burn in the middle of my chest and stomach.

Th: Okay, and the burn ... can you say a little more about it, and describe it, so I can get a good close sense of what it's like for you?

Cl: It's like a knot.

Th: Okay, a knot, yeah. And I assume the temperature but you tell me.

Cl: Yeah, it's hot, it's the burn, it's a hot knot.

Th: Hot knot. What would be ... maybe it's a weird question, but what's the color of it, if you imagine it has a color?

Cl: Definitely red, it's red-hot and tight.

Th: Okay, tight, hot, sounds intense, so, okay, let's go even one step further and imagine if this red hot tight knot, right there in the middle of your chest and stomach, if that knot could say something—I know it's an unusual question—but if it had something it wanted to say to you, the red-hot tight knot, what in the world would it say?

Cl: Say? Yeah, it *is* weird. *[There was a long pause.]*

Th: Yeah, as if the thing had a life of its own and it had a message for you, maybe an important one. What's the message?

Cl: *[With some renewed enthusiasm]* It would say, it would scream, "Run, avoid this. Don't talk to Melissa. 'Cause I can't tell her anything."

Th: Run, don't tell, don't say. Yeah, wow, what else, anything more?

Cl: No, just, "Don't say anything."

Th: Yeah, don't say anything.

Cl: *[Silence]*

Th: What's it like, that voice? What's it ...

Cl: It's smart; it knows what to do. *[This was one of the best descriptions I had ever heard of what is referred to in Coherence Therapy as implicit or unconscious "knowings."]*

Th: It's a smart one. It's so "don't say anything" smart. Don't say anything even if there's a lot to say?

Cl: I guess.

Th: Okay, so just keep imagining, what if you were to say something back to that voice that says, "Don't say anything, don't tell"? I know it takes some doing, but give it a try. You're answering it back. It said something to you and you have a response.

Cl: *[Contorted a bit in trying]* I'd say, "Okay, I'll do just what you say."

Th: Just do it exactly.

Cl: Yup.

Th: Just go ahead and don't talk.

Cl: Yup.

Th: 'Cause it's smart. It knows what's up.

Cl: Yup. You have a funny way of talking, ya know that?

Th: Haha. I've heard that. I think I get on a train of thought and I ... is it a bother?

Cl: No, I just have been noticing, you say things in a funny pace or ... I don't know; it's actually just fine.

Th: Okay ... the train just got a little derailed there. Let me ask you ... Does that sound familiar? Just not talking, not saying anything?

Cl: *[Contemplating for a few moments]* Yes. *[Delivered in a more serious and involved way than previously]*

Th: For sure, it seems like. What's familiar about it?

Cl: *[Banging it right out]* It's the way I was with my mother. I didn't talk to her.

Th: Oh, okay, like with your mother.

Cl: *[Launching into more animated speech, he sat up straight on the couch.]* Yeah, I was this total loser kid! I've always been really insecure. In school I was so unhappy, and even now I don't feel good-looking or in good enough shape and I think my penis is too small and my nose is too big. I've always thought that. I've always hated myself! When I was a kid I was a flop with girls and I couldn't make friends with the cool "in" kids.

Th: Man, sounds lousy, a real bust.

Cl: A complete bust. There was this guy Brian—he was a great athlete, had tons of friends, girls were nuts about him. I wanted to be like him. He was a winner, I was a loser. I hated who I was.

Th: Yeah, you felt like a loser, compared to him especially. And your mother … you were saying?

Cl: She would sit with me—it was like sixth grade—on the couch, she sat with me, and tried to get me to talk after school because I was always so grim and morose and bummed out, but I wouldn't. I never said a word about how or why I was feeling the way I was. I just shut up about it.

Th: Yeah, no talking. So, what might have happened … if you had talked with her?

Cl: Nothing. She would have been relieved. She used to say, "Honey, I can't help you if you don't talk to me."

Th: She would have been relieved if you talked, but you wouldn't talk. Even if you had lots to say, no matter. You just didn't say it.

Cl: Right. There you go again.

Th: There I go?

Cl: No problem.

Th: So, then, what would have happened if you had talked and given her some relief, if you had done what she wanted?

Cl: *[Silent and contemplating]* Then she would have won.

With these unexpected words, I realized I was hearing the first stirrings of some of the emotional logic underlying and necessitating the symptom. I didn't yet understand the connection between not talking and abusive drinking but now I knew that remaining verbally locked, unchanged and unchangeable, unreachable, was a position of safety, power, and autonomy for him.

Th: Oh, she would have won. You mean like a standoff to see who gives up first?

Cl: Yeah.

Th: So, how did it feel not to talk?

Cl: It felt great. I was like in control of her. I would just sulk and be miserable, and by not talking, I made her miserable. It was the only real power I had.

Th: Yeah—finally you had some control and power. Even though at school you had none, at home you did.

Cl: Exactly! I might have been messed up and everything, but I was in charge on that one. I held the cards—back then on that couch.

Beneath his "messed-up" exterior—as a morose, self-hating, insecure boy—Cliff had a secret place of triumph and agency. In this place, the selfhood gained by thwarting his mother was most successfully achieved by staying "messed up" and not being the cooperative son she wanted him to be. The underground coherence of the symptom of being an "alcoholic loser" was coming more and more into view.

Th: Ha, you sure did, you got "couch control"! So I think I get it. Even if you have to be in what seems like the messed-up role—silent, depressed, and miserable—the real truth is that you have the power, at least a lot of it. You really did find a way to get some of what you needed.

Cl: Yup, I did. At least with her I did.

Th: That's pretty resourceful for a little kid.

Cl: Yeah, I don't think I really knew, but I had a sense of some value, some pleasure in it.

Th: Value and pleasure, sure.

Cl: Yeah, I enjoyed it.

Th: Yeah, no wonder. Something felt good, finally.

Cl: Yeah, finally.

Th: It's good to get to hear all this about you.

Cl: Yeah.

Th: Now here you got me thinking, I'm thinking ... and let me know how this sounds, if it sounds true to you ... I'm thinking ... and I'm speaking for you here ... speculating, doing my own imagining, since you were willing to do that a few minutes back: "As bad as it is drinking a lot, feeling panicky about having to go to Melissa's events, then not going to the benefits or dinners or meetings or church and being depressed about that, as bad as all that is, and as much trouble as it causes Melissa and me, it's still better to be this messed-up guy than to have no power in the world. Because from down here at the bottom, I'm really on top and I rule, just the way I did with Mom."

Cl: *[Cliff's face flushed, his tone changed, and he looked directly at me, talking quite seriously, surprising me.]* If you help me, I'm going to be really angry.

Th: You'll be angry if I help you.

Cl: Yeah, that's right. If you help me you'll win and be the big shot, and I'll lose and have to go along with what you create for me. Then I'd be jealous of your success and pissed off.

Cliff's pro-symptom position—the wisdom and purpose of maintaining things just as they were—was now fully and energetically engaged, checkmating any attempt on my part to end his drinking, his social anxiety and isolation, or his unhappiness. In seeking only the coherence of his symptom, we had drawn into the open his real position of vehemently opposing any change, and why that was necessary emotionally. I recognized that, for the first time since our work had begun, Cliff was in the room with me in a fully authentic way.

Th: Jealous and pissed if I help you. Okay, okay, I think I get it. If I help you, it wouldn't be like help at all, right?

Cl: Right.

Th: The deal is kind of that if you keep the depressed, anxious role going, you have the power. So I could botch up the whole plan. Even by figuring it out we could botch things, wreck them. And then, in the mix, I'd end up coming across looking like that Brian character. I'd be the golden boy. And you'd have to be angry at me.

Cl: *[There was nearly a minute of silence while he looked away.]* I guess.

I was beginning to grasp how complex this work had been all along. Even in simply understanding Cliff and the two warring sides of his symptom picture, there was the danger of undoing his sense of safety.

Th: Cliff, I wouldn't want to do that, ya know, hear what you have to say or what's going on inside unless you wanted me to. I certainly wouldn't want you to change something you weren't ready to change.

Cl: Yeah. *[Cliff appeared a bit spacey and confused for a few moments, and then he spoke again.]* I have to think about things.

Cliff came to me because of his drinking, social anxiety, and weary years of feeling stuck. These were his presented symptoms and the only ones he knew about having. What we had just discovered together was that Cliff also had a painful unpresented symptom, a wound in his sense of self: a deep disempowerment, an expectation that others will always "win" and control him unless he secretly exerts a sense of control by defeating their attempts to get him unstuck. Focusing on this and only this would take our work in a new direction.

The session ended shortly after this exchange, with Cliff remaining facially flushed and out of touch, as if he were still living, for a few moments, in those areas where his attention never went. Disorientation of this kind is witnessed commonly in clients when for the first time they become consciously immersed in pro-symptom material and their own purposeful (though formerly unconscious) agency in maintaining symptoms. "Bumping into" the realization that all along they have been trying to solve a deeper life problem brings a sobering reassessment. The symptom has suddenly shown itself to be the conscious portion of an important but unrecognized core life dilemma, not a "personal defect." Although touching that dilemma revives a deep and familiar pain, it also puts clients in contact with a more resonant sense of who they are.

I wrote position statements on two index cards for between-session homework, in order to engrave the emotional truth and unrecognized logic of aspects of his symptoms:

> I always felt so powerless—that I had nothing going for me. I had such low self-esteem. I felt inferior to the popular, successful kids, and I was a flop with girls. The only power I've ever really known was the ability I developed with my mother to sulk, be depressed, and remain silent. This tormented her, but I refused to change—as much as she wanted me to. I was the one who was really in control. It's the same with Melissa. She may make all the money, she may be more successful, but I can torment and control her with my moods. I refuse to open up, I refuse to improve—no matter what. You can't make me! I'm in control ... here!
>
> I refuse to let you help me! I'd rather have a little power and control over others, even if I have to be miserable and messed up to keep that power. I'd rather suffer low self-esteem and have alcohol problems than feel powerless.

I tried to remain faithful to what had been verbalized by Cliff, adding no meanings or interpretations of my own to what he himself had discovered. Written cards like these are essential precisely because clients' discovery of buried emotional realities often occurs in such an altered state that they can easily forget both the words and the meanings of what they themselves have said, and so the discoveries can elude integration into conscious awareness.

My writing the words and handing Cliff the cards had the effect of putting us into this together—into the conditions of his pro-symptom world. For the first time, he was exposed, yet not judged, in his lonely strategy for selfhood. For me, getting to this most vulnerable material and doing nothing to overcome, argue against, or get away from it felt like an act of very tender joining.

The next session with Cliff revealed a drinking level that was even higher than the one he had come in with on the first day. He said he had read the position statement a number of times and shared it with his wife, who agreed that it sounded true to her. It was as though he hadn't actually "said" anything to her himself but rather used the cards as an intermediary, communicating some of what he may have been feeling without giving up his position of power that involved not telling or saying anything. I wondered to myself whether his having shared the position statement with his wife meant that, on some level, he truly wanted out of his trap, his dilemma and pain.

Cliff said, "I'm treating the medication as if it were my mother. I won't let it help me." He then began to discuss the possibility of a plan that he himself would craft to use alcohol in boundaried ways. He would be neither encouraged nor discouraged by anyone else but rather would take control in any way he wished.

These developments struck me as signs of true change being under way, despite Cliff's increased drinking. I saw his insight about not taking his medication, his plan to undertake his own treatment schedule, and his revealing to Melissa the emotional realities behind his intractability as all resulting directly from fully, consciously inhabiting his pro-symptom material for the first time in his adult life.

An axiom in Coherence Therapy is that a person cannot move away from a position that he or she does not yet knowingly occupy. In order to move forward, it is necessary first to find and inhabit one's actual psychological position. Only when "standing in that position" is it possible to step away from it or—in other words—to "change." Cliff couldn't act on his conscious position of "I want to stop drinking" because this position was completely at odds with his deeper, protective strategy for selfhood—a strategy that required him to continue drinking and remain "messed up" and unchanged.

During Cliff's process of finding his own way, much happened between us and a lot changed for him. I often wondered if Cliff was testing me to see if, by increasing his alcohol intake, he could entice me to his mother's side in the tug-of-war, trying to "help" him, "improve" him, get him not to be so "messed up." As much as possible, however, I attempted to maintain a neutral, non-interpretive, "non-helping," powerless stance, paying no mind to the burst of drinking in excess of 20 percent more alcohol than his presenting baseline.

Following our initial "bumping into" the long-unrecognized logic of Cliff's means of feeling some control and ruling his world passively from his emotional depths, the therapy process was characterized by a slow and cautious upward trek together. I had come to embrace fully the discovery that Cliff's real problem was not his drinking but rather a struggle to maintain control over his own existence. In this sense, drinking, avoiding social contact, being mired in negative routines—all of his presented symptoms—were actually Cliff's *solutions* to the *problem* of his sense of essential powerlessness. Being able to tease apart the two-layered structure of his symptom—the seemingly destructive, dysfunctional surface and its self-affirming underlying purpose—enabled me to maintain a non-counteractive stance with regard to his persistent symptoms. Now that I understood what was at stake, it was easier to keep myself from doing things that would actually oppose his deeper attempts at selfhood, which is what counteractive, anti-drinking interventions would have done.

Still, I often felt as if I were on a tightrope with Cliff or, more accurately, a trapeze, swinging between the two landing platforms of actually helping him on one hand and trying not to get seduced into the "help/don't help" tug-of-war on the other. How could I help him but avoid having him "lose"? During the months we worked together he sometimes interpreted the things I said to him and the questions I asked in sessions as my "trying too hard." On other occasions, when he spoke of overdrinking or avoiding social events with his wife, he viewed my silence as "not caring" about what he was enduring. I found it difficult to know what to do and how to be.

A few times I told him of my difficulties and my desire to find a way to connect with him, and he'd often reply with some variation of, "Hey, I'm not the doctor. Don't ask me." I'd attempt, on those occasions, to point out that there were two of us in the room, and that I needed some help from him to learn how best to interact with him. I think he liked the idea of *my* needing *his* help, but he was usually reluctant to offer it.

And there were times when I did inadvertently accept his invitation to take part in the "help me/don't help me" arm-wrestling match he was so practiced in performing. Of course I knew that the moment I locked hands with him, he'd slam the back of his own hand down onto the table and, though I landed on top of him, he would "win" from below, as my victim, empowered and showing his triumph in the following week by increasing his drinking. And even though I knew this, I couldn't stop myself, sometimes, from being "helpful." Cliff would accuse me again of "trying too hard." In reaction, I would occasionally remain silent and feel rigid, just listening while he informed me of his "failures" of that week, and I'd sometimes feel secretly as if I had failed as well. He was still overdrinking, unable to socialize, and being lax with the treatment protocol he was supposed to be following.

My attention occasionally wandered to the wind in the tall bamboo thicket outside the office windows and to other places outside the present moment with Cliff. At other times I remembered those Chinese straw "handcuffs" we placed on our fingers as children; the harder we tried to pull them off, the tighter they became. Often I was living in my head, attending not to Cliff but to endless skull-chatter. I often deliberated about what was right and wrong to say or do in the present moment with him, and in doing so I sometimes missed the present moment.

Cliff began to use humor from time to time, particularly about the way I sometimes asked questions or pursued information, which he thought was "weird." That had been our first point of play and now it felt as though a relationship was developing around it.

I have to admit that I felt twisted up by this man a number of times. The outpatient nurse manager wanted him out of the program because he wasn't following orders. She asked me more than once why I was allowing him to remain while he was "running his own show." My answers were never really clear and were generally unsatisfying to her. She was a consummate bureaucrat and had plenty of good company on staff. I had the feeling, though, that I should continue with Cliff and that a lot more could be gained through patience, steady presence, and empathy for his real dilemma than through medication, cognitive behavioral methods, or encouraging him to "follow orders." I was pursuing my genuine interest in him rather than following the protocol.

I frequently felt as though he were practicing emotional ju-jitsu at the level of a Grand Master, while I was a sheer white-belt in this special martial art form. The Zen notion of "fighting without fighting" became a way of staying non-counteractive. It was my guideline and I'd go with the flow as well as I could. I think he respected at least my willingness to try to understand how to be with him, and maybe that's why he stuck with me.

His sticking around led to us eventually finding a kind of benign standing before one another, neither running nor fighting. We had an expression we came up with to characterize how we learned to be together, and we used it meaningfully, frequently, and humorously. It was, "Hey, I'm right here." This meant that we were present, with no need to take off and hide, no need to struggle or persuade—just here. At one point, shortly before we terminated treatment, I asked him how he'd been feeling inside and whether he had changed. He said that he had. I asked him about the difference as he experienced it and he said something that felt both ordinary and profound: "I used to be angry, scared and insecure as hell, and now I'm just the guy who's right here, right now, talking to you, and that feels like a lot and enough." At that point I felt that he'd maintained his power, but that he had taken it from the cellar and brought it into the world and into a real relationship. He could be in the presence of another person and not have to sacrifice his well-being in order to have autonomy of self.

I would say that, over the long course of our work together, my ability to remain with Cliff in an accepting, non-counteracting way served to provide him with many instances of a juxtaposition experience at the exact moments he was consciously in touch with his overriding need not to conform to anyone else's requirements. My understanding of his selfhood wound kept me from being distracted by his drinking, his moods, and his other strategies for drawing me into struggling against him, and kept me focused only on accompanying him, only on witnessing, only on accepting the hidden truth of his symptoms. My way of being with him stood in stark contrast to all the counteractive, mother-replicating attempts at "help," "control," and "improvement" that he had experienced throughout his life. Over time he was able to disconfirm and transform his conviction that the only way to maintain power was to wield it from a position of enfeeblement and withdrawal.

In our process of getting to know and trust one another, and of finding ways to be together, Cliff's drinking began to decrease. From the follow-ups that the hospital did and from a couple of phone conversations I had with him as part of that process, I know that he had all but stopped drinking—meaning occasional use and no intoxication. As of this writing, he had begun taking courses toward a degree in a field that had long interested him, and was working part-time in that area while continuing with his many childcare responsibilities.

This outcome, in which all his symptoms were eliminated or reduced, meant to me that Cliff and I had found the master key—his governing pro-symptom position. All of his presenting symptoms, from drinking to social withdrawal, were actually his means of carrying out the one purpose of feeling self-empowerment in the only way he knew. Once that primary wound was welcomed out into the open, given sensitive attunement during its integration into Cliff's everyday awareness and brought into juxtaposition with new experiences of having his autonomy deeply respected by another human being, the presented symptoms fell away with no further work needed on them.

Alcohol abuse is complicated. There are layers of factors involved: underlying emotional reasons, habit, psychological dependence, physical dependence. In unlocking the emotional logic of a person's drinking, we can deal with many complicating issues. If, however, I hadn't made the effort to go to the root of Cliff's pain, if I'd been unwilling or unable to accompany him into the emotional core of his life and story, I would have risked engaging in a more superficial process. We could have missed the truth. Sorting out, unpacking, sifting through the underlying, out-of-awareness, unrecognized logic of alcohol overuse liberated him, at least sufficiently to begin a process that cut to the quick of his symptoms. And understanding the logic of Cliff's alcohol overuse enabled me to accept his lifelong double bind: both his hatred of his drinking and, at the same time, the necessity—the coherence—of exactly that behavior.

Cliff's story was one with a powerful unrecognized logic at its root, one which could not have been adequately guessed at or anticipated at the outset of our work. I was sufficiently able to maintain an "anthropologist's view," meaning that I committed myself to not knowing what Cliff was feeling or thinking until I had learned it from him, trusting all along that there was meaning to what he was doing. I was willing to acknowledge my awesome ignorance as to what constituted Cliff's "truth." I realized that the expert on what was (or wasn't) true sat not in my chair—but in his.

9

Bypassing Bypass Surgery: Using Emotional Coherence to Dispel Compulsive Eating

Niall Geoghegan[1]

Debbie, age 60, was referred to me by her primary care physician, who wanted her psychological state evaluated before she received gastric bypass surgery. In the large Health Maintenance Organization clinic where I work, I wear two hats: one for assessment and case consultation and the other for doing psychotherapy.

Debbie weighed about 320 pounds and told me she had been overweight since her childhood. She had a long history of dieting but was frustrated by her inability to maintain her target weight. Although she repeatedly succeeded in losing significant amounts of weight quickly, she always regained the extra pounds just as quickly. Debbie's doctor had told her that gastric bypass surgery would be the only way to alleviate the pain—at times excruciating—that she experienced in her knees and back. She was aware of the health risks that such an operation would involve.

To be eligible for gastric bypass surgery, Debbie would need to lose 10 percent of her body weight. With this requirement in mind, she had once again enrolled in a well-known national weight-loss program. She was finding, though, that her compulsive snacking, particularly on sweets, was making it impossible for her to reach her goal.

With about 20 minutes left in our first session, I asked whether she wanted this to be just a simple evaluation, or whether she would consider it preferable for us to do some therapeutic work that could result in her losing the weight without

1 Niall Geoghegan, PsyD, is a licensed psychologist in Berkeley, California, staff psychologist of the Kaiser Permanente Medical Center in Vallejo, California, and a certified trainer of the Coherence Psychology Institute.

surgery. She laughed and said, "I've been in therapy for years and I've probably been failing to lose weight since before you were born!" But she also said that the non-surgical option would, of course, be the better one.

I asked if she would be willing to try a "mental experiment," and she indicated that she would. I had her close her eyes and then began a process of symptom deprivation. In a slow cadence suitable for guided imaginal work I said, "I want you to imagine that, to your great surprise, we do some powerful therapeutic work here and that after a session or two, something shifts in you … and you begin to lose your desire to snack on sweets … and imagine that as you stop snacking, you begin to lose a pound or two … Our therapeutic work continues, and you start eating healthier food … You start following your diet plan faithfully … and week after week you continue to lose weight until … after the course of about a year and a half, you've gradually lost so many pounds that you have reached your target weight. [Longer pause.] What do you notice when you picture that?"

With eyes still closed, a faint smile played over her face, and she responded, "Well, I would probably feel successful, and good about myself, I would be more healthy, and would probably have more energy. I'd be able to go out and do more of the things I used to love to do. And my dog would be happy, 'cause I bet we'd go on more walks!"

Joining with her enthusiasm, I said, "Yes, it sounds as though you expect there would be a lot of positive results from stopping snacking and losing all that weight, and I hear you saying that it would *probably* feel great! But I'm wondering, is that the *actual* experience you're having as you imagine stopping snacking and losing all that weight, or is that just how good you think it would *probably* be?" As I asked her this, the smile dropped from her face.

Through slightly down-turned lips she said, "No, for some reason now I'm actually noticing a yucky feeling around here," and she pointed to her solar plexus. The symptom deprivation was working: A distress due to being without her excess weight was showing up.

I told her, "I'm curious to know more about the part of you that's feeling uncomfortable right now. Actually, this makes me think of a second experiment. I wonder how that uncomfortable part of you would end the sentence, 'If I stop snacking and lose all that weight …'" I had switched to using a sentence completion to guide her further into the symptom deprivation experience.

She paused and repeated my words, "If I stop snacking and lose all that weight … I won't get to eat all the yummy things that I love."

"Great," I encouraged her, "try it again. There's no one right ending, so keep seeing what other words might end that sentence, even if you don't like the endings or don't even fully understand what they mean."

She continued, "If I stop snacking and lose all the weight, I'll be deprived. If I stop snacking and lose all the weight, my husband will notice me more. If I stop snacking and lose all this weight, *other* people will notice me more. If I stop snacking and lose weight, I won't be safe!"

Picking up on this, I said, "Yes, it sounds as though there's a part of you that knows there's something *unsafe* about losing weight. I'm curious to hear more of what that part knows about that."

She visibly shrank back into her chair and in a small, low voice told me, "When I was really little I was cute and attractive, and around age six my uncle and his friends started taking the wrong kind of interest in me. I hated it, and wanted them to leave me alone, but they kept coming around. Right around then I started eating a lot, and I found that the fatter I got, the more they left me alone." I knew I had just heard the content of a young, very concrete, implicit learning, in which being fat was the solution necessary for safety from the problem of predatory male sexuality. She contemplated this for a moment and then appeared to be struck by a memory. "Years later, in my early twenties, I lost a lot of weight for the first time, and I remember that one of my male co-workers began to show interest in me and I got very scared and stopped dieting and gained it all back really fast."

I was not too surprised by this because I knew that excess weight is a common symptom in adults molested as children, yet I found it fascinating that Debbie's knowledge of the connection between being heavy and feeling safe—both at the age of six and as a young adult—seemed to exist in such a separate realm from her conscious desire to lose weight.

"Yes," I replied, "it sounds as though back then you learned that the way to avoid dangerous and unwanted attention was to eat and get big." As I talked, she nodded vigorously; so I continued: "And it sounds as though there's *still* a part of you *today* that knows that if you lose weight, men will start noticing you, and that will be very unsafe!"

Since she continued to nod, I said, "So I'd like to try one more thing before the end of the session. I'd like to give that part of you a voice. I'm going to suggest the closest words I can find for what that part of you might say, and I'd like you to repeat the words out loud, changing them if you need to until they feel true for you. If I'm hearing you correctly, then I'm guessing that part of you would say something like, 'I don't want to lose weight! If I do, men will notice me, and that's really dangerous. I've got to stay *big*—it's the only way to stay safe!'"

Debbie seemed to relax and grow bigger in her chair once again, no longer "shrunken" into her six-year-old emotional memory. With a broad smile returning to her face, she declared with enthusiasm, "I *want* to get as big and grotesque as possible. Then no one's ever gonna bother me!"

"Yes," I said with excitement, "and I would imagine that *this* part of you doesn't think that the diet is a very good idea at all!"

Clearly immersed in the material, and with her eyes still closed, Debbie exclaimed, "No way! I've been heavier before—I could still stand to gain a few more pounds—and *nobody* would notice me then!" The normally out-of-awareness part of herself that she was now speaking from had a very different target weight for Debbie from what her conscious personality had in mind.

Before the session ended we came up with a list of sentences on an index card, summarizing the newly discovered and newly owned emotional truth of a part of Debbie that was powerfully against dieting or losing weight. The card read:

I don't wanna lose weight!
If I get thin, men will notice me, and that's *way* too dangerous!
So I've gotta stay as big and grotesque as possible—then no one's *ever* gonna bother me!
Losing weight might help my knees and my back stop hurting,
but for me, it's more important to stay fat and safe!

When Debbie returned two weeks later, I asked her what it had been like to read the card several times each day. She reported that the words on the card had produced a remarkable shift in her conscious awareness. She had already been aware of the sexual abuse in her childhood, having done years of both individual and group therapy on that material, but she had never before recognized any connection between the molestation and her *current* eating patterns and overweight. Reading the index card between sessions had maintained her awareness of her fear of male attention and of how this fear was driving her ongoing resistance to dieting and losing weight. She added that she had been sticking to her diet plan for the last 10 days and proudly announced that she had already lost a few pounds.

The cause of that seemingly paradoxical change in behavior became apparent when she explained, "The first few days, the words on the card just felt completely true, but then it was as though another part of me began to realize that I'm at a different point in my life now, and that I'm probably *not* going to get that kind of attention no matter how much weight I lose, and even if I did, I could do things about it now!" Debbie was describing exactly the process of change sought in Coherence Therapy: She brought her pro-symptom position, "I *mustn't* lose weight because if I become thin I won't be safe" into direct, conscious, embodied experience, integrating it well into day-to-day awareness. This, in turn, allowed it to be exposed to sharply contradictory personal knowledge, in this case Debbie's existing knowledge in "another part of me" that she was now long since an adult, not a child, and was free of the dangers that had been present in childhood and had been built into her implicit learnings. The side-by-side juxtaposition of those opposite knowings had dissolved the key pro-symptom constructs. With many clients, as with Debbie, I have seen longstanding symptoms abruptly cease as soon as the underlying symptom-generating constructs were dispelled by an experience of juxtaposition.

Although this was not the end of our work together, it marked the beginning of a steady, gradual, and healthy weight loss over the next few years. Debbie realized after about a month that, in fact, she would not need surgery to lose the weight necessary to relieve her knees and back.

The molestations that Debbie suffered at age six were traumatic experiences that created traumatic memory, which she had largely resolved in her previous extensive therapy work. However, the solution of safety through obesity was a specific piece of emotional learning—stemming from the trauma—that her prior therapy had not addressed. In my experience, using Coherence Therapy for eating and weight problems has consistently revealed very specific underlying themes and purposes, as with Debbie, and as Ecker and Hulley (2008a) have described. I've seen a wide range in the number of sessions required for a lasting, liberating shift to occur. But cases like Debbie's have taught me to assume from the start of therapy that despite the long history and severity of a client's symptoms, a real breakthrough can be just a few coherence-focused steps away.

10

Hearing Hostile Voices: Ending Psychotic Symptoms at Their Coherent Roots

Timothy A. Connor[1]

When I was working with Emma, I had no thought of writing about her until near the end of her therapy. My formal progress notes are always kept brief. Such notes as I do take are intended to remind me of key statements by the client or to cue me about possible directions to pursue in the next session, so what follows is of necessity a reconstruction. I have not reconstructed exact quotations where I had no clear memory of them, which is why they are so few. Any gaps the reader may note in this account are the result of my effort to refrain from filling in gaps in my memory based on speculation about what probably happened. Emma read an early draft of this article and told me that her memories agreed with mine.

I met Emma in the clinic waiting room. She was a thin, angular woman in her late forties with a determined set to her jaw and an intense, almost fierce expression. She was in a wheelchair, and I knew nothing about her except that she had been referred by the psychiatrist who had been prescribing medications for her. I wheeled her down the ramp to my office on the lower level and asked her to describe her problem.

Emma told me that her neighbors, who lived in the other half of her duplex, had planted microphones and cameras in her side of the house and were spying on her. In addition, they had placed hidden speakers in her walls and commented on her activities, taunting her for being in a wheelchair and accusing her of faking her disability.

---

1 Timothy A. Connor, PsyD, is a licensed psychologist on the staff of Oregon State Hospital in Portland, Oregon.

I was taken aback. While I had worked with people with psychotic symptoms often enough, I rarely encountered them in the outpatient clinic of the facility where I worked at that time. As I continued to question Emma about her delusions, hallucinations and history, I became even more perplexed. Emma was in most respects a competent, "high-functioning" woman. She owned her home and car, managed her finances well, was active in her church, and helped care for her elderly father, who lived in a local retirement community. Apart from her implausible beliefs about and perceptions of her neighbors, her thinking was logical and coherent. She was somewhat depressed and anxious, but she seemed in control—perhaps too much in control—of her emotions. She did not fit the typical pattern of schizophrenia, which was the diagnosis she had been given.

Over the next few months I learned more about her history. It emerged slowly, in part because of the pressing nature of her practical difficulties and immediate distress, and in part because of her deeply ingrained reticence, which continued almost to the end of the two years we worked together. Trained as a nurse, she had worked in a major hospital in another city until she had become disabled 13 years before, at the age of 36. She had been standing on a window seat in her second-story apartment in order to hang blinds, and had fallen through the open window. After landing on her back, she had lain there, immobile, for some time before she was discovered. Her severe spinal injuries had left her confined to her wheelchair, and even though she had pursued physical therapy with a grim determination to recover, she had never walked again. Before her accident, she had been very athletic—a devoted bicyclist, hiker, and basketball player—and she felt the loss of these activities keenly. She was also unable to work; and though her disability pension was sufficient to live on, it did nothing to compensate for the loss of her identity as a worker and helper.

Emma became depressed, and her doctor prescribed medication, which seemed to help a bit. She did not seek psychotherapy. A few years after the accident she began to have neurological symptoms, which were identified as multiple sclerosis. About 10 years after the accident she moved to the small town where her parents had retired, to be close to them and care for them in their old age. She built a duplex and sold one side of it, while she lived in the other. Her neighbor was a middle-aged woman whose daughter and son-in-law visited frequently on weekends.

About a year after moving to her parents' town, she went outside to bring her garbage can back from the curb. Her wheelchair tipped over backward, landing her yet again on her back, helpless and in pain. It was the middle of the day in a suburban neighborhood with no foot traffic, and she lay there for 45 minutes before she was able to right herself and make her way back to her house.

She had re-injured her spine and soon found that her already limited mobility had been further reduced. A few weeks later, her mother died suddenly. Her father became depressed and began drinking heavily, and her own mood sank.

In the autumn, shortly before the anniversary of her original accident some 12 years earlier, she began hearing voices. At first they were subtle and indistinct, but soon they became clearer. They spoke to each other, describing Emma's actions. They also spoke directly to her, taunting her for being a useless cripple, telling her she could get up and walk if only she were willing to try. They seemed to be able to see her in the dark, in every room in her house, even under the blankets in her bed.

Having observed that her neighbor's son-in-law worked for a cable television company, Emma came to the conclusion that he had placed microphones, cameras, and speakers in her side of the house to torment her and drive her out of her home. She became even more depressed. After she began to have suicidal thoughts, she was hospitalized for two weeks and was prescribed antipsychotic medication.

Emma heard no voices in the hospital, but when she returned home the voices started again. Shortly after that, she had surgery on her back to treat her recent injury. The operation was unsuccessful. This time as well, although the voices had stopped while she was in the hospital, she heard them again once she was back home. This strengthened her conviction that the voices came from outside of her and were not "all in her head."

She continued to see the psychiatrist who had treated her during her hospitalization. He tried various antipsychotic medications and increased dosages, with no effect. Emma remained depressed, convinced she was being persecuted by her neighbors. Increasingly she withdrew, leaving her house only to shop or go to medical appointments. It was at this point that she was referred to me for psychotherapy.

It was not practical to begin by trying directly to resolve the seemingly psychotic symptoms, because she was unwilling to regard them as symptoms at all. She did acknowledge depression as a symptom, but saw it as a reasonable and inevitable response to persecution, so she could not see any hope of relief unless her neighbors' behavior changed. Her history, with no previous indication of hallucinations or delusions before age 49, gave me grounds for doubting the diagnosis of schizophrenia. Nevertheless, my initial approach was to be supportive and hope that medications would clear up the hallucinations and delusions soon.

This they completely failed to do. If anything, the voices became more intense and intrusive, their messages more hostile. The failure of the medications became further evidence in Emma's mind that the voices were real.

In the face of her absolute conviction concerning the objective reality of the voices, I could not yet find a path into using Coherence Therapy to dispel them. I therefore tried a range of counteractive methods for moderating and managing symptoms, methods that were quite alien to my usual way of working. Since Emma could not relate to working on making the voices go away, I tried helping her learn to live with them. This involved training her in mindfulness techniques for refocusing her attention away from the voices and onto other thoughts and activities.

We began with a basic meditation technique—focusing one's attention on the breath and returning to that focus when drawn away by distracting thoughts or emotions. We then expanded this to include observing the flow of thoughts and emotions in a nonjudgmental way—not attempting to suppress or change them—and developing the skill of accepting even painful experiences without reacting. In addition, we worked on the capability of choosing whether to attend to a particular experience or not (Hanh, 1999; Kabat-Zinn, 1990). I also tried cognitive restructuring (Beck, 1979) to reduce the emotional importance of the voices, encouraging Emma to challenge rationally the belief that her neighbors' opinion of her mattered.

The mindfulness practice gave her some relief, whereas standard cognitive therapy seemed to do little. Her mood improved slightly. The voices did not diminish, nor did their harsh content soften. Every week I was astonished that she came back at all.

Trying to find some way of doing useful sessions, I began to focus more on the content of the messages in the voices. I wanted to understand the meaning that those messages had for her. It was through this approach that the applicability of Coherence Therapy to Emma's situation finally became apparent to me.

Since our first session, I had been struggling to view Emma's symptoms within the framework of Coherence Therapy (Ecker & Hulley, 1996, 2008a) but I was finding it difficult to implement, since her conscious position was that the voices were not symptoms and she demanded only that her neighbors stop harassing her. She had no stated goals for change in herself, but now I began to seek what emotional coherence I could by asking her what it meant to her that the voices attacked her for being disabled, that they accused her of being worthless because she was in a wheelchair and needed help with basic tasks, and that they called her a fake, telling her that she could easily get up and walk if she chose. It was then that she began to tell me what it *meant* for her to be disabled.

She talked about how important her athleticism had been to her and how enormous a loss it had been to be unable to engage in intense physical activity. She told me of having been determined to defy the doctors' predictions that she would not walk again, and of remaining convinced for years that she would eventually regain her mobility, abandoning hope only when she had her second injury. She confessed her feelings of shame at needing help with ordinary tasks, when she felt she could not reciprocate. She also expressed frustration about the demands of caring for her father, as well as some resentment about having moved away from her previous home to care for him, while her able-bodied siblings who lived farther away gave little assistance.

I was struck by how closely these feelings paralleled the voices' attacks. I could see the faint outline of a pro-symptom position generating the voices, but I found no way to inquire more directly as long as Emma was unwilling to consider the voices to be symptoms. My few attempts at discovery through Coherence

Therapy techniques such as sentence completion and symptom deprivation yielded no pro-symptom material at all.

I began to ask Emma more about the accidents themselves and her feelings and memories about them. My questioning brought about the first intense display of emotion I had seen from her, as her iron self-control broke down and she became tearful, describing the feelings of helplessness and despair that had overcome her as she lay on the sidewalk in her overturned wheelchair. The depth of her pain suggested unresolved traumatic stress, and after further assessment I suggested that we try EMDR (Eye Movement Desensitization and Reprocessing; Shapiro, 2001). At this point I had been working with Emma for about four months.

At the first EMDR session, Emma chose to focus on the second accident (she said that the first one no longer disturbed her), especially the memory of lying on her back in the wheelchair, waiting for help that did not come. The negative cognitions associated with the memory were: "No one wants to help me and I can't help myself," "I'm all alone," and "I'm incompetent." The positive cognition she wished she could believe was: "I can reach out to people." She was aware of tension throughout her body as she recalled her fear, helplessness, and pain.

After the first set of eye movements, Emma reported only more intense awareness of pain and fear. After the second set, she burst into tears and nearly shouted, "I hate myself for being in this chair!" I was stunned. The self-hatred that until now had been so dissociated that it could show up only in external voices had suddenly been experienced by Emma as her own feeling. The last thing I had expected was such a direct emergence and passionate statement of a pro-symptom position. I asked her to repeat the statement, which she did, a bit more calmly, changing it to "I hate myself for being helpless."

After pausing to check that Emma was willing and able to continue, I invited her to focus on her awareness of this self-hatred, and continued with sets of bilateral eye movements. What followed was an improvised synthesis of the eye-movement technique with the methodology of Coherence Therapy, guided more by Emma's responses than by my direction, as I tried to draw out more and more of her pro-symptom position while being attentive to the underlying trauma scenario and Emma's level of emotional arousal. It was initially disorienting for me to think in Coherence Therapy terms while trying to use EMDR. Should I try to bring Emma's attention back to the trauma that we were supposedly trying to resolve (using the standard EMDR protocol) or should I now follow the Coherence Therapy path of step-by-step inquiry into her unconscious, symptom-requiring positions, a path that had just opened up by itself?

As it turned out, Emma herself resolved my dilemma. Her central focus never returned to the physical incident (her second accident). Rather than focus on images or memories as we continued the eye movements, she chose to focus on each new bit of revealed emotional truth. The eye movements seemed to free her to be aware of feelings and associated meanings that were usually inaccessible to her. In this way the discovery process of Coherence Therapy seemed to unfold largely by itself. With each set of eye movements she elaborated on her initial retrieval, verbalizing feelings of being selfish for wanting help and support from others, and especially for not caring for her father as well as she felt she should have. Not wanting to take sole responsibility for her father's care and not having the ability to do so meant to her that she was profoundly unworthy, and she felt this unworthiness intensely. "I can reach out to people for help to some degree," she said, "but it's hard." She then further discovered that she felt she deserved to *receive* care only to the extent that she could *give* care, and her ability to give care had become severely limited.

In the pro-symptom position or "part" of her that had emerged in this session, her entire identity and worth depended on taking care of others. Nothing, not even becoming disabled, was an acceptable reason for failing to do so, and she deserved scorn, taunting, and persecution for lacking the strength to overcome her injuries and resume the care of others. Certainly she did not deserve to receive care herself. This model of worth/worthlessness was her emotional truth, and until now it had been too painful and frightening to face or feel.

Emma had now achieved an awareness of her negative view of herself, and though this created no sense of resolution, her subjective distress decreased slightly. We had used eye movements throughout, yet the session had more the feel of Coherence Therapy, in that the eye movements seemed to release a process that allowed her symptom-requiring constructs to come into direct, experiential awareness without blockage. I therefore continued along the lines of Coherence Therapy and for homework gave Emma an index card summarizing the emotional truths she had unearthed about her self-hatred, in order to promote integration of it. The exact wording has been lost, but the sense was this:

> I want to reach out to people for support, but I'd better not do that because I'm sure they'll hate me as much as I hate myself for letting my disability stop me from helping others.

This was significant progress in the direction of Emma experiencing how, in essence, she felt herself to be exactly as the voices had been telling her she was: hateful for being disabled and for needing help. Her stark words would serve as a placeholder and point of departure in the next session. She was to read the card daily. I had some concerns about whether Emma might be overwhelmed by such a blunt statement of her self-disdain, and checked with her about this, but she assured me she could handle it, and I took her at her word.

At the next session, Emma said that during the past week she had been preoccupied with the awareness of her aloneness and how much of a struggle her life had become. She chose to have the session's eye-movement work begin again with a focus on the memory of lying on her back in the wheelchair in the street, with the negative thought, "I'm weak and helpless and I hate myself for it." Her desired belief was: "Even in the wheelchair I can take care of myself and be okay."

Again Emma quickly moved away from the concrete features of the incident to the emotional truths it entailed for her: "I'm ugly and worthless," with "nowhere to go," and "I blame myself for being disabled—I was stupid." Most poignantly, she encountered a deep inner conflict between a desire to be taken care of and a conviction that needing care automatically made her unworthy of it. This conflict emerged gradually as I guided Emma through sets of eye movements and between the sets pursued a Coherence Therapy style of discovery. I would ask a question designed to elicit more awareness of the emerging material and invite her to focus on the question as she did eye movements, and then explore the meanings that arose. When she seemed to have reached the momentary limit of her new awareness, I would help her embody it in a new question or a statement of emotional truth, then perform another set of eye movements. It was the kind of link-by-link retrieval that Ecker and Hulley (1996) term "serial accessing." "What would it mean if you really felt able to take care of yourself?" led to a feeling of being independent and "okay" but too alone. On the other hand, the question, "What would it mean if someone wanted to take care of you?" led to a sense of unworthiness and vulnerability to abandonment, but also to a desire to "just lie in bed and let somebody take care of me."

As the session neared its end, I asked Emma to feel and hold these two positions in her mind at the same time: her desire for total independence and her craving for nurturance. With her focused on both, we did more eye movements. I felt intuitively that prompting contact and integration between these very split-apart, conflicting positions would somehow move forward Emma's process of bringing to light the entire dilemma, whatever we would find it to be. What emerged over the course of two or three sets of eye movements was an awareness that, unless she blamed herself for her disability and believed that with a strong enough will she could reverse it, she would have no alternative but complete surrender to helplessness and passivity. That, in turn, would—according to her constructs—render her utterly worthless and contemptible, forever undeserving of care and forever alone. With this major discovery there was new awareness of a seemingly unresolvable dilemma that had been unconscious until now. It was summed up on her index card:

> I'm not yet willing to forgive myself for being disabled, because I'm afraid that would mean giving up completely and being worthless and alone for the rest of my life.

I understood now that Emma's self-blame was essential and her only way to avoid collapsing into a state of utter helplessness and abandonment. Self-blame was, in a sense, giving her the illusion of control over what had happened to her and thereby the ability to keep struggling against her disablement.

Emma was in a slightly better mood the next week; she attributed this to a visit from her sister. The voices always stopped when other people were present, and that relief was surely a factor as well. Checking on whether the card had promoted integration as intended, I asked Emma what it had been like living for the past week with awareness of her self-blame. She said it had brought her to a deeper recognition of feeling that her inability to give care made her utterly unworthy of receiving any of the love, respect, or care that she wanted and needed for herself. It still felt emotionally true to her to say, "I'm worthless if I can't take care of others," but in becoming more conscious of having this position, she noticed she was able to detach enough from it to recognize that, at the same time, this was not a standard that she would apply to anyone but herself.

It seemed to me that Emma was beginning to intellectualize about the dire things she was saying rather than actually experiencing their emotional impact. In order to recover the experiential engagement needed for successful Coherence Therapy, I asked her to focus on her depression from the position of believing herself unworthy. I then guided her to do so using Gendlin's (1982, 1996) focusing process, in which the client attends to the felt bodily sense of an experience, allowing meaning to emerge from direct contact with the felt sense.

After a few minutes of this, I asked her to imagine what her body would feel like if the depression were gone. In response to this step of symptom deprivation, she said she felt "resistance" even to *imagining* being without depression. Understood according to Coherence Therapy, her resistance to being without her depression was a response coming directly from her pro-symptom knowings requiring the depression. This is not to say there weren't many understandable reasons for Emma to feel depressed, but the discovery that she was *uncomfortable* giving it up indicated that her depression also served an unknown, coherent purpose. This resistance was itself a point of contact with, and access to, her pro-symptom position generating this aspect of her depression. I therefore asked her to focus on the sensation of resistance in her body, without in any way trying to overcome it, and she was able to feel and name a mixture of fear and guilt about the prospect of letting go of her depression.

Emma had now fully recovered the experiential quality that had previously faded. She said that the fear she had just described was tied into a feeling of being scrutinized by others; but there was not enough time left in the session to follow that line of discovery further. I wrote and handed over to her this index card:

> I'm not yet willing to give up my depression because if I can't take care of myself I don't deserve to be happy.

She read it aloud and let out a laugh of recognition—the first time I had ever seen her laugh! A sudden, free-energy laugh upon revisiting a pro-symptom position often occurs in Coherence Therapy and can be a marker of the onset of a fundamental change in that position. It remained to be seen whether such was the case.

At the next session Emma's improved mood continued, but she seemed less willing than she previously had been to focus on the emotional truths that had emerged during the last session regarding the importance of remaining depressed. When I tried to lead her into awareness of her unwillingness to do without that depression, my attempts fell flat, resulting mostly in her making statements about the senselessness of hanging onto the depression.

Exploring the significance of what she imagined others thought about her proved to be more productive. Emma said that she avoided leaving her house because she felt that "others don't see me, they just see the chair." She imagined that other people—strangers, at least, not necessarily those close to her—did not understand her disability and would not believe how difficult it was for her to do the things she did. She spoke of her reluctance to ask for help, even from friends and family, because she could not respond in kind: "There's nothing I can do for them." I tried a series of sentence completion exercises. The sentence stem, "If I can't take care of other people ..." yielded endings such as "I'm not myself," "I'm worthless," "I feel empty," and "I'm nobody." Her longstanding identity as a caretaker (both in her professional life as a nurse and in her family of origin) had been her way of feeling worthy. The feelings of emptiness, invisibility, and loss of identity seemed to her to make her depression as unavoidable as gravity. Clearly, in the deeper regions of her depressed mood, was an understandable sense of despair. Her index card at the end of this session had these words of discovered emotional truth:

> If I can't take care of myself and others, I feel like nobody and depression seems inevitable because I'm less myself.

When I asked her a week later about her response to that card, she said it had made her think more of being active, and she had begun to feel more interest in resuming certain activities (such as riding her specially adapted bicycle). This, however, had intensified her anxiety about being scrutinized and judged: "I'd feel better if I got out of the house and did things, but when I think about doing that I feel scared and I just want to get in bed and pull the covers over my head."

We explored her fear using visualization exercises combined with Focusing. She imagined herself being observed in activities and imagined the thoughts of the people observing her. She found herself imagining that they were thinking, "That's not something a person in a wheelchair should be able to do." If she were able to do anything for herself, she would be expected to do more: "If she can get in and out of her van, why can't she walk?" The more active and competent she became, the more would be expected of her and the more she would be suspected of faking her disability in order to get people to care for her—and the more she would feel empty and inadequate in the face of their expectations and her own. Her index card for the coming week read:

> I want to do all I can for myself, but I'm afraid that if I do, everyone will think I should do more and I wouldn't dare ask for help with anything, and

that's scary and depressing—so even though it's also depressing to hide and do nothing, that's better than looking like a fake.

Emma had rarely mentioned the voices during this series of sessions, except to note that they had stopped when her sister came to visit. At the next session, Emma announced that the voices had not returned since her sister's departure three weeks earlier. She also revealed that she had stopped taking her antipsychotic medication at about the time her sister arrived, before the voices had stopped.

When I asked Emma about her experience of reading her index card, she said that becoming aware of her fears of others' judgments had led her to realize that the actual problem had been her own judgments of herself, and that "what people think doesn't seem like such a big deal now." Her statement that a previously tormenting preoccupation with how she appeared to others no longer felt real indicated that Emma was slowly starting to see that her own thoughts and what she previously had projected onto others were one and the same. Emma now rated her mood at a level of seven (on a 10-point scale, where 10 meant the best possible mood), and she scored in the non-depressed range on a depression screening test. In addition, she was not emotionally reactive to a discussion of her second accident. She started making plans for activities and gradually began reaching out to others for companionship.

The sudden cessation of Emma's major symptoms brought intense relief to her—and to me, too. These developments led, however, to a significant error on my part. Because the voices had disappeared, I assumed that the pro-symptom position that had created them—Emma's hatred of herself for being limited in her ability to care for others, plus her need not to feel that self-hatred—had dissolved completely. Emma's own statements seemed to support my assumption; however, had I inquired more specifically, I would have learned that she had not yet actually experienced her agency in creating the voices, nor had she fully recognized her own purpose of protecting herself from awareness of her own negative self-judgments. As she told me later, she still felt embarrassed about the voices and clung to the notion that they might have been real experiences of persecution rather than hallucinations. In gratefully accepting the apparent resolution of a longstanding, perplexing problem, I neglected to cement the final block in her therapy.

This abatement of Emma's symptoms lasted for about four months, until her father's health began to deteriorate. At that point, her feelings of inadequacy as a caretaker reasserted themselves. The entire spectrum of symptoms recurred, beginning with depression, which then led to anxiety about the experience of persecution returning, followed rapidly by the reappearance of the voices two weeks before the anniversary of her first accident (her fall from the window), which she had claimed no longer distressed her.

This re-experiencing of the voices served to confirm for Emma that the previous experience of them had not been hallucinatory after all; therefore it was necessary for us to start from scratch, in effect. She was now even less willing than she had been a year earlier to view the voices as symptoms. However, she hesitantly agreed to proceed as if they were symptoms when I pointed out that I had nothing to offer her that would stop actual harassment by the neighbors. I reminded her that the eye movements had seemed to help her get "unstuck" the first time we had used them in a session, and I suggested trying them again. This time I proposed focusing on the first accident, from 14 years before, even though she still denied feeling distress over that memory. The recurrence of symptoms so close to that accident's anniversary seemed to indicate that it was still a significant trigger, albeit perhaps unconsciously so.

The next eye movement session, one week after the anniversary, confirmed this. Emma's anger at herself for allowing the accident to happen and for being helpless re-emerged, but in addition she re-experienced a profound sense of abandonment, as she recalled lying on the ground below her window, desperate for her parents to come to her aid. Another component of pro-symptom meaning that now became explicit was "anybody can look at me," an overwhelming sense of being exposed in her helplessness and mortification.

This second round of therapy was, by and large, a repetition of the first, a rediscovery of the same pro-symptom positions using the same approaches. These pro-symptom positions included self-hatred for needing help, shame that she couldn't help others, and conflict over being or appearing too independent—because how then could she get help or escape censure?

It was slower and more laborious, however. On some days Emma needed to talk about the immediate struggle of coping with her father's decline, rather than the voices and her sense of victimization. She began having suicidal ideation at one point, and several sessions were devoted to ensuring her safety, setting other possible topics aside.

The greatest obstruction to progress, however, was Emma's apparent inability or unwillingness to take seriously the idea that the voices came from her own mind, even though she accepted the fact that everyone else, myself included, believed that they did. My efforts to lead her to experience herself as the creator of the voices fell flat, although she was able to acknowledge intellectually that she shared many of the negative views of herself that the voices expressed.

Finally, at the end of a session, in a moment of either inspiration or desperation, I made a suggestion that I hoped would be a step in the direction of having Emma touch on discovering her own agency in manifesting the voices. She had mentioned that she sometimes talked back to the voices, telling them to go away and leave her alone. I proposed that she try the "experiment" of agreeing with them. When they accused her of pretending to be disabled, she should say, "Yes, I can walk, I'm just faking being unable to walk." If they called her names she should accept and agree with the insults. "Just an experiment," I said. "You'll be doing something they won't expect." She showed no enthusiasm, but agreed to try it.

The next week she reported that she had done as I asked and told me that, to her surprise, "it kind of shut them up," especially when she agreed with them that she could walk. This again indicated that the voices existed only as a result of Emma's disowning her self-condemning views and feelings. I asked her to imagine what it had felt like for "them" (the voices) to hear her agree that she was able to walk, but she was unable to place herself so directly within that perspective. She did recognize, however, that there was something about saying, "I can walk" that felt true, even if it seemed crazy. I gave her an index card simply stating that it felt true to agree that she was able to walk.

She began the next session with a surprising acknowledgment: She had discovered that part of her refused to accept her inability to walk. She said she had experienced this part through replying to the voices by agreeing with them. I saw that we had now discovered the implicit coherence of why she felt so "hateful": *she was a fake.* Her pro-symptom position was labyrinthine: She was a woman who couldn't walk, yet a part of her believed she was faking that she couldn't walk. I asked myself, "And why is this necessary? Why is it necessary to deny so fiercely that she is unable to walk?" To find the answer to this question I began, for the moment, by viewing that construct—"I can walk"—as the symptom and guided a symptom deprivation exercise in the hope of uncovering why it was essential to believe this was so. I asked her to imagine what it would be like for *that part* of her to recognize that she really could *not* walk.

After a long pause, she said, "It's like it's all my fault." We closely considered what she meant by that. It was this: The important thing was to avoid believing that she herself was to blame for carelessly causing her own permanent disablement, the loss of her identity as a caregiver and, with it, her value as a human being—and the only way to avoid believing it was to deny that the disability existed and believe and insist that she was faking it. It was as if Emma were saying, "It never happened. I am still the person I was the day before the accident—unafraid, active, athletic, helpful to others and fully self-sufficient. I am still myself."

Emma was now in touch with this pro-symptom position of denial with great clarity, including her own core purpose of protecting herself from the intense pain of seeing the ruinous fall through the window as being her own fault.

Then, by focusing on the bodily sensations she experienced while saying these things, Emma was spontaneously able to become aware of how much another part of her— a part that wanted care and felt neglected and abandoned—resented and refuted the harshly self-blaming part that insisted she was faking it. Her index card for this session read:

> I need to believe I can walk because if I don't believe it I have to blame myself for the accident and that's unbearable—so I have to keep believing I can walk no matter what the evidence, and blame myself for not making it happen.

Therapy was disrupted at this point because her father experienced a series of health crises, so we could not further develop the implicit disconfirmation that was starting to emerge between two very different parts of Emma. Her father died about a month after that session. She canceled appointments because of various demands, and the sessions that did occur were more supportive than exploratory. Emma admitted that she had little time or energy to look at or think about the last card. I simply encouraged her to keep it handy and read it when she could.

Over the next five weeks, without drama, the voices faded in frequency and intensity, as well as becoming less real-feeling to her. When Emma and I met for the first session after her father's funeral, the voices had been entirely absent for a week. We talked about what it meant to her to see that they had been a product of her own mind. Emma told me that she had felt ashamed of hearing voices and had not wanted to believe they came from her, but said that hearing voices now seemed no crazier to her than hating herself for being disabled and needing support. She seemed to have no difficulty accepting the voices as expressing her disowned rage at her own neediness, and now it was no longer necessary for her to invalidate and reject her own need to be cared for. Now she was able to see herself from the perspective of "Emma the nurse and caregiver" and feel compassion rather than disgust. By finally excavating the enormous self-blame that had developed from the first few moments and days of her original fall, she was able to render these angry and condemning constructs available for disconfirmation by other attitudes, beliefs, adult experiences and learnings she also possessed, in a separate part of herself, the compassionate nurse. The key therapeutic experience consisted of these two opposing sets of knowings or attributed meanings coming in contact with one other, ending their encapsulation from each other.

It was not until a few weeks later that I learned why Emma had installed such self-condemning learnings to begin with. With the voices gone, it became possible to focus on other pressing issues such as Emma's discomfort with emotional expression and her anxiety about reaching out to friends. In the course of this work, she revealed a critical piece of her history that made clear why her pro-symptom position of denying the actuality of her disability had been so deeply entrenched. She began one session by saying, "I want to tell you something I've never told you before." When she was nine years old, she confided, she had suffered a herniated disc, a spinal injury that is very unusual in children. She was hospitalized for two weeks for surgery, and it was during this period that she was first diagnosed with multiple sclerosis. Her parents were very attentive to her medical needs and for the next six months her mother took her to see specialists all over the western United States. Nevertheless, from her parents she received a strong, unspoken message, which became an implicit emotional learning, that she should not display any distress about the situation, because that would be a sign of weakness. As she put it, "I had to be tough for my mother." In addition, because her MS was asymptomatic for many years, she had had much practice in being able to blot it out of her awareness and, at times, even convinced herself that the diagnosis had been a mistake. This history told me that from a very young age she had learned the use of denial and had learned that denial was required within the terms of acceptance and approval in her family. It must have been quite frightening to her as a child to spend so much time in hospitals and to receive the MS diagnosis but to have to pretend that none of it mattered. What was real had to be treated as *not* real. Failure was defined by her mother (and perhaps by both parents) as succumbing to—or even admitting—her disabilities. I asked Emma why she had never mentioned this before, and she acknowledged that she had always felt embarrassed about it. It was only after she had been seeing me for over a year that she felt she could trust me not to see her as weak and unworthy for having felt abandoned and unloved during her childhood. I suspect—at least I hope—that, had I known she had been carrying such intense shame about a back injury and MS for 40 years, my therapeutic efforts would have been more focused and more effective from the beginning. It seems evident that in tandem with disconfirmations of the pro-symptom constructs driving persecutory voices, there was also a naturally occurring disconfirmation of her self-condemnation by virtue of our relationship. I did not minimize her suffering or see her as weak for admitting the hard reality of her physical struggles, as her family unwittingly had done. For Emma, this nonjudgmental acceptance was a very new experience.

Emma's sessions with me came to an end when I left my practice to move to another city. At that point she had not heard voices for several months. Her mood was good and she was focused on improving her relationships and becoming more comfortable with expressing feelings and emotional needs. Our final session was to take place one week after the 15th anniversary of her first accident. As the anniversary date approached she became apprehensive, afraid the voices might come back. "I think I'd know I was making them," she said, "but I'm not sure of that." The voices did not return.

I referred Emma to another therapist when we said goodbye, but when I called to follow up a few months later and asked her to review the first draft of this account, she said that she was no longer seeing him. She was cheerful, her social life was active, and she was having no problems with her neighbors. Emma had been free of her major symptoms for a year.

How did change take place?

Emma's various pro-symptom themes always revolved around the implicit sense that facing the actuality of her disablement would be too ruinous to bear. All of her pro-symptom meanings and strategies, as well as the symptoms implementing them, followed from the core knowing that it was urgent for her *not* to face the actuality of her disablement, in order—it emerged—to comply with her parents' attachment demands. It was this implicit knowing—that she *must not* succumb to being disabled—that again and again came into juxtaposition with a contradictory experience of *facing* the actuality of her disablement and finding it workable and non-devastating to do so. She developed trust in the reliability of receiving non-judgmental understanding and acceptance from me, which disconfirmed and dissolved her lifelong expectations of abandonment, learned from her parents. This allowed her to bring her denial-necessitating learnings into awareness, which in turn made it possible for Emma to relinquish the position of denial and give herself the compassion and understanding that she, as a nurse, was so able to give others. The repeated, implicit juxtaposition of "It will destroy me to face my disability" and "I'm able to face my disability" finally dispelled the realness of "It will destroy me to face it." Preventing herself from admitting the reality and hardship of her disablement—because to do otherwise would have made her a weak and disgusting child in her mother's eyes—was the purpose of most of Emma's symptoms, so naturally they ceased as soon as that specific purpose no longer existed.

A major question is the role of bilateral eye movements in Emma's therapy. I introduced portions of the EMDR protocol because there appeared to be unresolved post-traumatic stress from her accidents, but my use of side-to-side eye movements certainly did not follow the standard EMDR protocol. There was little evidence that her therapeutic process involved the construction of a coherent narrative from fragmentary traumatic memories, one of the more common formulations of the trauma resolution process. It seemed more as though the eye movements spontaneously brought specific, unconscious emotional themes and purposes into awareness, helping to carry out Coherence Therapy's discovery process when other techniques had failed to work for that purpose. This was all the more impressive because emotional awareness and expression were quite threatening for Emma, being associated in her mind with weakness and neediness. It was very difficult for her to get in touch with limbic states through verbal approaches, and it was often impossible for her to sense affect in her body, even using guided methods such as Focusing (Gendlin, 1982) or Gestalt body-awareness techniques. I have since learned that other therapists who use both Coherence Therapy and EMDR have likewise found that the eye movements can be effective for the emotional retrieval process of Coherence Therapy in situations where other techniques fail.

Once Emma had opened that door into her underlying emotional truths, we were able to proceed using more typical Coherence Therapy methods most of the time, utilizing eye movements or other structured techniques as needed. This flexible use of techniques for the discovery work allowed Emma to guide her own process and find the courage to face and master her shame and her fears about being disabled.

Glossary

accessing sequence: the initial, preparatory steps (A–B–C) of the *therapeutic reconsolidation process*, consisting of symptom identification, retrieval of target learning (corresponding to the discovery and integration phases of Coherence Therapy), and identification of disconfirming knowledge (the initial step of Coherence Therapy's *transformation phase*).

anti-symptom position: the client's initial, conscious view and stance regarding the presenting symptom, consisting of constructs that define the symptom as senseless, completely undesirable, involuntary, and caused by deficiency, defectiveness, illness, irrationality or badness.

coherence empathy: empathy focused on the emotional truth of the symptom: how the client's symptom is necessary to have and makes sense to have according to underlying, adaptive emotional learning; the specialized use of empathy in Coherence Therapy and a key practice for swift, successful retrieval of implicit symptom-generating emotional learnings.

Coherence Therapy: a unified set of methods and concepts for experiential individual, couple and family work based on the clinical observation that symptoms exist because they are emotionally necessary to have according to adaptive, implicit emotional learnings; a therapy of *transformational change* as distinct from *counteractive change*; the form of psychotherapy that has a procedural map and methodology that explicitly calls for and guides each step of the *therapeutic reconsolidation process*.

construct: any internal representation of self or world, in any mode of experiencing: sensory/perceptual; narrative/linguistic/conceptual; emotional; kine/somesthetic. A construct is a model of reality that operates as a unit of knowing; when applied, its representation seems real. A cluster of linked constructs form a *schema*, a mental model more elaborate than that of a single construct.

constructivism: a conceptual paradigm or epistemology that describes how the mind forms and organizes knowledge and responds according to that knowledge; based on the view that the mind of the perceiver actively if unconsciously shapes and constructs the experienced "reality," and actively bestows the meanings that this "reality" appears to have in itself; utilized to guide psychotherapy in various forms, one implication being that the therapist does not possess an objectively "correct" knowledge of reality to impart to the client.

contradictory/disconfirming knowledge: living knowledge that is fundamentally incompatible with the person's target emotional learning, such that when both are experienced together, both feel true but cannot possibly both be true; the finding of which is Step C of the *therapeutic reconsolidation process.*

counteractive change: the cultivation of preferred responses through new learning that suppresses and overrides unwanted responses but does not dissolve or nullify the existing learning that produces the unwanted response; as distinct from *transformational change.*

discovery phase: the process of using experiential methods in order to elicit into explicit awareness for the first time a therapy client's implicit emotional knowledge maintaining a symptom of behavior, mood or thought; the first part of the retrieval step (Step B) in the *therapeutic reconsolidation process* and the first phase of Coherence Therapy.

emotional brain: refers collectively to subcortical and cortical brain regions involved in the many aspects of emotional experiencing, conscious and non-conscious; including the subcortical limbic system and regions in the right cortical hemisphere. Among the many functions of the emotional brain are the formation of *emotional learning and memory* and the unlearning and erasure of *emotional memory.*

Emotional Coherence Framework: a unified body of clinical and neurobiological knowledge of (1) how emotional learning and memory operate, particularly the deep sense and adaptive cogency inherent in non-conscious emotional learnings and responses, (2) the unlearning and deletion of emotional implicit knowledge through memory reconsolidation, as demonstrated in laboratory research, and (3) the clinical application of reconsolidation using the *therapeutic reconsolidation process.*

emotional learning/emotional memory: learning that occurs in the presence of strong emotion includes the formation, in non-conscious or "implicit" memory networks of the brain, of a mental model (template or schema) that is the individual's adaptive generalization of the raw data of perception and emotion. Emotional implicit memory operates to detect the arising of similar situations and generates a self-protective or benefit-seeking response with compelling power and speed.

emotional truth of the symptom: the client's non-conscious emotional knowledge that makes the presenting symptom compellingly necessary to have in pursuit of safety, well-being or justice; also termed the symptom-requiring schema, the *pro-symptom position,* and the coherence of the symptom.

erasure sequence: Steps 1–2–3 of the *therapeutic reconsolidation process,* consisting of reactivation of the symptom-requiring schema, concurrent activation of disconfirming knowledge, and repetitions of the pairing of schema with mismatching knowledge; synonymous with *"transformation sequence,"* which is used in the clinical context, with "erasure sequence" used in the neuroscience and laboratory context.

experiential dissonance: an extension of the phenomenon of cognitive dissonance, involving whole-body experiencing of the emotional and sensory aspects of the mutually incompatible knowledges forming the dissonance.

experiential work: any step of work during a therapy session in which the client's attention is mainly or wholly on nonverbal, non-intellectual material; not to be equated narrowly with catharsis or highly intense or dramatic techniques. In Coherence Therapy, "experiential" means the client is subjectively in, and speaking from, the emotional reality of his or her symptom-generating emotional schema as a present-tense, first-person experience.

"I'm in memory" practice: a technique of experiential work in which the arising of an emotional distress, such as acute fear or hopelessness, or a compulsive behavioral response, such as relentless helpfulness, is used by the client as a cue to recognize and feel how the current situation is reminding him or her of an earlier severe suffering, and that the feeling is a living memory of what was felt originally.

implicit knowledge/implicit memory: acquired knowledge that the individual is unaware of possessing or having learned, even as such learnings respond and drive responses of behavior, mood, emotion, or thought.

index card task: a technique for structuring a between-session task designed to maintain or further the discovery, integration, or transformation of pro-symptom material in Coherence Therapy, by client's daily reading of a few sentences written on a pocket-sized index card; client uses card to remain in touch, on an emotional level, with key material arrived at during the session.

integration phase: the process of prompting a therapy client to make his or her recently discovered pro-symptom schema routinely conscious, through repeated experiences of inhabiting and knowingly expressing that schema or position, with no attempt to change its content or emotional truth; the second and final part of the retrieval step (Step B) in the *therapeutic reconsolidation process* and the second phase of Coherence Therapy.

juxtaposition experience: simultaneous experiencing, in the same field of awareness, of two sharply incompatible personal knowledges, each of which feels emotionally real, and one of which is retrieved symptom-generating knowledge; the core process of change in Coherence

Therapy's *transformation phase* and in the *therapeutic reconsolidation process*, where it occurs in Steps 2 and 3 of the *erasure (or transformation) sequence.*

limbic language: a style of phrasing used in Coherence Therapy for fostering the retrieval and experiencing of emotional implicit knowledge; it is highly candid emotionally, succinct, present-tense, and alive in maximally personal terms and use of personal pronouns, with the client speaking from and within the subjective experience of his or her pro-symptom knowledge.

limbic system: also known as the mammalian brain and the medial temporal lobe, this subcortical region comprises a number of structures that have major roles in emotional learning and memory—such as the amygdala and hippocampus—making our knowledge of this system particularly relevant to psychotherapy.

memory reconsolidation: a type of neuroplasticity which, when launched by the specific series of experiences required by the brain, unlocks the synapses of a target *emotional learning,* allowing that learning to be re-encoded or "re-written" in memory (during a time period of several hours) according to new learning experiences, resulting in either full nullification (erasure), weakening, modification, or strengthening of the original learning, depending on characteristics of the new learning.

mental model: any internal representation of the nature, meaning, or functioning of anything; one of the main contents and forms of acquired knowledge, whether conceptual, perceptual, emotional, or somatic; consists of component constructs and linked groups of constructs or schemas, all actively and adaptively created by the individual's mind for organizing and responding to experience.

mismatch detection: an automatic function of the brain in response to a conscious experience of new, unfamiliar knowledge that, in many cases, efficiently brings forward into awareness existing contradictory knowledge; a kind of vetting of each newly retrieved implicit construct in relation to the individual's vast library of existing conscious knowledge; one of the most important resources utilized in Coherence Therapy in the search for contradictory knowledge (TRP Step C) after a pro-symptom schema has been retrieved (TRP Step B).

neuroplasticity: the brain's many forms of adaptive activity of revising or reorganizing neural circuits or networks, using many different neurobiological mechanisms.

overt statement: a technique consisting of a succinct, emotionally candid, present-tense I-statement (limbic language) of part or all of the emotional truth of the symptom (the retrieved symptom-necessitating implicit knowledge), spoken aloud during a session under the therapist's guidance; and spoken directly to either the emotionally relevant person(s), visualized or in person, or to the therapist; one of Coherence Therapy's basic techniques used for facilitating discovery, integration, transformation, or verification of transformation.

pro-symptom position: one of the phrases used in Coherence Therapy to denote the client's initially non-conscious, learned emotional *schema* that makes the presenting symptom compellingly necessary to have; synonymous with *symptom-necessitating schema* and *the emotional truth of the symptom.*

psychotherapy integration: any framework for a unified understanding and/or utilization of a wide range of psychotherapy systems. Several different guiding principles of integration characterize the various frameworks that have been developed. The "common factors" principle defines the category that contains both the non-specific common factors framework as well as the very different framework of *transformation-specific factors,* which is the type of integration provided by the *therapeutic reconsolidation process.*

reconsolidation: see *memory reconsolidation.*

schema: a modular *mental model* of the functioning of self or world, consisting of a cluster of linked *constructs* (relatively simpler internal representations). Schemas formed by the emotional brain are nonverbal and either are implicit and do not themselves appear in conscious awareness (though their adaptive responses are apparent consciously), or, if conscious, are experienced as the nature of reality, not as a model formed by oneself.

sentence completion: an experiential, projective technique with a long history of use in various fields, and adapted for use as one of Coherence Therapy's basic techniques for discovery (i.e., initial elicitation) of the non-conscious emotional knowledge necessitating symptom production. A custom-made first part of a sentence or stem is designed by the therapist and spoken aloud by the client, who has been instructed to simply allow the sentence to complete itself, without pre-reflection or conscious choice of the ending that arises; and is repeated, with the same stem, until no new endings arise.

serial accessing: a process of sequential, experiential discovery in which any one emergent element of a symptom-generating emotional schema is experienced with full attention and then serves as a station of awareness from which the next directly linked construct becomes subjectively evident and accessible, either spontaneously or with facilitation by the therapist.

symptom coherence: the core principle of symptom production and symptom cessation in Coherence Therapy; the view that a therapy client's presenting symptom occurs entirely because it is compellingly necessary according to at least one of the client's non-conscious, adaptive *emotional learnings* or *schemas*, and that a symptom ceases to occur when there is no longer any emotional schema that necessitates it, with no other symptom-stopping measures needed.

symptom deprivation: an experiential technique of discovery for drawing an implicit, symptom-generating emotional schema into explicit awareness, utilizing the underlying emotional necessity of the symptom; by guiding an imaginal experience of being without the symptom in the very circumstance in which it has occurred and noticing the resulting, unwelcome effects, the adaptive necessity of the symptom begins to be revealed; one of Coherence Therapy's basic techniques.

terms of attachment: a client's acquired knowledge or constructs (largely or wholly non-conscious/implicit in most cases) that define the forms of available connection with significant others in attachment relationships, as well as the specific behaviors, thoughts and feelings required and forbidden in order to be accepted in such relationships; the individual's detailed, living knowledge of the conditionality of love.

therapeutic reconsolidation process (TRP): the sequence of tasks and experiences required in psychotherapy sessions in order to use *memory reconsolidation* to nullify a target *emotional learning* underlying a presenting symptom.

transformation phase: permanent dissolution or revision of key constructs making up the client's *pro-symptom schema*, so that there no longer exists an emotional reality (or part or ego-state) driving a response that entails the symptom; achieved through *juxtaposition experiences* in TRP Steps 2 and 3; the third and final phase of Coherence Therapy.

transformation sequence: Steps 1–2–3 of the *therapeutic reconsolidation process*, consisting of reactivation of the symptom-requiring schema, activation of disconfirming knowledge, and repetitions of the pairing of schema with mismatching knowledge; synonymous with *erasure sequence*; occurs within Coherence Therapy's *transformation phase*.

transformation-specific factors: the sequence of tasks and experiences constituting the *therapeutic reconsolidation process* viewed as a set of factors required for *transformational change* and shared by psychotherapies of *transformational change*.

transformational change: change in which problematic emotional learnings are actually nullified and dissolved, so that symptoms based on those learnings cease and cannot recur; as differentiated from *counteractive change*, which is incremental and necessitates ongoing managing and suppression of symptoms because their underlying emotional learnings remain intact.

References and Further Reading

Ainsworth, M. (1967). *Infancy in Uganda: Infant care and the growth of love.* Baltimore, MD: Johns Hopkins University Press.

Arden, J. B., & Linford, L. (2009). *Brain-based therapy with adults: Evidence-based treatment for everyday practice.* Hoboken, NJ: Wiley.

Badenoch, B. (2008). *Being a brain-wise therapist: A practical guide to interpersonal neurobiology.* New York, NY: W. W. Norton.

Badenoch, B. (2011). *The brain-savvy therapist's workbook.* New York, NY: W. W. Norton.

Baikie, K. A., & Wilhelm, K. (2005). Emotional and physical health benefits of expressive writing. *Advances in Psychiatric Treatment, 11,* 338–346.

Bandler, R., & Grinder, J. (1979). *Frogs into princes: Neuro linguistic programming.* Moab, UT: Real People Press.

Barry, R. A., Kochanska, G., and Philibert, R. A. (2008). G × E interaction in the organization of attachment: Mothers' responsiveness as a moderator of children's genotypes. *Journal of Child Psychology and Psychiatry, 12,* 1313–1320.

Bateson, G. (1951). Information and codification: A philosophical approach. In J. Ruesch & G. Bateson (Eds.), *Communication: The social matrix of psychiatry* (pp. 168–211). New York, NY: W. W. Norton.

Bateson, G. (1972). *Steps to an ecology of mind.* New York, NY: Ballantine.

Bateson, G. (1979). *Mind and nature.* New York, NY: Bantam Books.

Beck, A. (1979). *Cognitive therapy and the emotional disorders.* New York, NY: Plume.

Bouton, M. E. (2004). Context and behavioral processes in extinction. *Learning and Memory, 11,* 485–494.

Bowlby, J. (1988). *A secure base: Clinical applications of attachment theory.* London, UK: Routledge.

Bowlby, J. (1998). *Attachment and loss, Vol. 2: Separation.* New York, NY: Vintage/Ebury.

Brewin, C. R. (2006). Understanding cognitive-behaviour therapy: A retrieval competition account. *Behaviour Research and Therapy, 44,* 765–784.

Cammarota, M., Bevilaqua, L. R. M., Medina, J. H., & Izquierdo, I. (2004). Retrieval does not induce reconsolidation of inhibitory avoidance memory. *Learning & Memory, 11,* 572–578.

Cassidy, J., & Shaver, P. (Eds.) (2008). *Handbook of attachment: Theory, research, and clinical applications* (2nd ed.). New York, NY: Guilford Press.

Connors, M. E. (2011). Attachment theory: A "secure base" for psychotherapy integration. *Journal of Psychotherapy Integration, 21*, 348–362.

Cozolino, L. (2002). *The neuroscience of psychotherapy: Building and rebuilding the human brain.* New York & London, UK: W. W. Norton.

Cozolino, L. (2010). *The neuroscience of psychotherapy: Healing the social brain* (2nd ed.). New York, NY: W. W. Norton.

Deacon, B. J., Fawzy, T. I., Lickel, J. J., & Wolitzky-Taylor, K. B. (2011). Cognitive defusion versus cognitive restructuring in the treatment of negative self-referential thoughts: An investigation of process and outcome. *Journal of Cognitive Psychotherapy, 25,* 218–228.

Debiec, J., Doyère, V., Nader, K., & LeDoux, J. E. (2006). Directly reactivated, but not indirectly reactivated, memories undergo reconsolidation in the amygdala. *Proceedings of the National Academy of Sciences of the United States of America, 103,* 3428–3433.

DeCasper, A. J., & Carstens, A. A. (1981). Contingencies of stimulation: Effects on learning and emotion in neonates. *Infant Behavior and Development, 4,* 19–35.

Dell, P. (1982). Beyond homeostasis: Toward a concept of coherence. *Family Process, 21,* 21–41.

Della Selva, P. C. (2004). *Intensive short-term dynamic psychotherapy: Theory and technique.* London, UK: Karnac.

Dick, D. M., Meyers, J. L., Latendresse, S. J., Creemers, H. E., Lansford, J. E., Pettit, G. S., et al. (2011). CHRM2, parental monitoring, and adolescent externalizing behavior: Evidence for gene–environment interaction. *Psychological Science, 22,* 481–489.

Dobson, D., & Dobson, K. S. (2009). *Evidence-based practice of cognitive-behavioral therapy.* New York, NY: Guilford Press.

Dodes, L. (2002). *The heart of addiction.* New York, NY: HarperCollins.

Dudai, Y., & Eisenberg, M. (2004). Rites of passage of the engram: Reconsolidation and the lingering consolidation hypothesis. *Neuron, 44,* 93–100.

Duncan, B. L., Miller, S. D., Wampold, B. E., & Hubble, M. A. (Eds.). (2009). *The heart and soul of change: Delivering what works in therapy* (2nd ed.). Washington, DC: American Psychological Association Press.

Duvarci, S., Mamou, C. S., & Nader, K. (2006). Extinction is not a sufficient condition to prevent fear memories from undergoing reconsolidation in the basolateral amygdala. *European Journal of Neuroscience, 24,* 249–260.

Duvarci, S., & Nader, K. (2004). Characterization of fear memory reconsolidation. *Journal of Neuroscience, 24,* 9269–9275.

Ecker, B. (2003). The hidden logic of anxiety: Look for the emotional truth behind the symptom. *Psychotherapy Networker, 27*(6), 38–43, 58.

Ecker, B. (2006). The effectiveness of psychotherapy. Keynote address, 12th Biennial Conference of the Constructivist Psychology Network, University of California, San Marcos, CA. Transcript: www.coherencetherapy.org/files/ecker2006cpnkeynote.pdf

Ecker, B. (2008). Unlocking the emotional brain: Finding the neural key to transformation. *Psychotherapy Networker, 32*(5), 42–47, 60.

Ecker, B. (2011, January 13). Reconsolidation: A universal, integrative framework for highly effective psychotherapy. Retrieved January 31, 2012, from www.mentalhelp.net/poc/view_index.php?idx=119&d=1&w=487&e=41665

Ecker, B., & Hulley, L. (1996). *Depth oriented brief therapy.* San Francisco, CA: Jossey-Bass.

Ecker, B., & Hulley, L. (2000a). Depth-oriented brief therapy: Accelerated accessing of the coherent unconscious. In J. Carlson & L. Sperry (Eds.), *Brief therapy with individuals and couples* (pp. 161–190). Phoenix, AZ: Zeig, Tucker, & Theisen.

Ecker, B., & Hulley, L. (2000b). The order in clinical "disorder": Symptom coherence in depth oriented brief therapy. In R. A. Neimeyer & J. D. Raskin (Eds.), *Constructions of disorder: Meaning-making frameworks for psychotherapy* (pp. 63–89). Washington, DC: American Psychological Association Press.

Ecker, B., & Hulley, L. (2002a). Deep from the start: Profound change in brief therapy. *Psychotherapy Networker, 26*(1), 46–51, 64.

Ecker, B., & Hulley, L. (2002b). DOBT toolkit for in-depth effectiveness: Methods and concepts of depth-oriented brief therapy. *New Therapist, 20,* 24–29.

Ecker, B., & Hulley, L. (2008a). Coherence therapy: Swift change at the core of symptom production. In J. D. Raskin & S. K. Bridges (Eds.), *Studies in meaning 3* (pp. 57–83). New York, NY: Pace University Press.

Ecker, B., & Hulley, L. (2008b). *Compulsive underachieving.* [Video, transcript, commentaries.] Oakland, CA: Coherence Psychology Institute. Online: www.coherencetherapy.org/resources/videos.htm

Ecker, B., & Hulley, L. (2008c). *Down every year.* [Video, transcript, commentaries.] Oakland, CA: Coherence Psychology Institute. Online: www.coherencetherapy.org/resources/videos.htm

Ecker, B., & Hulley, L. (2008d). *Stuck in depression.* [Video, transcript, commentaries.] Oakland, CA: Coherence Psychology Institute. Online: www.coherencetherapy.org/resources/videos.htm

Ecker, B., & Hulley, L. (2011). *Coherence therapy practice manual and training guide.* Oakland, CA: Coherence Psychology Institute. Online: www.coherencetherapy.org/resources/manual.htm

Ecker, B., & Hulley, L. (2012). *Manual of juxtaposition experiences: How to create transformational change using disconfirming knowledge in Coherence Therapy.* Oakland, CA: Coherence Psychology Institute. Online: www.coherencetherapy.org/resources/juxt-manual.htm

Ecker, B., & Toomey, B. (2008). Depotentiation of symptom-producing implicit memory in coherence therapy. *Journal of Constructivist Psychology, 21,* 87–150.

Eichenbaum, H. (2004) An information processing framework for memory representation by the hippocampus: The cognitive neuroscience of knowing one's self. In M. S. Gazzaniga (Ed.), *The cognitive neurosciences III* (pp. 1077–1089). Cambridge, MA: MIT Press.

Eisenberg, M., Kobilo, T., Berman, D. E., & Dudai, Y. (2003). Stability of retrieved memory: Inverse correlation with trace dominance. *Science, 301,* 1102–1104.

Elliott, R., Greenberg, L., & Lietaer, G. (2003). Research on experiential psychotherapy. In M. Lambert (Ed.), *Bergin & Garfield's handbook of psychotherapy & behavior change* (pp. 493–539). New York, NY: Wiley.

Feinstein, D. (2010). Rapid treatment of PTSD: Why psychological exposure with acupoint tapping may be effective. *Psychotherapy: Theory, Research, Practice, Training, 47,* 385–402.

Festinger, L. (1957). *A theory of cognitive dissonance.* Stanford, CA: Stanford University Press.

Fisher, R. (2011). Dancing with the unconscious: An approach Freud never dreamed of. *Psychotherapy Networker, 35*(4), 59–63.

Foa, E. B., & Kozak, M. J. (1986). Emotional processing of fear: Exposure to corrective information. *Psychological Bulletin, 99,* 20–35.

Foa, E. B., & McNally, R. J. (1996). Mechanisms of change in exposure therapy. In R. M. Rapee (Ed.), *Current controversies in the anxiety disorders* (pp. 329–343). New York, NY: Guilford Press.

Folensbee, R. W. (2007). *The neuroscience of psychological therapies.* New York, NY: Cambridge University Press.

Forcato, C., Argibay, P. F., Pedreira, M. E., & Maldonado, H. (2008). Human reconsolidation does not always occur when a memory is retrieved: The relevance of the reminder structure. *Neurobiology of Learning and Memory, 91,* 50–57.

Forcato, C., Burgos, V. L., Argibay, P. F., Molina, V. A., Pedreira, M. E., & Maldonado, H. (2007). Reconsolidation of declarative memory in humans. *Learning & Memory, 14,* 295–303.

Fosha, D. (2000). *The transforming power of affect.* New York, NY: Basic Books.

Fosha, D. (2002). The activation of affective change processes in AEDP (Accelerated Experiential–Dynamic Psychotherapy). In J. J. Magnavita (Ed.), *Comprehensive handbook of psychotherapy, Vol. 1* (pp. 309–344). New York, NY: Wiley.

Fosha, D. (2003). Dyadic regulation and experiential work with emotion and relatedness in trauma and disordered attachment. In M. F. Solomon & D. J. Siegel (Eds.), *Healing trauma: Attachment, trauma, the brain and the mind* (pp. 221–281). New York, NY: W. W. Norton.

Fosha, D., Siegel, D. J., & Solomon, M. F. (Eds.) (2010). *The healing power of emotion: Affective neuroscience, development & clinical practice.* New York, NY: W. W. Norton.

Franklin, T. B., Russig, H., Weiss, I. C., Gräff, J., Linder, N., Michalon, A., et al. (2010). Epigenetic transmission of the impact of early stress across generations. *Biological Psychiatry, 68,* 408–415.

French, G. D., & Harris, C. J. (1998). *Traumatic Incident Reduction (TIR).* Boca Raton, FL: CRC Press.

Freud S. (1916/1966). The sense of symptoms (Lecture 17 in *Introductory lectures on psychoanalysis,* James Strachey, Ed. & Trans.). New York, NY: W. W. Norton.

Freud S. (1923/1962). *The ego and the id (The standard edition of the complete psychological works of Sigmund Freud,* James Strachey, Ed. & Trans.). New York, NY: W. W. Norton.

Frojan-Parga, M. X., Calero-Elvira, A., & Montano-Fidalgo, M. (2009). Analysis of the therapist's verbal behavior during cognitive restructuring debates: A case study. *Psychotherapy Research, 19,* 30–41.

Gable, S. L., & Haidt, J. (2005). What (and why) is positive psychology? *Review of General Psychology, 9,* 103–110.

Galluccio, L. (2005). Updating reactivated memories in infancy: I. Passive- and active-exposure effects. *Developmental Psychobiology, 47,* 1–17.

Gazzaniga, M. (1985). *The social brain.* New York, NY: Basic Books.

Gendlin, E. T. (1966). Research in psychotherapy with schizophrenic patients and the nature of that "illness." *American Journal of Psychotherapy, 20*, 4–16.

Gendlin, E. T. (1982). *Focusing* (2nd ed.). New York, NY: Bantam Books.

Gendlin, E. T. (1996). *Focusing-oriented psychotherapy: A manual of the experiential method.* New York, NY: Guilford Press.

Gorman, J.M., & Roose, S.P. (2011). The neurobiology of fear memory reconsolidation and psychoanalytic theory. *Journal of the American Psychoanalytic Association, 59*, 1201–1219.

Greenberg, L. S. (2010). Emotion-focused therapy: A clinical synthesis. *Focus, 8*, 32–42. Online: http://focus.psychiatryonline.org/cgi/reprint/8/1/32

Greenberg, L. S. (2011). *Emotion-focused therapy.* Washington, DC: American Psychological Association Press.

Greenberg, L. S., & Elliot, R. (2002). Emotion focused therapy: A process experiential approach. In J. Lebow & F. Kaslow (Eds.), *Comprehensive handbook of psychotherapy* (pp. 213–241). New York, NY: Wiley.

Greenberg, L. S., Rice, L., & Elliott, R. (1993). *Facilitating emotional change: The moment-by-moment process.* New York, NY: Guilford.

Greenberg, L. S., Warwar, S. H., & Malcolm, W. M. (2008). Differential effects of emotion-focused therapy and psychoeducation in facilitating forgiveness and letting go of emotional injuries. *Journal of Counseling Psychology, 55*, 185–196.

Greenberg, L. S., & Watson, J. C. (2005). *Emotion-focused therapy for depression.* Washington, DC: American Psychological Association Press.

Guidano, V. F. (1995). A constructivist outline of human knowing processes. In M. J. Mahoney (Ed.), *Cognitive and constructive psychotherapies* (pp. 89–102). New York, NY: Springer.

Hanh, T. N. (1999). *The miracle of mindfulness.* New York, NY: Beacon Press.

Hardt, O., Wang, S.-H., & Nader, K. (2009). Storage or retrieval deficit: The yin and yang of amnesia. *Learning & Memory, 16*, 224–230.

Hayes, S. C., Strosahl, K. D., & Wilson, K. C. (2003). *Acceptance and commitment therapy: An experiential approach to behavior change.* New York, NY: Guilford Press.

Heatherton, T. F., & Wagner, D. D. (2011). Cognitive neuroscience of self-regulation failure. *Trends in Cognitive Sciences, 15*, 132–139.

Held, C., Vosgerau, G., & Knauff, M. (Eds.) (2006). *Mental models and the mind: Current developments in cognitive psychology, neuroscience and philosophy of mind.* Amsterdam, The Netherlands: North-Holland Publishing.

Hernandez, P. J., & Kelley, A. E. (2004). Long-term memory for instrumental responses does not undergo protein synthesis-dependent reconsolidation upon retrieval. *Learning & Memory, 11*, 748–754.

Hesse, E. (1999). The Adult Attachment Interview: Historical and current perspectives. In J. Cassidy & P. Shaver (Eds.), *Handbook of attachment: Theory, research, and clinical applications* (pp. 395–443). New York, NY: Guilford Press.

Hesse, E., & Main, M. (2000). Disorganized infant, child, and adult attachment: Collapse in behavioral and attentional strategies. *Journal of the American Psychoanalytic Association, 48*, 1097–1127.

Högberg, G., Nardo, D., Hällström, T., & Pagani, M. (2011). Affective psychotherapy in post-traumatic reactions guided by affective neuroscience: Memory reconsolidation and play. *Psychology Research and Behavior Management, 4*, 87–96.

Howe, D. (2005). *Child abuse and neglect: Attachment, development, and intervention.* New York, NY: Palgrave Macmillan.

Hupbach, A. (2011). The specific outcomes of reactivation-induced memory changes depend on the degree of competition between old and new information. *Frontiers of Behavioral Neuroscience, 5,* 33.

Hupbach, A., Gomez, R., & Nadel, L. (2009). Episodic memory reconsolidation: Updating or source confusion? *Memory, 17,* 502–510.

Hupbach, A., Gomez, R., Hardt, O., & Nadel, L. (2007). Reconsolidation of episodic memories: A subtle reminder triggers integration of new information. *Learning & Memory, 14,* 47–53.

Husserl, E. (2010). *The idea of phenomenology.* Norwell, MA: Kluwer Academic Publishers.

Johnson, S. M. (2004). *Creating connection: The practice of emotionally focused marital therapy* (2nd ed.). New York, NY: Brunner/Routledge.

Judge, M. E., & Quartermain D. (1982). Alleviation of anisomycin-induced amnesia by pre-test treatment with lysine-vasopressin. *Pharmacology Biochemistry and Behavior, 16,* 463–466.

Jung, C. G. (1964). *Man and his symbols.* Garden City, NY: Doubleday.

Kabat-Zinn, J. (1990). *Full catastrophe living: Using the wisdom of your body and mind to face stress, pain, and illness.* New York, NY: Delta.

Kagan, J. (2011). Bringing up baby: Are we too attached to attachment theory? *Psychotherapy Networker, 35,* 28–33, 50–51.

Kandel, E. R. (2001). The molecular biology of memory storage: A dialog between genes and synapses. *Bioscience Reports, 21,* 565–611.

Kegan, R., & Lahey, L. L. (2001, November). The real reason people won't change. *Harvard Business Review,* 85–92.

Kindt, M., Soeter, M., & Vervliet, B. (2009). Beyond extinction: Erasing human fear responses and preventing the return of fear. *Nature Neuroscience, 12,* 256–258.

Kobak, R. (1999). The emotional dynamics of disruptions in attachment relationships: Implications for theory, research, and clinical intervention. In J. Cassidy & P. Shaver (Eds.), *Handbook of attachment: Theory, research, and clinical applications* (pp. 21–43). New York, NY: Guilford Press.

Kreiman, G., Koch, C. and Fried, I. (2000). Imagery neurons in the human brain. *Nature, 408,* 357–361.

Kurtz, R. (1990). *Body-centered psychotherapy: The Hakomi method.* Mendicino, CA: LifeRhythm.

Lah, M. I. (1989). Sentence completion tests. In C. S. Newmark (Ed.), *Major psychological assessment instruments, Vol. II* (pp. 133–163). Boston, MA: Allyn and Bacon.

Laing, R. D. (1967). *The politics of experience.* New York, NY: Pantheon.

Laing, R. D. (1995). The use of existential phenomenology in psychotherapy. In J. R. Zeig (Ed.), *The evolution of psychotherapy: The 3rd conference* (pp. 203–210). New York, NY: Brunner/Mazel.

LeDoux, J. (1996). *The emotional brain: The mysterious underpinnings of emotional life.* New York, NY: Simon & Schuster.

LeDoux, J. E., Romanski, L., & Xagoraris, A. (1989). Indelibility of subcortical emotional memories. *Journal of Cognitive Neuroscience, 1,* 238–243.

Lee, J. L. (2009). Reconsolidation: Maintaining memory relevance. *Trends in Neuroscience, 32*, 413–420.

Lee, J. L., Milton, A. L., & Everitt, B. J. (2006). Reconsolidation and extinction of conditioned fear: Inhibition and potentiation. *Journal of Neuroscience, 26*, 10051–10056.

Levine, P. (1997). *Waking the tiger: Healing trauma.* Berkeley, CA: North Atlantic Books.

Lewis, D. J., & Bregman, N. J. (1973). Source of cues for cue-dependent amnesia in rats. *Journal of Comparative and Physiological Psychology, 85*, 421–426.

Lewis, D., Bregman, N. J., & Mahan J. (1972). Cue-dependent amnesia in rats. *Journal of Comparative and Physiological Psychology, 81*, 243–247.

Lipton, B., & Fosha, D. (2011). Attachment as a transformative process in AEDP: Operationalizing the intersection of attachment theory and affective neuroscience. *Journal of Psychotherapy Integration, 21*, 253–279.

Mactutus, C. F., Riccio, D. C., & Ferek, J. M. (1979). Retrograde amnesia for old (reactivated) memory: Some anomalous characteristics. *Science, 204*, 1319–1320.

Mahoney, M. J. (1991). *Human change processes: The scientific foundations of psychotherapy.* New York, NY: Basic Books.

Mahoney, M. (2003). *Constructive psychotherapy: A practical guide.* New York, NY: Guilford Press.

Main, M. (1995). Recent studies in attachment: Overview, with selected implications for clinical work. In S. Goldberg, R. Muir, & J. Kerr (Eds.), *Attachment theory: Social, developmental, and clinical perspectives* (pp. 407–474). Hillsdale, NJ: Analytic Press.

Main, M., & Hesse, E. (1990). Parents' unresolved traumatic experiences are related to infant disorganized attachment status: Is frightened and/or frightening parental behavior the linking mechanism? In M. Greenberg, D. Cicchetti, & E. Cummings (Eds.), *Attachment in the preschool years: Theory, research, and intervention* (pp. 161–182). Chicago, IL: University of Chicago Press.

Mamiya, N., Fukushima, H., Suzuki, A., Matsuyama, Z., Homma, S., Frankland, P. W., et al. (2009). Brain region-specific gene expression activation required for reconsolidation and extinction of contextual fear memory. *Journal of Neuroscience, 29*, 402–413.

Martignetti, C. A., & Jordan, M. (2001). The use of DOBT in pastoral psychotherapy. *American Journal of Pastoral Counseling, 4*, 37–51.

Matzel, L. D., & Miller, R. R. (2009). Parsing storage from retrieval in experimentally induced amnesia. *Learning & Memory, 16*, 670–671.

McCarthy, K. S. (2009). *Specific, common, and unintended factors in psychotherapy: Descriptive and correlational approaches to what creates change.* Unpublished doctoral dissertation, University of Pennsylvania. Available online: http://repository.upenn.edu/edissertations/62

McGaugh, J. L. (1989). Involvement of hormonal and neuromodulatory systems in the regulation of memory storage. *Annual Review of Neuroscience, 2*, 255–287.

McGaugh, J. L. (2000). Memory—A century of consolidation. *Science, 287*, 248–251.

McGaugh, J. L., & Roozendaal, B. (2002). Role of adrenal stress hormones in forming lasting memories in the brain. *Current Opinions in Neurobiology, 12*, 205–210.

McLeod, J. (2001). *Qualitative research in counselling and psychotherapy.* London, UK: Sage.

Mileusnic, R., Lancashire, C. L., & Rose, S. P. R. (2005). Recalling an aversive experience by day-old chicks is not dependent on somatic protein synthesis. *Learning & Memory, 12*, 615–619.

Miller, S. D., Hubble, M. A., & Duncan, B. L. (1996). *Handbook of solution-focused brief therapy.* San Francisco, CA: Jossey-Bass.

Milner, B., Squire, L. R., & Kandel, E. R. (1998). Cognitive neuroscience and the study of memory. *Neuron, 20,* 445–468.

Misanin, J. R., Miller, R. R., & Lewis, D. J. (1968). Retrograde amnesia produced by electroconvulsive shock following reactivation of a consolidated memory trace. *Science, 16,* 554–555.

Missirlian, T. M., Toukmanian, S. G., Warwar, S. H., & Greenberg, L. S. (2005). Emotional arousal, client perceptual processing, and the working alliance in experiential psychotherapy for depression. *Journal of Consulting and Clinical Psychology, 73,* 861–871.

Mones, A. G., & Schwartz, R. C. (2007). The functional hypothesis: A family systems contribution toward an understanding of the healing process of the common factors. *Journal of Psychotherapy Integration, 17,* 314–329.

Monfils, M.-H., Cowansage, K. K., Klann, E., & LeDoux, J. E. (2009). Extinction–reconsolidation boundaries: Key to persistent attenuation of fear memories. *Science, 324,* 951–955.

Morris, R. G., Inglis, J., Ainge, J. A., Olverman, H. J., Tulloch, J., Dudai, Y., et al. (2006). Memory reconsolidation: Sensitivity of spatial memory to inhibition of protein synthesis in dorsal hippocampus during encoding and retrieval. *Neuron, 50,* 479–489.

Nader, K. (2003). Memory traces unbound. *Trends in Neuroscience, 26,* 65–72.

Nader, K., & Einarsson, E. O. (2010). Memory reconsolidation: An update. *Annals of the New York Academy of Sciences, 1191,* 27–41.

Nader, K., Schafe, G. E., & LeDoux, J. E. (2000). Fear memories require protein synthesis in the amygdala for reconsolidation after retrieval. *Nature, 406,* 722–726.

Neimeyer, R. A. (2009). *Constructivist psychotherapy.* New York, NY: Routledge.

Neimeyer, R. A., & Bridges, S. K. (2003). Postmodern approaches to psychotherapy. In Gurman, A. S. & Messer, S. B. (Eds.), *Essential psychotherapies* (2nd ed., pp. 272–316). New York, NY: Guilford Press.

Neimeyer, R. A., Burke, L. A., Mackay, M. M., & van Dyke Stringer, J. G. (2010). Grief therapy and the reconstruction of meaning: From principles to practice. *Journal of Contemporary Psychotherapy, 40,* 73–83.

Neimeyer, R. A., & Raskin, J. D. (Eds.). (2000). *Constructions of disorder: Meaning-making frameworks for psychotherapy.* Washington, DC: American Psychological Association Press.

Neimeyer, R. A., & Raskin, J. D. (2001). Varieties of constructivism in psychotherapy. In K. S. Dobson (Ed.), *Handbook of cognitive-behavioral therapies* (2nd ed., pp. 407–411). New York, NY: Guilford Press.

Norcross, J. C., & Goldfried, M. R. (Eds.) (2005). *Handbook of psychotherapy integration* (2nd ed.). New York, NY: Oxford.

Ochsner, K. N., & Gross, J. J. (2005). The cognitive control of emotion. *Trends in Cognitive Science, 9,* 408–409.

Oei, T. P. S., & Shuttlewood, G. J. (1996). Specific and nonspecific factors in psychotherapy: A case of cognitive therapy for depression. *Clinical Psychology Review, 16,* 83–103.

Oei, T. P. S., & Shuttlewood, G. J. (1997). Comparison of specific and nonspecific factors in a group cognitive therapy for depression. *Journal of Behavior Therapy and Experimental Psychiatry, 28*, 221–231.

Ogden, P., Minton, K., & Pain, C. (2006). *Trauma and the body.* New York, NY: W. W. Norton.

Olineck, K. M., & Poulin-Dubois, D. (2005). Infants' ability to distinguish between intentional and accidental actions and its relation to internal state language. *Infancy, 8*, 91–100.

Panksepp, J. (1998). *Affective neuroscience: The foundations of human and animal emotions.* New York, NY: Oxford University Press.

Papp, P., & Imber-Black, E. (1996). Family themes: Transmission and transformation. *Family Process, 35*, 5–20.

Parnell, L. (2006). *A therapist's guide to EMDR: Tools and techniques for successful treatment.* New York, NY: W. W. Norton.

Pedreira, M. E., & Maldonado, H. (2003). Protein synthesis subserves reconsolidation or extinction depending on reminder duration. *Neuron, 38*, 863–869.

Pedreira, M. E., Pérez-Cuesta, L. M., & Maldonado, H. (2002). Reactivation and reconsolidation of long-term memory in the crab *Chasmagnathus*: Protein synthesis requirement and mediation by NMDA-type glutamatergic receptors. *Journal of Neuroscience, 22*, 8305–8311.

Pedreira, M. E., Pérez-Cuesta, L. M., & Maldonado, H. (2004). Mismatch between what is expected and what actually occurs triggers memory reconsolidation or extinction. *Learning & Memory, 11*, 579–585.

Pennebaker, J. W. (1997). *Opening up: The healing power of expressing emotion.* New York, NY: Guilford Press.

Perez-Cuesta, L. M., & Maldonado, H. (2009). Memory reconsolidation and extinction in the crab: Mutual exclusion or coexistence? *Learning & Memory, 16*, 714–721.

Phelps, E. A., Delgado, M. R., Nearing, K. I., & LeDoux, J. E. (2004). Extinction learning in humans: Role of the amygdala and vmPFC. *Neuron, 43*, 897–905.

Pluess, M., Velders, F. P., Belsky, J., van IJzendoorn, M. H., Bakermans-Kranenburg, M. J., Jaddoe, V. W. V., et al. (2011). Serotonin transporter polymorphism moderates effects of prenatal maternal anxiety on infant negative emotionality. *Biological Psychiatry, 69*, 520–525.

Polster, E., & Polster, M. (1973). *Gestalt therapy integrated: Contours of theory and practice.* New York, NY: Brunner-Mazel.

Prenn, N. (2011). Mind the gap: AEDP interventions translating attachment theory into clinical practice. *Journal of Psychotherapy Integration, 21*, 308–329.

Przybyslawski, J., Roullet, P., & Sara, S. J. (1999). Attenuation of emotional and nonemotional memories after their reactivation: Role of beta adrenergic receptors. *Journal of Neuroscience, 19*, 6623–6628.

Przybyslawski, J., & Sara, S. J. (1997). Reconsolidation of memory after its reactivation. *Behavior and Brain Research, 84*, 241–246.

Quirk, G. J., Paré, D., Richardson, R., Herry, C., Monfils, M. H., Schiller, D., et al. (2010). Erasing fear memories with extinction training. *Journal of Neuroscience, 30*, 14993–14997.

Repacholi, B., & Gopnik, A. (1997). Early understanding of desires: Evidence from 14 and 18-month-olds. *Developmental Psychology, 33*(1), 12–21.

Rhode, A. R. (1957). *The sentence completion method.* New York, NY: The Ronald Press.

Richardson, R., Riccio, D. C., & Mowrey H. (1982). Retrograde amnesia for previously acquired Pavlovian conditioning: UCS exposure as a reactivation treatment. *Physiology of Psychology, 10*, 384–390.

Rodriguez-Ortiz, C. J., De la Cruz, V., Gutierrez, R., & Bermidez-Rattoni, F. (2005). Protein synthesis underlies post-retrieval memory consolidation to a restricted degree only when updated information is obtained. *Learning & Memory, 12*, 533–537.

Rodriguez-Ortiz, C. J., Garcia-DeLaTorre, P., Benavidez, E., Ballesteros, M. A., & Bermudez-Rattoni, F. (2008). Intrahippocampal anisomycin infusions disrupt previously consolidated spatial memory only when memory is updated. *Neurobiology of Learning and Memory, 89*, 352–359.

Roediger, H. L., & Craik, F. I. M. (Eds.) (1989). *Varieties of memory and consciousness: Essays in honour of Endel Tulving.* London, UK: Psychology Press.

Roozendaal, B., McEwen, B. S., & Chattarji, S. (2009). Stress, memory and the amygdala. *Nature Reviews Neuroscience, 10*, 423–433.

Rosen, G. M., & Davidson, G. C. (2003). Psychology should list empirically supported principles of change (ESPs) and not credentialed trademarked therapies or other treatment packages. *Behavior Modification, 27*, 300–312.

Rosenberg, M. B. (1999). *Nonviolent communication: A language of compassion.* Encinitas, CA: Puddledancer Press.

Rossato, J. I., Bevilaqua, L. R. M., Medina, J. H., Izquierdo, I., & Cammarota, M. (2006). Retrieval induces hippocampal-dependent reconsolidation of spatial memory. *Learning & Memory, 13*, 431–440.

Rossato, J. I., Bevilaqua, L. R. M., Myskiw, J. C., Medina, J. H., Izquierdo, I., & Cammarota, M. (2007). On the role of hippocampal protein synthesis in the consolidation and reconsolidation of object recognition memory. *Learning & Memory, 14*, 36–46.

Rothschild, B. (2000). *The body remembers: The psychophysiology of trauma and trauma treatment.* New York, NY: W. W. Norton.

Roullet, P., & Sara, S. J. (1998). Consolidation of memory after its reactivation: Involvement of beta noradrenergic receptors in the late phase. *Neural Plasticity, 6*, 63–68.

Rubin, R. D. (1976). Clinical use of retrograde amnesia produced by electroconvulsive shock: A conditioning hypothesis. *Canadian Journal of Psychiatry, 21*, 87–90.

Rubin, R. D., Fried, R., & Franks, C. M. (1969). New application of ECT. In R. D. Rubin & C. Franks (Eds.), *Advances in behavior therapy, 1968* (pp. 37–44). New York, NY: Academic Press.

Rumelhart, D. E., & McClelland, J. L. (1986). *Parallel distributed processing: Explorations in the microstructure of cognition* (2 vols.). Cambridge, MA: MIT Press.

Sara, S. J. (2000). Retrieval and reconsolidation: Toward a neurobiology of remembering. *Learning & Memory, 7*, 73–84.

Satir, V. (1972). *Peoplemaking.* Palo Alto, CA: Science & Behavior Books.

Schiller, D., Monfils, M.-H., Raio, C. M., Johnson, D. C., LeDoux, J. E., & Phelps, E. A. (2010). Preventing the return of fear in humans using reconsolidation update mechanisms. *Nature, 463*, 49–53.

Schore, A. N. (1994). *Affect regulation and the origin of the self: The neurobiology of emotional development.* Mahwah, NJ: Lawrence Erlbaum Associates.

Schore, A. N. (1996). The experience-dependent maturation of a regulatory system in the orbital prefrontal cortex and the origins of developmental psychopathology. *Development and Psychopathology, 8*, 59–87.

Schore, A. N. (1997). A century after Freud's project: Is a rapprochement between psychoanalysis and neurobiology at hand? *Journal of the American Psychoanalytic Association, 45*, 807–840.

Schore, A. N. (2003a). *Affect dysregulation and disorders of the self.* New York, NY: W. W. Norton.

Schore, A. N. (2003b). *Affect regulation and the repair of the self.* New York, NY: W. W. Norton.

Schore, A. N. (2009). Right brain affect regulation: An essential mechanism of development, trauma, dissociation, and psychotherapy. In D. Fosha, D. J. Siegel, & M. F. Solomon (Eds.), *The healing power of emotion: Affective neuroscience, development, clinical practice* (Chapter 5). New York, NY: W. W. Norton.

Schwartz, C. E., Kunwar, P. S., Greve, D. N., Kagan, J., Snidman, N. C., & Bloch, R. B. (2011, September 6). A phenotype of early infancy predicts reactivity of the amygdala in male adults. *Molecular Psychiatry.* Retrieved December 16, 2011 from www.nature.com/mp/journal/vaop/ncurrent/full/mp201196a.html

Schwartz, R. C. (1997). *Internal family systems therapy.* New York, NY: Guilford Press.

Schwartz, R. C. (2001). *Introduction to the internal family systems model.* Oak Park, IL: Trailheads Publications.

Sekiguchi, T., Yamada, A., & Suzuki, H. (1997). Reactivation-dependent changes in memory states in the terrestrial slug *Limax flavus. Learning & Memory, 4*, 356–364.

Shapiro, F. (2001). *Eye movement desensitization and reprocessing: Basic principles, protocols and procedures* (2nd ed.). New York, NY: Guilford Press.

Shapiro, F. (2002). EMDR treatment: Overview and integration. In F. Shapiro (Ed.), *EMDR as an integrative psychotherapy approach: Experts of diverse orientations explore the paradigm prism* (pp. 27–55). Washington, DC: American Psychological Association.

Shapiro, F., & Forrest, M. S. (1998). *EMDR: The breakthrough "eye movement" therapy for overcoming anxiety, stress, and trauma.* New York, NY: Basic Books.

Shapiro, R. (Ed.) (2005). *EMDR solutions: Pathways to healing.* New York, NY: W. W. Norton.

Siegel, D. J. (1999). *The developing mind: Toward a neurobiology of interpersonal experience.* New York, NY: Guilford Press.

Siegel, D. (2001). Toward an interpersonal neurobiology of the developing mind: Attachment, relationships, mindsight, and neural integration. *Infant Mental Health Journal, 22*, 67–94.

Siegel, D. J. (2006). An interpersonal neurobiology approach to psychotherapy. *Psychiatric Annals, 36*, 248–258.

Siegel, D. J. (2010). *Mindsight: The new science of personal transformation.* New York, NY: Bantam.

Siegel, D. J., & Solomon, M. F. (2003). *Healing trauma: Attachment, mind, body, and brain.* New York, NY: W. W. Norton.

Soeter, M., & Kindt, M. (2011). Disrupting reconsolidation: Pharmacological and behavioral manipulations. *Learning & Memory, 18*, 357–366.

Soley, L. C., & Smith, A. L. (2008). *Projective techniques for social science and business research.* Milwaukee, WI: The Southshore Press.

Solomon, J., & George, C. (1999). The place of disorganization in attachment theory: Linking classic observations with contemporary findings. In J. Solomon & C. George (Eds.), *Attachment disorganization* (pp. 3–32). New York, NY: Guilford Press.

Solomon, R. W., & Shapiro, F. (2008). EMDR and the adaptive information processing model: Potential mechanisms of change. *Journal of EMDR Practice and Research, 2,* 315–325.

Sroufe, L. A., & Waters, E. (1977). Attachment as an organizational construct. *Child Development, 48,* 1184–1199.

Stollhoff, N., Menzel, R., & Eisenhardt, D. (2005). Spontaneous recovery from extinction depends on the reconsolidation of the acquisition memory in an appetitive learning paradigm in the honeybee (*Apis mellifera*). *Journal of Neuroscience, 25,* 4485–4492.

Stricker, G., & Gold, J. (Eds.) (2006). *A casebook of psychotherapy integration.* Washington, DC: American Psychological Association Press.

Sullivan, H. S. (1948). The meaning of anxiety in psychiatry and in life. *American Journal of Psychiatry, 11,* 1–13.

Suzuki, A., Josselyn, S. A., Frankland, P. W., Masushige, S., Silva, A. J., & Kida, S. (2004). Memory reconsolidation and extinction have distinct temporal and biochemical signatures. *Journal of Neuroscience, 24,* 4787–4795.

Thomson, J. E., & Jordan, M. R. (2002). Depth oriented brief therapy: An ideal technique as hospice lengths-of-stay continue to shorten. *Journal of Pastoral Care & Counseling, 56,* 221–225.

Toomey, B., & Ecker, B. (2007). Of neurons and knowings: Constructivism, coherence psychology and their neurodynamic substrates. *Journal of Constructivist Psychology, 20,* 201–245.

Toomey, B., & Ecker, B. (2009). Competing visions of the implications of neuroscience for psychotherapy. *Journal of Constructivist Psychology, 22,* 95–140.

Tronson, N. C., & Taylor, J. R. (2007). Molecular mechanisms of memory reconsolidation. *Nature Neuroscience, 8,* 262–275.

Tryon, W. W. (2005). Possible mechanisms for why desensitization and exposure therapy work. Clinical Psychology Review, 25, 67–95.

Tsankova, N., Renthal, W., Kumar, A., & Nestler, E. J. (2007). Epigenetic regulation in psychiatric disorders. *Nature Reviews Neuroscience, 8,* 355–367.

Vaknin, S. (2010). *The big book of NLP, expanded: 350+ techniques, patterns & strategies of Neuro Linguistic Programming.* Prague, Czech Republic: Inner Patch Publishing.

van der Kolk, B. (1994). The body keeps the score: Memory and the evolving psychobiology of post traumatic stress. *Harvard Review of Psychiatry, 1*(5), 253–265.

van der Kolk, B. (1996). Trauma and memory. In van der Kolk, B., McFarlane, A., & Weisaeth, L. (Eds.), *Traumatic stress: The effects of overwhelming experience on mind, body, and society* (pp. 279–302). New York, NY: Guilford Press.

Van Nuys, D. (2010a, May 1). An interview with Bruce Ecker, MA, on memory reconsolidation and psychotherapy. Text and podcast retrieved January 31, 2012 from www.mentalhelp.net/poc/view_doc.php?type=doc&id=36397&cn=91

Van Nuys, D. (2010b, June 1). An interview with Leslie Greenberg, PhD, on Emotion-Focused Therapy. Text and podcast retrieved January 17, 2012 from www.mentalhelp.net/poc/view_doc.php?type=doc&id=36618

Volkman, V. R. (2008). *Traumatic Incident Reduction: Research and results* (2nd ed.). Ann Arbor, MI: Loving Healing Press.

Walker, M. P., Brakefield, T., Hobson, J. A., & Stickgold, R. (2003). Dissociable stages of human memory consolidation and reconsolidation. *Nature, 425*, 616–620.

Wampold, B. E. (2001). *The great psychotherapy debate: Models, methods, and findings.* Mahwah, NJ: Lawrence Erlbaum Associates.

Wang, S.-H., & Morris, R. G. M. (2010). Hippocampal–neocortical interactions in memory formation, consolidation, and reconsolidation. *Annual Review of Psychology, 61*, 49–79.

Weinberger, J. (1995). Common factors aren't so common: The common factors dilemma. *Clinical Psychology: Science and Practice, 2*, 45–69.

Winters, B. D., Tucci, M. C., & DaCosta-Furtado, M. (2009). Older and stronger object memories are selectively destabilized by reactivation in the presence of new information. *Learning & Memory, 16*, 545–553.

Wylie, M. S., & Turner, L. (2011). The attuned therapist: Does attachment theory really matter? *Psychotherapy Networker, 35*, 19–27, 48–49.

Xue, Y.-X., Luo, Y.-X., Wu, P., Shi, H.-S., Xue, L.-F., Chen, C., et al. (2012). A memory retrieval-extinction procedure to prevent drug craving and relapse. *Science, 336*, 241–245.

Zinker, J. (1978). *Creative process in Gestalt therapy.* New York, NY: Vintage.

Online Supplements

Resources for readers of *Unlocking the Emotional Brain* are available online at: www.CoherenceTherapy.org/discover/ueb-supplements.htm

Supplements include a listing of published case studies organized by symptom, with free download in many cases; an online discussion group for *UEB* readers; a list of the defining features of Coherence Therapy; searchable copies of the subject index and glossary of this book; and other related materials.

Author Index

Ainge, J. A. *214*
Ainsworth, M. 95, *207*
Arden, J. B. 14, 31, 35, *207*
Argibay, P. F. *210* (2)
Badenoch, B. 5, 14, 20, 31, 35, 53, 94, 150, *207* (2)
Baikie, K. A. 155, *207*
Bakermans-Kranenburg, M. J. *215*
Ballesteros, M. A. *216*
Bandler, R. 45, *207*
Barry, R. A. 96, *207*
Bateson, G. 45, *207* (3)
Beck, A. 189, *207*
Belsky, J. *215*
Benavidez, E. *216*
Berman, D. E. 24, *209*
Bermidez-Rattoni, F. *216*
Bevilaqua, L. R. M. 22, *207*, *216* (2)
Bloch, R. B. *217*
Bouton, M. E. 16 (2), *207*
Bowlby, J. 98, 103, *207* (2)
Brakefield, T. 18, *219*
Bregman, N. J. 17 (2), *213* (2)
Brewin, C. R. 35 (2), *207*
Bridges, S. K. 41, 55, 120, 122, *209*, *214*
Burgos, V. L. *210*
Burke, L. A. 41, *214*
Calero-Elvira, A. 59, *210*
Cammarota, M. 22, *207*, *216* (2)
Carstens, A. A. 7, *208*
Cassidy, J. 93, 94, *207*, *211*, *212*
Chattarji, S. 15, *216*
Chen, C. *219*
Cicchetti, D. *213*
Connors, M. E. 94, 98, 100, *208*
Cowansage, K. K. 24, *214*
Cozolino, L. 14, 16, 31 (2), *208* (2)

Craik, F. I. M. 14, *216*
Creemers, H. E. *208*
Cummings, E. *213*
DaCosta-Furtado, M. *219*
Davidson, G. C. 155, *216*
De la Cruz, V. *216*
Deacon, B. J. 59, *208*
Debiec, J. 23, *208*
DeCasper, A. J. 7, *208*
Delgado, M. R. 16, *215*
Dell, P. *208*
Della Selva, P. C. 35, *208*
Dick, D. M. *208*
Dobson, D. 35, *208*
Dobson, K. S. 35, *208*
Dodes, L. 45, *208*
Doyère, V. 23, *208*
Dudai, Y. 19, 24, *208*, *209*, *214*
Duncan, B. L. 35, 153, *208*, *214*
Duvarci, S. 18, 24 (3), *208* (2)
Ecker, B. *xv*, 5, 8, 14 (2), 15, 17, 20 (3), 35, 37, 39, 40 (2), 41, 44, 48, 51, 53 (2), 54, 55, 59, 62, 69, 71, 92, 105, 106, 152, 154, 165, 185, 189, 192, *208* (4), *209* (13), *218* (3)
Eichenbaum, H. 54, *209*
Einarsson, E. O. 20, 23, *214*
Eisenberg, M. 19, 24, *208*, *209*
Eisenhardt, D. 24, *218*
Elliott, R. 45, 136, 137, 155, *209*, *211*
Everitt, B. J. 24, *213*
Fawzy, T. I. 59, *208*
Feinstein, D. 20, *209*
Ferek, J. M. 17, *213*
Festinger, L. 58, *210*
Fisher, R. 5, *210*
Foa, E. B. 16, 35 (2), *210* (2)

Folensbee, R. W. 14, 31, *210*
Forcato, C. 21, 22, 25, *210* (2)
Forrest, M. S. 141, *217*
Fosha, D. 5, 14, 31, 35, 94 (3), 130 (2), 134, 136, *210* (4), *213*, *217*
Frankland, P. W. *213*, *218*
Franklin, T. B. 36, *210*
Franks, C. M. 17, *216*
French, G. D. 5, *210*
Freud S. 45, *210* (2)
Fried, I. 27, 86, 115, *212*
Fried, R. 17, *216*
Frojan-Parga, M. X. 59, *210*
Fukushima, H. *213*
Gable, S. L. 35, *210*
Galluccio, L. 21, 25, *210*
Garcia-DeLaTorre, P. *216*
Gazzaniga, M. *209*, *210*
Gendlin, E. T. 5, 45, 54, 100, 155, 170, 193, 200, *211* (3)
George, C. 102, *218*
Gold, J. 129, *218*
Goldberg, S. *213*
Goldfried, M. R. 129, *214*
Gomez, R. 25 (2), *212* (2)
Gopnik, A. 7, *216*
Gorman, J. M. 20, *211*
Gräff, J. *210*
Greenberg, L. S. 5 (2), 20, 45, 136 (3), 137, 155 (3), *209*, *211* (6), *214*, *218*
Greenberg, M. *213*
Greve, D. N. *217*
Grinder, J. 45, *207*
Gross, J. J. 35, *214*
Guidano, V. F. 55, *211*
Gurman, A. S. *214*
Gutierrez, R. *216*
Haidt, J. 35, *210*
Hällström, T. 20, *211*
Hanh, T. N. 189, *211*
Hardt, O. 25 (2), *211*, *212*
Harris, C. J. 5, *210*
Hayes, S. C. 35, *211*
Held, C. 54, *211*
Hernandez. P. J. 22, *211*
Herry, C. *215*
Hesse, E. 101 (2), 102, *211* (2), *213*
Hobson, J. A. 18, *219*
Högberg, G. 20, *211*
Homma, S. *213*
Howe, D. 98, *212*

Hubble, M. A. 35, 153, *208*, *214*
Hulley, L. *xv*, 5, 8, 20, 39, 40 (3), 48, 51, 53, 59, 62, 69, 71, 92, 105, 165, 185, 189, 192, *209* (11)
Hupbach, A. 25 (2), 26, *212* (3)
Husserl, E. 54, 55, 100, *212*
Imber-Black, E. 45, *215*
Inglis, J. *214*
Izquierdo, I. 22, 207, *216* (2)
Jaddoe, V. W. V. *215*
Johnson, D. C. *216*
Johnson, S. M. 45, 136, 137, *212*
Jordan, M. R. 40, 41, *213*, *218*
Josselyn, S. A. *218*
Judge, M. E. 17, *212*
Jung, C. G. 45, *212*
Kabat-Zinn, J. 189, *212*
Kagan, J. 94, *212*, *217*
Kandel, E. R. 14, 42, *212*, *214*
Kaslow, F. *211*
Kegan, R. 45, *212*
Kelley, A. E. 22, *211*
Kerr, J. *213*
Kida, S. *218*
Kindt, M. 23, 25 (2), *212*, *217*
Klann, E. *214*
Knauff, M. 54, *211*
Kobak, R. 98, *212*
Kobilo, T. 24, *209*
Koch, C. 27, 86, 115, *212*
Kochanska, G. 96, *207*
Kozak, M. J. 35, *210*
Kreiman, G. 27, 86, 115, *212*
Kumar, A. 36, *218*
Kunwar, P. S. *217*
Kurtz, R. 5, *212*
Lah, M. I. 73, *212*
Lahey, L. L. 45, *212*
Laing, R. D. 45, 54, 100, *212* (2)
Lancashire, C. L. 22, *213*
Lansford, J. E. *208*
Latendresse, S. J. *208*
Lebow, J. *211*
LeDoux, J. E. 14, 16 (2), 18, 23, 24, 31, *208*, *212* (2), *214* (2), *215*, *216*
Lee, J. L. 22, 23, 24, *213* (2)
Levine, P. 91, *213*
Lewis, D. J. 17 (3), *213* (2), *214*
Lickel, J. J. 59, *208*
Lietaer, G. 155, *209*
Linder, N. *210*

Linford, L. 14, 31, 35, *207*
Lipton, B. 94 (2), 130, 134, 136, *213*
Luo, Y.-X. *219*
Mackay, M. M. 41, *214*
Mactutus, C. F. 17, *213*
Magnavita, J. J. *210*
Mahan J. 17, *213*
Mahoney, M. J. 7, 45, 55, *211*, *213* (2)
Main, M. 100, 101 (3), *211*, *213* (2)
Malcolm, W. M. 155, *211*
Maldonado, H. 14, 18 (2), 21, 24 (4), *210*
    (2), *215* (4)
Mamiya, N. 24, *213*
Mamou, C. S. 24, 208
Martignetti, C. A. 40, *213*
Masushige, S. *218*
Matsuyama, Z. *213*
Matzel, L. D. 25, *213*
McCarthy, K. S. 154, *213*
McClelland, J. L. 54, *216*
McEwen, B. S. 15, *216*
McGaugh, J. L. 15 (2), 16, 213 (3)
McLeod, J. 54, *213*
McNally, R. J. 16, 35, *210*
Medina, J. H. 22, 207, *216* (2)
Menzel, R. 24, *218*
Messer, S. B. *214*
Meyers, J. L. *208*
Michalon, A. *210*
Mileusnic, R. 22, *213*
Miller, R. R. 17, 25, *213*, *214*
Miller, S. D. 35, 153, *208*, *214*
Milner, B. 14, 16 (2), *214*
Milton, A. L. 24, *213*
Minton, K. 87, *215*
Misanin, J. R. 17, *214*
Missirlian, T. M. 155, *214*
Molina, V. A. *210*
Mones, A. G. 45, *214*
Monfils, M. H. 24, 37, *214*, *215*, *216*
Montano-Fidalgo, M. 59, *210*
Morris, R. G. 21, 22, *214*, *219*
Mowrey H. 17, *216*
Muir, R. *213*
Myskiw, J. C. *216*
Nadel, L. 25 (2), *212* (2)
Nader, K. 18 (3), 19 (2), 20, 23 (2), 24 (4),
    25, *208* (3), *211*, *214* (3)
Nardo, D. 20, *211*
Nearing, K. I. 16, *215*

Neimeyer, R. A. 7. 8. 40 (2), 41 (2), 55 (3),
    120, 122, *209*, *214* (5)
Nestler, E. J. 36, *218*
Norcross, J. C. 129, *214*
Ochsner, K. N. 35, *214*
Oei, T. P. S. 155, *214*, *215*
Ogden, P. 87, *215*
Olineck, K. M. 7, *215*
Olverman, H. J. *214*
Pagani, M. 20, *211*
Pain, C. 87, *215*
Panksepp J. 14, 31, *215*
Papp, P. 45, *215*
Paré, D. *215*
Parnell, L. 5, *215*
Pedreira, M. E. 14, 18 (2), 21 (2), 22, 24
    (3), *210* (2), *215* (3)
Pennebaker, J. W. 155, *215*
Pérez-Cuesta, L. M. 14, 18 21, 24 (2),
    215 (3)
Pettit, G. S. *208*
Phelps, E. A. 16, *215*, *216*
Philibert, R. A. 96, *207*
Pluess, M. 96, *215*
Polster, E. 5, 45, *215*
Polster, M. 5, 45, *215*
Poulin-Dubois, D. 7, *215*
Prenn, N. 93, *215*
Przybyslawski, J. 18 (2), 19, *215* (2)
Quartermain D. 17, *212*
Quirk, G. J. 24, *215*
Raio, C. M. *216*
Raskin, J. D. 7, 8, 41, 55, *209* (2), *214* (2)
Renthal, W. 36, *218*
Repacholi, B. 7, *216*
Rhode, A. R. 73, *216*
Riccio, D. C. 17 (2), *213*, *216*
Rice, L. 45, *211*
Richardson, R. 17, *215*, *216*
Rodriguez-Ortiz, C. J. 21 (2), 216 (2)
Roediger, H. L. 14, *216*
Romanski, L. 16, *212*
Roose, S. P. 20, *211*
Roozendaal, B. 15 (2), *213*, *216*
Rose, S. P. R. 22, *213*
Rosen, G. M. 155, *216*
Rosenberg, M. B. 45, *216*
Rossato, J. I. 21 (2), 24, *216* (2)
Rothschild, B. 14, 16, 31, *216*
Roullet, P. 18 (2), *215*, *216*

Rubin, R. D. 17 (2), *216* (3)
Ruesch, J. *207*
Rumelhart, D. E. 54, *216*
Russig, H. *210*
Sara, S. J. 18 (4), *215* (2), *216* (2)
Satir, V. 45, *216*
Schafe, G. E. 18, *214*
Schiller, D. 18, 19, 23, 24 (2), 25 (2), 29, 37, *215*, *216*
Schore, A. N. 14, 16, 31, 53, 93, 94 (3), 117, 216, 217 (5)
Schwartz, C. E. 95, *217*
Schwartz, R. C. 5, 45 (2), *214*, *217* (2)
Sekiguchi, T. 18, *217*
Shapiro, F. 5, 20, 45, 141 (3), 190, *217* (5), *218*
Shaver, P. 93, 94, *207*, *211*, *212*
Shi, H.-S. *219*
Shuttlewood, G. J. 155, *214*, *215*
Siegel, D. J. 5, 14 (4), 16, 31, 53, 93, 94, 117, 149 (2), *210* (2), *217* (6)
Silva, A. J. *218*
Smith, A. L. 73, *217*
Snidman, N. C. *217*
Soeter, M. 23, 25 (2), *212*, *217*
Soley, L. C. 73, *217*
Solomon, J. 102, *218*
Solomon, M. F. 14 (2), *210* (2), *217* (2)
Solomon, R. W. 20, *218*
Squire, L. R. 14, *214*
Sroufe, L. A. 98, *218*
Stickgold, R. 18, *219*
Stollhoff, N. 24, *218*
Stricker, G. 129, *218*
Strosahl, K. D. 35, *211*
Sullivan, H. S. 45, *218*
Suzuki, A. 24 (2), *213*, *218*
Suzuki, H. 18, *217*
Taylor, J. R. 24 (2), 25, *218*

Thomson, J. E. 41, *218*
Toomey, B. 14, 15, 17, 20, 35, 37, 44, 53, 54, 55, 106, 152, 154, *209*, *218* (2)
Toukmanian, S. G. 155, *214*
Tronson, N. C. 24 (2), 25, *218*
Tryon, W. W. 35, *218*
Tsankova, N. 36, 37, *218*
Tucci, M. C. *219*
Tulloch, J. *214*
Turner, L. 93, 95, *219*
Vaknin, S. 5, *218*
van der Kolk, B. 14 (2), 16, 31, 45, *218* (2)
van Dyke Stringer, J. G. 41, *214*
van IJzendoorn, M. H. *215*
Van Nuys, D. 41, 136, *218* (2)
Velders, F. P. *215*
Vervliet, B. 23, 25, *212*
Volkman, V. R. 5, *218*
Vosgerau, G. 54, *211*
Walker, M. P. 18, 25, *219*
Wampold, B. E. 153 (2), *208*, *219*
Wang, S.-H. 22, 25, *211*, *219*
Warwar, S. H. 155 (2), *211*, *214*
Waters, E. 98, *218*
Watson, J. C. 5, 136, 137, *211*
Weinberger, J. 155, *219*
Weiss, I. C. *210*
Wilhelm, K. 155, *207*
Wilson, K. C. 35, *211*
Winters, B. D. 21, *219*
Wolitzky-Taylor, K. B. 59, *208*
Wu, P. *219*
Wylie, M. S., 93, 95, *219*
Xagoraris, A. 16, *212*
Xue, L.-F. *219*
Xue, Y.-X. 24, 25, *219*
Yamada, A. 18, *217*
Zinker, J. 5, *219*

Subject Index

abandonment 98, 132, 137, 145, 147, 148, 151, 192, 196, 197
abuse in childhood 82, 78, 110, 137; sexual 130
Accelerated Experiential Dynamic Psychotherapy (AEDP): and the therapeutic reconsolidation process 5, 10, 130–6
Acceptance and Commitment Therapy (ACT) 59
accessing sequence 63; definition 29, 30, 41; time required for 29; as transformation-specific factors 127; variations of 149, 152
accompaniment, therapist's 49, 109, 117, 132–3, 138, 148, 176, 178–9, 180
accountability, need for 79, 82, 99 , 120 , 140; see also justice
addiction, genetically-based 15, 34
affect regulation 33; see also emotional regulation
agency: disowning of 188–9, 195–7; retrieval and experience of non-conscious 50, 73, 80, 108, 114, 162–3, 175–6, 183, 195, 197
Ainsworth, Mary 95
alliance, therapeutic: and non-specific common factors 43, 153; and specific factors 155
aloneness 84, 101, 106, 110, 132, 191
amygdala 95
anger: case example 98–100, 159–67; as resistance to grieving 83
anniversary relapse 195–6
anxiety 9, 17, 37, 42, 69, 86–92, 102 , 110–19; avoiding, via self-blame 148; case study 43–63; maternal, during

pregnancy 96; social 6–7, 168–80; social predictors of 94
artistic domain of learning 96
athletic domain of learning 96
attachment: as defining focus for psychotherapy 93–4; as domain of learning 93–4
attachment learnings, insecure: absence/ presence revealed by retrieval 10, 97–100, 105, 98–100, 119–20, 150, 173–6; case examples of 71–7, 88–91, 105–23, 130–40, 148–51, 168–80, 198–200; cases unsuitable for reparative attachment work 104, 119–24; disconfirmed by therapist's empathy 105, 131, 150, 168–80, 199–200; disconfirmed other than by therapist's empathy 74–6, 82, 85–6, 88–91, 105, 110–24; examining childhood for 99–100, 106, 110, 120–1, 137–9, 172–4, 198–9; of family rules/ roles 91, 120–1; as not underlying all symptoms 10, 93–100, 104–5; primary vs secondary 103, 121; review of types/content of 100–2; role of client-therapist relationship in changing 32, 85–6, 97, 103–5, 110, 119, 153; role of, in development 32, 93–7, 148; role of, in symptom production 93–7; terms of attachment in 102–4, 111, 119–20, 173–7, 198–200; transformation of 71–86, 91, 103–123, 130–6, 150–1, 179, 198–200; see also disconfirmation: of attachment learnings; empathy, therapist's; juxtaposition experience: targeting attachment schemas; reparative attachment therapy

attachment patterns, insecure 4, 16;
coherent basis of 73, 100–2; dismissive
type 101; as emotional learning/schema
14–15, 81, 100–2; infant's learning
of 100–2; insecure-ambivalent 101;
insecure-avoidant 100–1; insecure-
disorganized 101, 110; insecure-
resistant 101; and merging 73–7;
preoccupied type 101; self-blame in
148; unresolved type 102
attachment relationship 104; definition
of 98; as required for reparative
attachment 123–4
attachment research 93; by Mary
Ainsworth 95; by Mary Main 100
attachment therapy: other than reparative
attachment work 71–86, 91, 105,
110–24; and psychotherapy integration
93–7, 124
autism spectrum disorders 8, 15, 34
autobiographical memory 14–15, 39, 117;
non-impairment of 14, 23, 39
autonomy 173, 179–80
avoiding emotional intimacy: case studies
106–9, 148–51

Badenoch, Bonnie 149
betrayal 95, 99
between-session index card task: eliciting
results of 12, 52; for integration 51–3,
80, 160, 162–3, 176, 184, 191–5, 197;
for juxtaposition 76, 165–6; *see also*
index card
bilateral stimulation 190–2, 196
bodily experiencing 50, 52, 87, 116–17,
170–2, 112, 131, 135, 140, 143–5,
150–1, 182, 193, 197
bottom-up versus top-down causation 33,
35–6, 42, 62, 66
boundary conditions: allowing
reconsolidation 23; between
reconsolidation and extinction 23–4
Bowlby, John 98, 103
brain, emotional: coherence of 6–8, 47, 102,
117, 128, 147–8; functioning of 6–8, 27,
31, 36, 47, 55, 62, 86, 102, 115, 149
brain imaging 95
brain's rules for memory erasure/updating
4, 26, 126, 149; and psychotherapy
integration 152; *see also* erasure/
deletion/dissolution; reconsolidation;

reconsolidation research; therapeutic
reconsolidation process; unlearning
Bridges, Sara K. 120
bullying 95

case example of AEDP: emotional self-
suppression, shame (Daniel) 130–6
case example of EFT: depression (Trish)
119, 136–40
case example of EMDR: panic attacks
(Susan) 141–8
case example of IPNB: avoidance of
intimacy (Cerise) 148–51
case examples of Coherence Therapy:
alcoholism, social anxiety, low self-
worth (Cliff) 168–80; anger (Raoul)
98–100; anxiety/panic/perfectionism/
low-self-worth/PTSD (Regina) 110–19;
anxiety/self-doubt/low self-esteem
(Richard) 43–63, 69–70; avoiding
emotional intimacy (Travis) 106–9;
compulsive eating/obesity (Debbie)
181–5; delusions/hallucinations/
depression/isolation (Emma) 186–200;
guilt/self-blame/depression/anger/
isolation/perfectionism (John) 159–67;
marital sexual aversion (Carol) 120–3;
obsessive attachment (Charlotte) 71–7;
stage fright/PTSD (Brenda) 86–91;
summary listing of 92, 125; under-
achieving/complex trauma (Ted) 77–86
causation of symptoms *see* symptoms,
causation of
chair work 48, 138–40
characterological avoidance of emotional
vulnerability 34
class, social 94
client-therapist relationship: choice of
use of 10, 97, 106, 119, 153; reparative
attachment work using 106–9, 148,
168–80, 199–200; role of, in outcome
research 153; schema-specific use of 97
clinical discovery of erasure sequence
39–41, 59
codependency 95, 97; as emotional
learning 14, 102
cognitive-behavioral therapy 35, 59
cognitive defusion 59
cognitive dissonance 58
cognitive insight 146; and transformational
change 12, 59, 118

cognitive re-appraisal techniques 59
cognitive regulation 33, 35
cognitive restructuring 59, 189
coherence: of autobiographical narratives
      7, 117, 155, 200; of emotional brain
      6–8, 47, 102, 117, 128, 147–8, 155;
      of implicit-learning-based symptoms
      4, 6–8, 36, 44–7, 54, 73, 78, 87, 99,
      100–3, 106, 111, 150, 180; of insecure
      attachment patterns 100–2; of self
      65–6; *see also* symptom coherence
coherence empathy: definition 48; example
      50, 173–6, 179
Coherence Therapy: agency experienced
      in 50, 80, 108, 114, 162–3, 175–6,
      183, 195, 197; applicability of 43; for
      attachment work 71–7, 85–6, 88–91,
      105–23, 179–80, 198–200; between-
      session tasks in 51–3, 160, 162–3, 176,
      184, 191–5, 197; bilateral stimulation
      within 48, 190–2, 196; causes of
      complexity in 62–3; client populations
      suitable for 43; as clinical discovery
      of erasure sequence 39–42, 59;
      coherence empathy 48, 50, 173–6, 179;
      collaborative nature of 10, 176, 179;
      construed meanings in 46, 106, 113,
      144, 189–92, 196; counter-indications
      for 43; cross-cultural use of 43;
      defining features of, listed online 213;
      definition of 42–3, 49; as demonstrating
      therapeutic reconsolidation process
      xv, 9, 40, 43–64, 67–92, 105–25,
      129; discovery phase of 41, 45–9, 73,
      78–9, 87, 98–100, 106, 110, 120–1,
      160–5, 170–5, 182–3, 189–97; dream
      work within 48, 87, 90–1; and the
      Emotional Coherence Framework 42,
      55; emotional truth of the symptom in
      47–52, 99, 106, 111, 121, 170, 176–7,
      184, 190; experiential nature of 45,
      47–8, 50–2, 57–8, 61–4, 71, 73–6,
      78–9, 82–3, 85, 87–91, 100, 103, 106–9,
      111, 113, 115–18, 123–4, 162, 165–7,
      171–2, 182–4, 190–1, 193, 197–8;
      as explicitly matching therapeutic
      reconsolidation process 5, 9–10,
      40–3, 64, 129; finding contradictory
      knowledge step of 41, 55–6, 74–5,
      81–2, 87–9, 106–7, 111–13, 115–18,
      122, 165, 179, 184, 198; as focused on

symptom-requiring implicit learnings
      43–6, 77; Focusing used within 48,
      170–1, 193–4; functional symptoms 47,
      163, 174, 184; functionless symptoms
      48, 68; in historical context 40, 45;
      history of development of 40–1; index
      of published case examples of 213;
      integration phase of 41, 49–53, 73,
      79–81, 121, 175–6, 183–4, 191–7;
      juxtaposition experience, definition
      of 41, 64; juxtaposition experience,
      examples of 56–60, 74–6, 82–3, 88–9,
      106–8, 113–14, 165–7, 179–80, 184;
      map of interior depth in 165; markers
      of erasure observed in 19, 41, 58–60,
      76–7, 83, 85–6, 90–1, 113, 122–3, 165–
      6, 179, 184, 193, 198–9; mindfulness
      of therapist in 44–5; name changed
      from Depth Oriented Brief Therapy
      xv, 40; non-counteractive nature of
      51, 77, 176–7, 179; number of sessions
      needed in 62, 185; outlier sessions
      as source of 41; parts work within
      48, 73–5, 182–4, 197; pro-symptom
      position 47, 50, 52, 61, 160–2, 175–6,
      179–80, 184, 189, 190–1, 193, 198;
      reconsolidation cited as mechanism
      of change in 20; re-enactment used
      in 86–91; resistance addressed in
      11, 62, 83–5; stance of therapist in
      47, 59, 97, 100, 121, 161, 176–9, 180;
      steps of methodology of 41; symptom
      coherence as central principle of 43–4;
      symptom identification as first step in
      41, 44; symptoms dispelled by 41–2;
      target of change in 47, 62–3, 68–70;
      81–2, 111; technique of mismatch
      detection via overt statement 71–2,
      74, 77, 82, 111–13, 164–5, 184; the
      two sufferings 47, 163, 174, 184, 192,
      194–5; therapist's creativity within
      10–11, 200; transformation phase of
      41, 55–9, 74–6, 82–5, 87–91, 106–9,
      111–19, 122–3, 165–7, 176–7, 179–80,
      184–5, 198–200; verification of schema
      dissolution in 41, 58, 60–1, 64, 76–7,
      85–6, 184, 199; *see also* discovery
      phase; case examples of Coherence
      Therapy; contradictory knowledge,
      finding/creating ; integration phase;
      juxtaposition experience

Coherence Therapy for attachment work:
case examples 105–123, 168–80, 198–
200; disconfirmation by therapist's
empathy in 106–9, 168–80, 199–200;
disconfirmation other than by
therapist's empathy in 74–6, 82, 85–6,
88–91, 110–24; reparative attachment
in 106–9, 168–80
common factors *see* non-specific common
factors
common factors theory 153; critique of
154; limits of 11, 154–5; and specific
treatment effect 154; *see also* specific
factors
complex trauma: case studies 77–86,
110–19, 136–40
compulsive: attachment behavior 71–7;
behavior in response to trigger 15;
drinking 168–80; eating 181–5;
perfectionism 110–19, 159–67; pleasing
102; underachieving 77–86
Connor, Timothy A. 186
constructivist view of mental life 7, 55, 107
constructs, implicit: disconfirmation/
dissolution of 55, 58, 75–6, 83, 88–9,
165–7, 184; as knowings 6–7, 69, 121;
as maintaining illusion of reality 7,
55, 58, 70, 76, 83, 124; as operating
unrecognized 7, 9, 31, 55; recognized
as only constructs 55, 58, 70, 76, 83;
specificity of 185; *see also* knowings,
implicit
constructs, problem-defining *see* problem-
defining constructs
constructs, solution-defining *see* solution-
defining constructs
contextual range of schema 62–2, 108, 115
contradictory knowledge, finding/creating:
in AEDP 131, 133–4; in attachment
work 74, 82, 103–7, 111, 119, 121–2,
131, 133–4, 151, 179, 199–200; in
client's existing knowledge 70–1, 74,
81–2, 92, 111–13, 125, 165–6, 184, 198;
as differentiation 91; and eliciting full
clarity 75; in EMDR 143–5; as guided
by retrieved schema 29, 68–70, 81–2,
87; as launching transformation phase
of Coherence Therapy 41, 55, 82; as
needed for juxtaposition experience
56, 70, 111, 113, 134; as needed for
memory mismatch 28; in new learning

70–1, 87–9, 92, 106–7, 125, 131,
133, 151; resistance to 188–9, 195–7;
sources for 70–1, 92, 119, 125; as
Step C of therapeutic reconsolidation
process 28–30, 41, 55–6, 68, 92, 131,
151; suitability of new learning for
121–2; summary listing of examples
92, 125; techniques tabulated 92, 125;
for traumatic memory 87–91, 111–13,
115, 118–19, 144–7, 198–200; using
empowered re-enactment 86–92; using
I'm in memory practice 115–18, 125;
using imaginal techniques 87–89, 115,
151; using opposite current experience
56, 77, 88–89, 92; using overt
statement/mismatch detection 71–2,
74, 77, 82, 92, 111–13, 122, 125, 184;
using therapist's empathy/reparative
attachment 104, 106–7, 111, 121–2,
125, 131, 133–4, 151, 179, 199–200; *see
also* juxtaposition experience; memory
mismatch; transformation phase
contradictory knowledge: co-existence
with target schema 70, 74; definition
29, 68; experiential quality of 56–8,
74, 82, 87, 111, 113; as new learning for
mismatch/erasure of target learning 58,
64, 87–90, 149; *see also* contradictory
knowledge, finding/creating
control, need for 174–6
costs of solutions/symptoms: effects of
awareness of 74–5; as milder than
suffering avoided 175–7; unacceptable
costs as contradictory knowledge 74–5
counteractive methods of change:
affirmations 145; building social
support 77; in cognitive-behavioral
therapy 17, 35; definition of 34;
examples of 17; extinction as prototype
of 16, 35; oxytocin 17; in positive
psychology 35, 43; positive thinking
17, 145; relaxation techniques 17,
34; in solution-focused therapy 17,
35; suppressive effect of 16–17, 51;
thought-stopping 77; varieties of 35
counteractive reflex 51
counteractive strategy of change 32;
clinical situations requiring 34;
contrasted with transformational
change 4, 9, 17, 19–20, 26, 32–4, 51,
53, 59, 61, 77, 82, 127–8, 135, 141, 152,

counteractive strategy of change
(*continued*): 176–7, 179; definition
16–17, 34–5, 128; emotional regulation
as 33, 152; incremental change in
4; ongoing effort required in 17,
33; persistence of divided self in
33; preserves symptom's emotional
necessity 61, 128; repetition required
in 32; suppressive/competitive nature
of 4, 33, 16–17, 128, 135; susceptibility
to relapse in 17, 61; *see also* emotional
regulation
counter-indications: for Coherence
Therapy 51; for therapeutic
reconsolidation process 34
crisis intervention 34

decision path for reparative attachment
104, 111, 120–2
denial 197–9
dependency of client on therapist 95, 97
depersonalizing 131–2
depression 17, 35, 37–8, 42; case study
136–40; epigenetic correlates of 36–7;
hypothyroidism-induced 8, 15, 34;
social predictors of 94
Depth Oriented Brief Therapy book xv
despair 194
differentiation: from family rules/roles 91;
as a goal of therapy 95, 97
disconfirmation: accuracy of 107; of
attachment learnings 74–6, 85–6,
88–91, 100, 105–124, 131–2, 150, 179,
198–200; of cherished constructs 82,
85, 164–6; context-specific nature of
108, 115; by existing knowledge 70–1,
74, 81–2, 165–6, 184, 198; finding/
creating 29, 55–9, 68–71, 74–7, 81–2,
86–90, 106–7, 119, 121–2, 131–2,
139, 145–6, 150, 198; of generalized
learnings 109; in juxtaposition
experience 55–9, 70, 74, 82, 103,
106–9, 111, 123–4, 132, 165–7, 184,
198; of mental model/constructs
54–9, 62, 77, 87, 91, 97, 107–9, 114–5,
138–9, 145–6, 198; as necessary for
dissolution 55; by new learning 55–9,
70–1, 87–9, 106–9, 131–2, 179, 199–
200; in reconsolidation research 21–2;
in reparative attachment work 106–9,
131–2, 179, 199–200; swiftness of 145;

of terms of attachment 104, 106–7,
111–19, 121–3, 131–2, 179, 198–200;
in therapeutic reconsolidation process
definition 30, 41; of traumatic learnings
86–91, 118–19, 144–7, 198–200; in
traumatic memory 91, 145; *see also*
contradictory knowledge; erasure;
juxtaposition experience; memory
mismatch; transformation phase
discovery experiences in Coherence
Therapy 50; altered state during 49,
176; bilateral stimulation used for
190–2, 196, 200; creation of 45–6, 73,
78, 98–9, 106, 110–11, 120–1, 160–4,
170–5, 182–3, 193, 197; definition of
45; experiential nature of 46; failed
attempts at 164; "Is there something
familiar...?" 99–100; sentence
completion for 73, 164, 162–3, 182,
194; symptom deprivation for 46,
78, 160–1, 170–5, 182–3, 193, 197;
therapist stance in 46
discovery phase in Coherence Therapy
45–9, 73, 78–81, 87, 98–100, 106,
110, 120–1, 160–5, 170–5, 182–3,
189–97; client vulnerability in 48,
110; definition 48; experiential/non-
interpreting quality of 45, 47–8, 50,
100; focus/efficiency of 45, 47; as a
following of links 48, 110; selection
criterion in 47; as Step B of therapeutic
reconsolidation process 45; technique
flexibility of 48, 170, 182–4, 193, 200;
therapist learns from client 47; "What's
under this?" 99–100, 197
dissociation 49, 62, 100, 102, 118; *see also*
emotional safety/stability
dissolution cascade: definition 70
domains of experience/learning 10, 93–8,
124, 126, 128; case examples 98–100
dreams: as focus of discovery work 48, 87,
90; markers of change in 91
dyadic regulation of affect 105; *see also*
reparative attachment

economic factors: as predictor of
mood symptoms 94–5; role of, in
development 94–5
effectiveness of psychotherapy 105,
119; enhancement of, by using
reconsolidation 13, 26–7, 38; and out-

come research 154; and process research 154–5; and specific factors 154–5
EFT *see* Emotion-Focused Therapy
Elliott, Robert 137
EMDR *see* Eye Movement Desensitization and Reprocessing
emotion: as adaptive 136; experience of suppressed 116–17, 132–3, 136–7, 139–40, 143–4, 190–1, 200; experience of suppressed, as potent specific factor 154–5; suppressed/avoided 132, 164, 195
Emotion-Focused Therapy (EFT): parts work in 139–40; reconsolidation cited as mechanism of change in 20; and the therapeutic reconsolidation process 5, 10, 136–40
emotional brain *see* brain, emotional
Emotional Coherence Framework 117; characteristics of 5–6, 8; components of 4, 55; as de–pathologizing 6, 8, 102, 155; and the emotional brain's coherence 6–8,102, 147–8, 155; as guiding case conceptualization 6, 147–8; as guiding Coherence Therapy 55; as guiding clinical use of attachment theory 93, 96, 101–2, 104–5, 107–9, 124; as guiding the therapeutic reconsolidation process 9, 128; as non-theoretical 10, 128; as phenomenological 10, 55; as schema-specific approach 97
emotional deepening: examples 49–50, 78–9, 106–7, 110, 116–17, 135–6, 190–2; factors that enhance or block 51; retrieval as 47–8, 50, 79, 99, 106, 110, 190–2
emotional implicit knowledge/learnings/memory 28, 118, 126: adaptive, self-protective nature of 7–8, 11–12, 43–5, 141, 155, 177, 183; apparent indelibility of 3, 15–16, 18; attachment or non-attachment content of 10, 93–100, 104, 124, 134; clients' insecure attachment patterns as 106–11, 148, 198–9; clinical phenomena exemplifying 14–15; coherence of 4, 6–8, 44–8, 50–1, 54–5, 62–3, 73, 78–81, 87, 98–9, 111, 128, 155, 164–5, 180; construed meanings in 46, 106, 113, 144, 161, 189–92, 196; definition of 14–15; as emotional truth

of the symptom 47, 111; as erasable 13–14, 17–20, 22, 44; experience of disconfirmation/dissolution of 55, 57–8, 74–7, 83, 88–9, 106–7, 119, 121–2, 131–2, 139, 145–6, 150, 165–6, 179, 198; of family rules/roles 91; formation of, in early attachment experiences 32, 100–3; formation of, in existential experiences 95; formation of, in social experiences 94–5; as the Freudian dynamic unconscious 31; generalization of 107, 111; human complexity/sophistication of 6, 27–8, 124, 151; initial example of 6–7; and limbic system/subcortical brain 15–16, 31, 101, 149; mental models in 6, 15, 53–4, 68–70, 97, 106, 111, 148; and natural selection 8, 15; of necessity of symptom 6–7, 50, 53–4, 66, 111; non-conscious functioning of 6, 9, 31–2, 172, 183; as the past living in the present 7–8, 96, 116, 147–9; as procedural knowledge 14–15, 172, 183; "raw data" in 6, 53, 110, 120, 150; as repository of all domains of 96; and right cortical hemisphere 31, 149; as root of symptom production 3, 6–8, 11, 14, 16, 28, 36–7, 39, 63, 65, 111, 148–9, 180, 183; schema structure of 4, 6, 15, 53, 68–70, 111; of a specific suffering and how to avoid it 44, 46–7, 53–4, 68, 77, 99–101, 108, 110–11, 121, 183, 192, 197, 199–200; specificity of nonverbal constructs/knowings in 6–7, 47, 53–4, 68–70, 97, 185; symptoms not caused by 8, 15, 37; synapses of 3, 13, 16; tenacity of 3, 8, 15, 37, 96, 101, 147–8; terms of attachment as 102–3; in therapy field's history 8, 45; and unknown content of target learning 27; *see also* constructs, implicit; knowings, implicit; mental models; schema, implicit; symptom-requiring schema
emotional learning *see* emotional implicit knowledge
emotional memory *see* emotional implicit knowledge
emotional necessity of symptom: as adaptive implicit knowledge 44–7, 100–1, 165, 173, 183, 197, 199–200; as avoidance of suffering 44, 46–7, 52, 68,

emotional necessity of symptom
(*continued*): 73, 85, 99, 100–1, 108,
121, 163, 165, 174–5, 183, 192, 197,
199–200; as non-conscious learning
44–5, 47, 68, 76, 180, 183; as purpose
driving symptom 47, 52, 68, 84,
108, 121, 165, 170, 177, 183, 192,
197; retrieval and experience of 47,
108, 121, 163, 165, 183, 192, 197; as
root cause of symptom 44, 47, 108,
165, 180, 183, 192, 197, 199–200; as
symptom's coherence 44–5, 47, 163,
174–5, 180, 183, 192, 197
emotional regulation: basic process
and strategy of 32–3; competitive,
suppressive nature of 33; and concept
of dysregulation 33, 102; contrasted
with therapeutic reconsolidation
process 32–3, 152; effort required
to maintain 33; incremental change
in 33; persistence of divided self in
33; susceptibility to relapse in 33; as
top-down suppression of subcortical
responses 33; varieties of 35; *see also*
counteractive strategy of change
emotional safety/stability: detecting
clients' problematic reactions 49,
175; dissociation, signs of 49; in
EMDR 142–3; learning client's
emotional tolerances 49, 175, 191;
as a non-specific common factor
43, 153; permission to re-suppress
49; small enough steps 48–9, 110,
116; suicidal ideation 196 therapist's
accompaniment, role of 49, 109
emotional truth of the symptom 47–52,
99, 106, 111, 121, 170, 176–7, 184, 190;
definition 47–8; emergent emotional
truths 68, 80, 85, 107, 112, 123, 160–3,
165, 192–4, 200; *see also* pro-symptom
position; symptom coherence;
symptom-requiring schema
empathy, therapist's communication of
120, 137; to both sides of juxtaposition
experience , 57–9, 106–7; coherence
empathy as special form of 48, 50;
and decision path for reparative
attachment viability 104, 111, 120–2;
for disconfirmation of attachment
learnings 85–6, 100, 104–9,
150–1, 179, 199–200; and emotional

attunement 13–14, 48, 50–1, 68; as
experience of secure attachment 103–
6, 121–2, 131–3, 148, 150–1; function
of, in transforming attachment patterns
108–9, 153; as a non-specific common
factor 43, 153; and voice tone 51, 57,
106–7; *see also* coherence empathy
empirically supported principles of change
155
epigenetic correlates of clinical symptoms
9, 36; as caused by emotional implicit
memory 36–7
erasure/dissolution of implicit emotional
learnings/models 4; in attachment
work 74–6, 82, 85–6, 88–91, 103, 105,
110–24, 131, 150, 168–80, 199–200;
autobiographical memory unaffected
by 14, 23, 39; behavioral sequence for
25–7, 126, 149; brain's rules/readiness
for 4. 26, 34, 65, 126–7, 149; client's
experience of change 55, 58, 60–1,
76–7, 85–6, 90–1, 113, 122–3, 133–6,
139–40, 146–7, 151, 165–6, 179, 184,
193, 195, 198–9; clinical discovery of
behavioral sequence for 39–40, 59; as
ending the control of the past 96–7;
grief in response to 83–5; identifying
target construct for 68–70, 111, 122;
markers of 19, 41, 58, 60–1, 64, 90–1,
95, 113, 122–3, 146–7, 151, 165–6, 179,
184, 193, 198, 199; as occurring in
definite moments 57–8, 75–6, 83, 88–9,
145; permanence of symptom cessation
9, 19, 39, 67; precision of 14, 23, 25;
as profound unlearning 39, 63, 67, 96;
requires emotional brain's consent
62, 83–5, 148; requires juxtaposition
experience 70, 103, 117–8, 123, 149,
153; research demonstrating 17–27;
resistance to 62, 68, 83–5, 163–4;
summary listing of case examples
92, 125; suitability of new learning
for achieving 27; swiftness of 8, 149,
153, 184; in traumatic memory 87–90,
111–19, 147–8, 198–200; understood
as memory "updating"/"rewriting"
25; *see also* contradictory knowledge;
erasure sequence; disconfirmation;
reconsolidation; therapeutic
reconsolidation process; transformation
sequence

erasure sequence 27–30; clinical discovery of, 39–42, 59; and complexity of target learning 27–8, 151; context-specific nature of 63, 108, 115; definition of 26–7, 30, 41; finding mismatch material for 28, 63; integrative features/value of 27, 149, 152; preparatory steps for 28, 63; repetitions for range of contexts 60, 63, 108, 115; as requiring knowledge/ retrieval of target learning 27–8, 63; research demonstrating 20–27; as sole process for erasing existing learning 34, 127; swiftness of 8, 29; technique and theory independence of 27; as unification of neuroscience and clinical findings 41–2; unknown content of target learning 27–8; unrecognized or serendipitous occurrence of 29, 127, 152; *see also* transformation sequence
ethnicity 94
evolution: and tenacity of emotional implicit memory 8, 15–16, 20, 36, 38
existential domain of learning: examples 95, 100
existential issues 85
expectation, implicit learning–based 6–7, 70, 100–1, 115, 121–4, 131–2, 134, 151, 175
experiential dissonance 58
experiential work: definition of, in Coherence Therapy 46, 50; examples 45–6, 49–50, 52, 56–8, 73–6, 78–83, 87–90, 98–100, 106–8, 111–14, 116, 131–3, 135–6, 138–40, 143–6, 150–1, 160–6, 170–6, 182–3, 190–4, 196–7; limbic language for 50; tone of voice for 56–7, 60, 99, 112, 182; *see also* bodily experiencing; techniques, experiential; *and* "experiential" *under* Coherence Therapy; discovery phase; integration experiences; juxtaposition experience; retrieval of symptom-requiring schema; symptom-requiring schema; therapeutic reconsolidation process; transformational change
exposure therapy: as extinction training 35
extinction: as neurologically distinct from reconsolidation 23–4; temporary nature of 16, 19;
extinction training: competitive/ counteractive nature of 16, 19; in

exposure therapy 35; as prototype of counteractive methods 35; during reconsolidation window 24
"extinction-induced erasure" as misnomer 24
Eye Movement Desensitization and Reprocessing (EMDR): within Coherence Therapy 190–2, 196; dual stimulation in 141; reconsolidation cited as mechanism of change in 20; and the therapeutic reconsolidation process 5, 10, 141–8

family of origin rules/roles: defining attachment 100–2, 108; as emotional learning 15; *see also* attachment learnings; attachment patterns
family system 91
flashback: affective 90; external projection of 117
Focusing 48, 170–1, 193–4, 194, 200; felt sense 60, 170, 193; and the therapeutic reconsolidation process 5
Fosha, Diana 130
functional symptoms: as avoiding a worse suffering 47, 163, 174, 184; case examples 47, 163, 174, 184; definition 47, 68
functionless symptom: case examples 48, 101; definition 48, 68

gender 94, 97
Gendlin, Eugene 170
generalization of implicit learning 107, 111
genetic predisposition: as inborn temperament 95–6; research findings 95–6; role of implicit memory in 15; role of, in schema formation 96; role of, in symptom production 95–6
Geoghegan, Niall 181
Gestalt therapy 87; and EFT 136; and the therapeutic reconsolidation process 5
glossary, online 213
Greenberg, Leslie 136
grief /grieving 42, 61, 84–5, 99, 117, 133, 137–9, 144, 147–8, 165; resistance to 83–5, 132, 163–4
guilt: case studies 143–5, 147–8, 159–67, 193

Hakomi: and the therapeutic
    reconsolidation process 5
Hebb's law 32
history, client's: searching in 12, 99–100,
    106, 110, 120–1, 137–9, 172–4, 198–9;
    see also original sufferings, revisiting
human studies of reconsolidation 25
hypervigilance 15, 101

ideal fantasy outcome 197
identity: defined by terms of attachment
    106, 111, 164, 198–200; implicit model/
    constructs of 111, 146, 191–4, 197; loss
    of 146, 191, 197; protection of 197; as
    unlovable/worthless 106, 111, 192–4,
    197; *see also* low self-esteem; self
I'm in memory practice 115–18, 146;
    calming/de-pathologizing effects
    of 116, 118; index card for 116; as
    integration of original sufferings
    116–17; juxtapositions created by 118;
    as mindfulness of retriggering 117
imaginal work 20, 45–6, 52, 56–7, 63, 73,
    78, 80, 85, 88–89, 106, 112–14, 119,
    150–1, 160–1, 170–5, 182–3, 193–4,
    197; brain's response to 27, 86
implicit knowledge *see* emotional implicit
    knowledge/learnings/memory
implicit to explicit knowing 7, 10, 46,
    48–9, 53, 55, 63, 69, 73, 100, 109, 117,
    153; examples 7, 50, 54, 98–100, 106,
    139–40, 143, 150; verbalization for 47,
    106, 111, 139–40, 148–9, 190–2; *see
    also* retrieval of symptom-requiring
    schema
incremental change: as inherent in
    competitive new learning 4, 33;
    ongoing effort required in 9, 33
index card for between-session task 76,
    84; eliciting/reviewing results of 52,
    74, 81, 111, 163–6, of 184, 192–5;
    instructions for 51, 53, 60, 81, 114,
    191; for integration experiences 51–3,
    73, 80, 84, 111, 121, 160, 162–3, 176,
    184, 191–5, 197; for juxtaposition
    experiences 60, 76, 84, 114, 165; and
    resulting markers of erasure 60, 122–3,
    165–6, 184, 198; and resulting markers
    of integration 52, 74, 162, 184, 193–5
integration experiences in Coherence
    Therapy 49; definition 49–50;

experiential, visceral quality of 50,
    52, 197; felt purpose of symptom in
    49–50, 79–80, 111, 115–17, 121, 160,
    162–3, 175–7, 183, 197; *I'm in memory*
    practice 115–18; as mindfulness of
    symptom-requiring schema 51–3; overt
    statement technique 49–50, 52, 73, 80,
    160–1, 163–4, 183; verbalization for
    52, 54; *see also* between-session task;
    index card; integration phase; markers
    of integration
integration of brain functions 149
integration of psychotherapy *see*
    psychotherapy integration
integration phase in Coherence Therapy
    49–53, 73, 79–85, 115–18, 162–5,
    175–7, 183–4, 191–7; as acceptance/
    non-counteracting 51, 53, 172–7, 183;
    completeness of 54–5; as completing
    retrieval/Step B of therapeutic
    reconsolidation process 49, 53;
    definition 49; experience of purpose/
    agency in 50, 52, 73, 79–80, 108, 114,
    121, 160, 162–3, 175–6, 183, 195, 197;
    as focused mindfulness 51–3; *see also*
    integration experiences; markers of
    integration
Internal Family Systems (IFS) therapy:
    and the therapeutic reconsolidation
    process 5
Interpersonal Neurobiology (IPNB):
    reconsolidation cited as mechanism
    of change in 20; and the therapeutic
    reconsolidation process 5, 10, 148–51
invisibility 102, 194
isolation 136–40, 159–67, 186–200

Johnson, Susan 137
Jung, Carl 53
justice/injustice/unfairness 44, 79, 81, 84,
    99, 120, 163–5
juxtaposition experience: client's
    experience of 58, 65, 107, 144–5;
    clinical discovery of 59; and cognitive
    defusion 59; and cognitive dissonance
    58; and cognitive restructuring 59;
    confirmed by markers of erasure
    65, 123, 127, 130, 133–4, 151, 198;
    context–specific nature of 63, 108,
    115; definition 58, 64; as devoid of
    counteracting/pathologizing 57, 59,

76, 82, 179; as dissolving problematic constructs/meanings 77, 97, 113–15, 117–8, 123, 135, 140, 144–5, 153, 198; as empathy toward both sides 57–9, 75, 107, 113; ending suppression of feelings 109, 131; examples 56–60, 74–6, 82–3, 88–9, 106–9, 113–14, 131, 140, 144–5, 151, 165–7, 179–80, 184, 198–200; as experiential disconfirmation 57–9, 70, 75–6, 82–3, 88–90, 103, 106–9, 117–18, 123–4, 132, 139, 144–6, 151, 165–7, 184, 198; explicitness of 65, 83, 90, 105, 109, 133–5, 152; fulfills Steps 1–2–3 of therapeutic reconsolidation process 41, 57–8, 67, 71, 130, 134, 151, 153; via *I'm in memory* practice 118; imaginal creation of 63, 83, 88–9, 112–15, 151; index card for repetition of 60; as mismatch required for unlocking synapses 57, 59, 64, 68, 71, 82; as observable moments of deep change 57–8, 75–6, 83, 88–90, 145; prompting mindful awareness in 57, 106; via re-enactment 89–91; repetition after resistance work 62, 85; repetitions for range of contexts 60, 63, 108, 115; repetitions of, in Step 3, 57–8, 60, 64, 68, 71, 75–6, 82–4, 107–8, 113–14, 132, 145–6, 179–80; resistance to 83–5, 104, 134, 188–9, 195–7; resulting from mismatch detection 82, 113–14, 122–3, 153, 165, 184; as specific factor in transformational change 59, 66–7, 70, 104–5, 153; as Steps 2–3 of erasure sequence 41, 56–60, 64, 66–8, 71, 107, 127, 130–4, 136, 140, 144–6, 151, 153; tacit/unnoticed occurrence of 65, 90, 133–5, 138–9, 152; targeting a master construct 69, 71, 88–90, 113–14, 122–3; targeting attachment schemas 103–9, 113–14, 119, 122–4, 131, 133–4, 151, 179–80; via therapist's empathy 106–8, 131, 133–4, 151, 179–80, 199–200; *see also* contradictory knowledge; disconfirmation; erasure; erasure sequence; memory mismatch; transformation phase; transformational change

Kagan, Jerome 94–5
Kandel, Eric 42

knowings, implicit 6, 7, 45–7, 51, 56–9, 62, 64, 69, 74–6, 84–5, 90–1, 103, 108, 114, 139–40, 143, 145, 150, 172, 184, 193, 198

laughter as marker 58, 60
learning preferred responses counteractively: competitive, suppressive nature of 33; incremental change resulting from 33; myriad repetitions required for 32; as not erasing 33; ongoing effort to maintain 33; susceptibility to relapse of 33; as top-down control 33
limbic language: definition 50–1; examples 50, 114;
limbic system 50; and Freudian unconscious 31; power of, over apparent reality 7, 16, 20, 127;
Lipton, Benjamin 130
living knowledge 7, 28–9, 50, 53, 55–6, 70, 74, 92, 102, 119, 124
living memory 183
low self-esteem/self-worth: as adherence to terms of attachment 111, 198–200; as emotional learning 14 as badness 144; case studies 43–63, 106–19, 130–40, 168–80; coherence of 45–7, 49–50, 106, 113–14, 198–200; as inner critic 139 as not mattering 106–8, 175–80; as perfectionism 111–14, 161, 164; as response to mistreatment 106, 110–11, 138–9; as response to powerlessness 144, 190; as self-blame 114, 137, 144–8 as feeling incapable 44, 137; as shame 137; as unlovable/worthless 111, 191–4, 197; *see also* identity; self

Main, Mary 100
Maldonado, Héctor xix
map of schema contents/structure 53–4
marital sexual aversion 120–3
markers of erased emotional response: as aiding therapist's learning 64–5; as caused by reconsolidation only 19, 41, 64, 127; client's report of 58, 60–1, 76–7, 83, 85–6, 90–1, 113, 122–3, 133–6, 139–40, 146–7, 151, 165–6, 179, 184, 193, 195, 198–9; as confirming juxtaposition experience 65, 123, 127, 130, 133–4, 151, 198;

markers of erased emotional response
(*continued*): as confirming reactivation
and mismatch 23, 127, 149; definition
19, 64, 127; with emotion marker of
compassion 60, 140, 198; with emotion
marker of grief/distress 60, 83, 113–14,
146, 165; with emotion marker of
mirth/laughter/joy 58, 60–1, 91, 123,
133, 135, 193; as not due to extinction
19; as verification of erasure 30, 41,
60–1, 64, 76–7, 85–6, 90, 131, 133,
135–6, 139–40, 146–7, 151, 179–80,
184, 199
markers of integration: awareness of
themes 52, 74, 177, 184, 193–5;
disorientation 165, 175–6; decrease of
symptoms 162, 193–5; dystonic feeling
174; experience of agency/purpose
50, 52, 73, 80, 108, 114, 175–6, 184;
recognition of coherence/sense 50, 184;
relief of de-pathologizing 50, 80, 108,
114, 116, 175–6
Martignetti, C. Anthony 168
master construct: definition 69; examples
69–70, 81, 122, 165; how to identify
69; presupposed possibility type of 82,
163, 197; as primary target 69
mattering 102, 106–8
meaning, implicit constructs of 46,
106–7, 113, 121, 144, 147, 161, 189–92,
196
mechanism of change: reconsolidation
cited as 19–20, 41–2, 154
memory consolidation 16–19
memory mismatch: brain's detection of
71–2, 77, 122; through contradiction
21–2, 25, 64; finding material for
28; inferred from markers 23; as
juxtaposition experience 59, 64;
through novelty 21–2, 25; as required
for reconsolidation 20–3, 26, 57, 59,
72; as Step 2 of erasure sequence 26–7,
30, 41, 57, 64; understood as prediction
error signal 22; understood as violation
of expectation 21–2, 26; *see also*
contradictory knowledge; juxtaposition
experience; mismatch detection; new
learning used for unlearning/erasing
a target learning; reconsolidation;
reconsolidation research

memory reactivation: as required for
reconsolidation 17–19, 26; as Step 1 of
erasure sequence 26–7, 30, 41, 56, 64,
71, 131, 149, 151; of target construct 27,
71, 151
memory reconsolidation *see*
reconsolidation; reconsolidation
research
"memory retrieval-extinction" procedure:
critiqued as misnomer 24
memory types: anatomical separateness of
15, 23, 31, 70; autobiographical 14–15,
23, 25; classical fear conditioning
25; context-specific 60, 63, 108, 115;
contextual fear 21; cue-triggered
heroin craving 25; declarative 21, 25;
distributed 60, 63, 115; episodic 15,
25; explicit 23; motor 20, 25; object
recognition 21; operant conditioning
21, 25; procedural knowledge
14–15; semantic 20; spatial 21; taste
recognition 21; traumatic 62, 86–91,
110–19, 141–8, 186–200; *see also*
autobiographical memory; emotional
implicit knowledge; traumatic memory
mental model: constructs within
6–7, 53–4, 68–70, 97, 111, 165;
disconfirmation/dissolution of 54, 56,
62, 77, 87, 91, 97, 107, 109, 114–15,
138–9, 139, 145–6; dissolution of,
blocked by resistance 62, 83–5, 163–4;
as driver of symptom production 54,
111, 148, 175, 191; examples 6–7,
53–4, 69–70, 77, 100–1, 106, 111,
114–15, 138–9, 145–6, 164–5, 175,
191; as expectation of how world
functions 6–7, 26, 53–4, 100–1, 107,
111, 131, 164–5, 175, 191; formed
in infancy 7, 100–1; as implicit
emotional learning 6, 15, 53–4, 68,
106, 111, 148; in traumatic memory
87, 111, 143, 191; map of structure
of 53–4; modular nature of 54; as
non-conscious instruction to self 54;
as non-disconfirmable when implicit
56, 118; non-verbal nature of 6, 68;
as prime target for erasure 54, 114,
175; "problem" defined in 53–4, 73,
79, 81, 100–1, 107, 111; of self/world
106, 111, 138–9, 145–6, 164–5, 175,
191; "solution" defined in 54, 73, 79,

81, 100–2, 107, 111; specificity of 6, 53–4, 68–70, 97, 185; as template of experiences 15, 100–1; of terms of attachment 102–3, 106, 109, 131, 175, 191; *see also* constructs, implicit; emotional implicit knowledge; knowings, implicit; schema, implicit; symptom-requiring schema

mindfulness, practice of: in integration experiences 9, 51–3, 117; in juxtaposition experiences 57, 106, 132; for learning preferred responses 32, 188–9; therapist's 44–5, 68

Minuchin, Salvador 94–5

mismatch detection 71–2, 77, 122; creates initial juxtaposition experience 74, 82, 153, 165, 184; *see also* contradictory knowledge, finding; juxtaposition experience; memory mismatch

Neuro-Linguistic Programming (NLP): and the therapeutic reconsolidation process 5

neuroplasticity, reconsolidation as type of 4, 13, 16, 26, 39

neuroscience's implications for psychotherapy: as changed by reconsolidation research 9, 13–14, 31–4; erasure sequence as unification 41–2; implicit memory as source of symptom production 6, 8, 16, 36, 149

new knowings used for erasing a target learning 39, 41,49; in attachment work 103, 105, 107–8, 113–15, 135, 153, 179–80, 199–200; disconfirming quality of 26–8, 58, 89, 103, 144–6, 179–80, 198; during reconsolidation window 25, 64; in EMDR 144–5; experiential quality of 27–8, 144–5; identifying target construct for 68–70; imaginal techniques for accessing 27, 86–90, 112–15; via juxtaposition experience 58, 64, 103, 135, 144–5, 179–80, 198; as Step 3 of erasure sequence 26–7, 64, 145; via synaptic re-encoding 33–4, 41; as transformational change 4, 20, 33–4, 64, 179–80, 198; for traumatic memory 88–91, 110–19, 144–8, 198–200; *see also* juxtaposition experience

non–specific common factors: catalytic role of 108–9, 153–4; components of

43; as distinct from specific factors in therapeutic reconsolidation process 43; as not creating transformational change 153–4; as prerequisites of Coherence Therapy 43; in relation to specific factors 153; and reparative attachment therapy 123–4; and secure attachment 123–4; and therapist as attachment figure 123–4; *see also* common factors theory

obsessive attachment 71–7, 92

online supplements 11, 41, 219

original sufferings, revisiting: as allowing emotional healing 137–9, 151; and awareness of retriggering by reminder 116, 146–7, 149; and de-pathologizing of self/symptoms 116–17, 137–8, 146–7, 175–6; as emotional integration 137–9, 149, 151; and forming coherent narratives 117; and grieving 117, 137–9, 144, 151; and past/present discernment 146–7, 149; requires small-enough steps 116; as requiring empathetic accompaniment 117, 137–9, 148, 151; as schema retrieval in original context 106,120–1, 137–9, 143–4, 164, 183; and self-compassion 116–17, 137–9, 198; *see also* history, client's

outlier sessions: in creation of Coherence Therapy 41; in outcome research 154;

overt statement technique 85, 164; examples 49–50, 52, 73–4, 80, 83, 160–1, 163–5, 183; as integration technique 49–50, 52, 73–4, 160–1, 163–4, 183; as launch of mismatch detection 71–2, 74, 77, 82, 111–13, 164–5, 184; as verification technique 85; *see also* techniques, experiential

oxytocin 17

panic 110–19, 141–8

paradoxical intervention 53

parts work 48, 73–5, 139–40, 182–4, 197

past/present distinction 118, 146–7, 149

perfectionism 14, 111–14, 119, 161, 164

pharmacological treatment 34

phenomenological view of mental life 7, 100, 145; *see also* constructivist view; mental model

phenomenology 54–5, 129

positive psychology 35, 43
post-traumatic symptoms (PTSD):as
    emotional learning 14; therapeutic
    strategy for 34–5
post-traumatic symptoms (PTSD), case
    studies of: using Coherence Therapy
    86–91, 110–19, 186–200; using EMDR
    141–8; using *I'm in memory* practice
    116–18; using re-enactment 20, 87–91;
    see also complex trauma; traumatic
    memory
powerlessness/helplessness 87–91, 99 ,
    101, 114, 163, 169–70 , 176–7, 190, 196
"problem" and "solution": as components
    of mental model 53–5, 73, 76, 79, 85,
    99, 100–1, 107, 111, 114, 150, 175–6;
    in early attachment learning 100–1;
    retrieval of 73, 79, 81, 177, 183, 197
problem-defining constructs 68–70;
    construed meanings as 76–7, 106,
    113; insecure attachment learnings as
    100–1, 104, 106–7, 111, 121, 198–200;
    as knowledge of how world/self
    functions 6, 53–4, 76, 88, 107, 121; as
    knowledge of vulnerability to specific
    suffering 6–7, 11–12, 44, 53, 68–70,
    76, 79, 87, 99, 106–7, 111, 119–21,
    150, 177, 183–4, 199; as prime target
    for erasure 46–7, 54; summary list
    of examples 92, 125; *see also* mental
    model; solution-defining constructs;
    symptom-requiring schema
procedural knowledge 14–15; *see also*
    constructs, implicit; emotional implicit
    knowledge; knowings, implicit;
Process-Experiential Psychotherapy 137;
    see also Emotion-Focused Therapy
pro-symptom position 47, 50, 61,
    160–2, 175, 179–80, 184, 189, 195–8;
    ownership of 52, 190–1, 193, 195–6,
    198; resistance to ownership of 188–9,
    195–7; *see also* emotional truth of the
    symptom; mental model; purpose;
    symptom-requiring schema
psychoanalytic therapy: reconsolidation
    cited as mechanism of change in 20
psychodynamic psychotherapy 35, 154
psychotherapy integration: and
    attachment-focused therapy 93–7, 124;
    and deep structure of transformational

therapies 127–30, 149, 152; and specific
    factors 127–8; by the therapeutic
    reconsolidation process 27, 124, 126–55
PTSD *see* complex trauma; post-traumatic
    symptoms; traumatic memory
purpose, implicit, maintaining symptom:
    adaptive nature of 8, 119–20, 162,
    175–7, 183, 197; as component of
    symptom-requiring schema 46, 68,
    79–80, 121, 195; de-pathologizing
    effect of recognizing 8, 47–8, 50, 80,
    114, 175–7; as implicit construct 68,
    175–6, 183; as key goal for retrieval
    50, 170,195; retrieval/experience of 46,
    50, 52, 73, 79–80, 114, 121, 160, 162–3,
    175–6, 183, 197; *see also* emotional
    truth of the symptom; mental model;
    pro-symptom position; symptom-
    requiring schema

racial/ethnic oppression 95
reconsolidation: as brain mechanism for
    erasure of target learning 13, 17–20,
    25–7, 33–4; chemical disruption of
    18; cited as mechanism of change in
    psychotherapy 19–20, 154; computer
    analogy for 22; de-consolidation/
    destabilization/labilization of memory
    circuits in 18–22; definition of 19;
    discovery of 17–18; introduction to
    psychotherapists of 14; mismatch of
    target memory as requirement for
    20–3, 149; as neurologically distinct
    from extinction 23–4, 33–4; as not
    induced by reactivation alone 18,
    20–3; as only type of neuroplasticity
    that erases 10, 13–14, 19, 26, 64, 127;
    permanence of symptom cessation
    from 19, 34, 39; reactivation of target
    memory as required for 17–18, 20–2,
    149; precision of erasure in 23, 25; re–
    encoding of synapses in 33–4, 41, 154;
    and strategy of psychotherapy 20; and
    transformational change 20, 26, 33–4;
    see also reconsolidation research;
    reconsolidation window; therapeutic
    reconsolidation process
reconsolidation research 38–9; with
    anisomycin 21; on biomolecular and
    genetic processes 24–5; on boundary
    conditions 23–4; on chemical

disruption for psychotherapy 25; as corroboration of clinical discovery 39–42; with cycloheximide 21; electroconvulsive therapy in early 17; with human subjects 25–6; and juxtaposition experiences 58; markers of memory erasure in 19, 41; memory mismatch requirement 20–3; origins and progression of 13–21; on precision of erasure 23, 25; reconsolidation window 18, 24–6, 64; species studied in 20–1; types of memory studied in 20–1, 25; *see also* reconsolidation; reconsolidation window; therapeutic reconsolidation process

reconsolidation window: duration of 18, 25, 64; erasure of target learning by new learning during 18, 24–6, 64; extinction training during 24; *see also* reconsolidation; reconsolidation research; therapeutic reconsolidation process

re-enactment, empowered 34; counter-indication for 91; for dissolving traumatic memory 86–91, 119; *see also* post-traumatic symptoms

re-encoding of synapses in reconsolidation 33–4, 41, 154

relaxation techniques 34

reparative attachment therapy: within AEDP 130–6; case examples 106–9, 121–2, 148–51, 168–80, 198–200; within Coherence Therapy 106–9, 121–2, 168–80, 198–200; and common factors 123–4; conditions of fulfillment of 123–4; as creating experiential disconfirmation 104, 106–7, 111, 121–2, 125, 131, 133–4, 151, 179, 199–200; critique of 95, 115; decision path for suitability 104–5, 111, 120–2; and emotional regulation 35; within IPNB 148–51; as optional for attachment work 77, 97, 104–5, 110–11, 119–22; rationale for 103–4, 148; as requiring non-adult emotional identity 123; schema-specific suitability of 97, 98–100, 104–5, 111, 119–24; unsuitability of, examples of 98–100, 119–24; *see also* attachment learnings; attachment patterns; disconfirmation: of attachment

learnings; empathy, therapist's; juxtaposition experience: targeting attachment schemas

reparenting 95, 97, 103, 105

research: on psychotherapy outcome 153–4; on psychotherapy process 154–5; randomized controlled trials 154; *see also* attachment research; reconsolidation research

resistance 123; to alcohol restriction 168–80; case examples 68, 83–5, 163–4, 188–9, 193, 195–7; coherence of 12, 62, 83–5, 163–4, 193; Coherence Therapy's approach for 11, 62, 83–5; dissipation of 83–5; honoring 12, 62; to integration of schema/emotional truth 188–9, 195–7; to juxtaposition experience 104, 188–9, 195–7; overt statement of 83, 163; to schema dissolution 62, 68, 83–5, 163–4; to symptom deprivation 193; to weight loss 181–5 utilization of 12, 193

resource utilization 34

retrieval of symptom-requiring schema: accuracy in 8, 46, 107, 176; agency experienced in 50, 80, 108, 114, 162–3, 183–4, 195; as awareness of symptom's emotional necessity 9–10, 46–7, 50, 67, 73–4, 79, 98–9, 120–1, 143–4, 150, 164–5, 183–4, 190–2, 197; as basis for finding contradictory knowledge 55, 68, 97, 105, 107, 121–2, 134, 177; collaborative nature of 11; completeness of 53–5, 73; consisting of traumatic material 87, 110–11, 143–4, 190–2, 196–7; as de-pathologizing symptom 48, 50, 65–6, 80, 108, 114, 116, 175–7; discovery phase of 73, 78–80, 87, 110, 160, 162–4, 170–5, 182–3; as emotional deepening 47–8, 50, 79, 99, 162, 190–2, 106, 110; as empirically supported specific factor 155; experiential nature of 10, 50, 52, 100, 150, 162, 183–4, 190–1, 197; as finding symptom's coherence 73, 78, 87, 98–100; imaginal work for 52, 78–9, 150–1, 160–1, 170–5, 182–3, 197; integration phase of 49, 53; as launching mismatch detection 71–2, 74, 111–13, 165, 184; limbic language for 114; mindfulness tasks for 9, 51, 53;

retrieval of symptom-requiring schema
(*continued*): non-counteractive nature
of 51, 176–7; non-interpretive nature of
100, 176; non-theoretical nature of 100;
as not dissolving schema 153, 191; as
opening schema to disconfirmation 56,
184; as revealing construed meanings
46, 106, 113, 144, 161, 189–92, 196;
as revealing domain of learning 10,
97–100, 104, 121; as revealing mental
model/constructs 54, 68, 73, 79, 81,
87, 97, 106–7, 110–11, 139, 143, 162,
164–5, 191; as revealing "problem" and
"solution" 53–5, 73, 79, 81, 98–9, 111,
150, 175–7, 183–4, 197; as revealing
coherence/purpose necessitating
symptom 7, 45–7, 50, 52, 73, 78–80,
98–9, 106, 110–11, 114–17, 120–1,
162–5, 175–7, 183–4, 192, 195, 197;
as revealing target learnings 46–7,
54, 62–3, 77, 81–2, 111, 114, 117–18,
175; as revealing terms of attachment
106–7, 110–11, 119–20, 198–200; as
revealing top-down coherent causation
of symptoms 7, 36; by revisiting
original sufferings 106, 120–1, 137–9,
143, 164–5, 183; as shift from implicit
to explicit knowing 7, 10, 47, 50, 73–4,
98–9, 109, 143–4, 150, 153, 155; small
enough steps in 110, 116; as source of
coherent narratives 7, 117; as Step B
of therapeutic reconsolidation process
28–30, 41, 46, 53, 139, 143–4, 150;
swiftness possible in 8; tracking of
client's experience in 12; verbalization
as key aspect of 47, 50, 52, 68, 99,
102, 106, 111, 148–9, 183, 190–2; *see
also* discovery experiences; discovery
phase; integration experiences;
integration phase
reward 54
"rewriting" of implicit learning 25, 27, 33,
41, 64
Rice, Laura 137

schema, implicit 4, 15, 73; as structure
of emotional learning 6, 13; *see
also* constructs, implicit; knowings,
implicit; mental model; symptom-
requiring schema
Schnarch, David 95

Schoninger, Beverly 141
self: de-pathologized sense of 65–6, 108,
119, 175–6, 198–200; disconfirmation
of implicit constructs/model of
89–91, 108–9, 119, 138–9, 145–6,
179–80, 198–200; divided 33; implicit
constructs/model of 87, 91, 109, 111,
137, 175–80, 191–4, 197; unified
33, 175–6; *see also* identity; low
self-esteem
self-blame 114, 137, 144–8, 192, 197–8; as
avoiding helplessness 163–4, 197; case
studies 159–67, 186–200; coherence
of 148; *see also* guilt; low self-esteem;
self-hatred
self-compassion 116, 135, 198
self-doubt 69; case study 43–63; *see also*
low self-esteem
self-hatred 160, 190–1, 195–6; *see also*
low self-esteem
self-talk 44
sentence completion technique 73, 78–9,
83, 112, 162–4, 182, 194
serial accessing 164, 192
sexual abuse, childhood 130, 183–4
sexual orientation 43
sexual problem, case study of 120–3
shame/shaming 6, 15, 42, 78, 110, 132,
137–9, 149, 162, 189, 195–6, 198–200
Shapiro, Francine 141
Sibson, Paul 159
Siegel, Daniel 148
silence 51, 57–8, 106, 112–13
skill-building 34
small enough steps 48–9, 62, 110, 116
social anxiety, case studies of 6–7, 61,
110–19, 168–80
social domain of learning 94–5, 100
social factors: as predictor of mood
symptoms 94–5; role of, in
development 94–5
social narratives 97
solution-defining constructs 68–70; broad
purpose/strategy defined by 54, 68,
100–1; case examples of 54, 69–70, 74,
81–2, 120; construct of possibility in
82, 163, 197; dissolving and replacing
85; formed in attachment learning
100–1, 120, 198–9; fulfillment of 120;
non-conscious idealized outcome as
81–2, 197; as self-fulfilling prophecies

107; summary list of examples of 92, 125; as symptom's direct cause 54, 68, 99; symptoms expressing lack of 101–2; tactics defined by 54, 68, 74, 100–1, 108; as target for erasure 46–7, 54, 77; *see also* mental model; problem-defining constructs; purpose, implicit; symptom-requiring schema

Solution-focused therapy 35

specific factors: definition 153; feeling avoided emotional meaning as chief among 154–5; and psychotherapy process research 154–5; and psychotherapy integration 127–8; in relation to common factors 153; as required for transformational change 11, 127, 130, 154; steps of therapeutic reconsolidation process as 11, 127; *see also* non-specific common factors; transformation-specific factors

specific treatment effect: and common factors theory 154; definition 154; and transformation sequence 154; *see also* research

spiritual domain of learning 96

stage fright, case study of 86–91

stance of therapist: as anthropologist 97, 161, 180; learns from client 47, 97, 100, 121, 128, 161, 178, 180; non-counteractive 59, 176–7, 179; non-interpretive 47, 100; not-knowing 97, 100, 180; trusting client's capability to revise learnings 59, 151 176;

strategies of psychotherapy: counteractive vs transformational 20, 127–8, 152; *see also* counteractive strategy of change; transformational change

symptom cessation 4, 59, 67, 77, 81, 119, 127, 136, 139–40, 146, 151, 153, 165–7, 179–80, 184, 195, 198–9; permanence of 4, 33–4, 39; *see also* markers of erased emotional response

symptom coherence: as adaptive emotional necessity of symptom 45, 47, 108, 163, 174–5, 177, 183, 192, 197; as deep sense of having symptom 8, 48, 50, 66, 147–8, 177, 192, 194–5; definition 44; de-pathologizing effect of recognizing 50, 80, 108, 175–7; of functional symptoms 47, 100–1, 184; of functionless symptoms 48, 68, 101;

as guiding efficient retrieval 12, 45, 47; in insecure attachment 100–2; as knowing to avoid specific suffering 47, 73, 99, 108, 163, 175, 177, 183, 192, 197; lack of solution as symptom driver 101, 194; as purpose driving symptom 47, 52, 68, 84, 108, 121, 165, 170, 177, 183, 192, 197; as revealed through retrieval 73, 78, 87, 98–100; of self-blame 148; as symptom production model in Coherence Therapy 6–8, 36, 42–8, 50, 73, 78, 83, 87, 99, 117, 124, 128, 147–8, 150, 155, 170, 175, 180, 197; as two sufferings, with and without symptom 47, 163, 174, 184, 192, 194–5; *see also* Coherence Therapy; emotional necessity of symptom; emotional truth of the symptom; purpose, implicit; symptom-requiring schema

symptom deprivation technique 45–6, 78, 160–1, 170–5, 182–3, 193, 197; principle of 46

symptom identification: case examples 44, 72, 77, 86; definition 29, 44; as Step A of therapeutic reconsolidation process 29–30, 41, 44, 63

symptom-requiring schema: attachment vs non-attachment related 10, 97–100, 104, 134; coherence of 4, 7, 8, 73, 78, 87, 99–103, 106, 111, 165; complexity of 27–8, 151; contextual range of 60, 62–3, 108, 115; as durable mental object 48; embracing vs opposing the 12, 49–53, 73–4, 79–85, 162–5, 172–7, 179, 183; experience of 50, 52, 73, 79–80, 106; 171–2, 182, 197; as findable/accessible 11, 44, 46; as immune from disconfirmation when implicit 56, 118; as implicit knowledge of how to avoid a suffering 46–7, 68, 70, 100–1, 108, 121, 163, 183, 192, 197; as pro-symptom position 47, 50, 52, 61, 160–2, 175; reactivation of, as Step 1 of erasure sequence 30, 41; resistance to dissolu-tion of 62, 68, 83–5, 163–4; self-protective nature of 7, 43, 46–7, 100–1, 108, 183, 192, 197; specificity of 7, 44, 185; symptoms having more than one 59, 62, 76; tenacity of 15, 37, 96, 101; triggers of

symptom-requiring schema (*continued*):
53–4, 87, 90, 110, 115–16; *see also*
emotional truth of the symptom; of the
symptom; mental model; pro-symptom
position; symptom-requiring schema,
components of
symptom-requiring schema, components
of: agency 50, 73, 80, 108, 114, 162–3,
175–6, 183, 195, 197; attachment
tactics 73, 81, 108, 111, 173–7, 198–9;
construed meanings 46, 106, 113, 144,
161, 189, 190–2, 196; and findings
in phenomenology 54–5, 100; for
insecure attachment patterns 100–2,
173–7, 198–200; map of 53–5; mental
model in 53–4, 68–70, 97, 111, 191;
"problem" and "solution" 54, 68–70,
73, 76, 79, 81, 85, 99, 107, 114, 177,
183, 197; problem-defining constructs
53–4, 68, 100–1, 111, 150; purpose
driving symptom 46, 50, 52, 73, 79–80,
114, 121, 160, 162–3, 175–7, 183, 197;
"raw data" of perception/emotion/
somatics 53, 120, 150; solution-
defining constructs 54, 68, 74, 81,
100–2, 120, 150; suffering to avoid
53–4, 68–70, 73, 100–1, 108, 111, 121,
175–6, 183, 198–9; tactic 12, 54, 68–9,
74, 81, 100–2, 108, 131, 150; terms of
attachment 102–4, 111, 119–20, 173–7,
198–200; unsuitable for reparative
attachment work 98–100, 119–24; *see
also* emotional truth of the symptom;
mental model; pro-symptom position;
symptom-requiring schema
symptoms: as driven by client's solution
52, 68, 73, 77, 79, 81, 85, 99–101, 108,
121, 177, 183, 192, 197, 199–200;
emotional necessity of 81, 108, 121,
163, 165, 170, 173–5, 177, 183, 192,
197, 199–200, 44–7, 52, 68, 77, 84–5;
expressing lack of solution 101–2;
functional 47, 68, 99, 100–1, 108, 121;
functionless 48, 68, 101
symptoms, specific: addictive behaviors
15; alcohol abuse 168–80; anger
98–100, 159–67; anxiety 6–7, 9, 15,
17, 43–63, 86–91, 96, 102, 110–19,
168–80; attachment distress/insecurity
71–7, 105–23, 130–40, 148–51, 168–80,
198–200; avoiding emotional intimacy

106–9, 148–51; codependency 14, 102;
compulsive eating 181–5; confidence,
lack of 9, 43–63; delusions 186–200;
depression 15, 136–40, 186–200;
dissociation 102; guilt 143–5, 147–8,
159–67; hallucinations 186–200;
hypervigilance 15, 101; invisibility 102;
low self-esteem 14, 43–63, 106–19,
130–40, 168–80, 191–4, 198–200;
marital sexual aversion 120–3; merging
73; obesity 181–5; obsessive attachment
10, 71–7; panic 15, 110–19, 141–8;
perfectionism 14, 110–19, 159–67;
post-traumatic symptoms 10, 86–91,
110–19, 141–8, 186–200; rage 15;
self-criticism 15; self-doubt 9, 43–63:
sexual inhibition 15; shame 6, 15, 42,
78, 110, 132, 137–9, 149, 162, 189,
195–6, 198–200; social anxiety 6–7,
61, 110–19, 168–80; stage fright 10,
86–91; underachieving 10, 77–86,
119–20; *see also* case studies; symptom
identification
symptoms, causation of: by adaptive
purpose 47, 50, 162–3, 170, 175–6, 177,
183, 197; agency realized by client in
50, 80, 108, 114,162, 163, 175–6, 183,
197; by attachment or non-attachment
learnings 10, 93–100, 134; clinical
observation of psychological 37–8;
and epigenetics 36–7; by emotional
implicit learnings 3, 7–8, 11, 14, 16,
28, 36–7, 39, 44–5, 63, 65, 111, 148–9,
180, 183; by expecting and avoiding
a suffering 45–7, 68, 77, 85, 99, 108,
170, 173–5, 183, 192, 197, 199–200;
by genetics/inborn temperament 95–6;
psychotherapists' beliefs about 37;
by solution-defining constructs 46–7,
54, 68–70, 74, 81–2, 92, 120, 125;
symptom coherence as model of 6–8,
36, 42–8, 50, 73, 78, 83, 87, 99, 117,
124, 128, 147–8, 150, 155, 170, 175,
180, 197; top-down vs bottom-up 33,
35–6, 42, 62, 66; *see also* emotional
necessity of symptom; symptom
coherence

target construct/learning for erasure
16, 18, 23–30, 41, 43, 46, 54, 57–8,
63–4, 71, 134–5, 138–9, 144–5, 149;

examples 51–2, 69–70, 87–92, 111, 121, 125, 143, 183; examples of mismatch of 57, 75–6, 83, 89, 107, 113, 131, 138–40, 144–6, 151; examples of reactivation of 56, 75, 82–3, 88, 107, 113, 138–40, 146, 151; selection of master construct as 68–70, 81, 87, 111, 134, 143; summary list of examples 92, 125; in traumatic memory 86–90, 111, 143–4, 190–1; *see also* constructs, implicit; master construct; mental model; symptom-requiring schema, components of

techniques, experiential: applicable range of, 30, 48; asking inside 150; bilateral stimulation 30, 48, 141–8, 190–2, 196; chair work 30, 48, 138–40; dream work 48, 87; Focusing 30, 48, 170–1, 193–4; *I'm in memory* practice 115–18; imaginal 31, 46, 48, 52, 56–7, 63, 73, 78, 80, 85, 138–40, 150–1, 160–1, 170–5, 182–3, 193–4, 197; mismatch detection 71–2, 74, 82, 111–13, 165, 184; overt statement 49–50, 52, 71–5, 77, 80, 82–3, 85, 87, 111–13, 160–1, 163–5, 183; parts work 48, 197; re-enactment, empowered 34, 86–91; sentence completion 73, 78–9, 83, 112, 162–4, 182, 194; symptom deprivation 46, 78, 160–1, 170–5, 182–3, 193, 197; trauma therapy methods 30, 111–18, 141–8, 190–7; *see also* bodily experiencing; experiential dissonance; *and* "experiential" *under* Coherence Therapy; discovery phase; integration experiences; juxtaposition experience; retrieval of symptom-requiring schema; therapeutic reconsolidation process; transformational change

temperament, inborn: research findings 95–6; role of, in symptom production 95–6;

termination 61

terms of attachment: as defining identity 106, 111, 164, 194, 198–200; definition of 102–3; examples of 102; examples of retrieval and disconfirmation of 104, 106–9, 110–14, 120–3, 170–9, 198–200; as primary vs secondary attachment learning s 103, 119–21; and reparative attachment work 104;

sexualized 121; verbalization of 106, 111, 121; *see also* attachment learnings; attachment patterns

theory-free framework for psychotherapy xv, 4–5, 8–10, 27, 30, 40, 44–5, 100, 105, 126, 128

therapeutic reconsolidation process: in AEDP 130–6; applicability of 34–5, 126; for attachment schemas 103–24; as best practice when applicable 35; case studies of steps of 43–61, 106–7, 130–52; client's experience of 58, 63, 65, 71; as coherence-focused 51, 73, 78, 87, 99, 111, 128, 155; in Coherence Therapy 40, 43–63, 67–92, 105–25; collaborative nature of 10; confirmation of, by markers 30, 41, 60–1, 64, 76–7, 85–6, 90, 113, 122–3, 127, 131, 133, 135–6, 139–40, 146–7, 151, 179–80, 184, 199; as core process of therapies of transformational change 10, 27, 65, 127, 129–52; counter-indications for 34–5; cross-cultural use of 43; definition of 29–30, 41; in EFT 136–40; as embodying brain's rules of unlearning 4, 126, 149, 155; in EMDR 141–8; and the Emotional Coherence Framework 4, 9–10, 42, 55, 97, 109, 124, 128, 155; emotional depth in 40, 71; empathetic quality of 4, 9, 48, 50, 57–8, 68, 75, 105–9, 125; empirical support from process research 154–5; experiential quality of 4, 10, 45, 47–8, 50–2, 57–9, 61–4, 71, 73–4, 78–9, 82, 85, 87–91, 100, 108–9, 115–18, 130–51; as guiding reparative attachment work 106–9, 124; and implications of neuroscience for therapy 31–5; in IPNB 148–51; integrative features/value of 5, 9–10, 27, 126–55, 149, 152; as map for implicit emotional domain 10, 155; as new learning dissolving old learning 33–4,155; non-counteractive nature of 9, 19–20, 26, 32–4, 51, 53, 59, 61, 77, 82, 127–8; non-pathologizing nature of 33, 65–6, 128, 155; as not requiring lengthy repetition 32–3, 60; as outside of common factors theory 11, 43, 124, 154; permanence of symptom cessation 4, 33–4, 39; phenomenological quality of 9–10; re-encoding of synapses in

therapeutic reconsolidation process
(*continued*): 33–4; as schema-specific
approach 97; as sequence that erases
emotional learning 27–30, 40–1,
67, 126, 152; as specific factors for
transformational change 11, 127,
130, 153; step sequence in various
therapies 149, 152; steps listed 26,
29–30, 41, 127; steps of, as matching
Coherence Therapy 40–64, 129; steps
of, as well-defined 10, 63–4, 68, 71;
summary list of case examples 92,
125; target selection principles 68–70;
technique- and theory-independence of
5, 9–10, 30, 40, 64, 126, 128, 149, 152;
therapeutic effects of, vs emotional
regulation 32–4; therapists' freedom
within 4–5, 10, 30, 64, 71, 128; therapy
systems congenial to 5, 40, 149, 152;
for traumatic memory 86–91, 110–19,
141–8; as yielding more unified self
33, 66; as yielding transformational
change 4, 33, 65, 67, 127, 149, 152;
unrecognized occurrence of 40,
65, 127; *see also* reconsolidation;
reconsolidation research; target
construct; transformational change
therapeutic reconsolidation process, steps
of:
Step A, symptom identification,
definition 29; discussion 28, 63, 67;
examples (tagged) 44, 106, 130–1, 137,
150; Step A examples (untagged) 72–3,
77, 86, 98, 110, 120;
Step B, retrieval of target learning,
definition 29; discussion 28, 63, 67,
131, 137, 144; examples (tagged) 45–53,
106, 138–40, 143–4, 146, 150–1;
examples (untagged) 73, 78–81, 87,
98–9, 110–11, 120–1;
Step C, identification of disconfirming
knowledge, definition 29, 68;
discussion 28, 63, 67–8, 92, 131, 134,
137–9, 145, 143; examples (tagged)
55–6, 106, 138, 143, 150–1; examples
(untagged) 74–5, 76–7, 81–2, 87,
111–13, 122;
Step 1, symptom identification,
definition 26; discussion 63–4, 67, 131;
examples (tagged) 56, 107, 138–40,
146, 151; examples (untagged) 75,

82–3, 88, 113;
Step 2, retrieval of target learning,
definition 26; discussion 58–9, 63–4,
67, 131, 134, 143, 145; examples
(tagged) 57, 107, 131, 138–40, 144–6,
151; examples (untagged) 75–6, 83, 89,
113;
Step 3, identification of disconfirming
knowledge, definition 26; discussion
27, 58–9, 63–4, 67, 131, 138–9,
145; examples (tagged) 57–8, 107,
132–3, 138, 140, 145–6, 151; examples
(untagged) 76, 90, 113–15;
Step V, verification of erasure,
definition 26, 30; discussion 60–1,
64, 127, 131, 136; examples (tagged)
58, 60–1, 76, 85–6, 131, 133, 135–6,
139–40, 146, 151; examples (untagged)
77, 85, 90–1, 118–19, 122–3;
therapist freedom/creativity 10, 27, 64, 71,
128, 196–7, 200
therapist learning/growth: as enhanced
by choiceful process 12, 155; and
markers of change 64–5; by observing
juxtaposition experiences 65; by tracking client's step-by-step responses 12
therapist dilemmas 11–12
therapist satisfaction 3, 11–12, 39; from
effectiveness 12–13, 66, 155;
top-down versus bottom-up causation 33,
35–6, 42, 62, 66
transformation phase of Coherence
Therapy: as carrying out
transformation sequence 56–9; case
examples 55–9, 74–6, 82–5, 87–91,
106–9, 111–19, 122–3, 165–7, 176–7,
179–80, 184–5, 198–200; as creation
of juxtaposition experiences 55–9;
and discovery of transformation
sequence 59; experiential dissonance
in 58; resistance arising in 62, 68, 83,
163–4; as Steps C-1-2-3 of therapeutic
reconsolidation process 41, 55–9;
see also contradictory knowledge,
finding/creating ; disconfirmation;
erasure sequence; juxtaposition
experience; transformation sequence;
transformational change
transformation sequence 56, 58, 68; as
critical specific factors 65, 127, 153,
155; definition 26, 64, 71; as dissolving

problematic constructs/meanings 43–4, 57–8, 63, 85, 113, 153; as juxtaposition experiences 58–9, 63–8, 71, 75, 82, 130, 132–4, 146, 153; as methodology of Coherence Therapy 56–9; as only behavioral process that erases 65, 127, 154; as present in diverse therapies 65, 130, 149, 152; resistance in response to 62, 68, 83, 163–4; and specific treatment effect 154; swiftness of 59; as verifiable by markers 60, 85, 113, 127, 130; *see also* erasure sequence; juxtaposition experience; markers of erased emotional response
transformational change: and acceptance/non-suppression of causal material 12, 49–53, 73–4, 79–85, 162–5, 172–7, 179, 183; of attachment patterns 71–86, 91, 103–123, 130–6, 179, 198–200; brain's rules for 4, 26, 62, 83–5, 126–7, 148, 152, 154; case studies with steps of 43–63, 71–91, 106–7, 130–51; contrasted with counteractive change 4, 9, 17, 19–20, 26, 32–4, 51, 53, 59, 61, 77, 82, 127–8, 135, 141, 152, 176–7, 179; in diverse therapies 65, 128, 130, 149, 152; and emotional brain's resistance 62, 83–5, 148; experiential quality of 12, 57–8, 70, 75–6, 82–3, 88–90, 103, 106–9, 117–18, 123–4; of generalized learnings 109; grief accompanying 60, 83–5, 165; as having well-defined steps 10, 68, 130, 154; in identity/model of self 89–91, 108, 119, 135, 139, 145–7, 179–80, 198–200; markers of 19, 58, 60, 64, 76–7, 85–6, 90–1, 113, 122–3, 127, 134–6, 139–40, 146–7, 151, 179–80, 184, 193, 195, 198–9; of mental model/constructs 54, 56, 62, 77, 87, 91, 97, 107, 109, 114–15, 138–9, 139, 145–6; as new learning erasing old learning 44, 20, 33–4, 64, 179–80, 198; as occurring in definite moments 57–8, 67, 75–6, 83, 88–9, 145; in outlier sessions 41, 154; permanence of symptom cessation in 9, 19, 39, 67; persists effortlessly 9, 34, 44; psychotherapies of 127, 130, 152; as regular event in clinical practice 12, 66; in reparative attachment work 106–9, 179, 198–200; resistance to

62, 68, 83–5, 163–4; as requiring specific factors 11, 127, 130, 154; of solution maintaining symptom 85; and schema retrieval 12, 97, 179–80; by the therapeutic reconsolidation process 33–4, 127, 130, 149, 152, 154; of traumatic memory 86–91, 110–19, 144–8, 198–200; *see also* erasure; juxtaposition experience; markers of erased emotional response; transformation sequence
transformation-specific factors: as deep structure of transformational therapies 127, 130, 152; implications of, for common factors theory 153; steps of therapeutic reconsolidation process as 127, 152–3; *see also* common factors theory; specific factors
Traumatic Incident Reduction (TIR): and the therapeutic reconsolidation process 5
traumatic memory: affective flashback of 90, 110; dissociation of 62; dissolution/unlearning of 86–91, 110–19, 144–8, 198–200; as emotional learning 15, 87, 110–11, 148–9, 183, 185; flashback of 90, 117; and *I'm in memory* practice 115–18, 146; integration of 115–18, 147, 149; mechanism of change of 91; and past/present distinction 146–7, 149, 184; retrieval of 87, 110–11, 190–2, 196–7, 200; retriggering of 87, 90, 110, 115–18, 141, 143, 146–9, 196; *see also* post-traumatic symptoms

underachieving 77–86, 92, 119–20
unemployment 95
unlearning: brain's rules/readiness for 26, 126–7; client's experience of 58, 63, 65, 71; as dissolution via reconsolidation 4, 18, 24, 26, 37, 39, 63, 67; and Emotional Coherence Framework 4–7, 42, 55; identifying target for 68–70, 87, 111, 134, 143; in juxtaposition experiences 63–5, 67, 71; by new learning in reconsolidation window 18, 24, 26, 64; as synaptic re-encoding 41; as therapeutic reconsolidation process outcome 26, 63, 126–7; of traumatic learning 86–91, 110–19, 144–8, 198–200; using imaginal techniques

63, 83, 88–9, 112–15, 151; *see also*
  disconfirmation; erasure; juxtaposition
  experience; target construct;
  transformational change
unlocking of synapses 4, 10, 16, 18–20,
  22–3, 26, 41, 57, 64, 68, 71–2, 82
updating of implicit learning 33, 141;
  brain's rules/readiness for 24–6, 34,
  126–7

verbalization: examples 49–50, 80, 99,
  111, 119–20, 135, 144, 183; key role of,
  for retrieval 47, 50, 52, 68, 148–9, 183,
  190–2; of terms of attachment 102, 111;
  see also index card; integration phase;
  overt statement; retrieval of symptom-
  requiring schema; sentence completion

verification of dissolution of target
  learning: clinical markers of 19, 41, 58,
  60–1, 64, 77, 90, 122–3, 134–5, 139–
  40, 146–7, 151, 179, 184, 199; as final
  step (V) of therapeutic reconsolidation
  process 26, 30, 41, 60–1, 64, 127, 131,
  134, 139–40, 146–7, 151; in lab studies
  25–6; question initiating 58, 60, 76; by
  re-cueing target response 30, 58, 60–1,
  85; *see also* markers of erasure

Watson, Jeanne 137
well-being 7, 12, 39, 44, 60, 74, 81, 130,
  133, 135–6, 179
working through 134
worthlessness 111, 191–2, 194, 197